THE EFFECT ON ENGLISH DOMESTIC LAW OF MEMBERSHIP OF THE EUROPEAN COMMUNITIES AND OF RATIFICATION OF THE EUROPEAN CONVENTION ON HUMAN RIGHTS

The Effect on English Domestic Law
of Membership of the European Communities
and of Ratification of the
European Convention on Human Rights

edited by

M.P. Furmston
R. Kerridge
B.E. Sufrin

1983

Martinus Nijhoff Publishers

The Hague / Boston / London

224530
KE7

Distributors:

for the United States and Canada

Kluwer Boston, Inc.
190 Old Derby Street
Hingham, MA 02043
USA

for all other countries

Kluwer Academic Publishers Group
Distribution Center
P.O. Box 322
3300 AH Dordrecht
The Netherlands

Library of Congress Cataloging in Publication Data　　　　　　　　　　　　CIP

Main entry under title:

The Effect on English domestic law of membership of
    the European Communities and of ratification
    of the European Convention on Human Rights.

    Papers by members of the University of Bristol
Faculty of Law in celebration of the fiftieth
anniversary of the Faculty.
    Contents: Influences on judicial reasoning / David
Feldman -- Constitutional conundrums : the impact of
the United Kingdom's membership of the Communities
on constitutional theory / D.N. Clark and B.E. Sufrin
-- The impact of European law on equal pay for women /
Richard Townshend-Smith -- [etc.]
    1. International and municipal law--Great
Britain--Addresses, essays, lectures. 2. European
Economic Community--Great Britain--Addresses,
essays, lectures. 3. Civil rights--Europe--Addresses,
essays, lectures. 4. Great Britain--Constitutional
law--Addresses, essays, lectures. I. Furmston, M. P.
II. Kerridge, Roger. III. Sufrin, B. E. IV. University
of Bristol. Faculty of Law.
KD4015.E43 1983   341'.04'0941   82-24668

ISBN 90-247-2811-8

PRINTED IN THE NETHERLANDS

Table of Contents   v

Preface   vii

PREFACE

The Faculty of Law in the University of Bristol admitted its first students in 1933. 1983 marks, therefore, the 50th anniversary of the Faculty's foundation and this volume of essays has been written by members of the Faculty as part of the celebration of that jubilee. It is safe to say that in 1933 it would have occurred to few that the topic chosen for such a work would have been the influence on English Law of European Law but if there is one lesson that we have learnt from the writing of this book it is that that influence is now pervasive and reaches many areas of English Law, which would not have been suspected ten years ago, let alone fifty.

The authors of these essays are not, for the most part, specialists in European Law. The book is offered therefore not as a work by specialists for specialists but as an attempt by a number of English Lawyers to take a number of snapshots of the interaction of English and European Law. Since the target is large and moving fast the coverage does not attempt to be comprehensive and cannot be definitive. We hope, however, that by looking at the topics from a wide variety of aspects, sometimes narrowly focussed and sometimes with a wide angle, we have produced a work which will be of interest to a wide variety of English lawyers, and indeed to European lawyers, who are interested in the way in which our strange island race is responding to this great legal invasion.

The authors of the individual essays owe debts of gratitude to so many who assisted them that it is not practicable to compile a list. Colleagues in Bristol, law teachers in other universities, lawyers in the Home Office and in the Foreign Office, members and ex members of the Human Rights Secretariat in Strasbourg read drafts and commented on them. This is a work not only about European cooperation but of European cooperation. Nevertheless, we should be at fault were we not to acknowledge a special debt to the secretaries in the Bristol Law Faculty who had the task of typing out the first drafts and to The Secretary Machine of Clifton who produced the final camera ready copy. The publishers, Martinus Nijhoff, were kinder than we deserved and raised no difficulties over amendments to our original plans, changes in length and requests for permission to submit the text later than originally promised. It is due to their efficiency that the book will, after all, be produced in time for the anniversary which it is intended to honour.

M P Furmston

Roger Kerridge

B E Sufrin

Bristol
November 1982

INFLUENCES ON JUDICIAL REASONING*

David Feldman

I

This essay attempts to trace the ways in which exposure to the laws of the European Communities and the European Convention on Human Rights has affected (or not affected) the way our judges reason, and the reasons for the effects or lack of them. Modes of reasoning are ephemeral, and the range of evidence vast. Any study of them must be selective and impressionistic. The risks of superficiality and distortion can only be reduced by alerting readers to them at the beginning.

Much of the essay is about interpretation of statutes. Judges require themselves to hunt the snark of the meaning of the statute or the intention of Parliament. As has been written in a different context, 'Long study of the classics had quickened his faculty for seeing sense in passages where there was none.'(1) The approach is this: background problems of the judge's role are briefly sketched in section II; factors affecting the use of purposive reasoning are considered in section III (concentrating on the English judges) and section IV (looking at limits on purposive reasoning which apply to English and European judges); section V looks at the place of certainty as an influence; section VI is a depressing glance at English judges' reactions to human rights claims; and section VII tries to draw some tentative conclusions. Apart from section VI the essay concentrates on the EEC's influence. There is however, no reason to suppose that the Court of Justice and the Court of Human Rights adopt the same approach, or that any two of their judges inter se adopt the same approach , or that they have the same political prejudices. That cannot be assumed of English judges, and the judges on the supranational benches of Europe are a far more heterogeneous crowd than ours.

II

Strictly speaking, in considering the effect of European law on English judges the actual behaviour of the European courts is irrelevant. The only important question is, what do English judges <u>think</u> is happening on the other side of the Channel? They may have some odd ideas about that, but it is those ideas rather than the reality of European law which influence our judges. There is an idea, albeit mistaken, that there is a European approach to adjudication. The political background of the ECHR is highly individualistic; it is framed in a liberal-conservative tradition, with only limited exceptions to the freedoms it provides for. The political background of European Community Law is also individualistic. <u>Art.5</u> ECSC, provides that the Coal and Steel Community is to carry out its task 'with a limited measure of intervention', and 'with a minimum of administrative machinery'. There is no such provision in the EEC Treaty, but the EEC is dedicated to the free market economy (except as regards agriculture), the economic epitome of the theory of individualism. Yet the EC Commission has a major set of coercive powers, and the Court of Justice tends to uphold its use of them. To balance the powers, the Court of Justice has supplemented written Community Law sources with protection for fundamental rights and various general principles of Community Law which do something to restrain unreasonable Community interventionism. In balancing between individualism and interventionism, the judges can supplement their personal leanings with the stated objectives of the Treaties and Conventions to work out a theory of judicial activity.

English judges have not had the benefit of such ready-made principles of judicial behaviour. Where judges find a gap in the fabric of the law, are they to try to fill it as they think best, or should they refuse any remedy until Parliament has spoken? The problem revolves around a most difficult question: assuming that everything judges do has an effect on the law, should they set out to change it or not? Should they act as conscious legislators? Where does the sensible judge draw the line between necessary but limited legislation in the course of adjudication, and major legislation, arrogating to himself the task of Parliament?

The fullest English judicial discussion of the legislative/adjudicative dichotomy came from Lord Simon of Glaisdale in Miliangos v George Frank (Textiles) Ltd.(2) in a dissenting judgment where he underlined the dangers of judges changing settled law on an insufficient appreciation of the economic and social consequences or of the knock-on effects in related areas of law. Another limiting factor is the difficulty of judges introducing new legal rules where special machinery is needed to enforce them.(3)

At bottom, the answer to how far a judge may properly go is almost intuitive. It varies with the determination or temerity of the individual judge, but in general English judges, bowing perhaps with excessive respect to the legislative powers of Parliament, have adopted a position of self-restraint, expecially on political issues. Parliamentary supremacy is a convenient judicial doctrine in troubled times. Every judge needs a theory to explain his role. Without a theory of what judges ought to be doing, no judge would ever know whether he was acting properly. He would never be able to feel confident that he had reached the 'right answer'.(4) Neither would litigants nor the general public. Unless there is an underlying theory of law and the public and the practitioners find it generally acceptable the law would be unable to provide either certainty or what people could call justice. The guiding principles of judicial action for judges of the supranational Courts of Europe are provided within the Treaties and the Convention, in the same way that those of the United States federal courts are provided by the Bill of Rights. The principles themselves are thus non-controversial once one accepts the Treaties, Convention or Bill as the appropriate source of the principles. What remains controversial is how they are to be worked out in practice. Words can be given a more or a less extended meaning, depending on the way the judge sees his role under the constitution. Thus it has been argued in another essay in this volume(5) that the ECHR tends to be given an extensive interpretation by the European Court and Commission of Human Rights because those bodies would become redundant if they did not make a stand for the greatest possible judisdiction. The Court of Justice, too, tends towards an extensive meaning for Community instruments by recourse to the spirit of the Treaty, and these interpretations tend to be controversial.(6) They can easily be seen as empire building rather than judicial interpretation. The public is less likely to take that view of a court which is adjudicating on people's rights, as the European Court of Human Rights is, for that is the traditional role of courts. However, a legal process introduced into a new area has difficulties from the start. The Court of Justice deals with complex economic arguments. It reaches decisions which involve settling economic issues and applying standards which are sometimes only painted in with broad strokes of a wide brush in the Treaties. This seems an odd thing, at first sight, for judges to be doing. In addition, the Treaties and their secondary legislation create some rights and duties which can be litigated in the national courts of Member States, which have to consider what is meant by such terms as 'equal work' in the context of legislation drafted in a tradition rather different from that with which our Parliamentary draftsmen are familiar. The problems which faced our own National Industrial Relations Court from 1971 to 1974 and the Restrictive Practices Court were worse, however. Those courts did not have their 'deep theory' worked out for them in the Acts which set them up. They were staffed by judges who brought to the job some knowledge of industry, commerce and finance but were still rooted in the individual rights tradition of the common law. It is no criticism of them to say that they struggled to find a coherent basis for their activities; rather it is remarkable that they succeeded to the extent they did. Devlin J in the RPC was particularly successful in discovering and applying the policy of the legislation. In applying Community law, on the other hand, our judges have the advantage of being able to look to the Treaties to provide an account of their objectives. We must now look at the way they have used the opportunity.

III

In <u>Macarthys Ltd.</u> v <u>Smith</u>(7) Lord Denning MR, discussing Art. 119 EEC, expressed (not for the first time) the view that there is a 'European fashion' in the drafting of legislation. He said:

> 'It enunciates a broad general principle and leaves it to the judges to work out the details. In contrast the Equal Pay Act is framed in the English fashion. It states no general principle but lays down detailed specific rules for the courts to apply (which, so some hold, the courts must interpret according to the actual language used) without resort to considerations of policy or principle.'

As he had said in <u>Bulmer</u> v <u>Bollinger</u>,(8) the European approach requires a different judicial response. The English judges, he said, in interpreting EEC laws must follow the European pattern. 'No longer must they argue about the precise grammatical sense. They must look to the purpose and intent... They must divine the spirit of the treaty and gain inspiration from it. If they find a gap, they must fill it as best they can.' This approach commended itself to Lord Denning. That is not surprising. One consistent thread in his Lordship's career was the desire to do justice as he saw it between the parties, taking due account of the public policy issues involved. Before the EEC, the problem this raised was simple. It took him beyond the scope of a judge's conventional function, tending to turn him into a legislator, since he was not basing his decision on conventionally accepted sources of English Law. Perhaps because of the English style of statutory drafting, perhaps because of the historical importance of certainty, English judges have, as part of their deep theory, fought shy of doing anything that could be called legislating, preferring to leave that to Parliament in deference to its acknowledged legislative supremacy. Lord Denning's impatience with the slowness of legislators led him to make several adventurous forays into judicial legislation which left the more 'timorous souls' among his brethren far behind.(9) Europe has helped him. In <u>The Siskina</u>,(10) the plaintiff sought leave to serve a writ outside the jurisdiction. This was governed by RSC Ord 11, r 1, which provided that a writ could be served out of the jurisdiction only if in the action an order was sought requiring the defendant to do or refrain from doing something within the jurisdiction, whether or not damages were also claimed. The plaintiff sought to get round that by seeking a Mareva injunction in respect of insurance moneys representing the defendant's vessel which, the plaintiff alleged, had been fraudulently scuttled. Lord Denning was impressed by the fact that the plaintiff's only realistic chance of recovering damages might be to give the English courts jurisdiction, and he did that by holding that a Mareva injunction could be sought if any of the defendant's property was within the jurisdiction. He held that Ord 11, r 1 should be interpreted as giving jurisdiction in those circumstances: a claim to a Mareva injunction is enough. Lawton LJ reached the same result; Bridge LJ dissented. The House of Lords allowed the shipowners' appeal. As Lord Diplock pointed out, a Mareva injunction would only issue if there was an issue triable in the English courts. To treat the claim for the injunction as itself grounding jurisdiction 'appears to me to involve the fallacy of petitio principii or, in the vernacular, an attempt to pull oneself up by one's own bootstraps.'(11) From our point of view however, the case is principally interesting for the different approaches to construction used by the judges. Lord Denning relied on three lines of reasoning to support what he regarded as the just result. First, the legislative history of the provision. More will be said of such matters later.(12) Secondly, an analogy with cases where English courts had restrained a foreign party to foreign proceedings from dealing with moneys which were the subject matter of the foreign action. Here, however, the plaintiffs were not entitled to any interest in the money representing the ship, but only to damages. Thirdly, he relied on an argument based on Community law. He pointed to Art. 220 EEC, which deals with reciprocal enforcement of judgments. He pointed out that the Italian courts would have jurisdiction, and referred to the job of harmonising the laws of member states pursuant to Art. 3(h). He then said that the treaty is to be interpreted according to its spirit, not its letter. Referring to the doctrine of saisie conservatoire, which operates in several European countries, whereby property is protected if it is the subject of an action pending the outcome, he concluded that it was possible to say it was the English court's duty to grant the injunction. The Court of Justice would not have reasoned in that way, and Community law gives nothing like such a wide ranging discretion to judges in national courts. As Lord Hailsham pointed out in the House of Lords, harmonisation is to be achieved either through directly applicable Community law which leaves the national court no choice but to apply it, or through legislative action by the appropriate organ in each member state. Neither was to be found in that case: 'it is not for the courts in member states to anticipate the work of the diplomats and the legislative authorities.'(13) Lord Denning's reply to the accusation of acting legislatively had already been given in the Court of Appeal: justice required that the courts should not wait for the legislature to act, if there was any credible ground on which the courts could develop the law themselves.(14)

The response of Bridge LJ in his dissenting judgment was to use orthodox approaches to the question of enlarging the court's jurisdiction, arguing that the consequences of such an act might be considerable: '...Our forensic horizons are necessarily limited. We cannot hope to be fully seised of all the considerations which should affect a decision, not only as to whether the jurisdiction should be enlarged but also, if it should, as to any appropriate conditions and limitations subject to which it should be exercised.... For these reasons I am clearly of opinion that we should not allow the urgent merits of particular plaintiffs, whom we see in peril of being deprived of any effective remedy, to tempt us to assume the mantle of legislators.'(15)

The dispute about the proper relationship between judges and legislators has been going on a long time. It would be wrong to assume that Lord Denning has been influenced in his attitude to the problem by closer links with European systems of law. His attitude was exactly the same (right down to a reference to 'timorous souls') twenty-six years earlier when attempting to extend common law liability to auditors who negligently drew up accounts on which others relied to their detriment.(16) The difference was purely one of weaponry. The EEC gave him extra encouragement, and an extra string to his bow.

The European Communities Act 1972, section 3(1) can even be read as imposing on judges an obligation to use European interpretative methods when deciding whether directly applicable Community law applies to the case. Section 3(1) provides that questions as to the validity, meaning or effect of any instrument of Community law shall be determined in accordance with the principles laid down by and any relevant decision of the Court of Justice. As has been point out,(17) 'principles' is wide enough to include the Court's methods of interpretation. However, the Court rarely explains what its approach to interpretation is. That is left to individual judges in extra-judicial lectures and articles, so it is unlikely that one can properly talk of the Court's approach to problems of interpretation as 'principles laid down by ... the European Court.' But as remarked earlier, what matters from the point of view of the effect of Community principles in England is what the English courts think is happening in Luxembourg, not what is actually going on there. The apparent readiness of the Court to indulge in judicial legislation, dictated by the nature of the legislation which they have to apply and make sense of, reinforced by the fact that the legislative organs themselves are often hopelessly deadlocked, has been taken by Lord Denning to reinforce his arguments when dealing with a different style of legislation and a very different constitutional structure. He has often tried to discover ways of bringing Community law into cases where he wants to reform the law. In some of the cases, his fellow judges and the House of Lords on appeal have found ways to reach a similar result giving effect to an acknowledged purpose or policy from within the English system, using only the armoury available to Engish judges: distinguishing, explaining and occasionally overruling.(18)

This can be seen in a number of cases in which courts have used methods of reasoning more closely related to purposive than to literal interpretation. This is in some ways surprising, since there seems to be an idea that English judges are by nature more inclined to interpret statutes by trying to find the 'true' or 'literal' meaning of the words than by looking for the result which most closely reflects the intention of the legislature as made manifest through the words used. Many have supposed that the Europeans have a different way of approaching statutory interpretation, being more concerned with purposes and less with the grammar of the legislation. This view has been encountered in the quotation from Lord Denning's judgment in Bulmer v Bollinger given earlier.(19) The idea is less convincing when one looks at the facts.

First of all, the English courts were and are capable of using a purposive approach to interpretation. The 'Mischief Rule', which requires courts to look at the mischief which an Act was designed to remedy, and give it an interpretation which will allow it to achieve that purpose as far as that is compatible with the words of the statute, has been part of the English approach since 1584(20) if not before. This desire to look for the purpose of the Act is not an attempt to derogate from the legislative supremacy of Parliament. It is quite the reverse. It recognises that Parliament does not legislate in a vacuum, and seeks to give effect to the 'will', for want of a better word, of the supreme legislature. However, the English courts have always taken the words of the statute as the best evidence of the will of Parliament. Judges assume that Parliament says what it means and means what it says. The intention of Parliament is seen as being the intention appearing from the words of the Act, and there has been a reluctance to look to non-statutory materials when interpreting the words. Sometimes this can have odd results, mainly because Parliament and its draftsmen are not less fallible than other authors in the task of expressing themselves. What does one do with an Act which claims to be a consolidation Act but uses words which on their ordinary meaning produce a result different from that of the Acts being consolidated? The answer, according to Lords Wilberforce, Simon and Edmund-Davies in Farrell v Alexander(21) is that one does not look at the antecedents unless there is a real and

substantial difficulty or ambiguity which classical methods of
construction cannot resolve.(22) Consolidation is not merely a
matter of mechanical convenience. However, when an Act
does on its wording produce an ambiguity the court resolves it
by looking at the background.(23) That can only be second-
best evidence of Parliament's intention, though, to be used
when Parliament has failed to make itself clear. The danger
in being too ready to look at reports on social problems,
Hansard, draft Bills and similar material is that one may be
inclined to assume that Parliament, looking at them, decided
to adopt the same solution as one would have done in
Parliament's place. This risk is inevitably present whenever a
piece of text presents itself for interpretation. As has
recently been pointed out, the texts of judgments themselves
have an effect and life of their own apart from the intentions
of the judges who gave them,(24) and the same is true of
statutes. The judge's preference for one result over another
colours his view of what constitutes a 'real and substantial
difficulty or ambiguity' anyway, and one man's ambiguity is
another man's clear words leading to an unwelcome result.(25)
To let in non-statutory materials too readily may lead to a
danger constitutionally more serious than Parliament's
intention being thwarted on a particular issue, for Parliament
can always rectify the mistake through amending legislation;
looking beyond the statute may ultimately reduce the
legislative supremacy of Parliament by encouraging judges to
play fast and loose with the words of the Act to give effect to
the solution which seems to the judges, but not necessarily to
Parliament, to be sensible.

This can already be seen in the context of Community law's
relationship with national law. The Community view is clear:
when they conflict, national law is subordinate to Community
law.(26) English judges are, by virtue of the Treaty and
Section 2 of the European Communities Act, bound to
administer both Community and English systems of law, but by
pre-accession English law, statute is not subordinate to any
other authority. The question of the effect of accession on
what used to be know as the 'doctrine of parliamentary
sovereignty' has, for some reason, raised hackles and heat, but

it is a matter of no practical importance. What is important is the way our judges have coped with the discomfort of being sandwiched between two systems.

The Court of Appeal in Macarthys v Smith(27) was faced with a problem over the interpretation of Section 1(2)(a)(i) of the Equal Pay Act 1970, which provided: '(a) where the woman is employed on like work with a man in the same employment - (i) if (apart from the equality clause) any term of the woman's contract is or becomes less favourable to the woman than a term of a similar kind in the contract under which that man is employed, that term of the woman's contract shall be treated as so modified as not to be less favourable...' There were two questions for decision. The first was whether the Act was to be interpreted as meaning that the man and the woman had to be simultaneously doing like work for the Act to come into play. The second was whether the position was affected by Art. 119 EEC, which requires Member States to ensure the application of the principle that men and women should receive equal pay for equal work, and Council Directive 75/117, Art. 1, which defines the principle of equal pay as meaning 'for the same work or for work to which equal value is attributed, the elimination of all discrimination on ground of sex with regard to all aspects and conditions of remuneration.'

In the Court of Appeal there was a difference of opinion on the first question. The majority (Lawton and Cumming-Bruce LJJ) held that the Act was clear on its words, and required simultaneous employment before a court could decide whether a woman was receiving equal pay. They relied on the use of the present tense-' is employed'- in the section to support this view, an example perhaps of a concentration on the literal and grammatical methods of construction. Their attention was directed to the fact that the 'is' could refer to the job, not the time when the job is being done, thus producing an ambiguity which could be resolved by looking at the odd results of the favoured interpretation. The judges, however, thought that the results were only odd if one assumed that the intention of Parliament in the Act was to extend its effect beyond men and women in contemporaneous employment. The argument based on the anomaly was therefore circular.

This is true, but if it is to have the effect of excluding an examination of anomalous results of a particular interpretation in that case it may do so in every case, for an argument that a particular result would be anomalous can always be met with the reply, 'That depends on whether Parliament intended to do something silly'. In our constitutional structure, Parliament has the power to be as silly as it likes, and, since the Acts it produces do not set out their objects in the way that Community legislation has to, there is no sure way of knowing whether the result is any odder than the one intended by Parliament. One cannot even identify a result which is self-evidently absurd, since absurdity is a value which calls for the observer to apply his own standards which might differ from Parliament's. Indeed the idea that Parliament, an inanimate juristic entity, intends anything or has any standards is in itself absurd.(28)

Lord Denning, in the minority, was in effect prepared to dispense with attempts to find the true intention of Parliament. He wanted to interpret the Act together with Art. 119 and the Sex Discrimination Act 1975 as a single harmonious code designed to eliminate discrimination against women. He therefore looked to the Treaty, assuming that the policy of the legislature in 1970 was to eliminate discrimination by a harmonious scheme even though at the time the United Kingdom was not bound to the Community law parts of it. The reason above all others for giving the Act a meaning consistent with the Treaty was to avoid troublesome conflicts, a policy not based on the intention of Parliament at the time the 1970 Act was passed. Lord Denning's approach becomes more satisfactory if we abandon the notion that a multi-member legislature, British or European, 'means' or 'intends' anything at all when it passes a piece of legislation. This will be considered further in section IV.

When the court came to examine the second question, the judges took different views again, this time on whether Art. 119 was clear enough to enable the English courts to interpret it confidently. Lord Denning, in the minority once more, thought that the words of Art. 119 were clear enough to cover the case without difficulty. When he considered the Directive, it became 'clear beyond question'. For him, it was plain that Community law protected women who were doing the same job as a man in succession to him. He had not doubt about the true interpretation of Art. 119, and saw no need for a reference to the European Court; as he had said in Bulmer v Bollinger(29), there was no need to refer questions which the English court, applying European methods, was quite capable of sorting out for itself. Lawton and Cumming-Bruce, LJJ, on the other hand, thought that the matter was far from clear, at least on English methods of construction. As the answer to that would effectively dispose of the appeal, and the Court of Justice knew better than the English courts how to interpret the Treaty, there should be a reference for the Court's opinion under Art. 177. A reference was duly made, the Court of Justice decided that Art. 119 extended to men and women doing the same job in succession, and when the case returned to the Court of Appeal it was all over bar the argument about costs.(30)

We can learn certain lessons from that about the way English courts approach problems of Community law. The most important is that our judges on the whole do not yet feel comfortable or wholly confident in the use of Community law sources or methods. The Treaties rarely provide the clarity they expect of an Act of Parliament. The approach of the majority in Macarthys v Smith, to leave problems of Community law as far as possible to the Court of Justice, could considerably reduce the practice judges get in interpreting Community law; but that approach has commended itself to other judges as well. A notable example is Garland v British Rail Engineering Ltd.,(31) another case on Art. 119 EEC. The Treaty provisions, which were clearly relevant, had not been raised by counsel until the case reached the House of Lords. The House is a court of last resort, and thus must refer to the Court of Justice for a ruling any question of Community law on which a decision is necessary in order for the House to reach its decision.(32) The House made a reference. Lord Diplock said later:

'Although I do not believe that any of your Lordships had any serious doubt what answer would be given to that question by the European Court, there was not in existence at 19 January 1981, the date when the order of reference under Art. 177 was made, so considerable and consistent a line of case law of the European Court on the interpretation and direct applicability of Art. 119 as would make the answer too obvious and inevitable to be capable of giving rise to what could properly be regarded as "a question" within the meaning of Art. 177.'(33) ·

This shows a far greater reticence in the application of the new methods than one would expect if all judges held Lord Denning's view of their ability to apply Community law. English courts are, in practice, not generally regarding the answer to a question of Community law as too clear to need elucidation from the fount of Community legal wisdom except in very clear cases indeed. Thus references have been made by lower courts, which are under no obligation to refer any point at all under Art.177. The attempt in Bulmer v Bollinger to cut down the number of references by imposing restrictive guide-lines on the occasions when courts should refer points has finally foundered on considerations of convenience and the judges' lack of self-confidence in dealing with a novel type of law. Indeed, reticence is the right attitude from a Community point of view the so-called 'acte claire' doctrine (elements of which are present even in the question from Lord Diplock from above) is not regarded as a proper approach from the Community angle.(34)

Two further points emerge. First, in Garland's case Lord Diplock accepted that it is permissible to interpret UK statutes in the light of Community law where they overlap, because of the presumption that Parliament intends to fulfil its international obligations. He limited this, however, to statutes passed after the date when the Treaty was made. Thus in that case, where the relevant UK statute was the Sex Discrimination Act 1975, it would have been permissible to do as Lord Denning advocates and construe the provisions as a harmonious whole (so long as the words of the statute are reasonably capable of bearing such a meaning). It would seem not to be permissible to do the same to statutes which predate the relevant Treaty, despite what Lord Denning did in Macarthys Ltd v Smith. Secondly, the result of the reference under Art. 177 is usually to dispose of the case, as in Garland and Macarthys. But sometimes the English courts will adopt rather strained reasoning to avoid a decision which they dislike but which the European Court's ruling seems at first sight to force on them. For example, in R v Secretary of State, ex parte Santillo(35) the Court ruled in a way that might have suggested to a neutral observer that a recommendation for the deportation of a worker after conviction for a criminal offence became stale after a certain time. The Divisional Court and the Court of Appeal, however, would have none of this, and seized on the part in the Court's judgment where it said that delay between the commendation and the order for deportation was liable to render it void. 'Liable to' does not mean 'does', and the judges therefore felt able to hold a recommendation made $4\frac{1}{2}$ years before the deportation order based on it to be fully effective. This looks like the use of typical English formalistic legal reasoning, plus a dash of abhorrence for the man concerned, to frustrate the point of the judgment of the Court of Justice.

IV

As the English judges tentatively feel for a European approach, the Europeans are showing that a crude characterisation of their approach as broad, legislative, purposive or teleological is a distortion of reality. While they can behave like that, there is far more formalism than many give credit for. This is partly dictated by the need for certainty in EEC law as elsewhere, and perhaps partly betrays the influence of British legal method, however slight, on the Community. With successive English Advocates-General at the European Court since 1973, it would be strange if some elements of legal method had not crossed the Channel from north to south. This section considers English and European attitudes to the attempt to discover the intention of the legislature.

As regards a purposive interpretation of the Treaties and subordinate legislation of the Community, there can be no doubt that the Court is not unduly constrained by the words of many of the instruments it has to interpret. As noted earlier, this is the result of the form of the legislation, which tends to state principles and leave the practical working out to the Court and to national courts. Indeed the Court has had to come up with principles to decide which parts of the Treaties and Directives are, and which are not, directly effective in national courts without the need for implementing legislation.(36) In developing those rights which arise from directly applicable Community law, the Court has taken account of the need to give the Articles in question a meaning which furthers the spirit of the Treaty even in the face of the intention of the parties as afterwards protested,(37) and the need for reasonable certainty and consistency in the application of the Treaty in different parts of the Community.(38) This can be shown by the view of the Court and the Advocates-General in a few cases.

Where there is a dispute as to the effect of the Treaty the Court can look at the texts of the Treaty in all the official languages and see whether these texts, when compared, resolve any ambiguity there might be in one language taken on its own. In doing so, the purpose of the provision can be used where that can be discovered from the history of the provision. For example, in Worringham v Lloyds Bank Ltd(39) the issue was whether 'equal pay' in Art. 119 included the provision of pension fund benefits. Advocate-General Warner compared the various language texts, particularly French and English, of which the French was more apt than the English to include such benefits. He concluded that the French text was preferable. The main reason for this was that, as pointed out in Defrenne v SABENA(40) by Advocate-General Trabucchi, the Article is a word for word repetition of the French text of the ILO Convention, Article 1(a), which differs from the English text of that Article. This use of legislative history as a guide to construction is the same as the approach of the House of Lords in Farrell v Alexander(41), and amounts to a purposive interpretation which makes deductions about the intention of the legislators based on evidence other than the opinions of individual legislators or others about the reasons for their choice of words.

However, recent cases suggest that the Court does not use legislative history in any more extensive way. Advocate-General Warner, an Englishman (though with a French mother), several times pointed out the serious problems of trying to establish a meaning for a text by examining the travaux preparatoires or the opinions of individual judges, jurists or legislators. In National Panasonic (UK) Ltd v EC Commission(42) he said:

'As I ventured to point out in Milac v HZA Freiburg [1976]ECR 1639 at 1664, what the members of the Council do when they adopt a regulation is agree on a text. They do not necessarily all have the same views as to its meaning. That is to be sought, if necessary, by judicial interpretation of the text. It cannot be sought by inquiry from individual members of the Council. A fortiori can it not be sought by ascertaining the views of particular members of the Parliament or of the Commission, let alone members of the Commission's staff, however eminent and however much they may have been concerned in the preparation of the text.'

The Court ignored the opinions of such people in that case in holding that Regulation 17, Art 14 differed from Art 11 by not laying down a mandatory two-stage procedure for Commission investigations. It should be said, though, that opinions of writers on the subject had been divided.

This approach is closely in line with the traditional English view that judges ought not to make use of travaux preparatoires and Parliamentary debates when interpreting statutes.(43) It also shows that the Court is limited by the words of the Treaty and the Regulations and Directives it has to interpret. The form of the drafting may leave room for manoeuvre, but wide limits do not mean that there are no limits imposed by the words at all. The text has one or more

possible meanings on its words which may not represent any
genuine agreement between the members of the legislature
about the effect it is to have. As Professor Pescatore, now a
judge of the Court, has said, 'The art of treaty-making is in
part the art of disguising irresolvable differences between the
contracting States.'(44) The nature of the Council makes that
as true of Council (though not necessarily of Commission)
Regulations and Directives as it is of the Treaties. The
travaux preparatoires are useful in identifying the mischief to
be remedied; they are not the total answer to finding the
proper interpretation of the legislative response to it. Even
when filling lacunae in the legislative scheme, the words of
Felix Frankfurter hold good: 'While courts are no longer
confined to the language, they are still confined by it.'(45)
Writing is an art, and reading is also an art, though of a
different kind. Reading is a reconstitutive art, but the
interposition of the reader between author and text makes it
also a creative art. The job of a court construing a statute in
even a simple case has been summed up by Lord Simon of
Glaisdale in Farrell v Alexander:(46) the court 'places itself in
the position of the draftsman, acquires his knowledge,
recognises his statutory objectives, tunes in to his linguistic
register, and then ascertains the primary and natural meaning
in the context of the words he has used...' One may disagree
with the idea that ascertaining the meaning is temporally
posterior to the other parts of the activity Lord Simon lists;
they would seem to be part and parcel of the activity of
construction. However, subject to that the statement
captures the essentials of the job of any court, and the
methods used by any court, British or European. Only the
details vary, and the variations are the direct result of the
way the legislation which the courts interpret is drafted. If
the English system of construction is to become more
European in its details, the English system of legislative
drafting will have to change to make the aims and structure of
the Acts clear from the face of the Acts themselves. The
preamble will need to become an operative part of the
legislation instead of a formal prefix. As Lord Scarman said in
Davis v Johnson(47):

'It may be that, since membership of the European Communities has introduced into our law a style of legislation (regulations having direct effect) which by means of the lengthy recital (or preamble) identifies material to which resort may be had in construing its provisions, Parliament will consider doing likewise in statutes where it would be appropriate, e.g. those based on a report by the Law Commission, a royal commission, departmental committee or other law reform body.'

If that happens, and not before, English courts will be on an equal footing with the Court of Justice in the ability to adopt a fully purposive approach to statutory interpretation. It will remain to be seen whether they have the inclination.(48)

V

The Court of Justice recognises the need for certainty as an aspect of doing justice. The confidence of nationals of the several Member States as to the treatment they will receive at the hands of the law should not be betrayed if that can be avoided consistently with the demands of the Treaties and the requirement that Community law be applied and interpreted uniformly throughout the Community. The use made by the Court of general principles of Community law, derived from the laws of the Member States rather than from the Treaties directly,(49) and the protection given by the Court to fundamental rights(50) can both be viewed as aspects of this. Another example is the way the Court has used the tool of decisions having prospective effect.

In Defrenne v SABENA,(51) the Court ruled that Art. 119 EEC has direct effect in the Member States, giving individual employees the right to sue for discrimination as to pay on the ground of sex. This came as a surprise to many, since the Commission had by its conduct given the impression to Member States and employers that Art.119 required national legislation in each Member State to make it effective, and employers had acted on that assumption. If it had been possible to claim back pay, perhaps going back years, in the light of the Court's judgment, firms might suffer serious financial problems and even bankruptcy. The Court would not sacrifice the objectivity of the law by taking that sort of consideration into account when deciding what the law was to be for the future. (In refusing to do so, the Court took a different attitude from that of some English judges in certain cases. For example, the infamous case of Spartan Steel and Alloys Ltd v Martin & Co (Contractors) Ltd(52) saw Lord Denning MR using financial expediency and the 'floodgates of litigation' argument as reasons for refusing the plaintiff's claim for damages for negligently caused econmic loss. Such arguments were not used by Lawton LJ and would scarcely have commended themselves to the European Court.) Nevertheless, the Court went on to say at paras. 72-75:

'However, in the light of the conduct of several of the Member States and the views adopted by the Commission and repeatedly brought to the notice of the circles concerned, it is appropriate to take exceptionally into account the fact that, over a prolonged period, the parties concerned have been led to continue with practices which were contrary to Art. 119, although not yet prohibited under their national law.... In these circumstances, it is appropriate to determine that, as the general level at which pay would have been fixed cannot be known, important considerations of legal certainty affecting all the interests involved, both public and private, make it impossible in principle to reopen the questions as regards the past. Therefore, the direct effect of Art. 119 cannot be relied on in order to support claims concerning pay periods prior to the date of this judgment, except as regards those workers who have already brought legal proceedings or made an equivalent claim.'

This power in exceptional circumstances to declare the law prospectively has many advantages. The individual litigant does not lose out; the law is settled for the future in the way the Treaties require; but the legitimate expectations of the other people who have been led to believe in the past that they would not be immediately liable under Community law are protected. It is a compromise between the enforcement of rights (or the certainty of justice) and the expediency of fulfilling expectations (or the justice of certainty). Nothing of this sort has yet been tried in England, despite the difficulty of providing a rational justification for the common law system under which hard cases are decided, and principles settled, through judicial decisions which have retroactive effect, subject to the rules on the limitation of actions. Occasionally judges have suggested that decisions might be limited so as to have prospective effect in the extreme case where the House of Lords overrules one of its previous decisions.(53) It could be done, but as Lord Simon of Glaisdale said in Jones v Secretary of State for Social Services(54) it would be best done by statute, sorting out procedural problems and preventing the battle which would inevitably follow an attempt to do it judicially, the conservatives denying that such a fundamental change in the way decisions are reached could legitimately be made without legislation, even if making the change were thought to be a good idea. We are thrown back here as elsewhere on the intractable problem of the proper role of a judiciary which is not directly responsbile to any democratic institution and has no corpus of principles on the exercise of its powers laid down by any outside body, in cases where there seems to the judges to be an injustice which cannot be remedied from inside the previously established body of statute and common law principles. The orthodox view is that we must wait for legislation. Action comes from judges only if there is a combination of two things: a clearly illogical or unfair rule which is not absolutely binding on the judge, and a judge who is imaginative and creative and (if on a multi-member court) has enough dominance and charisma to carry some of his brethren with him. Such men are few.

VI

The rarity of that combination of circumstances can be seen in the failure of the European Convention on Human

Rights to affect the development of the common law. The Convention is not directly effective in English law, unlike some Articles of the EEC Treaty.(55) Not only that, but English judges have refused to allow it to affect their decisions on matters of immigration, telephone tapping and contempt of court, while admitting that it may be of value in interpreting statutes: the presumption of construction is that Parliament intends to comply with its international obligations.

The United Kingdom was one of the first signatories of the Convention. Since then, little has been done to establish in our law the rights and liberties which the Convention sets out to protect. Legislation has grudgingly followed decisions of the European Court of Human Rights in a few cases: a new rule was added to the prison rules after the Court held in Golder v United Kingdom(56) the restrictions under English Prison Rules on prisoners commencing litigation contravened the Convention; the ruling in Sunday Times v United Kingdom(57) (the thalidomide contempt case), that the decision of the House of Lords had left the UK in breach of its obligations under the Convention, was followed by the passing of the Contempt of Court Act 1981, which may or may not now satisfy the requirements of the Convention.(58) There is no real sign of any Bill of Rights: parties in opposition like the idea as a restriction on the arbitrary behaviour of the party in power, but once in power the idea loses its attraction. The common law has fared worse than statute in its attempts - fitful as yet -to protect individuals from breaches of the Convention. An obiter dictum of Scarman LJ in Pan-American World Airways Inc. v Department of Trade(59) on the applicability of international treaties which do not form part of English law indicated that the courts could have regard to the treaty if there were two courses of action open to the court under English law, one of which would be consistent with the UK's treaty obligations while the other would be inconsistent with them. The court could then, he thought, formulate the principle of law, or adopt the interpretation of the statute, which would be consistent with the treaty obligations. Lord Denning MR in dicta in a case on the

Convention indicated a readiness to give it effect in a suitable case;(60) he later withdrew the suggestion that the Convention might have direct effect on the English law through our domestic courts.(61)

When Mr. Malone came before Megarry V-C(62) seeking a declaration that (inter alia) he had a right to privacy which had been breached by the police who had tapped his telephone acting under a warrant from the Home Secretary, and relying on the Convention, he was asking the judge to take a major step in the development of the common law. Previously no right to privacy had been recognised protecting telephone calls in this country. The doctrine of confidentiality gave some protection to some communications, though not to criminal ones. The law of trespass did not help unless the police had interfered with some property right of the plaintiff, for example by trespassing to position a bug; in fact everything had been done on the premises of the Post Office. England has no equivalent of the US Federal Communications Act, nor of the Fourth Amendment to the US Constitution, which give protection against wiretapping. However, counsel for Mr. Malone argued that the UK was in breach of Article 8 of the Convention, by allowing taps to take place without any of the protections for the individual which had satisfied the Court in Strasbourg that the German surveillance law was compatible with the Convention in Klass v Federal Republic of Germany.(63) There was no procedure for control of tapping by law in the UK, thus denying the UK the 'prevention of crime' exception in Article 8(2), and there was no statutory right to an effective remedy for breach of Article 8(1), thus violating Article 13. If the judge did not hold that Mr. Malone had a right to privacy, and a right to bring an action to vindicate it if necessary, it would leave the UK in breach of the obligations under the Convention. However, it was argued that at common law there was no authority against the rights which Mr. Malone claimed. Therefore, it was said, the court had two courses open to it, and should choose the one which would leave English law in line with the Convention.

Megarry V-C accepted that the lack of independent control over taps made the British administrative procedure hard to justify under the Convention. However, he held that the rights under the Convention were not legal rights in English law, so no declaration could be granted in respect of them. He said, further, that it would not be proper for a judge to create a right of the sort claimed in English law. The common law might be able to recognise a new right, but the Convention allowed that right to be subject to limitations so long as they were subject to review by an independent authority which could give a remedy for abuse by officials. The safeguards would need to be operated by institutions which, he thought, only a legislature could set up. The Convention puts limits on surveillance; it is to be subject to controls. 'It is those circumstances, conditions and restrictions which are at the centre of this case; and yet it is they which are the least suitable for judicial decision.'(64)

The difficulties one finds with this line of argument are these. First, the common law is said to be a system devoted to the protection of rights. Yet Megarry V-C seems to forget whose rights it is protecting. In a conflict between the administration and the individual, the citizen has rights; the administration only has powers. Every act of the administration must be justified by law. To say that anyone is allowed to do anything not forbidden by law, as the judge did, and use that as an argument for not creating a right in Mr. Malone to freedom from interference with the telephone, is disingenuous. If it is correct, anyone can freely tap anyone's phone. There is no need for any sort of authorisation, or indeed any reason at all. When one person's 'rights' interfere with another person's ability to carry on a normal life, the former's 'rights' need to be restricted. The courts are as good a medium as any for deciding whether this is the case. Say, as the courts did in the 18th century warrant cases,(65) that a practice of the State is unlawful because no lawful authority can be found for it, and the State either submits or legislates. If it passes an Act which is capable of an interpretation consistent with the Convention, it should be so interpreted. If not, the English courts must follow the Act, but until there is an Act it is perverse to go out of one's way to put the UK in breach of its Treaty obligations. Secondly, it is not clear that there was a real difficulty about finding an appropriate procedure to apply the principles of the Convention to telephone tapping. A bold court would have claimed for itself the right to determine the need for a tap, just as the courts took on the job (in the person of magistrates) of issuing warrants to search for stolen goods in the 16th and 17th centuries, and the House of Lords asserted the right to decide whether certain executive claims to public interest privilege were justified in the 20th.(66)

Malone shows that the Convention is not a fertile source of material for the inventiveness of judges. This is partly because judges are not very inventive. Partly it is because judges are so unused to thinking about rights seriously that they do not recognise a claim to a right when they see one. It takes a certain amount of experience to see that a case raises a rights issue. This was shown in Home Office v Harman.(67) Lord Scarman, who is a long-standing advocate of judicial protection for human rights, and Lord Simon, one of our most careful thinkers on the role of the judiciary, decided that the Convention was relevant to a case about whether a solicitor had committed contempt by revealing documents already read in open court to a journalist who was writing a feature article on the matter to which the litigation related. Lords Scarman and Simon looked for guidance to the Convention, and decided that to hold the solicitor guilty of contempt might be inconsistent with Article 10. This was one plank in their argument that the law of contempt did not extend to that situation. (Taken as a whole, their argument appears to be unanswerable.) However, they were in a minority. The majority, Lords Diplock, Keith and Roskill, decided that it was simply a technical matter of the solicitor's duty to the court. They failed to recognise that however narrowly you frame an issue it is capable of having repercussions on people's rights which go beyond the merely technical. Lord Diplock even denied that the case was about freedoms, justice or human rights at all. He described the Convention as containing freedoms stated in absolute terms but followed immediately by very broadly stated exceptions. The way he turned the case into a purely technical matter says more about the blinkered approach of the judges to human rights than it does about the true nature of the case, the Convention or the case law of the European Court of Human Rights.(68) The European influence is small. One can only hope that the next generation of judges will follow the lead of Lords Scarman and Simon. If they are inclined to do so, they will be helped by the duty to follow decisions of the Court of Justice of the European Communities, which uses the Convention's statements of freedoms as guidelines.(69) Perhaps in time this will extend from economic matters within the scope of the EEC Treaty to other areas of English law. It is simply a matter of waiting to see how long it takes for a body of judges educated in the ways of the Convention to emerge from the system.

VII

Conclusions. The evidence of judicial attitudes considered here is a tiny part of the total, which would include every decision of each English court. However, this little survey does suggest a few conclusions.

First, the gap between English and European methods of interpretation of statutes is exaggerated.

Secondly, where a difference in approach exists it is not dictated by an inability of the common law to produce judges skilled in purposive reasoning. It stems from the form of the legislation, and in particular from the way that the Treaties provide judges with a series of stated objectives. Judges operating in the EEC system of law need not agonise over whether they should adopt an individualistic or socialistic theory of the judge's role, or whether they would be legislating illicitly and unconstitutionally by reasoning teleologically. Their role is set out for them in the stated objectives of the legislation.

Thirdly, when the stated objectives still leave the proper approach uncertain, European judges have as much difficulty as English ones.

Fourthly, the influence of the European Convention on statutory interpretation is no greater than that of any other treaty yet, but there are signs of improvement. However, the common law seems as obdurate as an old ass in its resistance to change through the influence of human rights. Bentham's attitude still prevails among the common lawyers (whom Bentham utterly mistrusted): the lack of a right is a reason for wishing one had it, but not a reason for saying that it exists. 'Want is not supply; hunger is not bread.'(70)

FOOTNOTES

* A mass of literature touches this subject. As regards continental methods of interpretation I owe a particular debt to the lectures by Norman S Marsh, Interpretation in a National and International Context, (Brussels, 1974), especially lecture 7; the reports of the Judicial and Academic Conference of the Court of Justice of the European Communities 1976, especially the papers by Judge Kutscher and M Dumon; CJ Mann, The Function of Judicial Decision in European Economic Integration (The Hague, 1972); Brown and Jacobs, The Court of Justice of the European Communities (London, 1977); R Cross, Statutory Interpretation (London, 1976); and 'Quotjudices tot sententiae,' (1981) 1 Legal Studies 165, by Shael Herman. On the will of the legislature, see G C MacCullum, 'Legislative Intent,' in Essays in Legal Philosophy, ed Summers (Oxford, 1970), p237. Other particular debts are acknowledged in the notes.

(1) PG Wodehouse, 'The Manoeuvres of Charteris', in Tales of St Austin's (London, 1903).

(2) [1976] AC 443 at pp479-482, 490-491.

(3) See Malone v MPC (No2)[1979] Ch 344 at p380, discussed in section VI. This problem has been tackled with varying degrees of success by American courts in school desegragation and busing cases: e.g. Swann v Charlotte-Mecklenburg Board of Education 402 US 1 (1971); cp. Milliken v Bradley 418 US 717 (1974).

(4) See Dworkin, Taking Rights Seriously (London, 1977), chapter 4 on theories of adjudication and the 'right answer'.

(5) See the essay by Roger Kerridge in this volume.

(6) E.g. Camera Care v E.C. Commission, Case 792/79R, [1980] ECR 119. See further text at note 37.

(7) [1979] 3 All ER 325, CA.

(8) [1974] Ch 401, at p426. If it suits its purpose, however, the Court of Justice can use grammar and literal construction as much as English courts. See, eg, National Panasonic (UK) Ltd v E.C. Commission, Case 136/79, [1980] ECR 2033, at para 12 of the judgment, for a literal construction of the word 'or'. A purposive approach was then used (para 13) to confirm the view taken as a result of the literal interpretation.

(9) See note 16 below.

(10) [1979] AC 210 (Kerr J, CA and HL)

(11) [1979] AC at p257.

(12) Below, this section and section IV.

(13) [1979] AC at p263.

(14) [1979] AC at pp235-236.

(15) [1979] AC at p243.

(16) Candler v Crane Christmas & Co.[1951] 2 KB 164, CA For 'timorous souls', see at p178, and cp, Asquith LJ at p195; The Siskina [1979] AC at p 236; Chief Constable of Kent v V[1982] 3 WLR462 at p465.

(17) Brown and Jacobs, op cit, p194.

(18) See eg Miliangos v George Frank (Textiles) Ltd[1976] AC 443; James Buchanan & Co Ltd v Babco Forwarding & Shipping (UK) Ltd [1978] AC 141, affirming on other grounds CA, [1977] QB 208. On the effect of deadlock in the Council on the Court's attitude, see Henry G Schermers, 'The role of the lawyer in a Europe without leaders', in Jubilee Lectures celebrating the foundation of the University of Birmingham (London, 1981), pp81-91; Defrenne v SABENA, note 36 below.

(19) Above, text at note 8.

(20) Heydon's Case (1584) 3 Co Rep 7a.

(21) [1977] AC 59 at pp73, 82, 97, HL.

(22) [1977] AC at p73, per Lord Wilberforce.

(23) Black-Clawson International Ltd v Papierwerke Waldhof-Aschaffenburg AG [1975] AC 591, HL; R v Bloxham [1982] 1 All ER 582, HL.

(24) Murphy and Rawlings, 'After the Ancien Regime', Part 2, (1982) 45 MLR at pp60-61.

(25) Examples of the refusal to invent ambiguities in the face of an unwelcome result are IRC v Hinchy [1960] AC 748, where the H.L. could not help a taxpayer subject to a penal provision producing an absurd result because there was held to be no ambiguity; and, after the advent of the European influence, Express Newspapers Ltd. v McShane [1980] AC 672 ('in contemplation or furtherance of a trade dispute').

(26.) Costa v ENEL., Case 6/64,[1964] ECR 585; Amministrazione delle Finanze dello Stato v Simmenthal SpA, Case 106/77, [1978] ECR 629.

(27) [1979] 3 All ER 325. For the background and facts, see the essay by RJ Townshend-Smith in this volume.

(28) Lord Simon of Glaisdale has suggested that one is only seeking the intention of the draftsman: Ealing LBC v Race Relations Board [1972] AC 342 at p360; but this turns the draftsman from a functionary into a legislator.

(29) [1974] Ch at pp420, 423, 424.

(30) Case 129/79, [1980] ECR 1275, [1980] QB 180.

(31) Case 12/81, [1982] 2 All ER 402, CJEC and HL.

(32) Article 177, third para., of the EEC Treaty.

(33) [1982] 2 All ER at p415.

(34) Worringham v Lloyds Bank Ltd., case 69/80, [1981] 2 All ER 434 (CA); R v Bouchereau, Case 30/77, [1977] ECR 1999 (magistrate); R v Saunders, Case 175/78, [1979] 2 CMLR 216 (Crown Court), are cases of references by lower courts. On acte claire, see T.C. Hartley, The Foundations of European Community Law (Oxford, 1981), pp269-272.

(35) [1981] 2 All ER 897. On that case see the essay by Brenda Sufrin in this volume.

(36) Eg Defrenne v SABENA, Case 43/75, [1976] ECR 455.

(37) Van Geld en Loos v Nederlandse Adminitratie der Belastingen, Case 26/62, [1963] ECR 1.

(38) Eg A M & S Europe Ltd v EC Commission, Case 155/79, [1982] 2 CMLR 264: refusal to allow questions of legal privilege to be settled by national courts according to national law because of the need for uniform application of Regulation 17.

(39) [1981] 2 All ER at p442.

(40) Case 43/75, [1976] ECR at pp484-487.

(41) [1977] AC 59.

(42) Case 136/79, [1980] ECR 2033, [1981] 2 All ER 1, at pp2066, 7.

(43) See Black-Clawson etc., note 23 above; Davis v Johnson [1979] AC 264, HL. The theoretical problems are compounded by the inconvenience of an ditional mass of material to cope with.

(44) Quoted in Brown and Jacobs, op cit, p201. See further Dumon, 'The Case-law of the Court of Justice', paper given at the 1976 Judicial and Academic Conference of the Court of Justice of the European Communities, pp97-106.

(45) 'Some reflections on the reading of statutes', 47 Columbia Law Rev 527 at p543 (1947).

(46) [1977] AC at p84. For reservations about the importance given to the draftsman, see note 28 above.

(47) [1979] AC 264 at p350.

(48) Some reluctance to become fully committed Europeans can be seen in the speeches of Lord Wilberforce, Viscount Dilhorne and (to a lesser extent) Lord Salmon, in James Buchanan & Co Ltd v Babco Forwarding & Shipping (UK) Ltd [1978] AC 141 at pp153, 156, 160-161. In any case, no English court is ever likely to take respect for the spirit of the Treaties to the extent of rendering a provision in a Regulation ineffective by interpretation going to the extent of judicial legislation, as the Court of Justice did in SA Fonderies Roubaix-Wattrelos v Societe nouvelles des Fonderies A. Roux, Case 63/75, [1976] ECR 111, to Art 1(2) of Regulation 67/67. The Commission has bowed to the Court's view by removing the provision from its new Draft Regulation, a curious reversal of the normal roles of adjudicative and legislative organs.

(49) Eg AM & S Europe v EC Commission, Case 155/79, [1982] 2 CMLR 264.

(50) J Nold, Kohlen-und Baustoffgrosshandlung v EC Commission, Case 4/73, [1974] ECR 491.

(51) Case 43/75, [1976] ECR 455.

(52) [1973] QB 27, CA.

(53) Jones v Secretary of State for Social Services [1972] AC 944 at pp1015 (Lord Diplock), 1026 (Lord Simon); Miliangos v George Frank (Textiles) Ltd [1976] AC 443 at p490 (Lord Simon). It is well used by the US Supreme Court, which purports to base the practice on the common law: see Andrew Nicol, (1976) 39 MLR 542.

(54) [1972] AC 944 at p1026.

(55) See R v Secretary of State for the Home Department, ex parte Bhajan Singh [1976] QB 198, CA; dicta on the duty of immigration officers to bear the Convention in mind disapproved in R v Chief Immigration Officer, Heathrow Airport, ex parte Salamat Bibi [1976] 3 All ER 843, CA.

(56) (1975) Publications of the Court, Series A, No. 18. See the essay in this volume by Gillian Douglas and Stephen Jones.

(57) (1979) 2 EHRR 245.

(58) See the essay by NV Lowe in this volume.

(59) [1976] 1 Lloyds Rep 257, CA, at p261. See the cases cited in note 55 above.

(60) Birdi v Secretary of State for Home Affairs, CA Transcript 67B of 1975 (February 11, 1975).

(61) R v Secretary of State, exparte Bhajan Singh [1976] QB 198.

(62) Malone v MPC (No 2)[1979] Ch 344. The unsuccessful plaintiff has taken the case to Strasbourg, and the Commission has declared his complaint to be admissible on the question whether there are adequate legal safeguards on the use of telephone tapping in England: Malone v United Kingdom (1981) 4 EHRR 330.

(63) (1978) 2 EHRR 214.

(64) [1979] Ch at p380.

(65) Wilkes v Lord Halifax (1763) 2 Wils 151; Entick v Carrington (1765) 2 Wils 275.

(66) Rogers v Home Secretary [1973] AC 388, HL.

(67) [1982] 1 All E R 532, HL.

(68) Exceptions to the freedoms in the Articles of the Convention are to be strictly construed: Sunday Times v United Kingdom (1979) 2 EHRR 245. Lord Diplock has used the Convention, but mainly to deny a litigant's assertion of a right: Haw Tua Tau v Public Prosecutor [1981] 3 All ER 14, P.C.

(69) See J. Nold etc., note 50 above; Hauer, Case 44/79, [1979] ECR 3727; S Ghandi, 1981/2 Legal Issues in European Integration, p1.

(70) Bentham, 'A critical examination of the Declaration of Rights', quoted in Tur, 'The leaves on the trees' 1976 JR 139 at p154.

CONSTITUTIONAL CONUNDRUMS
THE IMPACT OF THE UNITED KINGDOM'S MEMBERSHIP
OF THE COMMUNITIES ON CONSTITUTIONAL THEORY

D N Clarke and B E Sufrin

The constitutional issues raised by the United Kingdom's membership of the European Communities remain unresolved. The aim of this essay is to take stock, to examine how and to what extent primacy is accorded to Community law and to see if the words of reassurance given in 1972 proved to be correct, that "nothing in [the European Communities Act 1972] abridges the ultimate sovereignty of Parliament",(1) or whether we have witnessed the complete or partial demise of what Dicey termed as the "very keystone"(2) of constitutional law. The present discussion will be limited to the effect of Community membership on received constitutional theory; and will not extend to matters such as scrutiny of European legislation by Parliament.

THE CONSTITUTIONAL POSITION AT ACCESSION

Dicey described the sovereignty of the UK Parliament as the "dominant characteristic of our political institutions" and his exposition of the concept became the foundation of English constitutional law thinking. Yet there has never been agreement on the details of the theory or even whether the concept is indeed "a legal fact, fully recognised by the law of England" or only expresses a fact of political life, namely that Parliament is a continuing representative political assembly with an unrestricted power to legislate. It has been claimed that the doctrine has not even been made out.(3)

It is worth recalling Dicey's definition:
"The principle of Parliamentary sovereignty means neither more or less than this, namely, that Parliament thus defined has....the right to make or un-make any law whatever; and further, that no person or body is recognised by the law of England as having a right to override or set aside the legislation of Parliament".
Views may differ on whether Parliament can make any law; Dike suggested the doctrine is challenged "every time a court

construes or interprets an Act of Parliament" but the sentiment at the heart of the Dicean view is a deeply ingrained one, namely that Parliament is the supreme legislator; the Queen in Parliment forms the ultimate authority in constitutional law.

The orthodox view of sovereignty

Professor Wade defends Dicean orthodoxy maintaining that no Act of Parliament could be invalid; that in the case of conflict between two Acts the later repeals the earlier; and that no Parliament can bind its successors. The "United Kingdom Parliament is, in the eyes of the English courts, a continuously sovereign legislature which cannot bind its successors as to "manner and form" or anything else". The truth, he asserts, is that there is an "ultimate legal principle" or "grundnorm" that judges will obey statutes and Acts of Parliament have force of law.(4) No statute can establish that rule; equally no statute can alter or abolish that rule.

This traditional view of Parliamentary sovereignty was difficult to reconcile with constitutional realities even before 1972. Two issues were particularly prominent. First, the Parliament Acts 1911 - 1949 do seem - as Wade recognised -to alter the manner and form of legislation. To avoid this conclusion, he submitted they should be classed as a "species of delegated legislation".(5) Unfortunately, the 1949 Act, designed to reduce still further the period during which the House of Lords could delay a public Bill (other than a Money Bill) was passed under the provisions of the 1911 Act. On this view, the 1949 Act offended against the general principle that a delegate cannot enlarge his authority. Logically, as Hood Phillips recognises, proponents of this view must argue that the 1949 Act - and any legislation passed under its provisions - is invalid.(6) Most modern writers reject this analysis.(7) Secondly, there is the issue of abdication of sovereignty.(8) Transfer of the whole area of legislative power (e.g. to a new legislature under a written constitution) can be accommodated in the theory; but the transfer either of authority over a particular territory - as with the numerous Acts granting independence to members of the Commonwealth - or of power to legislate over certain matters (an issue pertinent to the issue of Community law) are matters which are less easily digested. Since Parliament remains in existence and could pass amending legislation, the grant of independence can always be repealed. On the Dicey/Wade analysis, the "theory has no relation to realities";(9) and it is argued that a later "legal revolution" occurs whenever the courts in the independent ex-colonial state naturally assert that the legal power of the UK Parliament has been cast off. It will be submitted that this traditional approach cannot be maintained either in the face of the 1972 European Communities Act nor in the light of developments since then.

Self Embracing Supremacy

A more modern rationale of Parliamentary sovereignty, sometimes termed "self embracing" supremacy, can be seen in the writings of Jennings, Heuston, Mitchell and de Smith.(10) On this view, which has some judicial support in the Privy Council,(11) while Parliament cannot impose limits on the content of legislation, it can change its procedure and the manner and the form in which it legislates. The statutes whereby Parliament has indeed altered its procedure and manner of legislating then become examples of the way "manner and form" change rather than difficulties which have to be explained away.(12) Conveniently, it becomes somewhat easier to reconcile the concept of Parliamentary supremacy with the United Kingdom's Community obligations.(13)

In cases which do not involve a question of Community law, the courts have re-affirmed their traditional views of legislative supremacy. In Manuel v Attorney General(14) Canadian Indian chiefs sued for declarations (inter alia) that the Parliament of the UK had no power to amend the constitution of Canada so as to prejudice the Indian nations of Canada without their consent; and that the Canada Act 1982 was ultra vires. Megarry V - C struck out the statements of claim as showing no reasonable cause of action and the Court of Appeal held that he was plainly right. The Vice Chancellor applied the "simple rule that the duty of the court was to obey and apply every Act of Parliament and the court could not hold any such Act to be ultra vires." Slade L J, delivering the judgment of the Court of Appeal, said the contention of the plaintiffs depended upon the establishment of 3 propositions:

i) That Parliament could effectively tie the hand of its successors if it passed a statute which provided that any future legislation on a specified subject should be enacted only with certain specified consents;

ii) That s.7(1) of the 1931 Statute of Westminster (which preserved the existing powers of the UK to legislate by way of repeal, amendment or alteration of the British North America Acts) did not absolve the UK Parliament from the need to comply with s. 4 of the Statute when enacting the Canada Act 1982 if the latter Act was to extend to Canada as an effective Act;(15)

iii)   That the conditions in s.4 had not in fact been complied with in relation to the Canada Act 1982.

With regard to proposition (i), Slade L J observed that "at first sight" it conflicted with the statements of Maugham L J in Ellen Street Estates Ltd v Minister of Health and Lord Sankey in British Coal Corporation v The King,(16) which statements - though obiter - are central to the arguments of the supporters of the traditional view of Parliamentary supremacy. However, he also noted the degree of support for the first proposition of the plaintiffs "in the writings of certain academic lawyers and possibly in Bribery Commissioner v Ranasinghe [1965] AC 172". For the purpose of the judgment "their Lordships were content to assume in favour of the plaintiffs that the first proposition was correct but they were not purporting to decide it". Consequently Manuel, as with all previous cases, merely adds further obiter dicta to the issue. All that can be said is that the 'new' view of the nature of legislative supremacy has been recognised as a contender -and perhaps an equal contender - for the crown of constitutional grundnorm.

The ground of decision in Manuel was that proposition (iii) was untenable; if s.4 of the Statute of Westminster did impose conditions to be complied with, the condition was an express declaration that the consents had been obtained and the

Canada Act contained such a declaration. A trial judge would be bound to apply Picken v British Railways Board(17) and could not enquire whether or not the consents had been given, or given in the manner required.

Though Manuel reaffirms the legislative supremacy of Parliament as far as the judiciary are concerned, it did not raise any of the problems at issue as a result of the European Communities Act. Significantly, for Megarry V-C, the "simple rule of the duty of the court to apply every Act of Parliament" was subject to the caveat that he could leave aside "the European Communities Act 1972 and all that flowed from it";(18) - judicial recognition of the difficulties raised and the fact that a case with a European element is no longer answerable by application of a 'simple rule'. The question of whether any view of Parliamentary supremacy can be maintained since entry into the Communities remains open.

Judicial obedience to statutes

At least one writer has attempted to show that the case for the doctrine of Parliamentary sovereignty has not been made out. Yet even there it was conceded that "the attitude of the courts is the guage for measuring the extent of the powers of Parliament".(19) It may be that no judical consensus is forthcoming on the exact parameters of such an all embracing concept: but on one issue there is unanimity -the judges acknowledge that they must bow to the expressed intent of the Queen in Parliament embodied in a statute. A judge may interpret or even read words into the enactment; he may apply presumptions or rules of statutory interpretation which produce a result which some would regard as contrary to the plain words of the statute;(20) but an Act of Parliament is not to be ignored. Phrases such as "the intent of Parliament" and "it is for Parliament to change the law" abound in the law reports. Manuel is the most recent affirmation of this principle where it was said "sitting as a judge in an English court his Lordship owed full and dutiful obedience to that Act". It is not the place to enter upon the question of how far such an attitude actually cloaks judicial activism; it is enough that judical obedience to statutes and ascertaining and applying the "will of Parliament" is ingrained as the basic concept. It shows the judiciary's acceptance of the authority of Parliament; while the use of presumptions and canons of construction has meant that the courts have been able to avoid facing the deepest constitutional issues raised by the primacy of Community law.

The challenge of the Communities

The above analysis has been very much that of the lawyer, and the political scientist would place much less emphasis on sovereignty when describing the political establishment and the way the constitution works. We all know that Parliament hardly "legislates" at all and it is the Government which produces legislation for scrutiny and debate. Nevertheless, only an Act of Parliament has legislative effect(21) and if the "will of Parliament" is an unreal concept, that of Parliament as the ultimate authority is not. Just as the Commons can in the last resort deny the Executive its further legitimacy, so the constituent elements of Parliament can deny - and occasionally do deny - the Executive its legislative programme.(22)

To such a constitutional framework, Accession of the UK to the Communities posed a direct challenge. The assertion of the primacy of Community law over national law contradicts the negative aspect of Dicey's formulation - the Community institutions are clearly bodies which claim the right to override legislation of Parliament; and the positive aspect is contradicted if Community laws truly 'occupy the field' and become laws which Parliament cannot make or unmake. For the proponents of the 'new' or 'self-embracing' view of sovereignty the challenge was more subtle. The assertion of Community law supremacy appeared an attempt to impose limits on the content of legislation - could this be met by amending the 'manner and form' of legislation? Such a procedural change might be accommodated in the theory. Yet the issue is not just one of theory - but of how far the Accession to the Communities and developments since then have resulted in a weakening of Parliament as the ultimate constitutional authority.

COMMUNITY LAW PRIMACY

Community law introduces a new element into the context of the two classic theories of the relationship of national and international law. According to "monism" both types of law belong in the same hierarchy of legal norms and international law is the higher whereas "dualism" considers the two systems to operate in separate spheres, with each state's own national law superior inside that state. The approach of the Court of Justice has been monist, while English constitutional law is still unhesitatingly dualist.

The fundamental principle of Community law with regard to the relationship between itself and the national laws of the Member States is refreshingly simple. It is that in the event of a conflict between a rule of national law and a rule of Community law, the latter must prevail. The application of this principle of primacy may give rise to complexities in some situations but while some national courts have hedged it around with limitations and qualifications and constitutional lawyers in the Member States have struggled to reconcile it with their own constitutional provisions, the Court of Justice has never wavered from upholding it without reservation. It is a pragmatic idea born of the necessity to uphold the unity and uniformity of Community law throughout the Community and without it the pursuit of the aims and objects of the Treaty would be jeopardized. As the Court said in Costa v ENEL "the obligations undertaken under the Treaty....would not be unconditional but merely contingent, if they could be called in question by subsequent legislative acts of the signatories."(23) By 1973 the idea of primacy and the other twin cornerstone of the Community legal order, the doctrines of direct applicability and direct effect, were clearly established so that the UK knew exactly what the constitutional implications of Accession were and had the opportunity from the beginning of accommodating them. Whether the European Communities Act 1972 shows that this opportunity was taken remains to be considered although the UK's constitutional legal theory makes such accommodation very difficult.

The principle of primacy

The principle of primacy was first laid down by the Court of Justice in Costa, a case in which the possible conflict was between Treaty Articles and subsequent Italian legislation. The Court held in Internationale Handelgesellschaft(24) that Community law prevails whatever the conflicting national law, even where the latter is a basic constitutional provision guaranteeing fundamental human rights, and in Amministrazione delle Finanze v Simmenthal,(25) that it prevails whatever the national procedural difficulties. In Simmenthal the conflict had arisen in a lower court unable, according to Italian law, to do anything but apply national law; only the constitutional court could set aside national law in favour of the Community provision. The Court held that the primacy entailed Community law being applied in any court in which a conflict arose. There should be no question of waiting for the matter to reach a superior court.

In Van Gend en Loos(26) and in Costa the Court spoke of Member States having "limited their sovereign rights" and having transferred powers to the Community. This could give Member States a basis on which to begin to recognise the theory of primacy since if a state has transferred sovereign powers in a particular field it can be argued that it cannot legislate therein except insofar as the transferee or the terms of the transfer allow. The difficulty comes when the Member State's constitutional law cannot recognise irreversible limitations of sovereignty, as with the UK's doctrine of Parliamentary supremacy, or when the constitution does not allow transfers of sovereign rights which would touch upon certain basic entrenched provisions - as the majority in the Bundesverfassungsgericht held in Internationale Handelgesellschaft to be the case with the German Grundgesetz. The principles of Costa and Internationale Handelgesellschaft were repeated yet more forcefully in Simmenthal:

"....any recognition that national legislative measures which encroach upon the field within which the Community exercises its legislative power or which are otherwise incompatible with the provisions of

Community law had any legal effect would amount to a corresponding denial of the effectiveness of obligations undertaken unconditionally and irrevocably by Member States pursuant to the Treaty and would thus imperil the very foundations of the Community."(27)

Thus, the transfer of power, the limitation of sovereignty and the principle of primacy stem from the signing of, or acceding to, the Treaty by the Member States. National constitutional adjustments are irrelevant and for the purposes of Community law enactments such as the ECA 1972 are cosmetic only. Until Simmenthal the Court of Justice did not spell out the effect of primacy upon conflicting national law, but there it said that the entry into force of Community provisions rendered conflicting provisions of current national law "automatically inapplicable" and precluded "the adoption of new incompatible national measures" thus avoiding the description of the offending national law as "void".(28)

Direct Applicability and Direct Effect

The issue of primacy is inseparable from that of the direct applicability and direct effect of Community provisions for while any breach of its Treaty obligations render a Member State liable to a direct action before the Court instigated by the Commission or another Member State under Art.169 or Art.170, it is where the Community law can be pleaded in a national court that the problems arise.

The generally accepted view is that direct applicability means that no transformation is required to bring the Community rule into the national legal order; while direct effect means that the individual can rely upon the rule in national courts. However, the exact meaning and use of these terms is not yet free from doubt; in particular there is controversy about whether all Regulations are directly effective as well as directly applicable, whether Directives can be directly effective without being directly applicable, and whether in fact the terms are or are not synonymous.(29) The Court of Justice usually uses the phrase "produces direct effects" when pronouncing a particular piece of legislation to have the vital characteristics which allow an individual to rely upon it in a national court.(30) In Van Gend en Loos, the case which first established that an individual can rely on certain of the Treaty provisions in a national court, the Court described Community Law as a "new legal order."(31) Wyatt(32) questions the correctness of this, saying that what is claimed to be its distinctive feature, direct applicability and direct effect, was already familiar in international law. This is true, but the Court has always scrupulously avoided using the international law term "self-executing", preferring "direct application" or "producing direct effects".

The idea either of a self-executing treaty or of a Treaty producing direct effects cannot be accommodated in English constitutional law because in a system in which the signing and ratification of Treaties is the perogative of the Crown, no treaty provision can be seen as self-executing without allowing the Crown to legislate without reference to Parliament. The Crown perogative of Treaty-making was affirmed by the Court of Appeal in the Blackburn v Attorney General(33), in which the plaintiff challenged Accession. Even if a treaty is self-executing in international law, it will have no effect on the rights and duties of individuals as enforced in the English courts unless its provisions are enacted in legislation, or a device such as s. 2 ECA is used. This aspect of sovereignty of Parliament which nobody has ever suggested was abrogated by Accession, makes it impossible that rights and duties arising under the Treaty could ever be enforced in English courts without some domestic legislation, thus maintaining the dualist position. There are some points at which English constitutional law and Community theory are absolutely irreconcilable. The idea of a self-executing international treaty is one; and the primacy of Community law as expounded Costa and Simmenthal would seem to be another.

THE EUROPEAN COMMUNITIES ACT 1972

"One of the problems of not having a constitution may be that you cannot easily formally adjust what you have not got ..."(34) If the UK had had a written constitution, then no doubt constitutional rules could have been altered just as other non-constitutional legislation was altered on entry.(35) On the other hand, the formality and the politics of entry were made much easier by not having to make such clear constitutional adjustments, but the consequence is (perhaps conveniently) that vital issues remain unresolved.

Ideas to Facilitate Reception of Community Law

The 1967 White Paper, "Legal and Constitutional Implications of United Kingdom Membership of the European Communities"(36), was coy about the constitutional difficulties. Only two paragraphs addressed themselves to the issues. It was recognised that legislation would have to include "acceptance in advance as part of the law of the United Kingdom of provisions to be in the future by instruments issued by the Community institutions" - a situation without precedence in this country. However, the Paper continued, "these instruments, like ordinary delegated legislation, would derive their force under the law of the United Kingdom from the original enactment passed by Parliament." In this manner, s. 2 ECA was foreshadowed. The only other concession was that inconsistent domestic law would be overridden, but that this "need not to be left to implication", and "Parliament could enact from time to time any necessary consequential amendments and repeals. It would also follow that within the fields occupied by Community law Parliament would have to refrain from passing fresh legislation inconsistent with that law for the time being in force." This was not seen as involving any constitutional innovation.

The confidence of these paragraphs was not widely shared and a range of ideas were put forward for better ensuring the primacy of Community law, or reconciling the proposed legislation with basic constitutional tenets, or both. None of these proposals were taken up; nor does it appear that in the ten years since 1 January 1973, have they been really required.(37) There were those who were critical of the diffidence of the approach evidenced both in the 1967 White Paper and in the ECA 1972 and wanted a more adventurous approach. Mitchell wanted to see "a carefully drafted provision (by no means impossible to draw) which combines the two elements of transfer of legislative capacity and reciprocal limitation,"(38) with the declared aim, not just of helping to ensure the primacy of Community law, but also of avoiding the fiction that Community law is not a separate and higher legal order. He also wished thereby to encourage UK courts to "play their full part in the working of the Community system", arguing that if the system of reference under Art. 177 was to be effective the courts had to be able to hold national law invalid or inapplicable. Mitchell, significantly, did not attempt to produce a draft of the provision he outlined and in effect he was suggesting an irrevocable instruction to the courts in an Act of Parliament to accord primacy to Community law. It is hardly surprising that the suggestion found little favour with either academics(39) or politicians who knew they would face a stormy Commons passage for any legislation to give effect to a Treaty of Accession.(40)

An alternative approach was to suggest 'mechanical' means of ensuring Community law primacy. Wade urged the expedient of a 'European Communities (Annual) Act' by which Parliament would once a year assert the primacy of Community law.(41) Alternatively, he preferred a change in the format of Acts of Parliament, by altering the words of enactment or by providing a form of words indicating or taken to mean(42) that the Act was subject to Community law. Such mechanical means would conveniently "reconcile Parliamentary sovereignty and Community law."(43) With hindsight, neither idea appears necessary or helpful. We have not needed Annual Acts; the change in the format of statutes might have offended traditionalists while at the same time conflicting with the idea of direct applicability of Community Law.(44) Other ideas included the creation of a new constitutional convention restraining Parliament from legislating adversely to Community law but the analogy of 'Parliament' not legislating for the Domiminions which was the foundation for the proposal, is not in point(45) and in any event, a convention of this nature emerges and is not created by legislation.(46) The whole problem of Community law primacy led to renewed arguments for a written constitution(47) but this does not provide any immediate practical solution.

Trindade proposed the establishment of a permanent Parliamentary Standing Committee for the Scrutiny of Legislation Concerning the European Communities, which would consider current Bills before Parliament (which, it was hoped, would lead to a self denying rule of not enacting proposed legislation when any incompatiability was revealed). There would be a statutory requirement that judges, faced with a question of conflict with Community law, must stay proceedings for consideration by the Committee with an opportunity for amending legislation.(48) Trindade thought the gravest objection to his proposal was that Parliament would be encouraged to amend legislation half-way through judicial proceedings; but the more substantial objection is the difficulty of reconciling his idea with Art. 177. Would the reference to the Standing Committee occur before the Art. 177 reference - in which case it may not be clear whether a possible conflict arises; or after - when staying the proceedings would be tantamount to denying the primacy of Community law until an amending UK statute was passed.

None of these suggestions were taken up; but with hindsight it seems that even if the 'mechanical' proposals had existed, the cases would have arisen anyway. For example, the interpretation and effect in English law of Art. 119 on equal pay could not have been foreseen. A moment's reflection will show how hopeless would have been scrutiny of proposed legislation to detect possible conflicts. One only has to consider some of the cases in which incompatibility of UK law with Community provisions has been alleged or found. In R v Henn and Darby the defendants, caught red-handed smuggling pornography through Felixstowe docks contended that the difference in wording between the Obscene Publications Act 1959 and s.42 of the Custom Consolidation Act 1876 rendered the latter provision contrary to Art. 36.(49) In R v Saunders,(50) a binding-over order imposing a condition that the defendant go to Northern Ireland and not return to England and Wales for three years was challenged as contrary to Art. 48 on free movement of workers, and in Kenny v Insurance Officer(51) a claim for Social Security in England by a man who during the period in question was imprisoned in the

Irish Republic involved the question of the rights given by <u>Art. 7</u> and <u>Art. 48</u> of the Treaty and Regulation 1408/71. How many of these defences or claims could have been forseen in advance by a Select Committee? A clever defence lawyer faced with a piece of English law solidly against him may well be able to see a conflict with Community law. In <u>R</u> v <u>Goldstein</u>,(52) the case had gone to trial and appeal without mention of Community law until the night before the hearing in the Court of Appeal when a QC came on the scene and thought of <u>Art. 30</u> and <u>Art. 36</u> of the Treaty as a defence to a charge of importing Citizen Band radios manufactured to an illegal wavelength. There is also the fact that Community law is interpreted by the Court of Justice in accordance with the 'spirit of the Treaty' and to fulfill the aims and objectives of the Treaty.(53) It would be impossible in advance to predict whether UK legislation might not become incompatible with a seemingly innocuous Community provision suddenly given a generous interpretation in Luxembourg.

This brief review of views and ideas current during the period 1967-72 enables a more realistic assessment of the achievement of the draftsmen of the ECA 1972 despite all the constitutional difficulties. Instead of "two major Bills, one to give effect in UK law to the treaty.....and one to secure the necessary degreee of harmonization",(54) one relatively brief Act sufficed. The vital implementation, raising the varied constitutional issues, was limited to the famous - if not notorious - sections 2 and 3.

Section 2(1)

The key provision of the 1972 Act is s.2(1) which provides:

"All such rights, powers, liabilities, obligations and restrictions from time to time created or arising by or under the Treaties, and all such remedies and procedures from time to time provided for by or under the Treaties, as in accordance with the Treaties are without further enactment to be given legal effect or used in the United Kingdom shall be recognised and available in law, and be enforced, allowed and followed accordingly; and the expression "enforceable Community right" and similar expressions shall be read as referring one to which the sub section applies."

In sweeping language, therefore, all Community rules which are by Community law directly applicable or effective are given legal effect in the UK without any further incorporation procedure. As the 1967 White Paper foresaw, Community rules derive their force in the UK from this section. Those who wish to see the primacy of Community law recognised in its own right may lament this fact but a familiar technique finds expression in a new context. It must be stressed that s.2(1) only applies to those provisions which are accorded direct effect or applicability. Neither s.2(1) nor the section as a whole incorporates the EEC Treaty "lock stock and barrel";(55) it does not "decree the Treaty .....henceforth to be part of our law".(56) A better picture than the famous "advancing tide"(57) might be that of a Channel Tunnel. Section 2(1) provides the means whereby Community rules can cross the Channel and be enforced in our courts. The section, applying as it does to Community law made after 1972 as well as pre-existing rules is always available to transport new Community measures.

Section 3

It will be convenient to mention s.3 of the Act at this point, since it is the necessary consequence of directing our courts to give direct effect to Community law. By s.3(1), in all legal proceedings, any question as to the meaning or effect of any of the Treaties or Community legislation is to be treated as a question of law and, if not referred to the European Court, shall be determined in accordance with the principles and relevant decisions of the European Court. Section 3(2) requires our courts to take judicial notice of the Treaties, the Official Journal of the Communities and of any decision or opinion of the European Court on Community law. The purpose of this provision is "to put this material on all fours with equivalent domestic material and to give effect to Community law as a legal system which the courts must apply."(58) There are two interesting points to observe:

i   The provision in s.3(1) that questions as to the validity meaning or effect are to be treated as a question of law was widely interpreted as merely avoiding the difficulty that foreign law is treated as a question of fact and, as such, to be determined with the aid of expert witnesses and other evidence.(59) In R v Goldstein, however, Lane LCJ held that s.3(1) had a wider meaning, so that the meaning and effect of a particular Article of the Treaty was to be treated as a question of law, even though it was disputed whether the Article covered the prohibition imposed by national legislation. This interpretation avoided, in that case, having a jury determine the issue in a criminal trial.

ii   S.3(1) may go beyond what is demanded by Community law itself. In requiring courts to determine matters of Community law "in accordance with the principles laid down by and any relevant decision of the European Court" the Act constitutes all judgments of the Court binding precedents. This is perhaps not surprising in a legal system so centred on the doctrine of precedent and certainly serves to reinforce the provisions of s.2. It is clear in Community law that some judgments of the Court have an effect erga omnes: those annulling acts of the institutions in direct actions under Art.   173, for example, have an absolute effect and destroy the very legal existence of the act.(60) In cases brought before the court under Art. 177 however it is a different matter. Art. 177 does not state the effect of a ruling given thereunder.   It is clear that it is binding on the referring court in that case(61) and any other national court to which the case is appealed or remitted but it is not clear how far, if at all, it is binding on courts in subsequent cases. The Court has established that a court even of last instance may properly rely on a previous Art. 177 reference instead of referring the case before it,(62) but equally a court is free to refer a point already ruled upon in Luxembourg should it so wish. A preliminary ruling does have at least a most weighty authority but it may be necessary to distinguish cases in which the Court gives an interpretation of the law from those in which it makes a declaration of invalidity.(63)

S.3(1) removes from English courts the temptation to emulate the Conseil d'Etat in <u>Cohn-Bendit</u>.(64) In that case the Conseil refused to admit that Directives can be directly effective, despite the copious case-law of the Court of Justice, all arising under <u>Art. 177</u> references, to the contrary.

Sections 2(2) and 2(3)

For measures which do require implementation into the national legal order, section 2(2) gives generous powers to a Government to implement such Community law by secondary legislation - either by Order in Council, or by regulations made by a designated Minister or department. The power is limited by Schedule 2, but only to prevent imposition of taxation, retroactive provisions, more serious criminal offences and to ensure such instruments do not themselves confer power to legislate. Though far reaching in importance since by s.2(4) secondary legislation is to prevail over Acts of Parliament, once again s.2(2), as a device, is by no means an innovation.(65) Nevertheless, the direction that the person entrusted with the power to legislate, or in the exercise of any statutory power or duty, may have regard to the objects of the Community is more interesting. In effect, while exercising powers given by any UK legislation, Community laws - and, indeed, the broad 'objects' of the Community - are a legitimate consideration. This provision may be considered in the context of the doctrine of ultra vires. On its face, it must mean that it can never be an irrelevant consideration to have regard to the 'objects' of the Communities; and it is entertaining to speculate whether the exercise of an administrative power or duty could be challenged on the ground of failure to have regard to appropriate Community rules or objectives. The authors know of no case where the issue has been raised; nor do the standard works on administrative law seem to advert to the point.

By s.2(3), the UK's financial obligations are a charge on the Consolidated Fund. There is no question of returning to the House of Commons for annual approval of payments, which besides, no doubt, being a relief to Governments faced with large 'net contributions' in recent years, is a large nail in the coffin of the constitutional principle of the House of Commons control over revenue and expenditure.

Section 2(4)

This section has attracted the most attention which, considering its aims and wording, is not surprising. It provides:

"The provision that may be made under subsection (2) above includes, subject to Schedule 2 of this Act, any such provision (of any such extent) as might be made by Act of Parliament, and <u>any enactment passed or to be passed other than one contained in this part of this Act, shall be construed and have effect subject to the foregoing provisions of this section</u>; but, except as may be provided by any Act passed after this Act, Schedule 2 shall have effect in connection with the powers conferred by this and the following sections of this Act to make Orders in Council and regulations."

This example of complex parliamentary draftsmanship is really a sandwich of three provisions. The first element is only concerned with ensuring that subordinate legislation made under s.2(2) has the effect of an Act of Parliament -thus enabling such delegated legislation to amend or repeal statutes as well as the common law. The concluding exception makes Schedule 2 applicable to the exercise of all powers to make regulations or Orders in Council under the Act. It is the filling to the sandwich, underlined above, which is intriguing. A number of possible meanings to this part of the section have been put forward and since it is not yet clear which of the various views will be adopted by the courts, it is worth rehearsing the various suggestions:(66)

1) Literally, the words could be linked to the preceding part of s.2(4), thus making only delegated legislation subject to the requirement to be construed and have effect subject to Community law, but not only are there technical objections,(67) but this is inconsistent with statements of all the judges sitting in <u>Macarthys</u> v <u>Smith</u>.(68)

2) These words in s.2(4) may only create a new principle of interpretation so that "wherever <u>possible</u> UK courts should

seek to interpret UK legislation in a manner which would avoid conflict with Community law".(69)   The idea is that in the absence of a clear express intention in a later Act, the rule of construction would be used to reconcile the national legislation and avoid possible conflicts. However, the majority in Macarthys did not adopt this approach. The issue in that case was whether the Equal Pay Act 1970 (as amended and brought into force by s.8 of the Sex Discrimination Act 1975(70) gave the female claimant entitlement to equal pay for 'like work' done not at the same time as a male employee but in succession to him. The majority (Lawton and Cumming-Bruce LJJ) held that the claim failed under the Equal Pay Act. Using familar approaches to construction, they held that the 1970 Act required 'like work' to be done at the same time, while men and women were working side by side. Both judges denied that Community law could be used as an aid to construction. "The meaning of the words...is clear and ...under our rules for the contruction of Acts of Parliament the statutory intention must be found within those words". "I do not think it is permissible as an aid to construction to look at the terms of the Treaty". Neither judge referred to s.2(4) in this context, but both expressly rejected the contrary interpretation of Lord Denning MR and Phillips J where the principle of equal pay expressed in Art. 119 was used to assist in finding an alternative meaning to the provisions of the Equal Pay Act - with the Master of the Rolls expressly referring to s.2(4).(71) Consequently, this approach to s.2(4) would appear to have been rejected by the Court of Appeal.(72) The best that can be deduced is that regard can be had to Community law if there is a 'patent or latent ambiguity', in the English statute.(73) However, to assign this meaning to s.2(4) would make the words of little import since the courts have always been ready to have regard to the UK's Treaty obligations in the case of ambiguity.(74)

Just such an ambiguity was found in Garland v British Rail Engineering,(75) a complaint of sex discrimination in the provision of concessionary travel facilities. After retirement, female employees were only allowed concessionary travel for themselves; male employees were given such facilities for their families. The defence was that the concessionary travel scheme was a "provision in relation to retirement" within the exception in s.6(4) of the Sex Discrimination Act 1975. The EAT adopted a narrow construction of s.6(4), and held it did not include a privilege which has existed in employment and is allowed to continue after retirement. The Court of Appeal preferred the broad view of the industrial tribunal that a "provision....in relation to retirement" included any provision about retirement. The possible application of Art. 119 was not raised until the House of Lords heard argument. On a reference under Art. 177 the Court of Justice held that travel facilities given to employees after retirement which were an extension of those enjoyed in employment enabled them to be treated as 'pay' within Art. 119. Since female employees did not receive the same facilities there was discrimination within Art. 119, which, the Court stressed, applied directly without the operation of Community or national measures. When the case returned to the House of Lords, the employers conceded that the narrow construction of s.6(4) was correct. Lord Diplock's opinion(76) was therefore brief. He referred to the principle of construction of statutes 'now too well established to call for citation of authority, that the words of a statute passed after [an ordinary international] treaty has been signed and dealing with the subject matter of the international obligation of the UK are to be construed, if they are reasonably capable of bearing such a meaning, as intended to carry out the obligation and not to be inconsistent with it. A fortiori is this the case where the treaty obligations arise under one of the Community treaties to which s.2 of the European Communities Act applies." Since s.6(4) could bear either meaning without undue straining of the language used, the narrow meaning which was not inconsistent with Art. 119 was to be preferred. Significantly, no reference was made to either s.2(4) in this context though it was mentioned elsewhere. Consequently, it seems that no new rule of construction has been recognised as arising from s.2(4).

3) The most extreme interpretation of s.2(4), at the other end of the scale, would be to say that the clause entrenches s.2 and 3 against express repeal or amendment in a later statute. Such a view would obviously be incompatible with

constitutional theory;(77) but there is no warrant for such an interpretation in the words themselves. It would be amazing if such a far reaching constitutional provision dealing with primary legislation should be sandwiched in the same sentence between two provisions clearly dealing with the effect of secondary legislation. There are plenty of indications that such an interpretation would be rejected in the courts. In Garland, Lord Diplock indicated that the case was not one, having regard to s.2(4) to consider if "anything short of an express positive statement in an Act of Parliament passed after January 1 1973" that an express breach of a Community obligation was intended would justify a court construing that provision in a manner inconsistent with Community law. The implication is that an express provision contrary to the 1972 Act or Community law (let alone a statute repealing the 1972 Act) would be given effect by an English court. This was more clearly articulated by Lord Denning in Macarthys -"If the time should come when our Parliament deliberately passes an Act - with the intention of repudiating the Treaty or any provision in it - and says so in express terms - then I should have thought that it would be the duty of our courts to follow the statute"; and by Lawton LJ - "Parliament's recognition of European Community law and the jurisdiction of the European Court of Justice by one enactment can be withdrawn by another".(78)

4) In the light of these statements there appears to be little room for a similar interpretation of s.2(4) advanced by Mitchell Kuipers and Gall.(79) They contended that s.2(4) does not prevent enactment of legislation which is in conflict with Community obligations, but rather denies effectiveness to such legislation which is thereby rendered "inoperative" - a view which would agree with the opinion of the Court of Justice in the Simmenthal case. They argued that the effect of any such conflicting legislation would be subjected to s.2(1) of the Act which, by directing the courts to full effect to "enforceable Community rights," would import the element of primacy and thereby render the offending enactment inoperative. The writers hoped, in 1972, to see judges accept this analysis so that the Community view of the 'establishment of the new legal order' could find a place in English law. Sadly, English judges failed to respond to the challenge.

5) If the above interpretations can be put on one side, then the true nature of s.2(4) can be discerned. It is more than a mere rule of construction; but will yield to an express positive statement in an Act of Parliament subsequent to 1 January 1973 that a particular provision is to take effect notwithstanding the obligation under a Community Treaty to the contrary. The most obvious interpretation(80) which falls between these parameters is to treat s.2(4) as entrenching against implied repeal, or amendment, by later UK legislation the whole of s.2 and s.3 and, consequently, the complete spectrum of Community law brought into force thereby. Such an interpretation would have the advantage that effect would be given to subsequent UK legislation only to the extent that it was in accordance with Community law, while respecting the theoretical validity of any future enactment expressly contrary to the 1972 Act. It has been argued that s.2(4) does not purport to do this(81) and by others that it could not do it.(82) On the other hand Auburn(83) argued that for Parliament to legislate against future implied repeal would be the best way to ensure primacy of Community law - an approach which can be accommodated within the 'new' view of Parliamentary sovereignty. It is submitted that s.2(4) does just that - an enactment 'to be passed' is to 'have effect subject to ...this section.' The effect of such a subsequent statute would be similar to that suggested by Mitchell, Kuipers and Gall - it would be inoperative; but within the narrower (but vital) ambit of implied repeal. It is fair to say that there is no clear judicial expression of such a view; but as we have seen, there is a marked reluctance to delve into the exact meaning of s.2(4). In Garland, Lord Diplock expressly left the consequence of the "express direction as to the construction of enactments 'to be passed' which is contained in s.2(4)" to a more appropriate occasion;(84) so it is necessary to review the decade of judicial decisions to see if any consensus emerges.

THE TREND OF NATIONAL CASELAW

During negotiations for the entry of the UK into the Communities, Mr Blackburn sought a declaration (in effect) that, by ratifying the Treaty of Rome Her Majesty's

Government would have unlawfully surrendered the Sovereignty of Parliament for ever;(85) after the Treaty of Accession had been signed, but before the enactment of the ECA 1972, the equally redoubtable campaigner Mr Ross McWhirter sought a declaration that the acts of the Executive in signing the Treaty of Accession were contrary to the Bill of Rights 1689.(86) Both sets of proceedings were struck out as disclosing no reasonable cause of action and the Court of Appeal affirmed:

a) The courts cannot impugn the Treaty-making power of the Crown and until embodied in an Act of Parliament "these courts take no notice of treaties".(87) Mr McWhirter sought to argue that there was a limitation of executive power resulting from the Treaty of Accession. From the point of view of Community law he may well have been right;(88) but it contradicted the prerogative of the Treaty making power.

b) The courts will only look to the Act of Parliament giving effect to the Treaty - and "then only to the extent Parliament tells us".(89)

Thus, from the outset, the courts confirmed their uncompromising dualist position.

THE TREND OF NATIONAL CASE LAW

The Early Decisions

Once the ECA was in force, the judiciary took a little time to accustom themselves to the new situation. In particular, the exact effect of s.2(1), s.2(4) and s.3 of the Act was not fully appreciated. The Treaty was taken to be incorporated into domestic law "precisely as if the terms of the Treaty were contained in an enactment of the Parliament of the United Kingdom."(90) This statement and others of Lord Denning referred to earlier do less than justice to s.2(1), ignoring the vital words 'as in accordance with the Treaties' and fail to appreciate that a Community rule must produce direct effects to be enforceable in national courts. Fortunately, this attitude, described by one commentator at the time as 'misconceived and somewhat naive'(91) has been superseded by an awareness of the issues of direct applicability and effect.(92) It was also said that the Treaty provisions were "equal in force to any statute".(93) It is likely that this was an attempt to emphasise that Community rules have force of law, but implied in such statements is a denial both of the overriding primacy of such rules and of the independent legal order from which they spring.

Consequently, it is not surprising at this early stage that the oft-quoted dictum of Lord Denning in Felixstowe Dock and Railway Company v British Transport Docks Board(94) came to be made. In that case, it was argued that the defendant Board were abusing a dominant position, contrary to Art. 86 of the Treaty, in seeking to take over the Port of Felixstowe. The Board, a creature of statute, required fresh Parliamentary authorization to complete the acquisition (agreed with the Plaintiff Company before it succumbed to a rival takeover bid) and a Bill was before Parliament at the date of the hearing. After deciding that there was no abuse within Art. 86, Lord Denning observed:-

"It seems to be me that once the Bill is passed by Parliament and becomes a Statute that will dispose of all this discussion about the Treaty. These courts will then have to abide by the Statute without regard to the Treaty at all".

A great deal of emphasis is placed on this statement by defenders of traditional constitutional tenets;(95) but it is submitted that little weight should be given to this obiter dictum at the end of a judgment. For all the judges(96) made it clear that they believed there was no abuse of a dominant position and that this accorded with the expressed views of two Parliamentary Committees; and Scarman LJ was of the opinion that this was not a case of possible conflict between the Treaty and a subsequent Act of Parliament in view of a clause expressly inserted into the Bill to prevent the Board diverting trade from the Port after any takeover. He added that, notwithstanding the Act, subsequent conduct of the Docks Board might give rise to an abuse of a dominant position within Art. 86 but that there was nothing "in the proposed Act of Parliament which is in any way inconsistent with the Treaty of Rome."(97) Admittedly this does not entirely explain the dictum of the Master of the Rolls, but it stands alone and is inconsistent with many other observations, including some later ones from Lord Denning himself. With the passage of time, it may become one of the last judicial expressions of traditional constitutional doctrine.

Spotting the Conflict

In some decisions the possibility of a conflict between national and Community law has not been appreciated. In Garland, the impact of Art. 119 and of three Directives had not been raised by counsel before the industrial tribunal, EAT, or the Court of Appeal - a point noted by Lord Diplock in the House of Lords with some amazement, no doubt because the provisions of Art. 119 ought to have been well known by then. In Bulmer v Bollinger a more subtle conflict was ignored. A major factor in refusing the Art. 177 reference in that case was that, should the French defendants succeed in their claim for passing off in the lower courts "it would not be necessary to decide the point".(98) The possibility that the law relating to passing off would conflict with, or be inadequate in the light of, the relevant Community Regulation was not considered. The refusal of a reference left such possible conflicts unresolved. In de Falco v Crawley B.C.,(99) a case on the Housing (Homeless Persons) Act 1977, possible problems as to discrimination against EEC nationals contrary to the rules relating to the freedom of movement were never really raised. In R v Santillo an Italian national about to be deported pursuant to the recommendation of the sentencing court at the time he was jailed claimed the UK's deportation procedure was contrary to Community law.(1) A reference was made to the European Court who duly interpreted the relevant provision. When the English courts came to consider the ruling, both the Divisional Court and the Court of Appeal were unanimous that our law does comply with that ruling. Lord Denning thought the matter worthy of congratulation; in his opinion it was a good thing the reference had been made and our law shown to be consistent with Community law. In fact it is doubtful whether the procedure is in accordance with Community law and, with respect, the English judges appear not to have seen all the implications of the provisions as interpreted by the Court of Justice.(2) Their views may also have been affected by the subject of the case; national courts are instinctively inclined to guard more jealously the state's traditional rights to deport aliens than to cling to particular minutiae in modern equal pay and sex discrimination statutes -perhaps the latter are not seen to be so fundamental to our way of life. As we shall see, the cases of greatest constitutional significance, where the courts have accepted and applied conflicting Community law have been concerned with modern 'social policy' legislation.

Community Law Primacy in Practice

To set against the Felixstowe dictum and despite the tendency to fail to appreciate the impact of Community rules, there is an impressive array of dicta and decisions which indicate our courts' readiness to accord primacy to Community rules even in the face of subsequent legislation - provided Parliament has not expressly indicated an intent to legislate contrary to the UK's community obligations. True, many of the statements, such as that of Bridge J in Esso Petroleum Co. Ltd v Kingswood Motors (Addlestone) Ltd(3) (where the provisions of the EEC Treaty and of secondary legislation "is in conflict with our domestic law the effect of the Act of 1972 is to require that the community law shall prevail") do not in specific terms recognise primacy over subsequent national legislation. However, in Shields v E Coombes (Holdings) Ltd(4) Lord Denning MR addressed himself exactly to this point in discussing the direct applicability of Art. 119 of the Treaty;

"Suppose that the Parliament of the United Kingdom were to pass a statute inconsistent with article 119; as, for instance, if the Equal Pay Act 1970 gave the right to equal pay only to unmarried women. I should have thought that a married woman could bring an action in the High Court to enforce the right to equal pay given to her by article 119".

Lord Hailsham was equally forthright in the Siskina.(5) Where, he said, Community law applies directly "it is the duty of the courts here and in other member states to give effect to Community law as they interpret it in preference to the municipal law of their own country over which, ex hypothesi, Community law prevails." The most recent statement in the same vein is by the Master of the Rolls in Garden Cottage

Foods Ltd v Milk Marketing Board(6) where Art. 85 and Art.86 of the Treaty were considered and applied and formed the basis for an injunction. No constitutional issue arose but Lord Denning said that the articles of the Treaty "have supremacy over anything in our own municipal law which is inconsistent with them."

A series of decisions of the National Insurance Commissioner have held that European law is to prevail not only over earlier UK social security legislation(7) (the National Insurance Act 1965) but also subsequent legislation (the Social Security Act 1975) - Re An Absence in Ireland.(8) In the latter case, the national legislation provided(9) that "benefit ... shall not be payable" during an absence from Great Britain; Council Regulation 1408/71 was held to override that ground of disqualification. No reference was made to possible constitutional difficulties. In Re Medical Expenses Incurred in France(10), the Commissioner was more forthcoming and the 1975 Act was said to be "subject to the EEC Regulations" by virtue of s. 2(4) ECA 1972. In both cases, the claimants had benefit paid to them in circumstances categorically disallowed under the 1975 Social Security Act. Similarly, in Re Residence Conditions(11), the claimant, an Irish national, was required by the 1975 Social Security (Attendance Allowance)(No.2) Regulations to have been resident in Great Britain for not less than 156 weeks in the period of 4 years prior to her claim - a condition she did not satisfy. However, attendance allowance was awarded under EEC Council Regulation 1408/71.

The most famous - and significant - case in this context is Macarthys v Smith.(12) It will be recalled that Mrs Smith claimed the right to the same salary as her male predecessor. The majority of the Court of Appeal held that the Equal Pay Act 1970 (which despite its date, was amended and re-enacted by the Sex Discrimination Act 1975 and is therefore subsequent to 1972)(13) did not give Mrs Smith the right to equal pay; but the court made a reference under Art. 177 to ascertain whether Art. 119 of the Treaty(14) applied.

In their judgment, given before the reference under <u>Art. 177</u>, all three judges adopted positions indicating:
(i) If Parliament enacts legislation subsequent to 1972 with the intent to amend or limit the application of the ECA, then the courts will give effect to that Act. As Lawton LJ said:

"Parliament's recognition of European Community law and of the jurisdiction of the European Court of Justice by one enactment can be withdrawn by another."(15)

Lord Denning MR emphasised 'the duty of the courts' to follow an Act deliberately passed with the intent of repudiating the treaty - but he did not envisage such a situation.

(ii) Unless and until such a clear intent is discerned, the courts will accord primacy to Community law notwithstanding the existence of a national rule to the contrary - and that was seen to be the effect of s. 2(1) and (4) of the 1972 Act. The statements according such primacy are unequivocal.(16) Lawton LJ thought that such an approach did not infringe the sovereignty of Parliament but it does accord a unique position to the 1972 Act and is contrary to previously accepted constitutional tenets. The old wisdom was that a later Act inconsistent with an earlier Act will prevail; the new wisdom in matters of Community law is "If the terms of the Treaty are adjudged in Luxembourg to be inconsistent with the provisions of the Equal Pay Act 1970, European law will prevail over that municipal legislation."(17) So it came to be; the Court of Justice interpreted <u>Art.119</u> in Mrs Smith's favour holding that <u>Art. 119</u> was not confined to situations where men and women were in contemporaneous employment; and the Court of Appeal gave effect to it and upheld Mrs Smith's claim for equal pay confirming, in the words of the Master of the Rolls, that "Community law has priority. It is not supplanting English law. It is part of our law which ... overrides <u>any</u> other part which is inconsistent with it."(18)

A full review of the cases where the application of <u>Art. 119</u> and its impact on English domestic law have been raised is inappropriate in an essay on constitutional fundamentals and the reader is referred elsewhere.(19) In <u>Commission of the European Communities</u> v <u>United Kingdom of Great Britain and</u>

Northern Ireland(20) the Court of Justice ruled that the Equal Pay Act 1970 does not meet the requirements of the Equal Pay Directive because it does not entitle a woman to claim equal pay for work of equal value unless and until her employer has agreed to a job evaluation scheme. Such a ruling may cause little surprise when it is considered how our courts have had to grapple with the impact of Art. 119 on the provisions of the 1970 Act. What is more striking is how clear cases and issues of conflict between Community and domestic law have been avoided or side-stepped - except in the cases of Macarthys and Garland. Sometimes this has been done by construing the Equal Pay Act 1970 broadly so as to give effect to the principle contained in Art. 119(21) (though Macarthys case now makes it clear that this can only be done if there is an ambiguity); or interpreting Community law in a manner so as to make it consistent with English law;(22) or declining to make a reference to the Court of Justice under Art. 177 which might have revealed such a conflict, or, basing themselves on passages in the judgment of Defrenne v Sabena(23) by denying that Art. 119 has direct effect to the issue before the court.(24) Where Art. 119 does have direct effect it will supplement the provisions of the Equal Pay Act, or even supplant them.(25)

Three cases are perhaps worthy of particular mention. In Hugh-Jones v St Johns College, Cambridge(26) (not strictly a case of equal pay but involving sex discrimination) the complainant's contention was that the exceptions contained in ss.43 and 51 of the Sex Discrimination Act 1975 were overriden by Directive 76/207 on equal treatment. It was held that she could not rely on the Directive, either because an individual cannot rely upon it in proceedings against another individual or because it was not directly effective since the period in which the obligation imposed on the State to implement legislation had not expired at the date of the job application. No reference under Art. 177 was considered to see if such views were correct and the possibility of the conflict between the Directive and ss. 43 and 51 of the Act did not materialize -though Slynn J indicated that if he were wrong on the above points the Directive did fulfil the requirements of precision and clarity necessary for direct effect.(27) In Jenkins v Kingsgate (Clothing Productions) Ltd(28) it was conceded that a claim by a part-time worker (a woman) whose hourly rate of pay was less than that of full-time workers would fail under the law as hitherto interpreted. The Court of Justice, on a reference under Art. 177, held that differences in rates of remuneration did not offend Art. 119 provided the difference was attributable to factors which were objectively justifiable and did not relate directly or indirectly to discrimination based on sex. In the light of the Court's judgment, the EAT decided there was an ambiguity in s. 1(3) of the Equal Pay Act and felt able to reconstrue that section to accord with Art. 119 - and declared that an earlier decision to the contrary was no longer good law. Once again, any conflict giving rise to constitutional issues was thereby avoided. Finally in Worringham v Lloyds Bank Ltd(29) the defendant bank's pension scheme for persons under 25 had different contribution rules for men and women. The Court of Appeal held their claim failed under English law because of s. 6(1A)(b) of the 1970 Act saying equality provisions do not operate in relation to terms related to death or retirement, but referred the question of Community law to the Court of Justice. There it was held that contributions to a retirement benefit scheme is pay within Art. 119 of the Treaty and consequently the Court of Appeal found in favour of the claimants. It might appear a case of Community law displacing the national rule; but in reality s. 6(1A)(b) of the Equal Pay Act will now be interpreted more broadly in the light of the House of Lords decision in Garland v British Railways Board.(30) However, Lord Denning MR did seem prepared to envisage that national legislation may be displaced by Community law which 'has priority.'

CONCLUSIONS
1 The English courts have shown no inclination to accept Community law's view of itself, ie as a new legal order having force of law by reason of its own specific original nature. Community rules have effect here by virtue of ss. 2 and 3 ECA. Such an approach, inevitable from the constitutional framework, results in the conclusion that any direct repeal of

the sections of that Act would result in English courts denying any effect to Community law. Lip service is paid to Community law, but the spirit is denied.

2 Nevertheless, the ECA has largely ensured 'primacy for the time being' both by the way it was drafted and by the way the courts have dealt with matters of Community law since 1972 - provided they have been aware of the Community issue involved. It has been contended that the ECA has "the status of a constitutional statute having a superior rank to ordinary legislation."(31) If by this it is meant that there is a limitation either on express repeal of that statute or enactment of provisions expressly stated to be contrary to it, it is incorrect, but the statute does rank superior to ordinary legislation in so far as s. 2(1) of the Act has a 'continuing effect' and, by virtue of s. 2(4) of the Act is able to take precedence over a later inconsistent Act of Parliament.

3 The best interpretation of 'filling to the s.2(4) sandwich' and one which is most consistent with the caselaw, is that it entrenches Community law against implied repeal but not against any provision stating, or interpreted as meaning, that it is to have effect notwithstanding Community law. Not only is Parliament taken to know the existence of particular Community rules, with the consequent presumption that a subsequent Act did not intend to transgress them, but also in those circumstances where such a presumption is insufficient, s. 2(4) operates so that later enactments only have effect in so far as they are consistent with that Community law. Ellis argues, contrary to this view, that Macarthys is not an authority indicating that s.2(4) protects the ECA 1972 from implied repeal and that in that case there was "no conflict between the European Communities Act and any other piece of legislation; the only inconsistency is as between Community law on sex discrimination and the English statute on sex discrimination. Accordingly, there is no question of the repeal of the European Communities Act or otherwise."(32) On this basis, s.2(4) merely allots priorities as between pieces of legislation and provides that sometimes the normal rule of lex posterior is reversed. In our view, this is just another way of

stating that s. 2(4) protects against implied repeal - for the inconsistency which Ellis admits existed in Macarthys was between national law and Community law which had effect by virtue of s. 2(1) and s. 3 of that 1972 Act. It is protected against implied repeal or alteration by subsequent national legislation which says something different to Community law. However this is expressed it is a constitutional innovation.

4   The theory of Parliamentary sovereignty survives as the constitutional grundnorm, not only reaffirmed in the recent case not involving a European element (Manuel v Attorney General) but also in dicta in European cases.   Yet only in its 'modern' or 'self-executing' version can it be reconciled to the necessary consequence of Community rules prevailing over subsequent national legislation.   An Act of Parliament remains the ultimate constitutional authority in the United Kingdom with clear indications that effect will be given to any legislation unmistakably expressed to be effective notwith-standing Community law.

FOOTNOTES

(1) Sir G Rippon 831 H C Debates 278 (15 Feb 1972).

(2) Dicey 'Introduction to the Study of the Law of the Constitution' (10th ed 1959) p70. The quotations which follow are from pp39-40.

(3) Chijoke Dike [1976] P L 283. The later quotation is at p291.

(4) [1955] CLJ 172 at 190 (Quoting Salmon, 'Jurisprudence' (10th ed) and Kelsen).

(5) Wade p193.

(6) Constitutional and Administrative Law (6th ed) p90 and 'Reform of the Constitution' 1970 at 18 and 91. The procedure has not yet been utilized.

(7) Eg De Smith Constitutional and Administrative Law (4th ed) p97. This approach has been analysed as the 'continuing' supremacy of Parliament, see Winterton 92 LQR 590 at 591-2 and 597-604 - an illuminating analysis.

(8) See Winterton's article and the authorities there cited.

(9) Recognised in the dictum of Lord Sankey in British Coal Corporation v The King [1935] AC 500 at 520 - perhaps the clearest judicial expression of the idea of the 'continuing' nature of Parliamentary supremacy. See Wade p192.

(10) Jennings 'The Law and the Constitution' (5th ed) 152-3; Heuston 'Essays in Constitutional Law' (2nd ed) 1964 Ch.1; Mitchell 'Constitutional Law' (2nd ed) 1968 74-82: De Smith p97-101.

(11) Bribery Commissioner v Ranasinghe [1965] AC 172.

(12) Eg Parliament Acts 1911-1949; Royal Assent Act 1967.

(13) The basis of the argument in Winterton's article 1976 LQR 591-617.

(14) Times 14 May 1982 (1st Inst.): Times 4 Aug 1982 (CA).

(15) Section 4 provides: 'No Act of Parliament of the UK passed after the commencement of this Act shall extend, or be deemed to extend, to a Dominion as part of the law of that Dominion unless it is expressly declared in that Act that that Dominion has requested, and consented to, the enactment thereof'.

(16) [1934] 1KB 590 at 597 and [1935] AC 500 at 520 respectively.

(17) [1974] AC 765. See De Smith p91-97 and Wade & Phillips p70-74 for discussion of the Pickin rule.

(18) The judge added 'and also the Parliament Acts 1911-1949 which do not affect the present case'.

(19) Dike [1976] PL 283 at 296. Mitchell, op. cit. 1968, and in (1967) 5 CLMR 112 at 119-120 comes close to outright denial.

(20) Consider eg the statutory interpretatiaon in Anisminic Ltd v Foreign Compensation Commission [1969] 2 AC 147.

(21) Bowles v Bank of England [1913] 1 Ch.57.

(22) For the Commons to deny major Government legislation is tantamount to a no-confidence vote; the successful 1979 no-confidence motion was the first for over 50 years; but both Houses are a source of amendments and Government defeats are less infrequent than was once the case. (see Norton [1978] PL 360).

(23) Case 6/64 [1964] ECR 585; [1964] CMLR 425.

(24) Case 11/70 [1970] ECR 1125; [1972] CMLR 255.

(25) Case 106/77 [1978] ECR 629; [1978] 3 CMLR 263.

(26) Case 26/62 [1963] ECR1; [1963] CMLR 105.

(27) [1978] ECR 629 at 643.

(28) Some consequences remain to be clarified. Difficulties have arisen over the parallel application of national and Community systems of competition law. See Cases 253/78 and 1-3/79 Procureur de la Republique v Giry and Guerlain [1980] ECR 2327; [1981] 2 CMLR 99 (some of the Perfume cases).

(29) Of the academic literature on this topic, see in particular, Bebr: (1970) 19 ICLQ 257; Winter: (1972) 9 CML Rev 425; J-P Warner (1977) 93 LQR 348; Hartley: The Foundations of European Community Law Ch.7; Bebr. Development of Judicial Control of the European Communities pp548-611.

(30) Although in Case 12/81 Garland v British Rail Engineering Ltd [1982] 1 CMLR 696 (the language was English) it was said 'the provisions of Art.119 apply directly'. It is a different matter when the provisions of a Directive are in issue.

(31) [1963] ECR 1 at 12.

(32) (1982) 7 E l Rev 147, but see also Bebr: op cit pp549-561.

(33) [1971] 1 WLR 1037.

(34) Mitchell (1967) 5 CML Rev 112 at 125.

(35) ECA 1972 ss 4-12; though elsewhere, eg Germany, constitutionally entrenched provisions, particularly over fundamental rights have caused difficulty.

(36) Cmnd. 3301 paras 22 and 23.

(37) Trindade (1972) 35 MLR 375 summarises most of the proposals.

(38) Mitchell (1967) 5 CML Rev 112 at 120.

(39) Who felt Mitchell's proposals were constitutionally impossible: Trindade p386-7.

(40) The EC Bill passed its Second Reading with a majority of only 8.

(41) (1972) 88 LQR 1-4. (cf March-Hunnings (1968-69) 6 CML Rev 50).

(42) Eg by definition in the Act of Parliament.

(43) March-Hunnings at p60.

(44) It is suggested that Annual Acts would have created more problems than they would have solved; eg, legal uncertainty might arise with injustice for a litigant. Trindade p380-382 has further objections.

(45) Refraining from extending legislation to an independent territory is one thing; imposing a non-justicable rule not to legislate on a whole range of issues where the extent of the restriction may not be clear is quite different. Compare the distinction proposed by March Hunnings between vertical severance of sovereignty and horizontal loss of sovereignty at p57-58.

(46) Martin (1968) 6 CML Rev 7 at 23 admitting a convention could not be 'created overnight'; but surely it cannot be created as envisaged at all.

(47) Eg Hood Phillips 'Reform of the Constitution at p145ff.

(48) Trindade proposed a period of a year - see p399.

(49) [1980] 2 CMLR 229. The Obscene Publication Acts make it an offence to publish 'obscene' material; the 1876 Act prohibits 'obscene or indecent material' - a wider restriction.

(50) Case 175/78; [1980] QB 72, ECJ.

(51) [1978] 1 CMLR 181; Case 1/78; [1978] CMLR 651.

(52) [1982] 2 CMLR 181. Counsel was L Blom Cooper QC.

(53) There are many examples of this - eg Continental Can, Case 6/72; [1973] ECR 215 [1973] CMLR 199.

(54) As envisaged by De Smith (1971) 34 MLR at 603.

(55) 'We have to give force to the Treaty as being incorporated - lock, stock and barrel - into our own law here'. Denning MR Re Westinghouse Uranium Contract [1978] AC 547 at 564.

(56) Bulmer v Bollinger [1974] Ch.401 at 418.

(57) A favourite of Lord Denning -eg in Bulmer v Bollinger at 418 and Shields v E Coombes (Holdings) Ltd [1978] ICR 1159 at 1167.

(58) Mitchell Kuipers & Gall (1972) 9 CML Rev 134 at 136-7.

(59) Halsbury's Statutes vol 42 p85; Wall p28; Mitchell Kuipers & Gall p136.

(60) Art.174(1): See e.g. Case 22/70 Commission v EC Council Re ERTA [1971] ECR 263 [1971] CMLR 335.

(61) Case 29/68 Milch, Felt-und Eierkontor v Hauptzollumt Saarbrucken [1969] ECR 165 [1969] CMLR 390.

(62) Case 28-30/62 Da Costa v Nederlandse Belastingsadministratie [1963] ECR 31 [1963] CMLR 224.

(63) A declaration of invalidity made under Art.177 does not have the automatic avoiding effect of an Art.173 ruling but it may have some legal effects for third parties. See Case 101/78 Granaria (the 3rd Skimmed Milk Powder Case) [1979] ECR 623 [1979] 3 CMLR.

(64) Minister of the Interior v Cohn-Bendit [1980] 1 CMLR 543.

(65) See Wade 'Administrative Law' (4th ed) p700 for earlier precendents.

(66) See Wade & Phillips p128-9; Jaconelli (1979) 1CLQ 65.

(67) Noted in Wade & Phillips p129, footnote(9).

(68) [1979] ICR 785 at 789, 796 and 798.

(69) Wade & Phillips p129; see Hood Phillips (6th ed) p96: Collins p20.

(70) The dates are significant. The latter Act is subsequent to ECA 1972.

(71) Lawton LJ at 793-794; Cumming-Bruce LJ at 798; Denning MR at 789 and Phillips J (EAT) [1978] ICR 500 at 504.

(72) As was recognised by Hood Phillips (1980) 96 LQR 31-34.

(73) Cumming Bruce LJ at [1981] 1 QB 201-2; Lawton LJ [1979] ICR at 793.

(74) See eg Waddington v Miah [1974] 1WLR 683.

(75) [1982] 2 WLR 918.

(76) At 932; Lords Edmund Davis, Fraser, Russell and Scarman concurred.

(77) Discussed earlier; it would also be contrary to virtually all that was said from Government benches during debates on the Bill.

(78) [1979] ICR at 789 and 796.

(79) (1972) 9 CML Rev 134.

(80) Suggested eg by Wade and Phillips p129.

(81) Wall p26.

(82) Relying on the Ellen Street Estates case [1934] 1 KB 590.

(83) (1972) 35 MLR 129.

(84) [1982] 2 WLR 918 at 935.

(85) Blackburn v Attorney-General [1971] 1WLR 1037; [1971] CMLR 784.

(86) McWhirter v Attorney-General [1972] CMLR 882.

(87) Blackburn at 1039.

(88) cf. Costa v ENEL 'The High Contracting Parties have restricted their sovereign rights'.

(89) Blackburn at 1039; McWhirter at 887 (Phillimore LJ).

(90) Application des Gaz v Falks Veritas [1974] Ch381, 399; Esso Petroleum Co Ltd v Kingswood Motors (Addlestone) Ltd [1974] 1QB 142, 151.

(91) Bridge (1975-6) EL Rev 13 - a valuable review of early decisions.

(92) See eg Shields v E Coombes (Holdings) Ltd [1978] ICR 1159 at 1166-7.

(93) Ld Denning MR in Bulmers case at 418.

(94) [1976] 2 CMLR 655 at 664-5.

(95) Eg Hood Phillips [1979] LQR 167 at 170.

(96) Ld Denning MR and Scarman LJ; Geoffrey Lane LJ concurred.

(97) At p666. The Bill was lost in the Lords (H L Debates c1753).

(98) [1974] Ch 401 at 426.

(99) [1980] 1 CMLR at 426.

(1) Case 131/79 [1980] ECR 1585; [1980] 2 CMLR 308 (CJEC) [1980] 3 CMLR 212 (Div. Ct.) [1981] 1 CMLR 569 (CA).

(2) See O'Keefe (1982) 19 CML Rev 55; Barav (1981) 6 EL Rev 139; Ellis (1981) 97 LQR 533.

(3) [1974] QB 142 at 151. For another example see Aero Zip Fasteners Ltd v YKK Fasteners [1973] CMLR 819 at 820.

(4) [1978] ICR 1159 at 1167.

(5) [1979] AC 210 at 262.

(6) [1982] 3 WLR 514 at 516; and see the Essay in this volume p108.

(7) Brack v Insurance Officer [1977] 1 CMLR 277.

(8) [1977] 1 CMLR 5.

(9) Social Security Act 1975 s.82 (5)(a).

(10) [1977] 2 CMLR 317.

(11) [1978] 2 CMLR 287; cf Kenny v Insurance Officer [1978] 1 CMLR 181.

(12) Case 129/79; [1979] ICR 785 (CA) [1981] QB 181 (ECJ and CA).

(13) Recognised in Macarthys case at 788, 790 and 796.

(14) Which applies directly - Defrenne v Sabena Case 43/74 [1976] ICR 547.

(15) At p796.

(16) Per Ld Denning MR at 789; Lawton LJ at 796.

(17) Per Cumming-Bruce LJ at 798.

(18) At 200; emphasis added. Though this sounds like a monist position, primacy is still seen to depend on an Act of Parliament.

(19) Thomson and Wooldridge LIEI 1980/2 1 and the Essay in this Volume p69

(20) Case 61/81; Judgment of 6 July 82 OJ 1982 C200/2; [1982] 1RLR 333.

(21) Snoxell v Vauxhall Motors Ltd [1978] QB 11.

(22) Eg Handley v A Mono Ltd [1978] ICR 147.

(23) Case 43/74 [1976] ICR 547.

(24) O'Brien v Sim Chen Ltd [1980] ICR 429 at 446.

(25) Macarthys case. Supra.

(26) [1979] ICR 848 (EAT).

(27) At 860. When Slynn J became Advocate-General he repeated similar views in <u>Becker</u> v <u>Finanzamt Munster-Innenstadt</u> Case 8/81 [1982]1 CMLR 499.

(28) [1980] 1 CMLR 81 (EAT); [1981] ICR 592 (ECJ); [1981] ICR 715 (EAT).

(29) [1979] ICR 174 (EAT); [1980] 1 CMLR 293 (EAT & CA); [1981] ICR 558, [1981] 2 CMLR 1 (ECJ); [1982] ICR 299 (CA). Quotation at p303.

(30) Discussed supra. In <u>Worringham</u>, in the EAT, the claimants had in fact succeeded on this interpretation of the 'pensions' exclusion clause.

(31) Thomson and Wooldridge at 42.

(32) (1980) 96 LQR 511 at 513.

THE IMPACT OF EUROPEAN LAW ON EQUAL PAY FOR WOMEN

Richard Townshend-Smith

INTRODUCTION

The position of women in society has undergone profound changes since the Second World War. One of the chief of these has been a dramatic change in the employment pattern. This development led to pressure for legislation supposedly designed to contribute to equal treatment for women. The Equal Pay Act, 1970, Sex Discrimination Act, 1975, and the Social Security Pensions Act, 1975 were regarded as milestones, despite the fact that large areas were omitted (1) and that, even within the immediate scope of the legislation, numerous and significant exceptions were built in.(2)

At the same time as the domestic developments, the E.E.C. has been similarly active. Art. 119 of the Treaty of Rome adopts a broad-brush approach in seeking to bring about equal pay for women, while three directives, the Equal Pay Directive,(3) the Equal Treatment Directive(4) and the Social Security Directive,(5) are relevant to the employment position of women throughout the Community, although the immediate applications and benefits of the three directives remain a matter of acute controversy.(6)

Art. 119 provides that "each Member state shall... ensure and subsequently maintain the application of the principle that men and women should receive equal pay for equal work." For the purposes of the Article, 'pay' is defined as "the ordinary basic or minimum wage or salary or any other consideration, whether in cash or kind, which the worker receives, directly or indirectly, in respect of his employment from his employer.

Equal pay without discrimination based on sex means:
a) that pay for the same work at piece rates shall be calculated on the basis of the same unit of measurement.
b) that pay for work at time rates shall be the same for the same job."

Legislation by no means always achieves its desired effect, even if there is any consensus as to what the aims might be. The benefits to women of the Equal Pay Act cannot be gleaned simply by an analysis of the decided cases, many of which only deal with exceptional situations. In particular, the domestic legislation is largely unable to benefit women who are entrenched in patterns of occupational segregation. However the European legislation has the potential of escaping from some at least of the domestic restrictiveness. The main thrust of this chapter is to attempt to assess the scope of that potential.

Consideration will first be given to women's employment patterns during the 20th century, with particular reference to the post-war period. Having briefly identified the facts, the reasons why the employment position of women is weaker than that of men will be examined. It is only when the causes of discrimination have been identified that one can begin to see whether legal intervention can hope to eliminate particular instances of discrimination. It is then intended to apply this information to the Equal Pay Act to identify the strengths and weakness of the British legislation. Finally the European law will be examined to see in what respects it is wider than the British domestic law, and, crucially, whether in each area the additional width amounts to a realistic addition to the rights of women or is merely a technical extension unlikely to benefit more than a handful of employees.

THE EMPLOYMENT POSITION OF WOMEN

The number of females in the work force in 1951 was 7.4 million, compared with 15.8 million males. By 1976 the figures were 9.01 million and 13.01 million. The percentage figure of female participation had increased from 31.8% to 40.1%.(7) This increase has come at a time of declining male participation, for which a shorter span of years in the workforce as well as increasing unemployment are the most likely explanations. However the figure for female employees overstates the case as it draws no distinction between full-time and part-time workers, the latter being almost exclusively a female phenomenon.(8) Putting the figures the other way round, in 1951 34.7% of women were active in the labour force whereas by 1975 this figure had increased to 45.7%. In the same period the male participation rate declined from 87.6% to 80.6%.(9)

Significant though these figures are, they are far less dramatic than the change in the pattern of married women's employment. It is clear that social changes are likely to have had more impact on the married than the unmarried. The proportion of married women who were economically active increased from 10% in 1931, a figure which had remained fairly constant throughout the century until that date, to 42.2% in 1971, the increase occuring at a fairly constant rate throughout that forty-year period.(10) As far as married women with children are concerned, their participation in the workforce increased from 26% in 1961 to 40% in 1971.(11) Indeed "rising activity rates among married woman now constitute the major source of additional labour in Britain, mainly because of the re-entry into employment of older married women".(12) For many years young marrieds had a higher involvement in the workforce than any other age-group of married women, but between 1961 and 1966 they were overtaken by the age-groups 35-44 and 45-54.(13) The changes in the participation rates in the older age-groups have been dramatic. It has been suggested that one of the inferences that can be gained from the figures is that of considerable movements by married women in and out of the workforce.(14) This factor may prove to be of considerable significance when examining the pay and occupational structure of women in the labour force.

Turning to the question of pay, the simplest comparison is that of women's take-home pay with men's. In 1970, the year the Equal Pay Act was passed, though of course it was not brought into effect until 1975, average female earnings were 63.1% of those of men. By 1975 the figure had reached 72.1%. It peaked at 75.5% in 1977 and retreated to 73.0% by 1979.(15) These figures suggest that the Act had a significant effect in its early years which petered out fairly rapidly; breaches of the Act are clearly not the only cause of inequality in matters of pay. The Act's impact can also be demonstrated by looking at the increase in male and female earnings starting with the base year 1969. Between that year and 1976 male average hourly earnings increased 185% and average weekly earnings 170%; for women the equivalent figures were 241.5% and 235%.(16) Thus in percentage terms the earnings of women rose more rapidly than those of men, though given the much worse starting position of women it is likely that in money terms the gap actually increased. One factor that makes the position of women worse still is that the basic comparisons all exclude overtime. In 1973 "overtime earnings accounted for 16% of the earnings of male manual workers and only 3% of the earnings of full-time female manual workers."(17)

The above statistics have all concentrated on comparisons, whereas it is also instructive to see in absolute terms the extent to which women predominate among the low-paid in Britain. The Royal Commission on Income and Wealth(18) defined low pay as being paid no more than that earned by the lowest 10% of male manual workers. The percentage of female manual workers who were within this definition declined from 85% in 1970 to 68% in 1977, whereas for female non-manual workers the decline was from 56% to 48%.(19) Another approach is to examine the percentage of male and female workers within given salary bands. In April 1976 only 5.2% of full-time men earned less than £50 per week, while the female figure was 43.2%. At the other end of the scale 61.7% of men earned more than £60 per week and only 16.5% of women.(20) The problem is not that "some women are paid less than others, but that women as a whole have much lower pay than men."(21) Any significant change would not simply concentrate on the lowest-paid women but would need to shift the whole female distribution closer to the male.

Research into the extent of occupational segregation in Great Britain has distinguished(22) horizontal and vertical segregation: the former is where particular occupations are largely reserved for one sex; the latter is the alleged tendency for the better and more prestigious jobs within occupations to be occupied by men.

Various ways of looking at trends in horizontal occupational segregation are identified. For example "the proportion of occupations without any women workers was relatively constant at around 9% from 1901 to 1961, but fell to 2% in 1971."(23) Again "in 1901 almost half of men were in all-male jobs compared to 11% of women in all-female jobs......... By 1971 over half of all men were still in occupations where they outnumbered women by at least 9 to 1,"(24) whereas only a quarter of women were in such a position.(25) By the end of the 1970s these figures were 58% and 27% respectively,(26) figures which hardly changed at all in the decade which saw the passing of the Sex Discrimination Act. Hakim concludes that "legislation had a very marked and dramatic impact within a very short space of time, [but] some or all of these gains were then lost in the reversed trend in the latter part of the decade."(27) Strict segregation between the sexes is thus still a common feature of British employment. Indeed during the 20th Century "the likelihood of working in an occupation where one's own sex predominated (at 90% or more of the work-force, or even at 70% or more of the work-force) became proportionately greater for men.(28) Suggestions that women have made sweeping inroads into what were formally all-male preserves are shown to be false.

Vertical segregation is more difficult to measure, as it depends on identifying what are regarded as the top jobs. None the less a few examples will assist: a recent survey(29) showed that 91% of all supervisory jobs, and 77% of all managerial jobs were male, while 62% of all personal service jobs were female.(30) Hakim's conclusion is that "in manual work the trend is towards greater segregation with men increasingly over-represented in skilled work and women contributing an increasing share of unskilled and semi-skilled workers."(31) The overall conclusion is that the impact of anti-discrimination legislation, while significant at least for a time, "is a neccessary but not sufficient condition for movement towards equality."(32) A vital question for the potential effectiveness of any form of Equal Pay legislation is how far inequalities in pay are due to unequal pay for the same job and how far to occupational segregation. The more they are due to the latter, the less effective any legislation is likely to be.

One of the most significant contrasts relates to part-time employment. The overall figure for women who work part-time rose from 33.5% in 1971 to 38.4% in 1977 largely concentrated in the service sector.(33) The figures for men reached 5.26% in 1975.(34) These figures have great significance for levels of women's pay. In 1979 "79.5% of part-time women workers....were earning less than £1.50 per hour, compared with 47.8% of full-time women and 12.5% of full-time men."(35) There is a high proportion of part-time workers in occupations where wages generally tend to be low for both male and female employees.(36) In fact 70% of female part-time employees work in three broad occupational groups, professional and scientific services, distributive trades and miscellaneous services.(37)

To conclude that part-time workers tend to work in low-paid industries raises the question why some occupations are lower paid than others, which of course is a much wider issue. Indeed it may be the fact that such industries are low paid that enables them to have such a high proportion of part-timers. If so, to require part-time workers to be paid at the same rate as full-time may tend to reduce the opportunity to work part-time.(38)

It is vain to expect women to receive equal pay with men so long as they are concentrated in lower paid jobs. Further, it is vain to expect equal pay within particular occupations so long as women's career structures differ so radically from those of men when pay depends so significantly on age and length of service. Any reliance on equal pay legislation requires examination of the degree to which job segregation is the real cause of inequality in pay, and then of why it is that job segregation exists. It is to these issues that we now turn.

EXPLANATIONS FOR INEQUALITIES OF PAY AND FOR OCCUPATIONAL SEGREGATION

Any assessment of the likely effectiveness of equal pay legislation requires some understanding of the causes of the fact that the average pay of women is below that of men. The characteristics of women's work, being concentrated in certain sectors of the economy, and often in jobs notoriously hard to unionise, demonstrate long-term employment patterns which are very hard to upset. A further factor relates to the shorter and more intermittent stays in the labour market characteristic of female employees.(39) This suggests that there may be explanations for pay inequality which are not dependent on discrimination by employers. It is however somewhat surprising that research has suggested that the most important factor in pay inequality is differences in earnings within each occupation rather than differences between typically male and typically female occupations.(40) There are two explanations for this. The first is the influence of gradings and incremental pay structures which tend to reward employees with long service. Secondly, and more significantly, it is suggested that within particular occupations women are concentrated in lower-paying establishments, which tend to be the smaller firms.(41) It seems unlikely that either of these factors is likely to be much disturbed by legislation.(42) A more uncertain question is the reason for this concentration. In particular are such firms lower paying because they have women worker's, or vice versa?

To conclude that occupational segregation is a key factor in pay inequality says nothing as to its origin. A distinction exists between discrimination before the market and discrimination within the market.(43) The former denies its victims the opportunity to use or develop their capabilities to the full, while the latter causes certain workers to be treated less favourably because of a given characteristic, be it sex, race, age or whatever. As far as the former is concerned, Phelps Brown further sub-divides into discrimination in upbringing, the relevance of which to female employment patterns hardly needs elaboration, and discrimination in opportunity, which concerns not entry into a particular job, but entry into an occupation as a whole, such as by licensing, apprenticeship, or trade influence via the craft system.

Neither of the above forms of discrimination entails any inequality when women do win entry to a particular occupation. Such inequality is only inherent in discrimination within the market which again is sub-divided. The first category here is what is called monopsonistic discrimination: normally an employer would be unable to pay men more than women and remain competitive over his rivals who employed only women. If however he is a monopsonist, namely a sole buyer of labour in a given area, such pure market points will not disturb him. His ability to do this will remain in the more common situation of his being one of a group of employers in an area who together have a monopsony or near monopsony. Even without this situation, employers may consider that a certain group of workers is of less value than another group. It is here that attempts have been made to explain apparently economically irrational discrimination on the basis of discrimination according to status.(44) It raises the important issue of how employers assess the value of women workers, and whether such assessment can be made more objective.(45)

Economists have concluded that the amount of discrimination within the market against women is less than is often imagined.(46) This may partly be due to assumptions about the job market. Phelps Brown considers that "even where men and women are performing the same work with equal efficiency....and the women are paid less, it is still possible that their work is worth less over a longer period of time, because they were more likely to leave when their experience was making them increasingly useful."(47) In legal terms this kind of issue may be reduced to one of what sort of evidence a court or tribunal is prepared to hear before being willing to accept such defence to pay inequality.(48) Phelps Brown's conclusion is that "it seems highly probable that the disabilities of women workers spring far more from our first two forms of discrimination, in upbringing and in opportunity, rather than in....discrimination by monopsony and according to status."(49)

In many respects women comprise a separate labour market from men. A distinction is made between the primary labour market, which is marked by high levels of skill and wages and by good prospects for advancement, whilst in the secondary labour market the characteristics are low pay, low skill factors, little opportunity for promotion and a high labour turnover,(50) with women providing the bulk of the secondary work force.(51) If this is correct, it entails that "no major change in the position of women in the labour force could be achieved without a restructuring of the labour market."(52) This would at the very least necessitate either a reduction in the emphasis placed on continuity in employment, or a social reordering whereby women were better able to achieve such continuity. Moreover one of the chief ways in which the dualism is maintained is through the internal labour market. The more that a firm promotes internally, the more likely it is that length of service plays a part in securing promotion. Such requirements may well be economically "rational" from an employer's point of view, even though statistically they may discriminate against women,(53) and therefore legislation by itself is most unlikely to be able to resolve this problem.(54)

It has been suggested that employers discriminate because they can only have very generalised information about any particular applicant, and thus are forced to rely on hearsay or what may be very inaccurate generalisations as to the productivity or work commitment of women.(55) The information on the relative costs of employing men and women may be either unavailable or expensive to obtain.(56) It is therefore argued that decisions are made on the basis of unproven assumptions about the status and behaviour of women. Furthermore, assuming that the potential costs of discrimination are one of the items on the balance sheet of the economically rational employer, it is rare that these will be large enough to act as a significant deterrent.(57)

Status may also operate in discrimination before the market, although the way in which the social status attached to a given job affects pay in that job is uncertain, especially as compared with the role played by market forces. Another approach raises the question of what has become known as the "family wage"; the assumption that men need to be paid more than women because in the normal course of events their wage needs to support more than one person whereas the woman's wage does not. "Women are primarily seen as domestic labourers whose wage labour is organised as subordinate and supplementary to men. The breadwinner's wage is conceptualised as the family wage supposedly sufficient to maintain a wife and children in a condition of dependency."(58) It is arguable that this view benefits men, who have consequential employment advantages, and employers, who can draw on a more compliant and malleable secondary work force.(59) If trade unions are male-dominated, then there is no incentive to seek radical change, which is why many people stress need for greater female involvement in the unions.(60) It can also be easily demonstrated that the factual assumptions of the family wage argument are misplaced. It is never used as an argument for reducing the pay of men without wives or children. And in the days of one-parent families, the assumptions underlying the argument could well be a contributory cause of a considerable amount of absolute poverty.

Another important issue which can only be touched on is the extent to which past trade union practices and collective bargaining have contributed to female pay inequality. There are many difficult points involved: why fewer women traditionally have joined unions, why 'female' jobs are regarded in unions as harder to organise, whether unions have contributed, consciously or subconsciously, to the maintenance of occupational segregation, and the extent to which union pressure through collective bargaining actually affects eventual rates of pay.

Taking the last issue first, it has been suggested that only some pay structures are "trade union orientated", two examples being printing and the construction industry.(61) Other situations, such as where there is a coherent labour market, or where the employer has a monopsony, or where labour costs are low relative to product costs, are less influenced by union demands. While it would be wrong to overstate the long-term influence unions have had on wage rates and patterns, two conclusions have been reached. Firstly, "a union that is sheltered from the direct or indirect competition of other labour will generally be able to push up the relative pay of its members without causing job losses.(62) Secondly, "sustained unionism has been associated with a raising of manual pay relative to white-collar pay, and among the manual with a relative raising of the unskilled."(63) Such results on average will depress average women's rates compared with those of men.

The proportion of female trade unionists rose from 18.7% in 1951 to 28.8% in 1975, in a period when the total female workforce rose from 31.8% to 40.8%.(64) However in 1976 only 4.4% of full-time officials and 10.7% of TUC delegates were women.(65) Whether it is the case that 'female'jobs are harder to organise, or whether it is simply that unions have made less effort in such workplaces is uncertain. Sloane hypothesises, that while unions may narrow the male-female differential in the firms in which they operate, they may have the effect of widening the overall differential because of entry barriers to particular occupations where union power is strongest.(66) It may be that unions "organise industries which are potentially high paying rather than [being] responsible for the high pay of the industries which they have organised."(67) The role of women in unions is often seen as crucial in any attempt to secure greater equality; this may overstate the economic clout possessed by unions.

THE IMPACT OF DOMESTIC LEGISLATION

Any attempt to assess the value and impact of European legislation requires an evaluation of how far along the road to equality the British Equal Pay Act has brought us.(68) Sloane concludes that "the vast majority of women are receiving equal pay as defined by the act",(69) but many women can never stand to benefit from the legislation. The first basis of comparison under the act is where a man and a women are engaged on "like work".(70) This is of no help where a situation of employment segregation exists. Furthermore, because the permitted area of comparison is employees "within the same employment",(71) there is no need for the occupational segregation to be on a national or even an area scale to exclude the operation of the act. It is only where the same job is being done by a man and a woman within the same firm that comparison is permitted. It seems that one result of the act was to spur on occupational segregation. Snell concludes that before the act most women in manual jobs earned less than any men in the organisation, and tended to be on a single "women's rate". But after the act "women were paid on or above the lowest male rate, although many were paid on rates below those of most men, and which they did not share with any men in the organisation."(72) There is no doubt that the simple "like work" basis of comparison was unable to do more than provide a one-off boost for women's wages in situations where patterns of occupational segregation had not become entrenched.

The second basis of comparison is where work is "rated as equivalent" under a job evaluation scheme.(73) The failure by the British legislation to contain any mandatory requirement to carry out a job evaluation exercise has been the cause of the United Kingdom being held to be in breach of the Equal Pay Directive as not ensuring "equal pay for work of equal value."(74) There are enormous theoretical and practical difficulties inherent in this decision, but "there is clear evidence that job evaluation; properly carried out, has resulted in significant increases in pay for many women who would not otherwise have been entitled to them."(75)

The final technique is section 3, which gives power to the Central Arbitration Committee to amend collective agreements which contain any provision "applying specifically to men or women only" so as to bring the lower up to the level of the higher. This covers the situation where employees are covered by the same collective agreement whether or not the work comes within the "like work" definition. The CAC adopted a broad approach and held that section 3 applied even if women had been formally admitted into previously all male grades or jobs if the reality was that the agreement or structure was still discriminatory.(76) However in R v CAC ex parte Hy-Mac (77) it was held that section 3 only applied where a provision referred specifically to men or women only. In other words only explicit discrimination was covered; implicit but effective discrimination was excluded. Of course even the CAC never considered that there was any power to extend the scope of collective agreements to cover employees not already within their terms. There was and is no legal basis to challenge the greater bargaining strength of male dominated trade unions or work groups as resulting in unfair or discriminatory wage structures.

The major employer defence to an equal pay claim is, by section 1 (3), if the employer "proves that the variation is genuinely due to a material difference (other than the difference of sex)". This section has produced a spate of litigation, but three cases stand out. In National Vulcan Engineering v Wade (78) the Court of Appeal held that it was enough if the employer showed that his grading scheme was not tainted with overt sex discrimination; he did not have to show that his subjective approach to grading was free of any question of sex stereotyping or discrimination by status. It follows from the decision that as long as the employer does no more than share generally accepted social values he is not to be held in breach of the legislation. In Fletcher v Clay Cross (Quarry Services)(79) it was held that the employer was not allowed to plead as a defence under this section that the only reason he offered the man more money was that the candidate he wanted would not have come for less. This is a socially desirable outcome. One's only caveat is to reconcile the assumptions underlying the decision with the dual labour market theory considered earlier.(80) Finally in Snoxell v Vauxhall Motors (81) it was held that the preservation of a higher rate for a particular employee than equal pay would justify -red-circling - was protected so long as the reason for such protection was personal to the individual and not due to a past record of discriminatory payment systems.

Ways have been found to escape the consequences of equal pay legislation. Access to overtime pay and bonus and incentive schemes "may reflect relative bargaining strength rather than differences in output or effort."(82) If so, what would almost certainly be accepted as a genuine material difference may conceal either deliberate manipulation or unverified assumptions as to the types of qualities or results which "ought" to lead to higher bonus payments. Even if there are breaches of the legislation, one must not ignore the difficulties that lie in the way of potential claimants. Two points can be made. Firstly, "most cases of possible non-compliance with the act were not recognised by the women concerned."(83) Secondly, it is argued that the procedures involved and especially the role played by ACAS conciliators, are no encouragement to women to proceed even with a cast iron claim.(84)

The economic assumption behind the act is that "inequality in wages exceeds any difference in productivity [between men and women] and that part of this is discrimination".(85) If this is not the case, equal pay would result in the overvaluing of female labour and thus an increase in female unemployment. Even if the assumption is correct, increasing women's wages is likely to have at least a marginal effect on the demand for the products thereby produced. The cost to particular firms of implementing equal pay legislation varied according to the significance of labour costs in a firm's total overheads. Two-thirds of firms considered that the costs were less than 5% of their total wage bill, while for a handful of firms the estimate was in excess of 20%.(86) Obviously the costs would differ according to the degree of occupational segregation prevalent in the firms or the industry: it is ironic that the highest costs would have fallen on firms already highly integrated when the act came into force but which still had discriminatory payment systems.

Equal pay legislation has failed to drive average female earnings to a figure higher than 75% of men's. While it is probable that the legislation will bring some marginal change in the attitude of employers towards the employment of women, this is unlikely to be enough to counter other factors, social and economic, which lead to occupational segregation and thus to lower pay for women. It is in this context that we turn to examine the impact of European law.

THE IMPACT OF EUROPEAN LAW

i) Equal pay for work of equal value.

The potentially most far-reaching European decision concerns the failure by the United Kingdom to implement the Equal Pay Directive, which requires equal pay "for work to which equal value is attributed". In Commission of the European Communities v the United Kingdom (87) the Commission brought an action against the United Kingdom alleging breach of this Directive. The particular failure in mind was the absence of any mechanism for establishing the value or comparative value of work without the employer's consent. This "amounted to a denial of the very existence of a right to equal pay for work of equal value where no [job] classification has been made." The court considered that it would be possible to force an employer to comply with a job evaluation study, which if necessary could be carried out by an Industrial Tribunal in the context of adversary proceedings, as the Tribunal could obtain "such information as might be required."

In order to evaluate the implications and usefulness of this judgement, the methods and purposes of job evaluation must be explained. The ACAS guide to job evaluation outlines four methods.(88) Job ranking simply entails putting a range of different jobs into an order, which can then be used to fix pay rates and scales. Paired comparisons is a slightly more sophisticated version whereby each job is compared with each other job and a view formed as to whether it is more valuable, equally valuable, or less valuable. This again enables an overall table of value to be drawn up. Job classification starts at the other end with jobs considered typical of those in particular grades; all other jobs are then compared with these benchmarks to see into which grade they should appear. None of these methods contains any analysis of the content of jobs;

the evaluators simply decide whether or not one job is worth more than another, so that the system is almost totally subjective, albeit simple to operate.

The most popular method is the points method. This breaks down each job into a number of factors, such as skills, responsibility, training, working conditions and so on. "Points are awarded for each factor according to a pre-determined scale and the total points decide a job's place in the ranking order."(89) This method is more analytical than the others. However at two crucial stages a subjective assessment remains to be made. Firstly, a maximum value is fixed for each of the factors which have been isolated. For example the scheme formulated at United Glass(90) had maxima which varied from 16 for surroundings, hazards and mental effort, to 36 for responsibility and 40 for physical effort. It follows that the assumptions of the evaluators as to the more important factors are crucial. For example it has been argued that manual dexterity, regarded as a "feminine" skill, is liable to be ranked below factors such as physical strength. The second subjective element involves deciding how many points out of the maximum for each factor each individual job should receive. While this is clearly subjective, it is perhaps less liable to "skew" the eventual results of the study.

Job evaluation does not by itself provide a salary scale. When the jobs have been ranked in order, it is still necessary to group them into grades. Thus at United Glass jobs with a total points value of 0-30 were placed in grade 1; the grades then rose in steps of 17 points so that workers with 150 or more points were in grade 9, the top grade. When this is done, the actual money wages need to be fixed for each grade, whether by collective bargaining or otherwise; particular attention needs to be given to the differentials between the grades. The task is still not completed, however, as the result will only be the basic rates of pay. Additional factors will include bonuses, incentives, overtime payments etc.

There are enormous difficulties inherent in any proposal in effect to make job evaluation compulsory. Some are technical: for example would all studies be acceptable or would there be any requirement for trade union involvement?(91) A more fundamental problem would be the range of employees in respect of which job evaluation would be required. At present "it is not feasible to develop factors which are suitable for the evaluation of both manual and white-collar jobs, since the skills and working conditions which apply are of a different order."(92) It is unclear how it will be decided what type of scheme is necessary and how it will be organised: most schemes involve committees with employer and union representation, and take a considerable amount of organisation and time. It is beyond the capacity and expertise of Industrial Tribunals to carry out a study if requested to do so by an employee. Women can only benefit from such studies if men and women are within the same study, so it will often be in the woman's interest to argue for a study on the widest possible basis. There is no suggestion in the case of a minimum number of employees in a work group before such a study becomes necessary. It may be that legislation could iron out some of the difficulties, but with working situations being so varied the writer is sceptical whether any legislation could work which did not leave huge discretion to employers.

Hyman and Brough demolish any attempt to argue that job evaluation can ever be fundamentally objective.(93) In the first place "there is no scientifically obtainable answer to the question, 'what aspects of behaviour should be rewarded?' for this answer can only be provided by reference to a belief system which contains ethical components..... To prove acceptable and hence effective, the practice of work study must be rooted in already existent norms of effort; its aim is to standardise and systematise such often imprecise normative assumptions."(94) From a very different political perspective Phelps Brown echoes this view: "In practice [the weighting factors] are chosen according to what experience suggests as representative and application shows to produce intelligible results."(95) There is therefore no objective value of what each job is worth or even what each job is worth in relation to each other job. This is of fundamental importance in relation to women's pay, because it suggests that job evaluation cannot

overcome discrimination against women. Indeed it may reinforce such discrimination by appearing to give it some
spurious objectivity. If equality can only effectively be
pursued by altering preconceptions about what particular jobs
and qualities are worth, job evaluation is not the way forward,
as it "tends to assume that the existing rank order of reward,
based on bargaining strength and industry tradition, is
essentially correct and that the job evaluation study should be
designed to systematise and legalise the acceptability of that
rank order."(96) (Author's emphasis.)

The idea that there exists a social consensus on the
relationship between payment levels has come under strong
criticism.(97) Arguments about differentials are invariably
used to justify why one group should receive an increase, and
often the basis of such argument is simply to restore the
situation as it is perceived always to have existed. Special
treatment for the low paid and the maintenance of existing
differentials can become self-contradictory aims, which may
explain union ambivalence towards equal pay for women.
There may well be no social consensus as to the direction
change should take, but that is not to say that there is a
positive consensus that the current situation is appropriate. If
tribunals become involved in job evaluation, it would be
unlikely that they could or would do more than reflect existing
values, which would act even further as a means of
institutionalising such values.

One cannot ignore, as the European decision appears to,
the role of collective bargaining. Job evaluation "is merely a
framework on which to base negotiation and bargaining;"(98)
thus most schemes which are regarded as having been
successful have involved unions from the start in the
preparation and details of the study. It follows that the
scheme is likely often to reflect the values of the
representative unions, which may fail to benefit women.
Husband quotes the example of foundryworkers who "lay great
emphasis on hazards and length of training....-far greater
emphasis than on the undoubted core of the job which is
decision-making."(99) There must be doubts whether a female

view on the values to be considered exists or, if it does, whether adequate notice of it is taken. This is most powerfully demonstrated in the case of traditional craft unions, where the proportion of female members is extremely low. The maintenance of "craft" and "skill" factors is a vital element in wage negotiations in such situations,(100) and any attempt to undermine it by job evaluation, whether at the behest of an employer or a tribunal, would lead to industrial disruption. This begs the question, as indeed the decision in Commission of the European Communities v United Kingdom does, of what criteria a tribunal would adopt. The argument here is that there is no way that any criteria could be adopted which would be sufficiently radical greatly to influence the overall pattern of women's wages. This is not to deny that there will be firms where the practical problems are fairly mild and the existing proportion of women workers reasonably high, such that compulsory job evaluation could considerably increase women's average wages in the company, but it is submitted that the effects of this decision will be no more than marginally to improve the overall pay position of women.

ii The "economic justification" cases

In domestic law the leading case is Fletcher v Clay Cross (Quarry Services).(101) The question was whether the payment of a higher wage to a man because had the employers not have done so they would not been able to attract him to the job constituted a defence to an equal pay claim as being a "genuine material difference" under Section 1(3). The Court of Appeal was unanimous that it did not, one strand in their argument was a belief that such a restrictive interpretation would harmonise English and European law. Lawton L.J. pointed out that under Art. 119 "there is no let out for the employer who pays a man more than a woman because the labour market is such that in order to get a worker....he has to pay a male applicant more than he is paying his women workers." Only factors personal to the two people involved in the comparison may constitute a genuine material difference, "but the Tribunal is not to have regard to any extrinsic [economic] forces which have led to the man being paid more." Lawton L.J. considered that this result would avoid the need for complicated statistical evidence "based upon such a vague conception as economic factors or market pressures."

The decision of the Court of Justice of the European Communities in Macarthys v Smith(102) suggests a wider defence is acceptable under Art. 119. A male employee had worked as a stockroom manager at £60 per week. When he left, the post was filled after four months by the applicant, who was paid £50 per week. The initial question was whether the Equal Pay Act covered this situation. The Employment Appeal Tribunal held that it did, being prepared to override the strict wording of the legislation in order, as they saw it, to ensure consistency with Art. 119.(103) The Court of Appeal, Lord Denning M.R. dissenting, took a different view,(104) holding that a strict construction required the man and the woman who were admittedly engaged on like work to be engaged in contemporaneous employment, but they referred the case to the European Court for it to be decided, inter alia, whether Art. 119 applied. It was held that the reference in the Article to equal pay for equal work, "is exclusively concerned with the nature of the services in question [and] may not be restricted by the introduction of a requirement of contemporaneity." This is clearly a respect in which European Law is wider than English Law. How many women stand to gain by the extension is, however, a matter of some doubt. It would appear only to be relevant in situations where men and women apply fairly interchangeably for posts, and where wages are fixed unilaterally by management. The facts of this case would be unlikely to occur where terms and conditions of employment were fixed or regulated by collective bargaining. A few women clearly benefit from this extension but their number will not be great.

Even those who are within such extension may not succeed under Art. 119. "It cannot be ruled out that [such] a difference in pay.... may be explained by the operation of factors which are unconnected with any discrimination based on sex." This shortly-expressed limitation is somewhat cryptic, giving no guidance as to which factors are considered relevant. The view of the Advocate-General was that if there was "an objective justification in the changing general or particular economic conditions [of the employer] .... there would no longer be any ground for speaking of unjustified and arbitrary discrimination in pay," and even the written submissions on behalf of the employee accepted that the principle of equality is only violated "if a given difference of treatment has no objective and reasonable justification." The position is, therefore, that while the conditions for presumptive liability are wider under European Law, at first sight the grounds of defence are also wider.

This issue arose in the subsequent English case of Albion Shipping Agency v Arnold.(105) A male employee was made redundant, at which time he was earning £73 per week, and Mrs Arnold, in effect, took over his job but continued at her old pay rate of £37 per week. Two years later, when she was also made redundant, she claimed that she should have received the same pay as her predecessor. The Industrial Tribunal held, following Fletcher, that a change in the volume of business could not constitute a "genuine material difference." The EAT, however, pointed out that if her only claim was by virtue of Art. 119,(106) the potential defence must be along the lines advanced by the European Court. However, if the claim was under the Equal Pay Act as impliedly amended by Art. 119, they were prepared to distinguish Fletcher on the grounds that "the kind of economic factors which arise in this case (ie a change in the volume of work and profitability of the business....)" could not arise there. The upshot is that in cases of equal pay where the employments are not contemporaneous, some economic factors are relevant, but only those relating to the economic health of the employer, factors which must be taken to apply equally to both jobs if they were being performed contemporaneously. The implication is that in neither case is the Court permitted to take into account the general position of women in the labour market. The former type of factor, while by no means easy to decide, is far more susceptible to a legal decision than more general considerations. But if the claim is eventually held to be based purely on Art. 119, it is likely that further consideration of the European Court decision in Macarthys will be needed to know whether that court intended any limitation of the range of economic factors which are potentially relevant in cases such as this.

It was further argued for the applicant before the European Court in Macarthys that in order to achieve the aims of Art. 119, the economic and social aims as outlined in Defrenne v Sabena(107), "the principle of equal pay necessarily has to apply to people who are unable to compare their work with that of persons of the opposite sex" for reasons of occupational segregation, horizontal or vertical. The question put was whether a woman can claim equal pay if she shows that she receives "less pay than would have been received by a man doing equal work for the same undertaking." This is the principle of the so-called "hypothetical man." While this extension was held unable to benefit the applicant in Macarthys, the reason for so holding is unclear. The European Court certainly holds that such a claim cannot fall within the type of discrimination to which Art. 119 is directly applicable as it is to be classed as "indirect and disguised discrimination." It is not however clear whether they take the view that such discrimination is none the less a breach of Art. 119, albeit not directly applicable at the suit of an affected individual.

The notion of a "hypothetical man" has implications wider even than the decision in Commission of the European Communities v United Kingdom. That decision only enables a woman to compare herself with a man also covered by the study. This limitation does not apply to the alternative approach, where the key problem would be in deciding what a man would have been paid. The Advocate-General considers that this is "undoubtedly possible when there is a means of referring to wages normally paid or offered to male workers for equal work within the same undertaking". This adds little to the decision: it seems to postulate a situation where the employer normally has male workers but happens not to have any at the moment the case is brought. Any attempt at a "hypothetical man" comparison where the employer does not and never has had female employees doing the particular job involves extremely difficult problems of assessment, particularly if one of the reasons for such absence is the low wages paid! Would such a comparison refer to male workers in the district or in the same industry elsewhere, assuming that any could be found? The problem of satisfactory evidence is very great and the end result might be enormously to increase an employer's wage bill. The causes of low pay and occupational segregation among women are too entrenched to be solved by a neat legal device such as the "hypothetical man".

The second group of "economic justification" cases concerns whether it is permissible to pay part-time workers at a lower time-rate than full-time workers. This amounts to indirect discrimination against women because of the enormously greater numbers of women who work part-time. The relevant issues are firstly whether such discrimination none the less can in some or all circumstances be justified under Section 1(3) of the Equal Pay Act, and secondly, whether it contravenes Art. 119.(108)

The issue first arose in the English courts in Handley v Mono.(109) The part-time workers in the employer's ladies fashion factory were paid a lower hourly rate than full-time workers. The argument that the inequality in pay was due to a "genuine material difference" was that the part-time workers contributed less "value overall to the productivity of the company, because .... the machine which the employee uses is idle when she is not there." This the employee countered by arguing that Fletcher limited the defence to factors personal to the employees and did not permit reliance on extrinsic factors, in which category the fact of part-time working was alleged to fall. Slynn J. held that the fact that the applicant in had chosen to work part-time was indeed a factor personal to her, and accepted that she was contributing at a lower rate to the employer's productivity, although this was simply stated by the employer with no attempt made to lead evidence in its support. Despite Fletcher economic factors were taken into account.

The EAT further held that there was no breach of Art. 119, both on the grounds that working full-time and working part-time did not constitute the same job under Art. 119 (b), and that, even if they did, the European Court would imply an exception along similar lines to Section 1(3). When Jenkins v Kingsgate (Clothing Productions) Ltd.(110) reached the EAT it was decided to refer these very issues for resolution by the European Court. The facts were that part-time workers, of which there were only six in the factory, including five women, were paid 10% per hour less than full-time workers as the employers "wished to discourage absenteeism... and to encourage all its employees....to work a full forty hour week so that its machinery should be used for as many hours every day as was possible." It was agreed that there was no intention to discriminate, but also that there was "no finding by the Industrial Tribunal or agreement between the parties that the differential was in fact effective or required to reduce absenteeism or to increase utilisation of the employer's machinery."

The first question was whether the part-time employees and the full-time employees were doing "the same job" within Art. 119(b), and thus entitled to equality in respect of time rates by the very wording of the clause. It is implicit in the judgement of the European Court that this view is rejected. The Advocate-General took the view that it did not follow from the fact that two employees were doing "equal work", which was clearly the case here, that they were necessarily doing "the same job", the two being alternative routes to the application of the Article. The second question was what, if any, reason for the inequality was sufficient to exclude the operation of Art. 119. The reasoning of the European Court permits inequality in rates as long as the distinction is not based on sex but is "contributable to factors which are objectively justified." However the formal ruling of the Court states that the difference in pay is only discrimination if it is "merely an indirect way of reducing the pay of part-time workers on the grounds that that group of workers is composed exclusively or predominantly of women." The decision of the Court is therefore ambiguous, in places suggesting that any distinction must be objectively justified -an approach based on indirect discrimination - whereas the ruling suggests it is enough if the employer negates a positive intention to discriminate. Whichever be correct, it is for national courts to decide whether or not the employer has satisfied them that his defence succeeds.

It must be the case that such pay inequality can only contravene either Art. 119 or the Sex Discrimination Act if it indirectly discriminates against women, in that a considerably smaller percentage of women can work for the requisite number of hours in order to earn the full time rate.(111) What is not made clear is over what group of workers that statistical assessment falls to be made. On the facts of this case there were 34 men and 49 women working full time, and one man and five women working part-time. These figures hardly suggest that any definite conclusions could be drawn merely by looking at the employer in question. It would be more sensible to look at the labour force as a whole and to assume that any inequality between full-time and part-time workers was automatically indirectly discriminatory against women. That this is the view taken receives support in that the Advocate-General referred to national statistics from different parts of the community, and there is no suggestion in the judgement that he was wrong to take such a broad perspective.

The approach of the European Court required the case to be returned to the British Employment Appeal Tribunal,(112) which pointed out the ambiguity of the European decision, and emphasised that it had not been shown that the inequality had any objective justification. Perhaps fortunately, the EAT felt able to decide the case without resolving the problem, by holding that Section 1(3) of the British Equal Pay Act requires the differential to be objectively justified. The effect is that Art. 119 adds nothing to the domestic legislation as now construed, although the interpretation placed on the Act in Handley v Mono was far more favourable to the employer, and it took the European Court decision to show the EAT that such approach was undesirable.

The distinction between this approach and that in Macarthys v Smith is important. In that case the EAT was and will be bound by any defence which the European Court is prepared to allow, because the claim there could only be by virtue of Art. 119, it being accepted that the domestic legislation did not apply. It would be strange if it were to be held that an applicant could rely on Art. 119 for the purpose of establishing presumptive liability, but could return to the domestic legislation to restrict the scope of defences more than the European Court would do. In Jenkins, on the other hand, the view of the EAT was that the claim of indirect discrimination was presumptively allowed both by Art. 119 and by the Equal Pay Act, so that there is no objection to construing United Kingdom statutes as conferring greater rights than Art. 119. The eventual outcome is that as far as part-time workers are concerned, no additional rights are conferred by European legislation than are enjoyed under domestic legislation.

No guidance is given by either court as to how the Industrial Tribunal should decide whether the inequality is necessary. If the analogy of Steel under the Sex Discrimination Act is relevant, the employer ought at least be required to show that he had no alternative means of achieving the same result. He will also need statistical evidence to demonstrate how his policy operates. The problems that this will cause, both to employers and to tribunals who have to comprehend this evidence, are obvious. The question has been asked whether the relevant statistics should "relate to the labour market as a whole, to individual industries, or .... to the employer in question." Whatever the answer, preparing for litigation in these cases will be horrendous. Finally, even if it is possible to overcome the practical problems, one may question the philosophy of permitting a defence based on objective economic necessity. The necessity is always that of the employer; the tribunal is not to consider the needs of the individual applicant or the female workforce as a whole. It is the employer's decision to employ part-time labour, and in this case if he wished to get rid of part-time working, which was his avowed aim, he could have done so much more directly. We have seen that it is arguable that employers also derive advantages part-timers,(115) advantages potentially capable of being measured statistically. "To allow the consequences of a management decision to be invoked as a genuine material difference is surely to repeat the error rejected in Fletcher v Clay Cross."(116) It may be that the assessment of the economic consequences of employing part-time labour are not assessable by an Industrial Tribunal, and that requiring equality might force out of the labour market some who can only work part-time. In any event it is vain to think that the law of equal pay and part-time work is ever going to assist the disadvantaged labour market position of women in general.

iii The meaning of "pay"

Art. 119 provides for equality in pay, which includes "any ....consideration ....which the employee receives, directly or indirectly, in respect of his employment ..." The Equal Treatment Directive extends equality to "access to employment, including promotion ....and as regards working conditions."(117) It is clearly vital to know whether this definition grants wider rights than the British legislation. If so, it may be important to know whether it does so under Art. 119, or by virtue of a directive, as this may affect direct applicability.

Major exemptions from the scope of the Equal Pay Act are those in relation to protective legislation, to pregnancy and childbirth, and to pensions and retirement. There are equivalent exemptions from the Equal Treatment Directive in the first two instances, so the cases have all considered the third issue, the first being Garland v British Railways Board.(118) On retirement male employees continued to enjoy valuable travel facilities for themselves and for their families, whereas female employees only received continued benefits for themselves personally. Under English law this claim was under the Sex Discrimination Act as the benefits were not paid by virtue of a contract of employment, and the claim failed because of Section 6(4), which exempts discrimination "in relation to death or retirement."(119) The European Court had little difficulty in holding that these benefits came within the Art. 119 definition of pay, and that Article contained no retirement exception.(120) Furthermore, there was no difficulty in holding that in this context Art. 119 was directly effective, the discrimination being so obvious that there was no need for further national or Community measures to define the form of discrimination with greater precision.

When the case returned to the House of Lords(121), Lord Diplock took the view that the effect of the judgement of the European Court was to modify the construction put upon Section 6(4) of the Sex Discrimination Act by the Court of Appeal so that it did not now apply to these facts. Mrs Garland's claim was therefore allowed under British legislation and not under Art. 119. This approach could only be taken because he regarded Section 6(4) as capable of bearing more than one meaning; this contrasts with Macarthys where the lack of ambiguity in the British legislation meant that the only route to success was by virtue of Art. 119, while in Jenkins the EAT took a view not dissimilar although not as decisively expressed as Lord Diplock's. If any parts of Art. 119 are in the future held not to be directly applicable, Lord Diplock's approach does have potential advantages for applicants. Meanwhile the precise inter-relationship between domestic and European law is left in confusion, although it is doubtful whether the English courts will ever allow it to work to the disadvantage of an applicant. The overall benefits to women are clearly limited to very particular and unusual circumstances.

Burton v British Railways Board(122) appears at first sight also to be about pay, in that the male applicant was denied access to a voluntary redundancy payment to which he would have been entitled had he been female. The employers asked for volunteers for redundancy, but male volunteers were required to be at least sixty while female volunteers only needed to be fifty-five. Mr Burton, a man of fifty-eight, claimed that this differentiation was unlawful. He failed under the retirement exception in the Sex Discrimination Act, but the case was referred to the European Court to find out, inter alia, whether Art. 119 and the Equal Pay and Equal Treatment Directives had been breached. It was held that Art. 119 was not infringed; had Mr Burton been of the correct age, the benefits he would have received would have been calculated on the same basis as the female employees with whom he sought to compare himself.(123) Therefore the discrimination existed not in the payments but in the conditions of access so that only the Equal Treatment Directive could possibly benefit the applicant. It was held that the word "dismissal" in the Directive includes "termination of the employment relationship between a worker and his employer, even as part of a voluntary redundancy scheme." However, the European Court referred to the Social Security Directive which is expressly stated to "exclude from its scope the determination of pensionable age" with its possible consequences for various benefits. The conclusion was that "the determination of a minimum pensionable age for social security purposes which is not the same for men as for women does not amount to discrimination prohibited by Community Law."(124)

This must be correct policy. If such differentiation were a breach, fashioning a remedy would be impossible. The difficulty arises whether the retirement age of men should be reduced to sixty, that of women increased to sixty-five, or some compromise position reached.(125) The cost would be great if the retiring age for men were reduced; the social costs of a high number of elderly non-working people are also high; the issue as to retirement is merely one aspect of how to deal with an increasing number of elderly people, many of whom are compulsorily retired when they have many years activity left. This is not a question to which it is reasonable to expect European Law in this particular context to answer.

If discrimination as to retirement ages remains lawful, so must the payment of state old-age pensions from the date of retirement, even though paid to women under different conditions from men. Occupational schemes raise different considerations which may be more susceptible of legal resolution, but the European Court has so far been unwilling to hand down judgements which will radically alter existing national practices. In Great Britain there were in 1975 some 65,000 occupational pension schemes. Of the 11.5 million employees who were members, 2.8 million were women.(126) However if one looks at full-time employment only, in 1970 55.3% of male employees were members and 36.0% of female employees. Under the Social Security Pensions Act 1975, women have a right of equal <u>access</u> to occupational schemes, that is the conditions under which membership of such schemes is granted must be the same. However there is no right of equality in respect of <u>benefits</u>. The commonest inequality concerns the absence of benefits to widowers as against widows. The vast majority of such schemes "contract-out" of the state pension scheme, which means that their members will, on retirement, only be entitled to the basic flat-rate state pension and not to the additional earnings-related element. Approving "contracting-out" is the responsibility of the Occupational Pensions Board, a body set up by the state, and so while occupational schemes are basically private in nature there is direct state involvement in their operation.

<u>Worringham</u> v <u>Lloyds Bank</u>(129) is a case of an employer who treated men and women differently for pension purposes. The reason for this was that a large number of female employees left the bank's employ before they reached the age of 25, and it was felt unprofitable to build them into the scheme. Only employees who had attained age 26 and had five years' service with the bank qualified for the scheme. Those who left without fulfilling both criteria could either have their pension rights transferred or receive a refund of their own, but not their employer's contribution. All male employees were required to contribute 5% of salary to the scheme from the date of the commencement of employment, while female contributions only started at 25. To compensate the men, those under 25 received a 5% addition to salary, which brought about inequality in gross pay, though of course the effect was that the 5% addition exactly equalled the 5% which went to the pension scheme. None the less this produced real inequality: if a man under 26 left he received a refund of contributions which a woman would gross receive, and a number of benefits, such as redundancy payments and unemployment benefit, are calculated by reference to gross pay.

The questions referred to the European Court were whether either or both of the employer's contributions and the employee's benefits under a pension scheme were covered by Art. 119 or the Equal Pay Directive. Consciously or not, the question was framed in the widest possible terms. None the less the answer given was that a contribution "by the employer in the name of the employee by means of addition to the gross salary which helps to determine the amount of that salary" is "pay" within Article 119. The European Court expressly confined its decision to the particular facts, and took no decision on the general question of whether employer contributions and employee benefits are covered. Thus when the case was returned to the Court of Appeal the remedy was that the women applicants were to receive a sum equal to that which they would have received by way of refund on leaving the employment had they been male.(130)

The question whether normally constituted occupational pension schemes require equality remains uncertain.(131) It would be strange if it were held that equality were required in occupational schemes when it is clear from the Social Security Directive that state schemes remain outside its scope. In technical terms state schemes were held to be outside the scope of Art. 119 in Defrenne v Belgium (132) where it was held that "pensions which are directly settled by law without reference to any .... consultation within the industry or undertaking concerned" fall outside the definition of "pay". One problem is to determine the criteria which separate a "state" scheme from a "private" scheme, particularly bearing in mind the different arrangements within the Community. In Defrenne v Belgium the scheme was held to be within the former category even though it was a special scheme governing the pension rights of air crews, because it was within the framework of a national legislative scheme. It could be argued that contracting-out provides in the British context a sufficiently close link with the legislative scheme that the same reasoning should apply, and this appears to have been the view of the Advocate-General in Worringham. If that were the case then Art. 119 could not apply to the contributions and benefits under any occupational scheme. It therefore follows from the decision in the European Court that this argument was rejected, so that British occupational schemes may in some circumstances fall within the scope both of Art. 119 and the Equal Pay Directive.

It seems that this is one context in which Art. 119 may be held not to be directly effective. In Defrenne v Sabena(133) it was held that Article 119 is only directly applicable in areas where a court can apply its provisions by reference to the simple criteria that those provisions themselves lay down; it can have no direct effect where implementing legislation is necessary to lay down the relevant criteria. That is why the European Court adopted a narrow line in Worringham: the inequality was patent. What equality is required in respect of contributions and benefits under ordinary schemes is certainly not so patent. Because women retire earlier and live longer higher contributions are necessary in order to provide them with the same pension as men. Equality of contributions either entails lower benefits for women or a subsidy of women's contributions out of men's contributions. Alternatively, equality of benefits could be said to require higher contributions from women. The real question is whether it is socially acceptable to treat women differently from men in the context of pension schemes. This question would remain even if there was equality in retirement age because of women's greater longevity.

It is submitted that benefits of and contributions to such schemes do not fall naturally within the context of "pay". However, the Equal Treatment Directive, in its reference to working conditions, is a possible way forward. On the other hand, it may be that this directive would be read subject to the Social Security Directive(134) which not only permits continued discrimination in respect of pensionable age, but also permits certain inequalities in benefits. It is not clear whether the British social security scheme will need any amendment to comply with this directive. While it does not apply to occupational pension schemes, it is unlikely that the European Court will grant greater rights to women in relation to such schemes than the Social Security Directive grants to beneficiaries of equivalent state schemes.

There are three basic problems for women in relation to pensions. Firstly, women may be disproportionately employed in non-pensionable employment. Secondly, their work patterns may make it difficult to build up a good pension record because of intermittent employment. The first problem cannot be solved by legislation, while there are great difficulties in the way of a legislative approach to the second issue. The third issue is one of equality within the scheme: here it is the obligation of the state to give a lead via legislation. The European Directives may provide a gentle push, but no more. Case law has little if anything to contribute in this area.

CONCLUSION

There is no doubt that both domestic law and European law have a contribution to make to the cause of equal pay, both in particular instances of inequality and by virtue of the educative functions of law. The aim of this chapter, however, has been to demonstrate that the causes of inequality are too deep-rooted to be overcome by legal intervention alone. It follows that, while strengthening the law might make some marginal contribution and should therefore not be excluded from consideration, greater attention needs to be devoted to the underlying social and economic causes of inequality. In this fundamental socio-political task the alleged additional contribution of European law, both that which has already been made and that which might be made in the future, is at worst a distraction and at best a relatively insignificant contribution to the cause of equal pay for women compared with the changes which are needed in other directions.

FOOTNOTES

(1) Issues of Tax, social security, family law and nationality law are entirely omitted from the coverage of the British legislation.

(2) Below, 95.

(3) Directive 75/117 of 1975 on Equal Pay provides:

Article 1: The principle of equal pay for men and women ....means, for the same work or for work to which equal value is attributed, the elimination of all discrimination on grounds of sex with regard to all aspects and conditions of remuneration. In particluar, where a job classification system is used for determining pay, it must be based on the same criteria for both men and women....

The Directive goes on to require domestic legislation to conform to Article 1, whether by way of the introduction of new legislation or the repeal of existing legislation.

(4) Directive 76/207 of 1976 on Equal Treatment for men and women provides:

Article 1: The purpose of this Directive is to put into effect....the principle of equal treatment ... as regards access to employment, including promotion, and vocational training and as regards working conditions.....

Article 2: ....the principle of equal treatment shall mean that there shall be no discrimination whatsoever on grounds of sex, either directly or indirectly by reference in particular to marital or family status.

There follow exemptions where sex is a genuine occupational qualification, and for protective legislation, particularly relating to maternity and childbirth.

(5) Directive 79/7 of 1978 on the Progressive Implementation of the Principle of Equal Treatment for Men and Women in Matters of Social Security.

Article 4:1 The principle of equal treatment means that there shall be no discrimination whatsoever on grounds of sex either directly or indirectly by reference in particular to marital or family status in particular as concerns:
- the scope of the schemes and the conditions of access thereto,
- the obligation to contribute and the calculation of contributions,
- the calculation of benefits including increases due in respect of a spouse and the dependants and the conditions governing the duration and retention of entitlement to benefit.

Article 7:1 This Directive shall be without prejudice to the right of Member States to exclude from its scope
(a) the determination of pensionable age...,
(b) advantages in respect of old-age pension schemes granted to persons who have brought up children; the acquisition of benefit entitlements following periods of employment due to the bringing up of children,
(c) the granting of old-age or invalidity benefit entitlements by virtue of the derived entitlements of a wife;

(d) the granting of increases of long-term invalidity, old-age, accidents at work and occupational disease benefits for a dependent wife.....
This Directive has a 6 year implementation period.

(6) On the question of whether directives have horizontal direct effects see, inter alia, Case 148/78 Pubblico Ministero v Tullio Ratti [1979] ECR 1629; [1980] 1 CMLR 96, and Case 8/81 Ursula Becker v Finanzamt Munster - Innenstadt [1982] 1 CMLR 499.

(7) Creighton: Working Women and the Law (1979),9.

(8) Below, 74.

(9) Elias: Labour Supply and Employment Opportunities for Women; in Lindley (ed): Economic Change and Employment Policy (1980), 182, Table 6:1.

(10) Creighton, 6.

(11) Chiplin and Sloane: Sex Discrimination in the Labour Market (1976), 12.

(12) Ibid, 20.

(13) Creighton, 7. The activity rate of the 20-24 age group increased from 36.5% in 1951 to 45.7% in 1971; that of the 35-44 age group from 25.7% to 54.5%, and that of the 45-54 age group from 23.7% to 57.0%.

(14) Chiplin and Sloane, 14.

(15) Coote and Gill: Women's Rights - A Practical Guide (3rd ed. - 1981),69. These figures represent take-home pay excluding overtime.

(16) Creighton, 10, Table 6.

(17) Mackie and Pattullo: Women at Work (1977), 40.

(18) Cmnd. 7175 (HMSO, 1978).

(19) Sloane (ed.) Women and Low Pay (1980), 4, Table 1.1.

(20) Creighton, 14, Table 9.

(21) Sloane, 2.

(22) Hakim: Occupational Segregation (1979), Department of Employment Research Paper No.9; also Sexual Divisions within the Labour Market (1978) D E Gazette 1264; Job Segregation - Trends in the 1970's (1981) D E G 521.

(23) Ibid, 22.

(24) Ibid, 23.

(25) More than half of all employed women work in three service industries: 17% in the distributive trades, 23% in the professional and scientific areas, and 12% in miscellaneous services, which include laundries, catering and hairdressing: Mackie and Pattullo, 40. In 1977 93% of girls beginning an apprenticeship were training to be hairdressers: Cousins: Equality for Women - Have the Laws Worked (1980) 24 Marxism Today 6. "A great many of the occupations in which women are over-represented are typically feminine in that they draw on skills exercised on an unpaid and non-specialised basis within the home." Hakim, 31.

(26) (1981) D E G 521.

(27) Ibid.

(28) Hakim, 23.

(29) McIntosh: Women at Work - A Survey of Employers (1980) 88 D E G 1142.

(30) The "correct" ratio would be approximately 6:4, mirroring the proportion of men to women in the workforce.

(31) Ibid, 27-9. This conclusion may contain a possible explanation of how discrimination occurs, in that typically "male" qualities may be classified as

skilled, whereas typically "female" qualities are classified as unskilled or semi-skilled.

(32) (1981) DEG 521.

(33) Creighton, 8.

(34) Creighton, 8. For these purposes part-time working is defined as working less than 30 hours per week.

(35) Coote and Gill, 111. They also state that such workers are seldom considered for promotion and are often the first victims of redundancy.

(36) Sloane, 24.

(37) Chiplin and Sloane, 35, Table 3.7.

(38) Hakim, 30, concludes that there is no relationship between part-time work and patterns of occupational segregation.

(39) Sloane, 200-01.

(40) Chiplin and Sloane, 44.

(41) Ibid, 46.

(42) Figures show that there is far less discrepancy between the pay of single men and single women, which might appear to suggest that the problem for married women is often a lack of accumulated work experience.

(43) Phelps Brown: The Inequality of Pay (1977) 145-48.

(44) Phelps Brown, 147 ff.

(45) Below, 83-7.

(46) Chiplin and Sloane, 138.

(47) Phelps Brown, 178.

(48) In particular, see Jenkins v Kingsgate (No.2) [1981] ICR 715, below, 93.

(49) Ibid, 159.

(50) Sloane, 151-4; Chiplin and Sloane, 68-70.

(51) Hakim, 47.

(52) Ibid.

(53) It is unlikely that an Industrial Tribunal would hold that a convention whereby promotion depended on, say, 5 years continuous service was "unjustifiable" within section 1(1)(a)(ii) of the Sex Discrimination Act.

(54) It has been argued that the dual labour market system has advantages for employers, as women can be used as a flexible army of labour, being hired when times are good and numbers reduced without the need for compulsory redundancies when recession strikes, by virtue of a high turnover, particularly in the case of part-time workers; Gardiner: Women, Recession and the Tories (March 1981) Marxism Today 5.

(55) Sloane, 232-4; Chiplin and Sloane, 73-6.

(56) Chiplin and Sloane, 110.

(57) In Case 69/80 Worringham v Lloyds Bank [1981] ECR 767 (ECJ); [1979] ICR 174 (EAT) the costs to the employer of losing were said to amount to over £2M. One cost which it is hard to estimate is that of the publicity of being known as an unlawful discriminator, though even that can often be minimised by an out-of-court settlement. This type of argument could be used to support the introduction of class actions and exemplary damages in an effort to persuade the employer of the economic good sense of complying with the legislation.

(58) Campbell: Not What They Bargained For (March 1982) Marxism Today 18.

(59) Aldred: Women at Work (1981), 48-50.

(60) Ibid, chapters 4 & 5.

(61) Husband: Work Analysis and Pay Structure (1976), 6.

(62) Phelps Brown, 328. He adds that "the general effect of trade unions on relativities is probably to conserve them against market forces making for change."

(63) Ibid, 99.

(64) Creighton, 5 & 89.

(65) Ibid, 90.

(66) Sloane, 42.

(67) Amsden, 29.

(68) See eg Chiplin and Sloane, Ch 6; Davies and Freedland, Labour Law - Text and Materials (1979) 296-320.

(69) Sloane, 47.

(70) Equal Pay Act, section 1(2)(a).

(71) Section 1(6) provides that to be employed by the same employer includes the situation where two employers are "associated employers" as long as the two "establishments" in question observe "common terms and conditions of employment either generally or for employees of the relevant classes."

(72) Snell: The Equal Pay Act and the Sex Discrimination Act (1979) 1 Feminist Review 37.

(73) Equal Pay Act, section 1(5). For a summary of the English Law on job evaluation schemes, see Creighton, 113-6; also (1978) 122 IRLIB 1.

(74) Case 61/81 Commission of the European Communities v United Kingdom [1982] IRLR 333.

(75) Snell, 39.

(76) Hepple and O'Higgins: Employment Law (4th ed, 1981) 201. The decision in Beechams and MATSA, CAC Award no.213 of 1978 quoted by Davies and Freedland, 317, demonstrates that such approach inevitably led the CAC to be concerned with fair differentials between different jobs done by highly different proportions of men and women, and that this "opened up to legal scrutiny the basic issues about fair structures, namely those of what are fair comparisons and fair differentials."

(77) [1979] IRLR 461.

(78) [1979] QB 32; [1978] ICR 800 (CA).

(79) [1979] 1 All ER 474; [1979] ICR 1 (CA).

(80) Above, 77. Hakim, 50, quotes the example of the advertisement that failed to attract any women applicants until the salary offered was reduced by over half in a re-advertisement. Surveys consistently report that women have higher levels of satisfaction with their pay than men, despite their lower average pay. These facts fit uneasily with the assumptions in Fletcher.

(81) [1978] QB 11; [1977] ICR 700 (EAT).

(82) Snell, 42. See also Chiplin and Sloane, 100.

(83) Snell, 43.

(84) Gregory: Equal Pay and Sex Discrimination - Why Women are giving up the Fight (1982) 10 Feminist Review 75. She points out that the number of equal pay claims declined from 2500 in the first year of the Act's operation to 81 in 1980. For proposals to strengthen the legislation see 1980 Annual Report of the Equal Opportunities Commission, Appendix 5.

(85) Chiplin and Sloane, 96.

(86) Ibid, 99.

(87) Case 61/81. [1982] IRLR 333.

(88) ACAS Advisory Booklet No.1: Job Evaluation.

(89) Ibid, 10. For a more detailed description of this method of job evaluation, see Husband, 51-4.

(90) 185 IRRR 6. For another example see: Joint Job Evaluation at Phillipps, 229 IRRR2.

(91) These problems exist at present, see note 90 above, and now Arnold v Beecham Group [1982] IRLR 307.

(92) Husband, 56. A survey of 114 large firms showed that none combined a scheme for manual and non-manual workers, although some used the same type of system. Gray: Towards National Job Evaluation - Trends and Attitudes in Great Britain and the Netherlands (1977) 7 Industrial Relations Journal 23.

(93) Social Values and Industrial Relations (1975), 30-31.

(94) Ibid, 13-16.

(95) Phelps Brown, 295.

(96) Husband, 129.

(97) Hyman and Brough, 32-7.

(98) Husband, 57.

(99) Ibid, 162.

(100) Phillipps and Taylor: Sex and Skill - Notes towards a Feminist Economics (1980) 6 Feminist Review 79.

(101) Note (79)above.

(102) Case 129/79 [1980] ECR 1275; [1980] 2 CMLR 205; [1981] QB 180; [1980] ICR 672.

(103) [1978] ICR 500 (EAT).

(104) [1979] ICR 785 (CA).

(105) [1981] IRLR 525 (EAT).

(106) The EAT accepted that Industrial Tribunals and therefore the EAT itself had jursdiction to hear claims based directly on Art. 119, which fall outside the Equal Pay Act. The reasoning was that the decision in Macarthys v Smith (No2) [1980] ICR 692 (CA) dismissing the appeal against the decision of the EAT must have been made on the assumption that that court had jurisdiction to hear and determine the case.

(107) Case 43/75 [1976] ECR 456; [1976] 2 CMLR 98; [1976] ICR 547.

(108) Under the Equal Pay Act, section 8(3), all cases involving the payment of money are dealt with under that Act and not under the Sex Discrimination Act. The question of when indirect discrimination is justifiable is equally relevant to both cases. See Steel v Union of Post Office Workers [1978] 2 All ER 504; [1978] ICR 181, also [1977] 6 ILJ 241.

(109) [1979] ICR 147; also Wallington [1979] 8 ILJ 237.

(110) Case 96/80 [1981] ECR 911; [1981] 2 CMLR 24: [1981] ICR 592.

(111) Reasoning by analogy from the Sex Discrimination Act, s.1(1)(b).

(112) Jenkins v Kingsgate (No2)[1981] ICR 715. The EAT then further remitted the case to the Industrial Tribunal.

(113) Kingsgate, a company of 90 workers, in fact decided that they were unable to bear the costs of being represented at the European Court.

(114) Syzszczak: (1981) 10 ILJ 259.

(115) Note 54 above.

(116) Wallington: (1979) 8 ILJ 237.

(117) Note (4) above. The Equal Pay Directive refers to "all aspects and conditions of remuneration," which appears to add nothing to the definition in Art. 119.

(118) Case 12/81 [1982] 1 CMLR 696; [1982] 2 All ER 402; [1982] ICR 420.

(119) [1979] IRLR 244 (CA).

(120) The argument for the appellant was that the benefits were granted as a result of the employment relationship; that "it is immaterial whether its actual receipt is deferred until after the termination of the employment"; and that it matters not that the difference concerns the families of employees, not the employees themselves, as "in human and economic terms," those interests are the same. The European Court did not need to answer the question whether the discrimination also constituted a breach of the Equal Pay and Equal Treatment Directives, but equivalent reasoning to that adopted in relation to Art. 119 would seem to lead to the same result.

(121) [1982] 2 All ER 402.

(122) Case 19/81 [1982] 2 CMLR 136; [1982] ICR 329.

(123) It might be argued that benefits dependent on length of service are indirectly discriminatory against women who are less able to accumulate long periods of service. This would raise the question of whether, eg, the award of redundancy payments on such basis could be justified on economic grounds.

(124) This decision avoided the need to answer the question whether individuals can enforce Directives.

(125) Equal Status for Women in Occupational Pension Schemes: Report of the Occupational Pensions Board (Cmnd. 6599, 1976), Ch 7.

(126) Ibid, 13, 82. Smith: Occupational Pensions (1980), 57. It was estimated in 1971 that 62% of male employees were members of schemes and only 28% of women employees.

(127) Ibid, 84.

(128) Smith, 59.

(129) [1979] ICR 174(EAT); case 69/80 [1981] ECR 767; [1981] 2 CMLR 1; [1981] 2 All ER 434; [1981] ICR 558 (ECJ).

(130) [1982] ICR 299 (CA).

(131) This issue has already been considered by Ellis and Morrell: Sex Discrimination in Pension Schemes - Has Community Law Changed the Rules (1982) 11 ILJ 16, esp. at 22-28. It is not intended to rehearse their argument in detail.

(132) Case 80/70 [1971] ECR 445; [1974] 1 CMLR 494.

(133) Case 43/75, note (107) above.

(134) Note 5 above.

THE IMPACT OF EEC COMPETITION LAW
IN THE UNITED KINGDOM

Richard Whish

1. Introduction

Art. 2 of the Treaty of Rome expresses the function of the European Economic Community as being "to promote throughout the Community a harmonious development of economic activities, a continuous and balanced expansion, an increase in stability, an accelerated raising of the standard of living, and closer relations between the States belonging to it". Art. 3 of the Treaty then specifies certain activities to be carried out by the Community for the purpose of achieving the objectives described in Art. 2. Art. 3(f) specifies as one of these activities "the institution of a system ensuring that competition in the common market is not distorted". Part III Title 1 Chapter 1 of the Treaty goes on to lay down detailed rules on competition. In particular Art. 85 prohibits agreements which prevent, restrict or distort competition and Art. 86 prohibits the abuse of a firm's dominant position.(1)

It was established at an early stage that Arts. 85 and 86 are directly applicable provisions of the Treaty(2) and in Wilhelm v Bundeskartellant(3) the Court of Justice of the European Communities made it clear that in any case involving a conflict between the domestic and Community competition rules, it is the latter which must prevail.(4)

In this chapter it is intended to discuss the impact that EEC competition law has had in the United Kingdom. It will be argued that the differences between the EEC and domestic systems of competition law are considerable and that this necessitates a major reappraisal by the UK business and legal communities of their attitude to competition matters.(5)

2. Economic Background of Competition Law

Systems of competition law attempt to regulate economic behaviour. The policies that inform such systems and the benefits claimed to derive from competition vary

However, there are certain economic conditions which typically feature when considering competition problems, even if their treatment varies according to particular value judgments, and some explanation of them and the esoteric terminology used should facilitate an understanding of the substantive law of the subject.(6)

A monopolist is the sole seller of a given product. The classical objection to the monopolist is that by controlling the volume of his own output he is able to affect the market price. By restricting his output he will be able to maximise his own profit.(7) As long as he has such market power he may become richer at the expense of his customers, inefficiency may arise in the conduct of his business(8) and society will be deprived of the extra output which the monopolist has suppressed. These effects are not inevitable: economic theory cannot account for the way in which the monopolist might actually choose to behave. But the point is that he does have freedom of choice and therefore some mechanism for controlling his market behaviour may be necessary.

Pure monopoly is extremely rare. Even the sole seller of a product may not have truly monopolistic power. A seller of any given product faces competition not only from other producers of that particular good but also from suppliers of other goods which purchasers might consider to be reasonably substitutable. Also there is always the possibility that someone else is ready to move into the monopolist's market if and when the level of the latter's profits seems to warrant the necessary investment. Therefore competition laws typically direct their attention not to pure monopoly alone but also to situations in which a firm has a sufficient degree of power over the market to be able to behave substantially independently of other competitors. Such dominant firms may be scrutinized not only to ensure that they are not exploiting their market position, for example by taking excessive profits, but also to check that they are not acting in a way designed to suppress or destroy competition from rival firms.

In conditions of perfect competition it is not possible unilaterally to fix the market price; rather the price at which any good can be sold has to be taken from the market.(9) There are so many producers that no one individually has the power to affect price by altering his output. An increase or decrease in output by any one firm will be imperceptible. The theory goes further and asserts that the price to be taken from the market will inexorably be no more than marginal cost, that is to say the cost of producing the last unit of output plus a reasonable element of profit. In such conditions, if anyone raises his price above marginal cost he will be deserted by purchasers who will buy elsewhere: and if he lowers his price below marginal cost, his competitors will not be affected since he lacks the necessary degree of market power to affect them substantially.(10) Furthermore in conditions of competition firms will have constantly to strive for greater efficiency and for technological improvement in order to hold on to their custom.

In highly simplified form, thus runs the classical economist's conception of perfect competition. In practice perfect competition is rare; however in many markets there is at least "workable"(11) competition which may produce benefits similar to, if not the same as, those of perfect competition. Systems of competition law may realistically strive to protect or engender workable competition even if perfect competition is regarded as only an analytical benchmark.

A typical problem for competition law occurs where competitors agree between themselves to abandon their economic freedom and instead to coordinate their behaviour, for example by fixing their prices or the volume of their output. Such firms are sometimes said to have formed a "cartel". In doing so the benefits of perfect or workable competition will be eliminated and instead artificial market power will have been created together with its potential disadvantages. Restrictive trade practices such as these, involving as they do an element of conspiracy against the public interest, are frequently dealt with more severely by systems of competition law than other antitrust problems and this is particularly true of UK law. An added complication is that in certain circumstances restrictive trading agreements can produce positively beneficial effects. For example two small firms, individually lacking the resources to develop a new product, may be able to do so through collaboration thereby increasing overall the competitive pressures in a market; while a manufacturer may be able to distribute his products more effectively by agreeing to protect his distributor in an allocated sales territory from outside competition.(12) Again, firms faced with a short term recession in their industry may only be able to survive by temporarily agreeing to suspend competition between themselves. The important point is that it is dangerous to generalize about restrictive trade practices, and indeed about competition matters generally, since in certain circumstances restrictions of competition can obviously be beneficial. The corollary of this is that competition laws must be sufficiently sensitive and flexible to be able to distinguish between desirable and undesirable restrictions.

Many markets are oligopolistic in structure. This means that output is concentrated in the hands of a few relatively large undertakings. The problem of such markets is that the beneficial effects of competition may be diminished as a result of the relative power of each firm. In perfect competition, the variation of price by any one supplier will not affect the market at large. A cut in price by an oligopolist, however, could cause such large scale desertion by other competitors' customers that corresponding price cuts by those competitors will be unavoidable. At worst the price may be forced below marginal cost and the price war could spell disaster for everyone. Conversely an oligopolist will not be able to raise his price since that will result in wholesale desertion of his own customers to his competitors. The conclusion is therefore that oligopolists must necessarily match each other's behaviour. "Conscious parallelism" is the only safe conduct.(13) Though no doubt the problem can be overstated, and oligopolists frequently compete albeit in ways other than through price,(14) two particular issues are raised as far as competition law is concerned: firstly, how does one distinguish consciously parallel conduct produced by oligopolistic market structures from collusively parallel conduct agreed upon by competitors; and secondly, how should the problem of oligopoly be dealt with at all? Although UK and EEC law approach the former problem in a similar manner,(15) it would seem that EEC law, unlike that of the UK, has no effective provision for dealing with oligopolistic market structures.

In the foregoing discussion, market power has been identified as a potential cause for concern, whether possessed by one firm or the members of a cartel acting collectively or by oligopolists. Assuming that market power is perceived to be a problem, therefore, a completely coherent and rational system of competition law ought also to contain provisions dealing with mergers between independent firms, since such mergers may result in the reduction of the number of competing firms in a given market and thus an increase in market power.(16) Again however mergers may produce beneficial results: for example the increased power of the combined undertakings may enable them to compete more effectively with larger firms or they may be able to achieve substantial economies of scale. As we shall see, EEC law is deficient as regards the control of mergers: a problem all the more serious in view of its inability to deal with oligopolies adequately. Indeed it is in these two areas that, in substantive terms, EEC law can be seen to be less developed than that of the UK.

3. UK Competiton Law

Laws designed to deal with restraints upon competition in the UK are of ancient origin.(17) In particular anti-competitive practices came under close scrutiny in the sixteenth and sevententh centuries, but thereafter both Parliament and the common law courts gradually retired from the control of the competitive process. Abstentionism by the courts reached its peak in Mogul SS Co. v McGregor Gow and Co(18) in which the House of Lords refused to condemn the members of a cartel, designed to keep competitors out of the tea-shipping trade, as having acted tortiously. The House held that it was lawful to conspire to harm trading rivals provided that this was done bona fide to further one's own business interests, or did not involve the use of unlawful means.

In the first half of the present century public opinion and Parliament tended for a variety of reasons to favour the restriction or elimination of competition. The result of this was that by the end of the second world war, the greater part of British industry was to some extent cartelized and competition was weak.(19)   The 1944 White Paper on Employment Policy,(20) which was the genesis of modern UK competition law, recognised that this was so and asserted that the new, post-war economy would have to be much more competitive if it was to provide the growth and wealth needed to ensure full employment.   However, the subsequent Monopolies and Restrictive Trade Practices (Inquiry and Control) Act 1948 approached the problem of encouraging more competition in a highly cautious, even diffident, way. This of course was hardly surprising given the experience of the previous fifty (and more) years. Legislation along the lines of the 1890 Sherman Act in the United States, which had introduced fines, imprisonment and treble damage actions as deterrents to anti-competitive behaviour, would have been a revolution that British industry could hardly have been expected to bear. What is interesting, however, is that the basic shape of the investigative system introduced in 1948 has remained the same to the present day, save that restrictive trade practices are now subject to a more rigorous system of law of their own. The investigative system is a mild weapon in the control of anti-competitive practices not caught by the Restrictive Trade Practices Act, particularly when compared with Art. 86 of the Treaty of Rome which prohibits the abuse of a firm's dominant position. The Competition Act 1980 may have sharpened up the impact of the investigative system to some extent. But it does seem that the exigencies of 1948 have cast an indelible pattern on the UK system of competition law which cannot or will not now be removed.

It is proposed now to consider, though inevitably only in outline form, the current UK competition law; firstly the Restrictive Trade Practices Act 1976 will be dealt with and then the Fair Trading Act 1973 and Competition act 1980 (which two are the descendants of the original 1948 Act). Thereafter the provisions of Arts. 85 and 86 of the Treaty of Rome will be analysed on a comparative basis.

(a) The Restrictive Trade Practices Act 1976

The early reports of the Monopolies and Restrictive Practices Commission(21) after the passing of the 1948 Act suggested that certain restrictive trade practices between independent firms would invariably be found to be against the public interest.(22) Parliament therefore in 1956 passed the Restrictive Trade Practices Act. This Act declared that certain restrictive agreements would be presumed to be against the public interest unless the parties to them could persuade the newly constituted Restrictive Practices Court that they were in some way beneficial; the Act specified the types of benefits that could be claimed for agreements in subsections of section 21 which have become known as the gateways. The 1956 Act has now been repealed and the relevant Act is that of 1976 which consolidated the legislation which had in the intervening twenty years been considerably modified and extended. However the legislation as it exists today is still of substantially the same nature and several of its characteristics require consideration in order to facilitate comparison with Art. 85 of the Rome Treaty.

Firstly, the 1956 Act was deliberately framed in such a way as to render economic problems susceptible of formal legal analysis. Industry had not been impressed with the MMC's machinations or the political control that lay at the heart of the 1948 Act's system. It favoured having the problem handed over to independent and impartial judges. The judges however were reluctant to be called upon to adjudicate on matters of economic complexity and political sensitivity.(23) The compromise was the attempt to purify the 1956 legislation of economic content and to reduce the issues involved to legal propositions such as might be found for example in a planning statute. The result is bizarre. The Act applies to any agreement in which two or more parties accept "restrictions" as to such matters as the prices to be charged for goods, the descriptions of goods to be supplied or the persons from whom they are to be acquired.(24) In certain circumstances restrictions are deemed to have been accepted while other restrictions must be disregarded.(25) Members of trade associations are deemed to have a contractual commitment to comply with certain recommendations of the association.(26) In certain circumstances agreements that would otherwise be caught by the Act are excepted by virtue of their subject matter.(27) Otherwise the parties must attempt to vindicate their agreement before the Restrictive Practices Court by relying on one or more of the gateways.(28)

This formalistic system is curious in many ways. To start with it is astonishingly difficult to understand: indeed there are major issues of principle which it is still not possible to advise upon with certainty.(29) Its incomprehensibility must inevitably affect the incidence of compliance with it. There has been plenty of (typically English) litigation over such matters as the tense of "to be" in section 6 (1) (a) of the 1956 Act, or the meaning of "descriptions" in section 6 (1) (c).(30) From time to time legislation has had to be passed to rectify the more anomalous consequences produced by this formalism.(31) But a more profound criticism of the legislation is that its applicability is determined - of course deliberately - without reference to the economic effects of the agreement in question. An agreement between a dominant firm and a customer whereby the latter agrees to purchase all his requirements of a particular product from the former for the next ten years may have serious effects on the competitive opportunities for other producers. But under UK law, since a restriction will only have been accepted by one party, the agreement will not be caught.(32) Again, an agreement between two firms carrying on a goods business and a services business respectively will be unaffected by the legislation. Conversely an agreement of no economic significance whatsoever can be caught for purely technical reasons. That may require a change in the legislation, abandonment of the agreement or administrative action to release from the Act's net what a less fine mesh would never have trapped.(33) These consequences of the form-based system may be considered tolerable if the predictability claimed to flow from such a technique was clearly apparent. However even this may be seriously doubted, as the litigation over the National Federation of Retail Newsagents amply illustrates.(34)

The Liesner Committee was asked in 1978 to report to the Secretary of State for Prices and Consumer Protection on the operation of UK restrictive practices policy. In its report(35) it considered, amongst other things, the merits and demerits of the form-based UK legislation when compared with the effects-based system contained in Art. 85 of the Treaty of Rome. Its conclusion was that, for all the drawbacks and demerits of UK law, it would be better to continue with the present system which is well known and has been in operation for over 20 years. The change to an effects system would cause problems of uncertainty, instability and over transition.(36) It would seem in the wake of this report that for the forseeable future there will be no fundamental change in our restrictive practices legislation. In other words, just as the UK investigative system, designed to meet the requirements of 1948, remains substantially unaltered today, the same is true of our restrictive trade practices legislation whose curious form was dictated by the needs of 1956.

The second issue raised by the RTPA is the treatment of beneficial collaboration. It was pointed out earlier that in certain circumstances restrictions of competition might produce desirable effects. The exemptions from the Act, for example of patent licensing agreements and exclusive dealing arrangements, and the gateways reflect an awareness of this.(37) However it is highly questionable whether in practice the legislation has really facilitated fruitful cooperation. The exceptions are very narrowly drawn and, anyway, are applicable according to mechanistic rather than economic criteria, while the difficulty, time and expense involved in attempting to pierce one of the gateways has all but resulted in the abandonment of any attempt to do so.(38) The last major successful case was in 1965.(39) Agreements of economic insignificance may be permitted by the Secretary of State without the necessity for a court hearing,(40) but more serious restrictions of competition are unlikely, overtly at any rate,(41) to be attempted. Thus for both formal and institutional reasons, UK law seems to have resulted in a de facto if not a de jure prohibition of all agreements restrictive of competition to the extent that the RTPA succeeds in catching them. This lopsidedness was recognised in the report of the Liesner Committee but its recommendation to introduce more flexibility into the system by, in effect, making the Director General of Fair Trading (DGFT) a court of first instance with capacity to permit certain beneficial agreements, was not acted upon when Parliament passed the Competition Act in 1980. EEC law is undoubtedly far more flexible in its treatment of beneficial collaboration.

The third important point about UK restrictive trade practices legislation is the relevant mildness of the sanctions available to ensure compliance with it. Before 1968 the only sanction against registrable agreements was the injunction; disobedience of the injunction was of course a contempt of court and a fine or even a term of imprisonment could be imposed.(42) The Restrictive Trade Practices Act 1968 further provided that registrable agreements not registered within the prescribed period should be void and that persons harmed thereby should have an action in damages against the parties to the agreement.(43) There does however seem to be a general reluctance in the UK to invoke the latter provision;(44) it is highly controversial at the moment whether actions for damages lie against breaches of Arts. 85 and 86. Unlike EEC law though, there is no power to fine recalcitrant firms for operating a registrable agreement except for disobeying an injunction. In other words, the first offence is not punishable. Under EEC law, Regulation 17 Art. 15 (2) empowers the Commission to fine undertakings up to 10% of their turnover in the preceding business year for any infringement of Arts. 85 and 86, and in recent years the EC Commission has been far from reticent in invoking this power.(45)

Fourthly, just as UK law's sanctions are relatively mild, so too are the authorities' powers to obtain information as to the existence and operation of restrictive agreements. By section 36 (1) of the 1976 Act the DGFT may serve a notice on a person whom he has reasonable cause to believe is party to a registrable agreement; if necessary that person can then be called upon to give evidence on oath before the Restrictive Practices Court. However, in Registrar of Restrictive Trading Agreements v W H Smith & Son(46) a very narrow view was taken of the Registrar's powers under this section. Since that case, evidence of fairly wide spread concealment of registrable agreements has accumulated.(47) One might therefore have thought that powers similar to those of the EC Commission(48) ought to be conferred on the DGFT. However there seems to be no immediate prospect of this happening: again there is a restraint in the UK law on competition that is lacking in that of the EEC.

(b) The Fair Trading Act 1973 and Competition Act 1980

Broadly speaking, competition problems which are not dealt with by the RTPA 1976 are controlled, if at all, by means of the investigative system established in 1948 and continued by these two Acts. Under the FTA the DGFT or the Secretary of State may, if they think fit, ask the MMC to investigate and report upon monopoly or complex monopoly situations.(49) The MMC in its report considers whether such situations operate against the public interest or alternatively whether any particular activity of the firms under investigation ought to be modified or discontinued. After its report has been published, it is then for the DGFT, acting on the instructions of the Secretary of State, to obtain appropriate undertakings from firms whose behaviour ought to be altered. Should it be necessary, the Secretary of State does have order-making powers, exercisable subject to Parliamentary scrutiny, which enable him for example to reduce a monopolist's prices, modify contractual conditions or even to order divestiture of assets.(50)

Part V of the Act provides powers to control mergers. Where a merger will be of more than a certain size, the Secretary of State (who acts upon the DGFT's advice(51)) may refer the matter to the MMC which again will report on the public interest implications and make appropriate recommendations which the DGFT will then attempt to implement through negotiation with the undertakings concerned.(52)

One of the biggest problems of the investigative system, particularly as regards anti-competitive practices by a single firm, is that experience has shown that monopoly investigations tend to be extremely protracted. The MMC feels that it is bound to study the industry in question exhaustively in order to establish market shares, normal commercial practices etc. before passing any judgment. Often, reports have taken several years to prepare and inevitably it has not been possible to carry out many investigations at the same time. The Competition Act is designed to overcome this problem to some extent by allowing the DGFT to investigate anti-competitive practices himself. If he establishes that a firm is indulging in such practices the Director is empowered to negotiate undertakings with the firm concerned designed to secure their discontinuance. The firm may decide not to give an undertaking in which case the matter is referred to the MMC which then proceeds much as under the FTA.(53) However, the Act does enable the Director to short-circuit the system in some situations when a firm decides that it is better to change its practices rather than incur the expense of further investigation.

There are several points about the investigative system which should be noted at this stage: as will be seen the EEC approach to the practices under consideration here is wholly different.

First, the separate treatment of restrictive trade practices and other competition problems is anomalous.(54) It does seem very strange that the Restrictive Practices Court has to adjudicate upon the merits of an agreement wherein two parties have accepted restrictions but only the MMC may be called upon to do so if only one restriction has been undertaken.

Secondly, when considering the public interest in monopoly and merger investigations, the MMC is required by section 84 of the FTA to take into account all matters which appear to them to be relevant including among other things the desirability of promoting competition. It is implicit in this that the Act is not committed above all other factors to the ideal of competition. The pragmatic UK approach to competition is evident again; under EEC law any substantial elimination of competition is likely to be forbidden.

Thirdly, the decision to investigate anti-competitive practices and mergers under UK law is entirely discretionary. For example by section 50 of the FTA the DGFT may make a monopoly reference "if he thinks fit". Only in the case of newspaper mergers is there any limitation upon this discretion.(55) Under the FTA there were 5 monopoly references and 3 merger references to the MMC in 1979; in 1980 the respective figures were 2 and 5. In those two years there was a total of 439 qualifying mergers.(56) It may be that the Competition Act will mean that more investigations will be carried out. But the point remains the same: the system is a remote one which lacks directly applicable rules and sanctions whereas Art. 86 prohibits the abuse of a dominant position and breaches thereof may have serious repercussions.

Fourthly, and closely related to the last point, is the fact that the investigative system does not give rise to obligations which are enforceable in normal domestic litigation. Thus the High Court is not called upon for example to consider whether clauses in a contract conferring discriminatory discounts upon a customer are void. The direct applicability of Art. 86 does have this consequence and one of the major questions to be resolved is whether the English courts will be capable of adjudicating upon the extremely complex issues raised thereby.

Fifthly, the FTA enables a monopoly reference to be made where a firm or firms control 25% of the supply of goods or services of any description.(57) However, an assessment of a firm's market share at this stage only operates as a trigger, enabling a monopoly reference to be made. It is not necessary when making a reference to actually decide whether the firm or firms in question do possess market power. That question is one for the MMC to consider in the course of its investigation at the same time as it decides upon market behaviour and public interest issues. However under Art. 86, the prohibition approach has led to the formulation of rules whose applicability depends upon a prior finding of market dominance. Thus the extremely complex problem of ascertaining market power tends to become separated from the question of whether a firm has somehow abused its position and is taken as a preliminary issue. Under Art. 86, therefore, the question of market power has a crucial role in controlling how certain firms may behave on the market which it does not have under UK law.(58)

The sixth point about the UK investigative system is that in two respects it provides more effective control over competition problems than EEC law. Oligopolists may be referred to the MMC under the FTA to the extent that competition is restricted between them other than through the operation of registrable agreements, and if necessary divestiture powers could be exercised following the MMC's report if it were thought necessary to produce a more competitive market structure. Many of the MMC's reports have concerned product markets that were oligopolistic. Also UK law does deal specifically with the problem of mergers; admittedly the law on this subject may require strengthening, but at least provisions do exist; EEC law has yet to deal with mergers effectively.(59)

The investigative system then is generally a rather benign one, lacking sanctions, pragmatic, involving political discretion rather than rules and obligations. In all these respects it differs from the corresponding provisions of EEC law.(60) However there are situations in which it might be argued that the blunter edge of UK law is more likely to produce a sensitive solution to some competition problem than the more aggressive EEC approach. For example, EEC law prohibits price discrimination by a dominant firm.(61) Economic theory however suggests that in certain circumstances price discrimination may have beneficial effects on output, income distribution and competition.(62) In prohibiting discrimination EEC law, particularly in view of the severity of its penalties, must inevitably discourage both detrimental and beneficial discrimination. It does seem that the more discreet UK approach is less likely to have such a deterrent effect on discriminatory practices and that its pragmatic style may lead to more sensitive conclusions in particular cases. Similarly oligopolists may be investigated under the FTA precisely because the system is not a prohibitory one: it would be most unreasonable to apply Art. 86 to oligopolists whose consciously parallel behaviour is explicable in economic theory.

4. EEC Competition Law

Much has been said in the foregoing discussion about the diffidence and pragmatism of UK competition law and about how this is reflected in the substantive law, the sanctions and the investigative powers that are available. EEC law differs fundamentally in terms of its doctrinal commitment to competition. As explained at the start of the chapter, the institution of a system of undistorted competition is one of the fundamental objectives of the Rome Treaty and this unequivocally pro-competition policy has informed much of the later development of the law on the matter.

The framers of the Treaty were in favour of a free market economy in the manufacturing and industrial sector, and thus the inclusion of antitrust provisions was not surprising. However it is crucial to recognize throughout any discussion of EEC law the additional function of the competition provisions, namely to facilitate and encourage integration of separate national markets. There would be little advantage in abolishing customs, tariffs and other restrictions on inter-state trade if undertakings themselves entered into agreements or acted in a way designed to prevent access to markets in other member states. The purpose of the common market is to enable firms to expand, to grow beyond the scale necessary to satisfy demand on their own domestic markets and through such expansion to become more efficient. By doing so such firms should then be able to compete effectively with foreign undertakings, particularly in Japan and the United States. Not surprisingly therefore anticompetitive practices designed to maintain the isolation of national markets have been consistently condemned and on occasions severely penalized.

The dynamic role of EEC competition law is also demonstrated by the positive encouragement which the EC Commission has given to certain forms of collaboration between small and medium sized undertakings.(63) Various agreements restrictive of competition have been permitted whose effect might be to enable small firms to combine and compete effectively with other, larger, enterprises. Again this may facilitate market integration by enabling small firms to operate on the market in other member states which, acting alone, they would have lacked the resources to penetrate.(64)

Arts. 85 and 86 prohibit anti-competitive agreements and abuses of dominant positions respectively. Common to both Articles is the further requirement that the practices in question must affect inter-state trade. This phrase therefore is of crucial importance expressing as it does the legitimate boundary of the applicability of EEC competition law. The phrase operates as a jurisdictional threshold. It is not an offence in itself to affect inter-state trade; indeed it has been held that the condition may be satisfied both by an increase as well as a decrease in such trade.(65) In a series of cases both the Commission and the Court have taken an extremely lenient view of what constitutes an effect on inter-state trade. For example in Commercial Solvents v Commission(66) the fact that a refusal to supply one particular manufacturer with a necessary raw material might entail his elimination from the market was in itself held to produce such an effect. In Vacuum Interrupters(67) an agreement between two UK companies whereby they would jointly develop sophisticated electrical equipment was held to affect inter-state trade since they might otherwise have been expected to develop such products independently and then to have sold them in competition with each other in other member states. Purely national restrictive agreements have been held to infringe <u>Art. 85</u>.(68)

This treatment of the inter-state trade clause is of course of considerable importance as to the impact of EEC law at the domestic level, for the direct applicability of EEC law pro tanto involves the subordination of domestic rules; and this is all the more serious in view of the many different provisions and policies of the two systems. Thus for example a fidelity rebate scheme operated by a dominant firm, which under the FTA might have been referred to the MMC for it to investigate, may well infringe <u>Art. 86</u> and attract a heavy fine and perhaps a damages action.(69) Much greater caution is required on the part of commercial undertakings and their lawyers than is called for by UK law.

It is intended now to consider separately the specific provisions of <u>Arts. 85</u> and <u>86</u>, comparing their treatment of various competition issues with that of domestic legislation.

(a) Art. 85

<u>Art. 85(1)</u> prohibits:
"all agreements between undertakings, decisions by associations of undertakings and concerted practices which may affect trade between Member States and which have as their object or effect the prevention, restriction or distortion of competition within the Common Market..."

Thereafter some examples are given of agreements that might be caught by this provision. <u>Art. 85(2)</u> provides that agreements caught by <u>Art. 85(1)</u> shall be automatically void. <u>Art. 85(3)</u> however provides that the provisions of <u>Art. 85(1)</u> may be declared inapplicable to agreements which contribute to the improvement of the production or distribution of goods or to technical or economic progress, which allow a fair share of the resulting benefit to consumers, and which neither contain dispensable restrictions nor substantially eliminate competition.(70)

The first point to emphasize is the simplicity of these provisions on restrictive trade practices when contrasted with the RTPA whose peculiarities and technicalities have already been referred to. Art. 85 looks straight to the economic effects of agreements and concerted practices rather than to their legal form. The result is that the anomalous inclusions and exclusions that arise under the UK Act are avoided and that, in policy terms, the applicability of the law is determined on rational and coherent grounds. Against this however it might be argued that a lot is lost in terms of predictability, although the real predictability of UK law is in fact questionable. It is not an easy task for a lawyer to advise his client on the likely economic analysis of his contractual terms and conditions. This difficulty is compounded by the obviously sensible requirement of the Court of Justice that the anti-competitive effects of an agreement can only be assessed by undertaking an analysis of the whole market in which it operates.(71) Furthermore the de minimis principle, whereby certain agreements falling within Art. 85(1) are ignored because of their economic insignificance, operates on economic criteria. The Commissions's Notice Concerning Minor Agreements(72) states that in its view Art. 85(1) does not apply to agreements affecting products which do not represent more that 5% of the volume of business in such products in the part of the common market where the agreement is effective and where the undertakings' turnovers do not exceed specified amounts. Difficult economic assessments are called for by provisions such as these; the same problems may also be met when dealing with the applicability of block exemptions and of Art. 86. Furthermore the direct applicability of these provisions means that not only managers of commercial undertakings and their legal advisers will have to consider these economic problems but so too will the judges of the High Court as the volume of domestic litigation involving Arts. 85 and 86 increases.

The much broader scope of Art. 85 than that of the Restrictive Trade Practices Act is obvious from an analysis of the cases that the Commission and Court has dealt with.(73) Requirements contracts, untouched by the UK Act because only one party accepts a restriction, are caught by Art. 85.(74) Any agreement which purports to confer absolute territorial protection on someone may be caught. For example in the Pioneer case the Commission fined four firms a total of 6,950,000 u.a., that is to say a figure in excess of £4 m., for taking part in concerted practices designed to prevent sales into France which might undermine the high level of prices prevailing for Pioneer products in that country.(75) Under UK law, a provision simply restricting the purchaser's ability to resell goods would actually be disregarded by virtue of section 9(3).(76) Again EEC law applies to agreements irrespective of whether the parties provide goods or services, whereas UK law maintains an extraordinary division between these two sectors.

Secondly the breadth of Art. 85(1) is such that much beneficial collaboration is also caught. However this is offset by the flexibility and willingness of EEC law to permit desirable restrictions of competition. Exemption of agreements caught by Art. 85(1) may be specifically applied for by notifying the agreement to the Commission. It may then grant an exemption if the agreement complies with the requirements of Art. 85(3). Many exemptions have been given.(77) By negotiation with the Commission undesirable restrictions of competition may be identified and abandoned and appropriate conditions imposed on the firms in question. The procedure is an administrative one unlike the judicial procedure adopted by the RTPA and there is no lack of willingness to apply for an exemption as is the case in the UK. This having been said however there is a major institutional weakness in the EEC system, namely that the Commission is so short-staffed that gaining exemption can take an extraordinarily long time. The problem is that, if in the end an exemption is not granted, the agreement will be void restrospectively;(78) this being so it would for example be very foolish for two firms to invest heavily in setting up a joint venture company to carry on research and development which may subsequently have to be wound up.

Because of this institutional problem the Commission has attempted to deal with the backlog of cases by sending out what are normally referred to as "comfort letters". Such letters might inform the parties that it would appear that an agreement does not infringe EEC competition law or that an agreement appears to benefit from a block exemption so that no individual decision is necessary.(79) It then states that it is going to close its file on the matter. Very many cases have been dealt with by sending such letters. However this understandable attempt to short circuit the decision-making system, produced by the fact that the Commission alone has power to grant an individual exemption,(80) does have serious drawbacks. In the Perfumes cases,(81) the Court held inter alia that such letters were not decisions binding on national courts, although national courts were invited to take them into consideration when dealing with a case. However they did put an end to the notification seeking an exemption. The consequence might therefore be that, upon the parties to the agreement litigating in a national court inter se or being sued by a third party, that court might decide after all that Art. 85(1) was infringed, that the Commission's view of the matter was erroneous, that it was unaffected by the comfort letter, and that the agreement was void and its operation unlawful. It could not consider the prospect of an exemption, that being the Commission's sole preserve.(82)

In its Eleventh Report on Competition Policy the Commission has conceded the difficulties produced by such letters.(83) It therefore is planning to revise its procedures if possible so that in future exemptions in some cases will be given more quickly and with less formality than at present and which will afford the parties necessary legal security. However the most important step that the Commission can take to deal with the exemption problem is to enact more block exemptions.

Block exemptions have so far dealt with exclusive dealing arrangements and specialization agreements.(84) A draft regulation on patent licensing agreements should soon come into effect and this will enable a very large number of the pending notifications to the Commission to be dealt with.(85) There are also proposals afoot to deal specifically with purchasing agreements in the petrol and beer sectors.(86) The advantage of block exemptions is that they are able to describe the types of provisions in certain agreements that the Commission will or will not tolerate and therefore agreements may be tailored to accord with them. Furthermore national courts are permitted to apply them in domestic litigation.(87) Thus the need to apply for an individual exemption is by-passed. There are some problems with them: for example their applicability normally depends on economic as well as legal criteria so that market analysis is again necessary; the teleological approach of the Commission and the Court of Justice in interpreting their scope is somewhat alien to the British approach to such problems;(88) and in the case of specialization agreements the exemption is rather narrow. However against this it is much easier to devise agreements against the background of a block exemption than against the need to plan for an individual exemption that might take years to acquire.

Despite the institutional problems of EEC law over the actual granting of exemptions, the cases show a flexibility and generosity towards certain types of collaboration that is lacking in UK law. Several joint ventures and research and development projects have been approved, even where large firms were involved that might otherwise have been in competition with each other,(89) as have other arrangements designed to achieve technological or distributive improvements.(90) To the extent that a lax view is taken of the inter-state trade clause of Art. 85(1) the increased penetration of EEC law into UK commercial activity has the beneficial effect of substituting for the inherent difficulties of pleading the RTPA's gateways this more sympathetic and flexible approach of the EEC.

The third point about Art. 85(1) is the question of sanctions. Unlike UK law, infringements of the EEC rules on restrictive trade practices may entail not only nullity of contract, injunctions and damages actions, but also the imposition of heavy fines. With increasing vigour the Commission has been fining undertakings found to have infringed Art. 85(1) and this only serves to emphasize the greater doctrinal commitment of EEC law to competition.(91) Added to this is the fact that the Commission has considerably greater investigative powers than those available under UK legislation. Regulation 17 Art. 14 enables officials of the Commission in certain circumstances to visit a firm's premises, without prior warning, and search its files for information concerning infringements of Arts. 85 and 86.(92) Practical assistance must be offered to the officials to enable them to perform their task(93) and recently the Commission has fined several firms guilty of supplying it with misleading information.(94) Under EEC law a less generous view is taken of the rules on self-incrimination and legal privilege than prevails in the UK.(95) All these factors reflect the sharper edge of the EEC antitrust legislation.

(b) Art. 86
Art. 86 prohibits
"[a]ny abuse by one or more undertakings of a dominant position within the common market or in a substantial part of it ..... insofar as it may affect trade between Member States."

The Article then proceeds to give some examples of the types of practice likely to come within its scope, such as the imposition of unfair purchase or selling prices or unfair trading conditions. Many of the most important of the Commission's decisions on competition law have involved the applicability of Art. 86 and several of them have been the subject of appeals to the Court. The law has developed very rapidly and for a variety of reasons about to be discussed has introduced a wholly novel approach to the problems of monopoly and mergers when compared with the UK investigative system.

The first point to make about Art. 86 is that it does not establish a distinct regime for the control of anti-competitive problems not produced by restrictive trading agreements. It will be remembered that under UK law the investigative system is wholly separate from the prohibition system of the RTPA. The EEC approach is a much more sensible and principled one which avoids the anomalous type of problem produced, for example, in the MMC'S report on Copying Materials(96) where it discovered in the course of its investigation several registrable agreements which it therefore had no jurisdiction to adjudicate upon. Arts. 85 and 86 are not mutually exclusive: for example in the Hoffman La Roche case(97) it was pointed out by the Commission that Roche's supply contracts might possibly infringe both Articles.

The second point requiring emphasis is that Art. 86 prohibits the abuse of a dominant position and that the Commission has, by virtue of Regulation 17, powers to order the termination of infringements and to impose considerable fines which may amount to up to 10% of an undertaking's turnover in the previous year. Several large fines have been imposed for infringements of Art. 86.(98) There are no corresponding provisions under UK law at all and the possibility of incurring such penalties under EEC law is rendered all the more likely by the rapid development of the scope of the Article.(99) Furthermore the wide investigative powers, already discussed in the context of Art. 85, are also available where breaches of Art. 86 are suspected and these are considerably greater than those provided by UK legislation.

Thirdly, and following on from the previous point, it is important to realize that, as a consequence of the direct applicability of Art. 86, it may be invoked in litigation in the domestic courts. Its availability as a defence to an action has never been doubted;(100) the question of whether it is also available to a plaintiff (for example who claims that he has been charged an excessive or discriminatory price) has tended to be more controversial. However, in two English cases at least an interlocutory injunction has been given to a plaintiff complaining of a wrongful refusal to supply by a firm in a dominant position contrary to Art. 86, the most recent of which was decided in the Court of Appeal.(101) Thus it would seem that injunctive relief is available to plaintiffs claiming

injury as a result of infringements of Art. 86 even if the
possibility of also being awarded damages remains a moot
point.(102) The significance of this is two-fold. It means that
anti-competitive practices by individual firms may now in
certain circumstances be directly attacked in domestic
litigation whereas under the law of the UK the most that
might be hoped for is a favourable political decision by either
the DGFT or the Secretary of State to investigate the problem
and perhaps refer it to the MMC. It also means that the High
Court will increasingly be called upon to deal with competition
matters which may raise issues of the utmost economic
complexity. Of course we have already seen that the
applicability of Art. 85 entails awkward economic
considerations; it is submitted that Art. 86 involves even
more complex questions. For example the premise of its
applicability is that a firm has a "dominant position". This
involves identifying the relevant product market, and then
considering the question of market power. As to the abuse
itself, it is an extremely difficult task to establish, for
example, whether a price is excessive or discriminatory.(103)
But it would seem that these are tasks which national courts
will increasingly be called upon to deal with, though it is
highly questionable whether they really provide a suitable
forum for doing so. One possible improvement might be to
insist on these issues being litigated, if at all, before the
Restrictive Practices Court which would at least have the
advantage that two lay members would be able to help the
judge on difficult economic matters.

Fourthly, Art. 86 differs from the UK system in its
approach to the question of market dominance. As was
explained earlier, the fact that a firm controls 25% of the
supply of any particular goods or services does not in itself
prejudice or inform the opinions eventually expressed by the
MMC: the issue is only of jurisdictional significance.
However, Art. 86 prohibits the abuse of a dominant position
and it is normal for the Commission to therefore start by
considering whether dominance exists. The Commission has
consistently taken a very narrow view of what constitutes the
relevant product market in which dominance is alleged to

exist, thus, of course, increasing the incidence of Art. 86.(104)
Two particular criticisms of the EEC approach can be made.
The attempt to isolate the identification of dominance from
the abuse itself is not entirely appropriate: it may be that one
of the vital indicia of dominance is the ability to act
abusively. Furthermore the range of abuses has been extended
greatly by the decisions of the Commission and the Court and
it would seem that many kinds of conduct will be considered
per se abusive if practised by a dominant firm.(105) Thus
prohibition of certain practices is hinged upon a finding of
dominance, a concept of great complexity. Indeed it has been
argued that the prohibition system of the EEC, operated in
this way, has led to several decisions that could have
undesirable effects. For example in United Brands v
Commission(106) the Court held that it was an abuse for a
firm with a dominant position to discriminate geographically
in the prices at which it sold its products to distributors.
Having confirmed the finding on dominance, the Court then
applied in effect a per se rule against price discrimination.
But the view taken as to dominance from which the
condemnation of the abuse flowed was highly questionable:
United Brand's market share hovered around the 40% level and
it faced competition from several other firms of some
considerable power; whereas it is by no means clear either
that there was in fact any price discrimination being practised
by UBC or that such discrimination necessarily ought to have
been condemned. Similarly in Nederland Michelin(107) the
Commission condemned that company's discounting practices
having first held that it was in a dominant position on the
heavy replacement tyre market in the Netherlands. In the
light of the finding of dominance, the condemnation was
inevitable given the previous case law on the matter. But the
dominance issue in that case is not free from doubt(108) in
which case the condemnation of the "abuse" may have been
most unfortunate. It has to be borne in mind that in many
markets rivalry on discounting firms is a normal and indeed
sometimes the only form of workable competition. Thus
improper prohibitions of the practice can produce adverse
economic effects both in the instant case and in the many
other commercial decisions that will be taken in reliance on it.

It may well be that in such complex areas the more diffident and cautious approach of UK law is more likely to produce a sensitive and appropriate solution. However the direct applicability of Art. 86 and the manner of its application require that the caution be exercised on the part of the business community and its legal advisers.

Fifthly, the substance of the prohibitions that flow from Art. 86 needs to be considered. We have already seen how under UK law any anti-competitive practice and certain mergers may be investigated. However, technical analyses are less important where the system is non-prohibitive and lacks sanctions than under EEC law where fines may be imposed and Art. 86 may be invoked in domestic litigation. These factors necessitate the formulation of rules which enable undertakings to form some idea of their legal position. Certain practices, such as for example entering into long-term requirements contracts, refusing to supply an existing customer and discriminating in price with no objective justification, seem likely to be always condemned by the Commission, and presumably national courts will follow its lead. Whether a rule can properly define improper discrimination or establish what consitutes an excessive price is highly questionable and has already been remarked upon. But an added problem for the British legal adviser is the teleological approach to the interpretation of Art. 86 adopted by the Commission and the Court.

For example in the Continental Can case(109) the Court approved the Commissions's decision that Art. 86 is infringed where a firm in a dominant position takes over a rival : and this irrespective of whether the former actually used its market power in order to do so. Art. 86 contains no explicit reference to mergers, nor does anything else in the Treaty deal with this delicate and highly political matter. However the Court's reasoning was that Arts. 85 and 86 had to be construed in the light of the fundamental objectives of the Treaty; that Art. 3 (f) required the institution of a system of free competition; and that Art. 86 therefore must be taken to comprehend actions which would lead to a substantial reduction in competition. This approach to statutory interpretation, of which this is by no means the only example, is radically different from that to which the English lawyer is accustomed. Familiarity with it however is vital in view of the serious consequences flowing from transgression of EEC competition law.

The sixth point raised by Art. 86, related to the previous discussion on substance, is that it does not contain any exemption provision or call upon the competition authorities to consider the effect of any practice on the public interest. Art. 85(1) is of course subject to the exemption provisions of Art. 85(3); under the RTPA attempts may be made to penetrate one of the gateways, and under the UK investigative system an extremely broad conception of the public interest is provided against which the MMC is required to make its recommendations. The deficiency of any such provision in Art. 86 obviously compounds the criticisms of it that have been made, for example that it may be applied to prohibit behaviour that ought to be permitted or that the complexity of the issues involved may inevitably result in "bad" or "wrong" decisions. It is particularly serious when one considers for example the mergers that (surprisingly) have been held to be caught by it. Suppose that the merger may enable the merged firm to compete successfully with an American or Japanese undertaking. Would it not then be in the public interest to permit it? But according to Art. 86, provided that the acquiring firm was in a dominant position, the merger would be prohibited and someone with sufficient interest may be able to get either the Commission or a national court to take action to prevent it.(110) Similarly, price discrimination may in some circumstances have beneficial effects; this being so one might have thought that the practice ought to be permissible in certain circumstances. Art. 86 in its present form however seems to be too rigid to accommodate such considerations. This inflexibility of Art. 86 coupled with its direct applicability thus means that many commerical practices have been brought within the scope of a prohibition system from which there is no escape which were formerly, in the UK context, only subject to the much more remote investigative one.

The seventh point raised by Art. 86 is that in some respect its scope is less than that of the FTA 1973. Under the latter Act markets which are oligopolistic in structure may in certain circumstances be referred to the MMC as may certain mergers, irrespective of whether one of the firms concerned already has market power. Under EEC law however it would seem that oligopolists may only be caught by the competition rules where they are guilty of collusion under Art. 85. The Court has indicated that Art. 86 does not apply to jointly held dominant positions so that they cannot be investigated under this provision.(111) This means therefore that there is no really effective way of dealing with the problem of conscious parallelism which may often be identified in oligopolistic markets and which may require the application of behavioural or structural remedies. This lacuna is not surprising in that Art. 86 is prohibitive : it would be inappropriate to prohibit parallel behaviour which economic theory explains is rational. However the gap is a serious one, especially in view of the increasing concentration in EEC industry. The FTA, because of its flexibility and lenience, is able to deal with oligopolistic industries in a more sensitive way. Similarly the application of Art. 86 to mergers is not particularly suitable, partly because of its lack of any public interest provision, but also because it may only be invoked where one of the merging firms already has a dominant position. Thus EEC law has no provision which can deal with undesirable acquisitions of market power through mergers between non-dominant firms.

Conclusions

In the foregoing discussion the domestic competition law of the UK has been contrasted with that of the EEC in several ways. It has been explained that the result of UK entry into the Common Market has not been some substantial alteration in domestic law: the direct applicability of Arts. 85 and 86 renders that unnecessary. It is certainly true that a somewhat more competitive approach has been adopted in the UK in recent years, culminating in the passing of the Competition Act, though it is a matter of speculation whether that is attributable to Common Market influences rather than a shift in political opinion in the UK. In some respects EEC influences have been resisted at the domestic level; for example the Liesner Committee's recommendations designed to facilitate beneficial collaboration have not been acted upon (such collaboration being more obviously encouraged at the European level); while the Liesner report itself declined to recommend the adoption of an effects system along the lines of Art. 85 to replace the anomalous form-based system contained in the RTPA.

The direct applicability of EEC competition law has however affected many commercial activities in the United Kingdom and the extremely liberal line taken by the Commission and the Court of Justice to the meaning of an effect on inter-state trade has meant that many firms that might only have had to contend with the problems raised at the domestic level have also had to ensure that they do not infringe the EEC rules. They face therefore a double-hurdle and the burden of this chapter has been to demonstrate the considerable difference between those two hurdles.

In the first place, the policies underlying UK and EEC law differ. Whereas the UK law has tended to adopt a cautious and pragmatic approach to dominant firms and to mergers, Art. 86 prohibits any abuse of a dominant position and the Commission and Court have considerably extended the scope of this Article in order to ensure the maintenance of competition. Admittedly both domestic and EEC law show a similar hostility towards restrictive trade practices, but here too the greater commitment of EEC law to this policy is demonstrated by its more extensive powers to investigate and punish. Furthermore there is the important role of EEC law in helping to achieve market integration which has resulted in a whole series of decisions - such as those in United Brands and Pioneer - with which domestic law would have had no concern. There is no doubt that the most serious infringment of community law that can be committed is one which results in the separation of one national market from another, and in recent cases the Commission has objected to several agreements whose effect would be to achieve such segregation albeit by indirect means.(112) Thus in advising on matters involving EEC competition law it is vital always to keep in mind the geographical implications of any agreement or practice.

Secondly, EEC law differs considerably from that of the UK in terms of legal technique. The UK lawyer now finds that he has to advise upon agreements and other commercial decisions in terms of their economic impact considered in particular market conditions. Judges will increasingly be called upon to decide complex economic matters - such as the definition of a relevant product market for the purposes of Art. 86 - as awareness of EEC competition law and the opportunites to invoke it increase. And in interpreting the provisions in question regard must be had to the continental approach to interpretation which has been referred to in the discussion on the Continental Can Case. These problems will require skills very different from those required in order to understand the workings of, for example, the RTPA.

Thirdly, at the substantive level, on the whole EEC law is considerably broader in scope than that of the UK. Certainly this is true as regards restrictive trading agreements, precisely because of the operation of an effects - rather than a form-based system. As regards other competition problems, since the investigative system in the UK involves a substantial element of discretion, exercisable by either the DGFT or the Secretary of State, there are no "rules" as such prescribing the ways in which firms should behave. On the one hand most practices and mergers of potentially anti-competitive effect may be made the subject of investigation. On the other hand, Art. 86 either prohibits certain practices entirely in which case fines and injunctions may be imposed or it does not apply at all (as for example to the oligopoly problem or to certain mergers). However, whereas in some respects UK law may be considered to be too lenient towards certain anti-competitive practices, it may well be that Art. 86 is a rather crude instrument for the control of complex economic problems.

Fourthly EEC law differs considerably from that of the UK at the enforcement level. Recalcitrant firms may be fined for "first offences" under Arts. 85 and 86, whereas no such fines can be imposed under domestic law except for contempt of a court order. Furthermore the EEC rules may be invoked in domestic litigation thus increasing substantially the armoury of litigants. This is particularly important in cases involving breaches of Art. 86 since under the UK investigation system, anti-competitive practices and mergers may only be the subject of an investigation by the DGFT or the MMC. There may also be cases where Art. 85 may be invoked by litigants in circumstances where the agreement in question is not caught by the RTPA. Furthermore, where breaches of the EEC rules are suspected, considerably wider powers of investigation are available to the Commission than any provided by domestic law to the DGFT; similarly the extent of privilege is more limited in the EEC law than in that of the UK.

Thus in many respects the UK business community together with its legal advisers is now confronted with a body of law which differs substantially from the domestic system to which it is accustomed. As the EC Commission enforces Arts. 85 and 86 with greater enthusiasm, and litigants plead them more frequently in domestic litigation, it will be vital to appreciate the nature and extent of these differences.

FOOTNOTES

(1) These articles only apply to the extent that anti-competitive practices affect the flow of trade between EEC Member-States: post p123.

(2) Case 13/61 De Geus v Bosch 1962 ECR 45.

(3) Case 14/68 1969 ECR 1.

(4) It follows that undertakings whose commercial practices are permitted by domestic competition law must also face the hurdle of complying with Community law: see eg the UK Sulphur Pool which has been considered both by the Restrictive Practices Court in the UK(1963 LR 4 R P 169) and by the E C Commission (1980 O J L 260/25 1980 3 CMLR 429).

(5) It is also arguable that certain changes in domestic law have been influenced by the Community rules: compare eg the language of s2(1) Competition Act 1980 with that of Art 85(1) of the Treaty.

(6) For more detailed accounts of the economics of competition see, eg Scherer Industrial Market Structure and Economic Performance 2nd Ed passim, Allen Monopoly and Restrictive Practices ChsI and II, Swann Competition and Consumer Protection passim.

(7) In pure monopoly, there being no other producers, the restriction in output will lead to a scarcity of the product and thus increase its market price. The monopolist has power over the market and is a price "maker"; in competitive conditions the price is "taken" from the market.

(8) Eg there will be no incentive to keep production costs down in order to be able to match competitors' prices.

(9) For an explanation of perfect competition see eg Scherer op cit pp9 -12.

(10) In oligopolistic markets a price-cutter would have sufficient market power to affect his rivals thus leading to the problem of conscious parallelism. See infra p111.

(11) Though prosaic, the term "workable competition" does have a place in the academic literature: see eg Allen op cit ChII.

(12) Eg it would be cheaper for the manufacturer to only have to despatch products to a relatively small number of distributors while the latter may only be willing to carry large amounts of a manufacturer's stock or provide an after-sales service if he is sure that his investment will be protected by freedom from other competition at the distributive level.

(13) For a more detailed explanation of oligopolistic interdependence see eg Sweezy Journal of Political Economy 47 pp568-573.

(14) Eg oligopolists may expend large sums of money on advertising or compete on terms and conditions or after-sales service.

(15) Both UK and EEC competition law catch arrangements falling short of being legally enforceable contracts whereby firms knowingly co-ordinate their behaviour: see eg the discussion of the term "arrangement" in s 43 of Restrictive Trade Practices Act 1976 in Cunningham's The Fair Trading Act 1973 pp202-216 and of the term "concerted practice" in A85(1) in Bellamy and Child's Common Market Law of Competition pp28-34. Conscious parallelism simpliciter however falls short of "knowing co-ordination".

(16) It is not inevitable that mergers will lead to an increase in market power in a particular product market: eg a conglomerate merger between two

undertakings from different economic sectors would be unlikely to do so.

(17) See eg Wilberforce, Campbell and Elles <u>Restrictive Trade Practices and Monopolies</u> 2nd Ed Ch1 for an historical survey of UK competition laws.

(18) 1892 AC 25.

(19) For an account of the restriction of competition in the UK in the first half of the twentieth century, see Allen op cit pp50-56.

(20) 1944 Cmnd 6257.

(21) This Commission has had two subsequent changes of name: it is now known as the Monopolies and Mergers Commission and henceforth will be referred to by the abbreviation "MMC" irrespective of its appellation at the time of any particular report.

(22) For an account of these early reports see eg Allen op cit ChsV and VI.

(23) For an interesting account of judicial resistance to the Restrictive Trade Practices Bill see Viscount Kilmuir's biography <u>Political Adventure</u> pp261-262. The judge in the R.P. Court is assisted by 2 lay members.

(24) See s 6 RTPA 1976; seperate provisions deal with the services sector (s 11); there are further provisions dealing with the exchange of information (ss 7, 12).

(25) See ss 6(3) and (4), 9, 17 and 18.

(26) See ss 8 and 16.

(27) See ss 28-34 and schedule 3.

(28) Now to be found in ss 10 and 19.

(29) Eg it is not clear to what extent clauses contained in a patent licence qualify as "restrictions" for the purposes of the RTPA: see eg the discussion of <u>Re Ravenseft Properties Ltd's Application</u> 1977 ICR 136 in Cunningham op cit (Supplement).

(30) See on the former issue <u>Re Blankets</u> 1959 LR 1 R P 208 and on the latter <u>Re Waste Paper</u> 1963 LR 4 R P 29.

(31) Eg the Restrictive Trade Practices Act 1977 was passed to exclude certain types of credit transactions from the Act; also see the various amendments to the 1976 Act in the Competition Act 1980 (ss 25-30).

(32) This formalistic approach of the RTPA inevitably results in considerable intellectual effort being expended in order to avoid its provisions: the effects approach of A85 precludes such avoidance.

(33) The Director General of Fair Trading may ask the Secretary of State to relieve him from the obligation of having to take registrable agreements before the Restrictive Practices Court where they are of no economic significance: s 21(2) 1976 Act. Under the de minimis principle in Community law, such an agreement would not be caught by A85(1) at all. See post p125.

(34) See on these cases Cunningham op cit pp250-253.

(35) A Review of Restrictive Trade Practices Policy 1979 Cmnd 7512.

(36) ibid. paras7.4-7.8.

(37) Exemptions are dealt with in ss 28-34 1976 Act and Schedule 3; the gateways are contained in ss 10 and 19.

(38) Out of 4626 agreements registered by the end of 1981 only 11 have successfully passed through the gateways, and in one of those the Court held that the harm to the public interest overall offset the benefit claimed: see <u>Re Yarn Spinners</u> 1959 LR 1 RP 118.

(39) Re Distant Water Vessels Development Scheme 1966 LR 6 RP 242.

(40) See note 33 supra.

(41) In recent years it has become clear that many registrable agreements have not in fact been registered: see eg the MMC reports on Flour and Bread 1977 HC 412 and Copying Materials 1976 HC 47; also many agreements have been found to be operating in the construction industries.

(42) For an example of the imposition of a fine see Re Mileage Conference 1966 LR 6 RP 49 where fines totalling £80,000 were imposed on firms held to have accepted price restrictions.

(43) See now s 35 1976 Act.

(44) So far as the writer is aware there are no reported decisions in which such damages have been awarded; see however the Annual Report of the DGFT for 1977 for details of an out-of-court settlement whereby the Post Office received £9 million from cable producers.

(45) It is possible that more penal sanctions may be adopted in the UK for some breaches of the RTPA: see eg the Liesner report (note 35 supra) at pp48/9,68; the Department of Trade did publish a Consultative Document on 30th July 1980 on the possibilities of introducing criminal penalties for collusive tendering, but so far the matter has proceeded no further. For fines imposed by the E C Commission see post note 91.

(46) 1969 LR 7 RP 122; the Registrar's functions were transferred to the DGFT by the FTA 1973 s 94. The CAP held that the section only applied where objectively ascertainable facts could be shown to exist indicating that there was a registrable agreement in operation; one might have thought that investigatory powers are required precisely where objectively ascertainable facts are lacking.

(47) See note 41 supra.

(48) See post p129.

(49) These terms are defined in ss 6-11 FTA; a complex monopoly situation is one in which two or more firms behave in a way which is uncompetitive without actually agreeing to act in a way caught by the RTPA 1976.

(50) See s 56 and Schedule 8 FTA.

(51) The DGFT actually presides over the Mergers Panel which advises the SOS: the discretionary aspect of the UK system is emphasised by the fact that on some occasions the SOS has declined to accept such advice: see eg DGFT's Annual Report for 1979 p41.

(52) The SOS does have Order-making powers, should they prove necessary: ss 73,74, Schedule 8 FTA.

(53) The Competition Act system is designed in such a way as to produce speedier conclusions than under the FTA. An important point is that public interest considerations can only be taken into account by the MMC, and not by the DGFT: s 8(2)(d) of the CA only relates to reports by the MMC.

(54) ss 10(2) FTA and 2(2) CA concretize this distinction by providing that those Acts do not apply to agreements registrable under the RTPA.

(55) See s 58 FTA.

(56) Figures taken from DGFT's Annual Reports for 1979 and 1980.

(57) See ss 6-8 FTA.

(58) At least under the FTA an improper finding by the MMC on market power may only entail an obligation to alter certain practices prospectively; under A 86 however a finding of abuse may have a retrospective effect and fines (and perhaps damages) may be imposed for past behaviour.

(59) In a Government statement on 1 July 1980 the Secretary of State announced that a more sceptical approach to mergers would in future be taken and the number of merger references has recently increased; the Government does not however plan any alteration in the provisions of the FTA as recommended by the Green Paper "A Review of Monopolies and Mergers Policy" 1978 Cmnd 7198: see DGFT's Annual Report 1980 pp9-11. On EEC law see p135 post.

(60) See also note 58 supra on the time factor; also the powers to acquire information are very limited and contrast considerably with the E C Commission's power to investigate: see post p129.

(61) See eg Case 85/76 Hoffman La Roche v Commission 1979 ECR 461 and Case 27/76 United Brands v Commission 1978 ECR 207.

(62) See eg Scherer op cit Ch11.

(63) See eg the Notice on Co-operation Agreements OJ C 75; the Block Exemption on Specialization Agreements 1972 JO L292/23 as amended by Regulation 2903/77 OJ L 338; and the 11th report on Competition Policy points 29-33.

(64) Market integration was also one of the policies informing the Block Exemption on Exclusive Dealing Agreements, Regulation 67/67 O J 1967,10.

(65) See eg Cases 54 and 56 Consten and Grundig v Commission 1966 ECR 299 at p341.

(66) Cases 6 and 7/73 1974 ECR 223.

(67) 1977 O J L48/32 1977 1 CMLR D 67.

(68) See eg Case 8/72 VCH v Commission 1972 ECR 977.

(69) See eg the Hoffman La Roche case (n 61 supra) where fines were imposed.

(70) It is noticeable that exemption will only be granted under A 85(3) where some competition in the market will remain: neither the RTPA nor the FTA demands in terms the maintenance of competition on the market in all circumstances.

(71) See Case 23/67 Brasserie de Haecht SA v Wilkin (No 1) 1967 ECR 407.

(72) 1970 J O C84/1.

(73) For a detailed account of the scope of A 85(1) see eg Bellamy and Child op cit Chs 2 and 3.

(74) See eg the Brasserie de Haecht case, note 71 supra.

(75) Re Pioneer Hi-fi Equipment 1910 O J L60/21 1910 1 CMLR 457.

(76) Assuming that the agreement is bilateral: see s 9(4) RTPA.

(77) See generally Bellamy and Child op cit Ch 6.

(78) Assuming that the agreement is a "new agreement" which, in the UK context, will mean an agreement entered into after 1 January 1973.

(79) Block exemptions are dealt with below.

(80) See Regulation 17 J O 1962, 204 Art 9(1).

(81) Several different actions were dealt with in these cases: see 1980 ECR pp2327, 2481, 2511, 3775.

(82) For a detailed account of the problems raised by comfort letters see Korah 1981 ELRev p14.

(83) See point 15.

(84) See notes 63 and 64 supra. New draft Regulations on Distribution, Purchasing and Specialization were published by the Commission in 1982 OJ C 172/3-16; they are due to come into effect on January 1st 1983.

(85) According to the Tenth Report on Competition Policy, 64% of the 4203 cases pending before the Commission related to patent licenses: see point 104 ibid.

(86) See the draft Regulation on Purchasing referred to in note 84 supra.

(87) See eg Case 63/75 Fonderies Roudaix v Fonderies Roux 1976 6 ECR 111.

(88) See eg Atka v B P Kemi 1979 O J L286/32 1979 3 CMLR 684.

(89) See eg Henkel/Colgate 1972 J O L14/4.

(90) As to which see Bellamy and Child op cit passim.

(91) For a useful account of the fines imposed so far by the Commission see Kerse EEC Antitrust Procedure pp178-181.

(92) See in particular Case 136/79 National Panasonic v Commission 1980 ECR 2033. In EEC law there is no distinction in powers according to whether the case involves a breach of A 85 or 86.

(93) Community v Fabbrica Pisani 1980 O J L75/30 1980 2CMLR 354 and Community v Fabbrica Sciarra 1980 O J L75/35 1980 2CMLR 362.

(94) See eg Community v C C I 1982 O J L27/31 1982 1 CMLR 440.

(95) See in particular Case 155/79 A M & S Europe Ltd v Commission 1982 2CMLR 264 in which the Court of Justice held that there was no legal privilege in Community law for correspondence between a company and its own in-house lawyer. Presumably this decision will be regarded by solicitors in private practice as having had a most favourable impact!

(96) See note 41 supra.

(97) See note 61 supra.

(98) See Kerse op cit on such fines.

(99) See Bellamy and Child op cit Ch7.

(100) See eg Felixstowe Dock and Railway Company v British Transport Docks Board 1976 2 CMLR 655 where A 86 was pleaded as a defence to a takeover bid. In the CAP no objection was raised as to the nature of the defence although on the facts of the case it was held to be unavailable. It is impossible under UK law to invoke the merger provisions of the FTA in domestic litigation.

(101) See Garden Cottage Foods Ltd v Milk Marketing Board 1982 2 CMLR 542; the earlier case, James Budgett v British Sugar Company Ltd, is unreported though it is noted in 1979 ELRev at p417.

(102) The same uncertainty exists in the case of infringements of A 85. Lord Denning's view in Application des Gaz SA v Falks Veritas 1974 Ch 381 at p396 that Arts 85 and 86 create new torts remediable in damages was obiter and has since been doubted by one of the other judges in that case (by Roskill L J as he then was in Valor International Ltd v Application des Gaz 1978 3 CMLR 87); in the Garden Cottage case Lord Denning and May L J both inclined to the view that damages might be available but again these comments, in an application for interlocutory relief, were obiter. For a fuller discussion of the damages issue, see Kerse op cit paras 10.15 et sequitur.

(103) By virtue of what legal rule can a price be branded as "excessive"? Is it possible for the High Court to decide what the price of a product would have been in competitive conditions? In discrimination cases it is extremely difficult to calculate whether a price differentiation is attributable to different supply costs of the product in question or to discriminatory selling prices.

(104) Presumably national courts dealing with A 86 will tend to adopt an approach similar to that of the Commission. It is important to appreciate that A 86 catches firms with dominant positions and not dominant (ie large) firms. Given the narrow approach taken by the Commission to the definition of the relevant product market it may be anticipated that many more firms will find themselves being attacked under A 86 than might at first have been expected.

(105) Such as entering into long-term requirements contracts with customers: see Hoffman La Roche note 61 supra.

(106) Note 61 supra: for criticisms see eg Bishop 44 MLR 282, Valguirata 1982 ICLQ 36.

(107) 1981 O J L353/33 as corrected in 1982 O J 11/28 not yet reported: the case is going on appeal to the European Court of Justice.

(108) See eg Korah 1982 ELRev p130.

(109) Case 6/72 Europemballage and Continental Can v Commission 1973 ECR 215.

(110) The Commission is aware of the unsuitability of A86 for the control of mergers, but until the Council agrees to a specific Regulation to deal with the probem, it is the only weapon available to it. The Commission has recently published a draft Regulation (1982 OJ 36) which amends its earlier draft of 1973, but it remains to be seen whether the Council will take action.

(111) See Hoffman La Roche note 61 supra at para 38 and Case 172/80 Zuchner v Bayerische Vereinsbank AG 1982 1 CMLR 313.

(112) See eg Re Zanussi's Guarantee 1978 O J L322/26 1979 1 CMLR 81 and RE ANSEAU-NAVEWA IP 81 240 1982 2 CMLR 193.

THE EUROPEAN COMMUNITY
AND ENGLISH COMPANY LAW

N E Furey and J E Parkinson

In this essay we intend first to outline the various ways in which membership of the EEC has had and may be expected in future to have an impact on English company law. We then propose to look at the impact on a particular area of company law, the law relating to groups of companies. This is a field where English company law is likely to see significant changes in the next decade, changes which will almost certainly be heavily influenced by an EEC Directive for the harmonization of national company laws.

The aims and methods of the EEC

(1) Freedom of establishment

The first question, however, is why membership of the EEC has any impact on company law at all. Art. 2 of the Treaty of Rome states that the aim of the EEC is to promote "a harmonious development of economic activities, a continuous and balanced expansion, an increase in stability, an accelerated raising of the standard of living and closer relations between the States belonging to it". These are to be achieved "by establishing a common market and progressively approximating the economic policies of Member States". Even that, however, does not indicate why company law should be particularly affected. The answer lies first in the important role companies play in the economy of Member States and hence in any common market. Thus the Green Paper on "Employee Participation and Company Structure"(1) in discussing the need for Community legislation observes that, "[t]he corporation with limited liability and a share capital is the typical form adopted by the majority of the Community's most important industrial and commercial enterprises. They have become the principal buyers and sellers of goods, the major borrowers and lenders of capital, and the most significant developers and users of new technology. They are the main producers of wealth, and as employers, they have an immediate impact on the lives of large numbers of the Community's citizens.   In sum they are institutions of strategic importance in relation to the economic and social systems of the Community".

Secondly, company law is affected because of the methods by which the common market is to be established.   These are set out in Art. 3 of the Treaty and include " the abolition, as between Member States, of obstacles to freedom of movement for persons, services and capital".   It is made clear in Chapter 2 of the Treaty dealing with the free movement of persons that the right of establishment applies to artificial persons, as much as to natural persons.(2)   The importance of this for companies is apparent from Art. 52 para. 1 which states that the abolition of restrictions on freedom of establishment of nationals of one Member State in the territory of another Member State, "shall also apply to restrictions on the setting up of agencies, branches or subsidiaries by nationals of any Member State established in the territory of any Member State".   One important aspect of freedom of establishment is that there must be no discrimination in one Member State against persons from another Member State.   Again so far as companies are concerned it is expressly provided in Art. 52 para. 2 that, "freedom of establishment shall include the right to ... set up and manage undertakings, in particular companies or firms ... under the conditions laid down for its own nationals by the law of the country where such establishment is effected".

So the United Kingdom, for example, must permit a company from any other Member State to trade in the United Kingdom on the same terms and conditions as United Kingdom companies.(3)   That example, however, illustrates a problem the draftsmen of the Treaty faced in deciding what should count as a company from another Member State and thus be entitled to the benefit of freedom of establishment. If it was sufficient for the company merely to be incorporated in a Member State that would allow, for example, a United States company to incorporate a subsidiary in Italy which would then have the right of establishment in every other Member State even though both parent and subsidiary were managed from outside the EEC. Read literally the wording of Art. 58 para. 1 would allow this. It requires that a company be incorporated in a Member State and have either its registered office, central administration or principal place of business within a Member State, which, however, need not be the same as the Member State in which it is incorporated. It would be perfectly possible therefore for the subsidiary of the United States company to be incorporated in England and have its registered office in England but to be managed from the United States. However, the General Programme for the abolition of restrictions on freedom of establishment(4) provides that companies may only enjoy freedom of establishment in the Community if, besides coming within Art. 58 para. 1, "their activity shows a real and continuous link with the economy of a Member State".(5)

(2) Harmonization of company law

Freedom of establishment therefore requires that Member States allow companies from other Member States to trade within their territory on the same terms as their own companies. In return for this freedom Member States needed to be sure about two things. First, that the law applicable to the formation and operation of companies in other Member States was broadly speaking at least as onerous as their own. There is an obvious danger otherwise that companies will be incorporated in the country with the most congenial and relaxed company law and then take advantage of the right of establishment to trade in other Member States.(6) Secondly, the Member States needed to be sure that, with companies free to trade anywhere in the EEC and investors free to invest anywhere in the EEC, the law applicable to companies contained at least the basic requirements for the protection of shareholders and others who deal with companies. So Art. 54(3)(g) provides that in carrying out the removal of restrictions on freedom of establishment the Council and Commission are to co-ordinate the safeguards for the protection of the interests of members and others with a view to making such safeguards equivalent throughout the Community.

It is clear from the wording of Art. 54 that co-ordination is not intended to make it easier for a company to establish itself in another Member State. The co-ordination is of laws protecting shareholders and others who deal with the company, not of laws providing for the establishment of companies. Co-ordination also aims at harmonization not unification. The safeguards are to be equivalent not identical. So it is not, for example, intended to establish a uniform procedure for forming companies throughout the EEC. The removal of restrictions on freedom of establishment is the positive side of the Common Market so far as companies are concerned. The programme for harmonization under Art. 54(3)(g) can be seen as the quid pro quo for freedom of establishment from the point of view of the Member States.

The programme for harmonization is carried out by means of Directives issued under Art. 54(2). In contrast to Directives issued under Art. 100 those under Art. 54(2) do not, since the ending of the first stage, need to be unanimously approved by Council. The use of Directives at all may be questioned on the ground that because it is left to Member States to implement them, the implementation may differ considerably in detail so that equivalence is not achieved except in a very broad sense. Problems may arise too in Member States failing to implement the Directive properly(7) or even at all.(8)

More serious criticisms though have also been made of the programme for harmonization itself. H. C. Ficker has argued that true harmonization cannot be achieved unless the national policies of Member States as to how company law should develop are themselves harmonized.(9) This, however, presupposes the existence of an EEC policy about how company law should develop in future. While there are signs of such a policy in relation to areas of company law reform like disclosure of information of employee participation, there is no overall policy for the future development of company law. The most that can be said in general of the EEC attitude to company law is that it should be harmonized.

A further question arising from the relationship between the Member States and the EEC itself is whether the Member States are or should be free to undertake independent reform of company law in those areas covered by an EEC Directive.(10) It might even be argued that there should be no independent reform of national company law at all since as Ficker points out(11) no area of company law can be isolated from all other areas and the programme for harmonization must therefore be regarded as affecting all areas of company law. Perhaps the explanation for Ficker's doubts about the harmonization programme lies in his suggestion that the contracting parties to the Treaty of Rome should have made unification of company law the aim instead of mere harmonization.(12) It cannot be stressed too much, however, in understanding and evaluating the harmonization programme that it is not aiming at unification. It may be that when the harmonization programme is successfully completed there may then be moves towards unification. It may be anticipated that they may come via the publication of a model EEC Code of company law which Member States will be encouraged to adopt when reforming a particular area of company law. All that however is a long way in the future. For the time being harmonization alone is the aim.

(3) Recognition of companies.

The right to freedom of establishment enables a company from one Member State to set up business in any other Member State on the same terms as companies from the Member State where the business is to be established. It would be a severe handicap to the foreign company, however, if, despite being allowed to set up business, it was not recognised as a corporate body with legal personality in the Member State where it has set up. It would be unable, for example, to sue in its own name in the courts of the Member State and this handicap would apply also to companies which without setting up a business in the Member State nevertheless made contracts with residents in the Member State and wished therefore to be able to enforce them in the courts of the Member State. This problem was appreciated by the draftsmen of the Treaty and so in Art. 220 they provided that:

"Member States shall... enter into negotiations with each other with a view to securing for the benefit of their nationals:
- the mutual recognition of companies or firms within the meaning of the second paragraph of Art. 58 [and] the retention of legal personality in the event of a transfer of their seat from one country to another."

In fact each of the original Member States had rules for the recognition of foreign companies that broadly speaking ensured that companies from one Member State could enforce contracts in another Member State. The difficulty was that the rules applied by the Member States were not uniform. The Netherlands applied a test, known as the place of incorporation test, whereby a foreign company will be recognised as having corporate personality in the Netherlands if it has corporate personality under the law of the place where it is incorporated. This is also the test adopted by most common law jurisdictions. So, for example, a company incorporated in the United States but which had a place of business in England could be sued in the English courts in its own name because it was recognised as a corporate body in the United States.(13) Conversely, when under the law of the U.S.S.R. a company incorporated in Russia ceased to exist English courts treated it as having ceased to exist in England as well.(14)

The advantage of this approach to recognition is the relative ease with which the test can be applied and the certainty with which the result can be predicted. The great disadvantage of the place of incorporation test is that it would allow a company to be incorporated in a jurisdiction with which it had little if any economic connection but which might have a relaxed and congenial company law. Having thus established corporate personality in its place of incorporation it could claim recognition in the countries of the common law world without having to comply with all the provisions of the domestic company law. To some extent the advantages to the company can be reduced by provisions like those in Part X of the Companies Act 1948 which require companies that establish their place of business in England or Wales to register at Companies House and to file certain information corresponding to the more important disclosure requirements of English company law.

The continental Member States, with the exception of the Netherlands, have responded to the danger by adopting a different test for recognition. They grant recognition if the company is recognised as having corporate personality by the law of the country where its central management and administration (siege reel) is carried on. This test has the merit of asking whether the company is recognised as a company by the law of the country with which it has its greatest economic connection. It is similar to the test used in United Kingdom revenue law for determining the residence of companies.(15)

Another consequence which stems from the test of recognition is the decision as to what law constitutes "the proper law of the company" and governs, for example, the relationship between the company and its members and the rights and duties of members inter se. Those countries that adopt a place of incorporation test for recognition similarly hold that the proper law of the company is the law of the place of incorporation. So English courts have treated the question of liability of members of a company for the debts of the company and the rights of preference shareholders to dividend as depending on the law of the place of incorporation. Once again the place of incorporation test has the advantage of certainty and so long as countries do not allow companies to change their place of incorporation (under English company law the domicile is the only clause of the Memorandum of Association that can never be changed) then the proper law of the company does not change.

On the other hand the siege reel theory has the advantage that the proper law of the company is the law of the country with which the company will probably have its greatest economic link. There is good sense in having, for example, the right of a company to distribute dividends to its shareholders governed by the law of the place with which the company has its strongest economic ties. The problem comes, however, if a company changes its siege reel. Does the proper law of the company change with it? The inconvenience of this has led to a suggestion that in German law a decision to transfer the siege reel automatically causes the dissolution and liquidation of the corporation.(17) Whatever the true legal position the siege reel theory presents substantial practical obstacles to the possibility of changing the siege reel from one country to another. This is why Art. 220 of the Treaty as well as referring to the mutual recognition of companies refers also to the retention of legal personality in the event of a transfer of a company's seat from one country to another.

Art. 220 provides for the Member States to negotiate to secure the aims specified. This has resulted in Conventions negotiated between representatives of the national governments and resembling in law treaties rather than Community legislation. The Draft Convention on Mutual Recognition(18) is one result of such negotiations. It deals, however, only with recognition and not with the migration of companies from one country to another. So far as recognition is concerned the general approach of the Convention is in favour of the place of incorporation test. Thus Member States must recognise enterprises covered by the Convention(19) if they are established under the law of a Member State which accords them legal personality (and possibly even if it does not, provided the enterprise has certain characteristics(20)) and have their registered offices within the Community. Since this approach is the same as that currently used in the United Kingdom the Convention will not have a great impact on the English courts' approach to recognition of foreign companies. If, however, we imagine a company incorporated in Italy with its siege reel in France, at present the Belgian courts will recognise that company as governed by French law whereas under the Convention they will have to recognise it as governed by Italian law. The Member States however, in discussions in 1979, agreed that the Convention should not affect the question of the proper law of the company and should only affect the question of recognition. Since as we saw above(21) recognition does not present real practical problems in any of the Member States it seems likely that the Convention on Mutual Recognition will be laid aside for the time being.

(4) Measures to promote transnational co-operation

The EEC proposals affecting company law that we have so far considered have all been concerned with making it easier for a company established in one Member State to trade within another Member State. From the outset the EEC has also been concerned to promote co-operation between enterprises established in different Member States within the EEC. Closer co-operation between companies within the EEC may give them economies of scale that may promote the "accelerated raising in the standard of living" referred to in Art. 2 of the Treaty. If the co-operation is between companies from different Member States it may promote "closer relations between the States" also referred to in Art. 2. The evidence, however, suggests that links between enterprises in different Member States are less likely to come about than either links between enterprises within one Member State or between an enterprise in a Member State and one in a non-EEC country.(22)

The reasons for this lack of co-operation must presumably include cultural, linguistic and psychological barriers but in so far as there are also legal barriers the EEC is proposing measures to overcome them. Art. 220 of the Treaty which as we have already seen provided for Member States to negotiate a Convention on Mutual Recognition also provides for them to negotiate "with a view to securing for the benefit of their nationals the possibility of mergers between companies or firms governed by the laws of different countries". Accordingly a Draft Convention on the International Merger of Public Companies(23) has been prepared. This lays down a procedure for mergers using the method whereby one company transfers all its assets and liabilities to another company in return for shares in the acquiring company or two companies transfer all their assets and liabilities to a new company in return for shares in the new company. This method of merger is relatively uncommon in the United Kingdom and it is doubtful whether the Convention when enforced will have much impact on United Kingdom companies.

The second idea for promoting cross-frontier co-operation is the proposal for a European Company. This idea is not mentioned in the Treaty which assumed that all companies would be formed under the law of one of the Member States. The concept of the European Company is of a company incorporated not under the laws of any one Member State, but, under a Regulation and registered at the Court of Justice in Luxembourg. Once incorporated a European Company would be able to trade, with legal personality, in each of the Member States. The idea was first suggested in 1959 by Professor Sanders and the current proposal is for a Statute for a European Company to be introduced via a Regulation under Art. 235 of the Treaty.(24) The present draft is restricted to mergers or the formation of joint subsidiaries by existing enterprises from at least two different Member States. Individuals may not take part directly; neither may enterprises incorporated outside the EEC.

The European Company is the most ambitious of the EEC projects involving company law since it entails the creation of a new body of company law independent of the law of any Member State. Not least of the problems the European Company will face will be the danger of diverse interpretation of this new body of company law in the national courts of the Member States. In part the problem is alleviated by the use of a Regulation which is ultimately subject to the interpretation of the European Court of Justice under Art. 177 and by making the Regulation as detailed as possible. Nevertheless cases will arise when national courts have to exercise jurisdiction over the European company and Art. 7 of the draft statute lays down how they are to proceed. In relation to matters governed by the Statute including those not expressly mentioned in it (in effect all matters of company or labour relations law), national courts are enjoined not to apply national law. Instead they must apply the Statute itself to matters mentioned in the Statute. In relation to matters governed by the Statute but not mentioned in it they must look first to the general principles on which the Statute is based and if that does not provide an answer then they must apply the rules or general principles common to the laws of the Member States. That seemingly Herculean task of identifying the general principles common to the laws of the Member States is not perhaps as difficult as it sounds. The harmonization Directives will provide a large body of material that can be taken to form a common threshold for the company law of the Member States on the topics covered by the Directives. So the harmonization Directives may ultimately be seen as more than mere harmonization measures and instead as forming the basis of a European company law.

The passing into law of the draft Statute for the European Company may still be some years away. Meanwhile a different format for transnational co-operation is also being developed. The European Co-operation Grouping(25) will in effect be an unlimited liability partnership consisting of firms or individuals all of whom must be resident within the Community for tax purposes and who come from at least two different Member States. The activities of the grouping will be restricted to providing services, which, however, may include the production, processing or packaging of goods, exclusively for the purposes of its members. The grouping will enjoy legal personality and in so far as no provision is made by the Regulation, the law applicable to it will be the law of the Member State where the head office is situated.

(5) Background to the Ninth Directive

This brief survey of the three main areas of impact of the EEC on company law may at least help to show how the areas relate to one another and in particular show how the harmonization programme ties in with the proposals on recognition and transnational co-operation. There is another way of categorizing the EEC measures on company law which reflects the fact that some of these measures cover topics which are already dealt with in the company law of most if not all of the Member States whereas other measures are entirely new. So, for example, the four harmonization Directives issued so far which cover the protection of parties entering into transactions with companies, the raising and maintenance of capital of public companies, the merger of public companies and the publication of public company accounts, all deal with topics already covered by domestic company law. They are true harmonization measures in that they harmonize existing provisions. Likewise the seventh draft Directive on harmonization of group accounts will fall into this category.

On the other hand the ninth draft Directive is concerned with the legal problems caused by groups of companies other than the issue of group accounts. It includes provisions that will allow groups of companies in certain circumstances to operate as a single enterprise. At present such provisions really only exist in German company law (on which the Directive is likely to be based) and so although this is a harmonization Directive its impact in most Member States will be to introduce a new concept in company law and a measure of genuine reform. This difference from other harmonization directives is reflected in the fact that this proposal emanates from a division within the Commission dealing with entirely new concepts like the European Company and the European Co-operation Grouping. The novel idea of allowing groups of companies to operate as a single enterprise and the potentially far-reaching implications this may have, make this topic one of the most interesting for United Kingdom company lawyers. We propose in the remainder of this essay to examine the English law relating to groups of companies and to assess the likely impact of the ninth Directive on English law.(26)

Problems which may arise in English law where companies operate as groups

Companies which are part of a group often operate as though they were departments of a single enterprise. They may have common directors who manage the affairs of the company in the interests of the group as a whole, and even where each company has separate directors they will generally follow the instructions of the dominant company. Thus, a subsidiary may be involved in trading practices which are not in its inidividual interests, for example, it may trade with other group companies at special prices, or transfer assets or provide services gratuitously or may divert business opportunities to the parent or other group companies. Whilst these and similar practices are often commercially desirable, since many advantages may spring from central co-ordination of group activities and resources, they are inimical to the interest of those who do not share in the fortunes of the group as a whole, namely the independent share-holders, creditors, and employees of the company. Such protection as English law offers against the exploitation of one company's ability to control another has arisen haphazardly, in contexts unrelated to the problems of groups. The result is that the law creates a number of obstacles to the operation of companies in groups, but at the same time fails to provide effective safeguards for the interests of minority shareholders, creditors and employees.

There is no definition of "group" in the Companies Acts, thought mainly for the purposes of accounting requirements,(27) the 1948 Act (section 154) defines the holding company/subsidiary relationship. A company is a subsidiary of another if the latter is a member of it and controls the composition of its board (in the sense that it has the power to appoint or remove a majority of the directors) or it holds more than half in nominal value of its equity share capital. A sub-subsidiary is treated as a subsidiary of the holding company. Problems created by groups may arise where a company has a holding of substantially less than a majority of voting shares (especially where the other shares are widely dispersed) and hence the expression "group" will be used in what follows to refer to a situation where one company is in a position to exercise effective control over another. Some of the legal implications of group enterprises will now be considered, under the following heads: (1) restrictions on transactions which are designed to benefit the group rather than the company itself and (2) the possibility of other group companies being liable for the debts of an insolvent group company.

(1) Restrictions on transactions designed to benefit the group rather than the company itself

(a) Ultra vires

A restriction on the ground of ultra vires would deny the company the capacity to enter into a transaction which was in the group interest but not its own. It has never been seriously suggested that a company will lack the capacity to enter a transaction which is not in its own interests where the transaction involves the exercise of one of the objects set out in the company's memorandum, for example, where a company sells its product to an associated company at less than the market rate. Until recently, however, the extent to which a company might rely on a power in order to enter into a transaction which is not for its independent benefit has been unclear.(28) The answer would now seem to depend on whether the power in question is implied or express. An implied power will only arise in respect of a particular transaction if that transaction is for the company's benefit, since the basis for the implication of a power is that it is necessary to enable the company to pursue its objects. On the other hand, benefit to the company is irrelevant where the power is contained in the objects clause and is not, as a matter of construction, or by reason of the nature of the power,(29) purely ancillary.(30) In Charterbridge Corporation v Lloyds Bank(31) Pennycuick J. rejected the argument that the capacity of a company to give a guarantee of indebtedness of an associated company, where the company has an express power to do so, depended on the directors' belief that they were benefiting the company itself. There was no justification for subjecting a power contained in the company's objects clause to such a limitation.

To hold a transaction ultra vires on the basis of a tenuous distinction between powers and objects would lead to highly capricious results, and for that reason alone the ultra vires doctrine is not a suitable device for controlling prejudicial group transactions.(32) The result of the cases is, therefore, that a company with an appropriately-drafted objects clause will have the capacity to enter a wide range of disadvantageous transactions with or for the benefit of associated companies, including, for example, the gratuitous transfer of assets to another group company. Where the recipient company is a shareholder in the transferor, however, a non-arm's length transfer of assets may be classified as an unlawful "distribution" (as involving a return of capital) if the company does not satisfy the requirements for paying a dividend.(33)

(b) Directors' fiduciary duties

The fiduciary status of directors imposes on them the duty to act in good faith for the benefit of the company. As a result of the corporate entity principle the person to whom these duties are owed is necessarily the individual company, and at least in principle, therefore, the directors will be in breach of duty where they prefer the interests of the group to those of the company.(34) A director of a subsidiary, if he is not also a director of the parent company, will owe no duty to the parent company and must not follow instructions given to him by it if carrying them out would be contrary to the interests of the subsidiary.(35) By the same token the directors of the parent owe no duty to the subsidiary.(36) A further component of directors' duties requires them not to place themselves in a position where their private interests, or another duty, may conflict with their duty to the company. This presents obvious difficulties where an individual is a director of several group companies with overlapping interests, for example, with regard to business opportunities.(37)

In some cases it may be possible to bring an action against the company in whose interests the directors in default are acting, and this will be of particular importance where the directors themselves are of insufficient substance to be worth suing. Where a company obtains property which it knows

results from a breach of duty, it will hold it as a constructive
trustee for the damaged company.(38) It is likely that in many
cases such knowledge would exist, especially where there are
overlapping directorships and central group control. There
may also be liability where a company has knowingly
participated in a fraudulent breach of duty by the directors of
the damaged company, even though the first company has not
received the proceeds of the breach of duty, and on the basis
of conspiracy.(39)

In practice, however, these remedies are difficult to
invoke, for a number of different reasons. First, the duty to
act in good faith for the benefit of the company is largely a
subjective one: the directors must act bona fide "in what they
consider - not what a court may consider - is in the interests
of the company".(40) Where companies are economically
interdependent a contention that what is good for an
associated company is good for the company in question will
often be difficult to resist, given the courts' well-known
reluctance to consider the merits of "business decisions".

Secondly, and even more importantly, many damaging
transactions simply never come to light.(41) Where they do,
most minority shareholders will be deterred from bringing an
action by the expense, and if there is a market in the
company's shares, they are likely to sell rather than to stay on
and fight.

Thirdly, the breaches of duty referred to above are wrongs
done to the company and company law doctrine insists, with a
number of vaguely-restricted exceptions, that any action in
respect of them must be brought by the company itself.(42)
One of these exceptions allows a derivative action to be
brought by minority shareholders where there is a "fraud on
the minority" and it is probable that, at least in theory, this
will be available where the directors have deliberately harmed
the company in order to benefit the group.(43) Creditors
(where the company is not in liquidation) and employees will
have no standing, however, to complain of breaches of duty
which harm their interests. Whilst there is increasing

recognition by the courts that the interests of creditors must be taken into account in board decisions,(44) creditors do not have an independent cause of action. Similarly, section 46 of the Companies Act 1980 requires the directors to consider the interests of the company's employees, but again the duty is owed to the company and there is no mechanism which would allow the employees to enforce it.(45)

Where a company is a wholly-owned subsidiary there is obviously no possibility of prejudice to minority shareholders, but there is, if anything, a greater risk to creditors, in that the inhibiting influence of the outside shareholders is removed and also because of the increased possibilities of breaches of duty being ratified. Where the directors deliberately inflict harm on the company their breach of duty will not be ratifiable by a majority vote of the shareholders,(46) but it is not clear that unanimous ratification would be ineffective.(47) Where a company is wholly-owned and its directors act under the instruction of the parent company ratification would, in effect, be automatic.(48) Thus, in addition to the creditors' inability to intervene when the company is a going concern the liquidator may be deprived of the right to complain of the relevant breaches of duty when the company is in liquidation, since they will have ceased to be breaches.

(c) Unfairly prejudicial conduct

Minority shareholders may find a petition under section 75 of the Companies Act 1980 a more attractive means of seeking redress, as it is not necessary to establish a breach of duty by the directors and there are no problems of standing, since the Rule in Foss v Harbottle does not apply.(49) The section may be invoked where the affairs of the company are, or have been, conducted in a manner which is unfairly prejudicial to some part of the members (but not creditors or employees(50)). It offers a flexible range of remedies: the majority may, for example, be required to buy the shares of the minority, or the court may make an order regulating the affairs of the company in future. The section provides an opportunity, therefore, for the court to intervene in the relationship between majority and minority shareholders; the wording of the section, which suggests an element of improper discrimination is apt to cover many of the problems which may arise in a group company which has an outside minority. As considered above, however, it may be impossible for a shareholder to discover that damaging practices have been carried on and it might also be wondered how willing the courts will be to question intra-group transactions which might be seen to involve matters of "business judgement", for example, the reorganisation of group administration, or the reallocation of commercial opportunities amongst group companies.

(2) Liability for debts of group companies

The limited opportunities for the liquidator of an insolvent company to recover compensation for damage inflicted on the company from the directors responsible or some other group company which is party to the directors' misfeasance have been noted above. A different, but related issue, which has given rise to great controversy over recent years, concerns the extent to which other group companies should be liable for the debts of an insolvent subsidiary. The corporate entity doctrine dictates that liability should be restricted to the group itself and should not extend to the parent company. There are, however, a number of persuasive arguments(51) which support a modification of the limited liability principle as it applies to group enterprises; for reasons of space, these may only be mentioned briefly. First, a company's creditors will often be misled into believing that the assets of the group back its debts , where, for example, the company is described as a member of the "XYZ Group" or uses a name similar to that of its parent company. Secondly, it is felt that companies should not be able to indulge in high-risk ventures at the expense of their creditors, especially given the ability of the parent to determine the financial structure of its subsidiary, whereby the subsidiary may largely be funded by secured loans from the parent which will rank ahead of ordinary creditors in the company's liquidation. It might be argued that a company which has taken advantage of its subsidiary to the detriment of the latter's creditors has chosen to ignore the separate status of the subsidiary and hence should not be allowed to invoke it where the subsidiary has become insolvent.

Despite these considerations, a parent will in English law very rarely be liable for its subsidiary's debt. The principles in accordance with which the court will lift the "corporate veil" are extremely uncertain, but there are no reported decisions in which a parent has been held liable for its subsidiary's debts in the absence, for example, of an express agency. Additionally, section 332 of the Companies Act 1948 imposes liability for "fraudulent trading"; the court may declare persons who knowingly participate in the carrying on of a business with intent to defraud creditors liable for all or any of the company's debts. Whilst there will often be no difficulty in showing that a parent has played an active part in the affairs of the company, it will be much more difficult to establish the element of fraud.(52)

Since the directors of the parent company owe their duties to it, and owe no duty to a subsidiary or its creditors, if they were to decide that the parent should discharge an insolvent subsidiary's debts, this might involve a breach of duty. For reasons of reputation, however, if not commercial morality, this would in many cases be justified as being in the parent company's interests, and the court would doubtless be unwilling to interfere with a judgment to that effect.

The EEC proposals relating to group companies

The strategy of the ninth Directive will almost certainly be to provide for a formal group structure which group enterprises may at their discretion adopt, together with measures to strengthen the protection for minority shareholders and creditors where companies remain outside the formal structure. The proposals will only apply to dependent public companies, owing to the diverse range of non-public companies in the member states, but there appears to be no reason why they could not be applied in the United Kingdom to public and private companies alike. The importance of the proposals would otherwise be significantly reduced, since in Britain even subsidiaries of major enterprises are normally private companies. The dominant undertaking may be of any form, including that of a natural person, and hence the provisions apply beyond what is normally understood as a "group"; the measures to prevent abuse by a dominant undertaking (where the formal structure has not been adopted) would apply, for example, to the human major shareholder of an individual company.

(1) The formal group structure

It is thought that the Directive will follow German company law and provide for a group structure on the basis of a "control contract". Under this arrangement the dominant enterprise guarantees the minority shareholders in the dependent company an agreed return on their shares in exchange for the right to manage the company in the group interest. Where a control contract has been entered into there will also be additional safeguards for creditors of the dependent company, which will be considered below. A contract would normally be made between companies where one already has a substantial shareholding in the other, with a view to avoiding restrictions on group operations of the kind referred to above, but there would be no required minimum shareholding.

Entry into a control contract would probably be dependent on a resolution supported by a three-quarters majority of shareholders. It seems likely that the Directive will follow German law and permit the dominant enterprise to vote its shares; to provide otherwise would give what is considered to be disproportionate power to what may be a very small minority of shareholders. Where the dominant company has the appropriate shareholding the effect of the proposals will be that entry into a control contract, relegating the interest of the minority to a purely financial one unrelated to the future performance of the company, will be entirely at the option of the dominant enterprise. In the light of this it is essential that there be effective safeguards to ensure that the terms of the contract are fair to the minority shareholders.

The provisions for securing the interests of minority shareholders are likely to follow those contained in the draft Statute for European Companies.(53)   Minority shareholders will be given the choice of disposing of their shares to the dominant enterprise, by selling or exchanging them for shares in the latter, or receiving an "annual equalisation payment".(54) The effect will be to enlarge the ability of the dominant enterprise to acquire the shares of a minority shareholder where the latter opts to dispose of his shares rather than accept the annual equalisation payment.(55)   The level of income obtained by the minority from their shares will be largely severed from the fortunes of the company, leaving the company to be run in the group interest without prejudicing the minority.   The annual equalisation payment would either be an annual sum calculated on the basis of the expected average earnings per share as if the contract had not been entered into, or be related to the earnings of the dominant enterprise's shares, where it is a company.   In negotiating the level of the annual equalisation payment, the minority shareholders will be in a weak bargaining position where the dominant enterprise holds more than three-quarters of the shares in the company, since it will be in a position to compel the company to enter into the contract. The Directive will probably provide for a mechanism to scrutinise the level of compensation offered, requiring it to satisfy a minimum test of adequacy, by providing for the compulsory appointment of independent assessors and giving the right to the minority to challenge the level of payment offered in the court.(56) What an adequate level of compensation is may be highly speculative, especially where the annual equalisation payment is based on the projected earnings of the dependent company. The minority are, in effect, selling their right to future participation in the company, and how important the lack of an objective basis of valuation is will depend on the effectiveness of the independent supervision of the terms of the contract in overcoming any inequality in bargaining power.

Allowing the dependent company to be operated in the group interest is potentially prejudicial to the company's creditors. It is thought that the Directive will deal with this problem by providing that the dominant enterprise will, in some circumstances, be liable for the debts of the dependent company. It seems, however, that liability will be limited to the extent that the dominant enterprise has exercised a deleterious influence over the affairs of the company; there would be no liability simply on the basis that the company was undercapitalised or that its trading as part of the group had created the impression that group assets would back its indebtedness. It is likely, however, that the onus will be on the dominant enterprise to show that the company's failure to discharge its obligations is not the result of its influence.

The interests of minority shareholders and creditors having been safeguarded, the dominant enterprise would be permitted to operate the company in the group interest. This would require the fiduciary duties of the directors of the dependent company to be modified to permit them to act in the group interest where this conflicts with the interests of the company. The restrictions on distributions in Part III of the Companies Act 1980 would need to be removed, and the ultra vires doctrine, so far as relevant, would have to be excluded. Whilst the dependent company would cease to be protected against transactions which are contrary to its individual interests, its directors would remain liable for other forms of misfeasance and it is likely that a new duty would be imposed on the dominant enterprise requiring it to exercise its powers of management over the dependent company in the group interest, and with reasonable care. It seems that this duty would be owed to the dependent company and enforceable by it,(57) though it is difficult to see who would be interested in bringing an action, since breach would not affect the annual equalisation payment(58) and the creditors' interests are protected by the direct liability of the dominant enterprise. A remedy against the directors of the dominant enterprise, enforceable by its shareholders, would be of more use since it is the dominant enterprise which will suffer if its directors conduct the affairs of the dependent company in a way contrary to the group interest.

The Directive will probably provide that a control contract may be terminated by mutual consent or subject to certain safeguards, unilaterally. The dominant enterprise might wish to bring the contract to an end where, for example, a fixed annual equalisation payment has become excessive in relation to the contribution of the dependent company to the group. Where the reverse occurs, for instance, some asset or expertise of the dependent company unexpectedly increases in value, it would be desirable to permit the minority shareholders to terminate or require the contract to be varied, though it is doubtful whether such a mechanism will be provided for.

(2) Provisions relating to group enterprises where the formal structure is not adopted

In cases where a company does not opt for the formal structure, the object of the Directive will be to strengthen the protection of minority shareholders and creditors. This will require a definition of the relationship between companies that will bring the protective provisions into play. If the criteria were to be based on voting strength or share ownership(59) this might result in some forms of abuse escaping control and encourage the formation of structures designed to evade the provisions. Such criteria are also insensitive in that a given percentage shareholding may be consistent with situations where the degree of actual control exercised varies considerably. It seems likely, therefore, that the definition contained in the draft seventh Directive on group accounts which employs the flexible concept of dominance will ultimately be adopted.(60) A relevant group relationship would be identified as one in which an enterprise is able to exert, directly or indirectly, a dominant influence over another company. The consequence of an open-ended definition of this type, making the policy of the Directive difficult to evade, however, is a level of uncertainty in marginal cases, which may require court proceedings for a solution, assisted by a series of rebuttable presumptions.(61)

The Directive will extend the range of remedies available where a company has suffered damage as a result of its acting in the interests of the group rather than exclusively for its own benefit. This will probably be done by imposing liability on the dominant enterprise where the latter has exercised its influence over the company to cause it to enter into a damaging transaction, or to prevent it from entering into a beneficial transaction. As considered earlier, the likelihood that many damaging transactions will never be discovered and the practical difficulties in proving them present considerable problems to those whose interests have been harmed. In order to remedy this, it is thought that the Directive will provide that a dependent company must produce an annual report, to be circulated to the shareholders and certified by the company's auditors, stating particulars of all transactions entered into with or at the request of the dominant enterprise, or transactions which the company has failed to enter into at the dominant enterprise's request. The report will be required to state whether these transactions have resulted in damage to the company. Where the report indicates that there have been detrimental transactions, it will be provided that an application may be made to the court by a minority shareholder, creditor (who has failed to achieve satisfaction from the company) or employees' representative, requesting the appointment of special auditors, whose function would be to investigate the transaction in question and quantify the damage caused to the company. Armed with this information, the complainants would be in a much stronger position to bring proceedings against the dominant enterprise. As a further protection, it is likely that the directors of the dominant enterprise would be jointly and severally liable with it.

This new remedy would to some extent overlap with the remedies already available in English law discussed above. It will generally be more favourable to plaintiffs, however, in that it offers a direct remedy against the dominant enterprise, simply on the basis that damage has been caused to the company, that is, it is not necessary to show that the dominant enterprise is a party to a breach of duty by the directors of the dependent company and there would be no need to show "unfair prejudice".(62) Another advantage would be that the remedy could be invoked by creditors, even though the company is not in liquidation, and by employees' representatives, as well as minority shareholders. Any award made by the court would be payable to the dependent company; as far as creditors are concerned this would increase the company's ability to discharge its obligations. One novel feature as far as English law is concerned is that in calculating the compensation payable to the dependent company, the value of benefits conferred on it by the dominant enterprise would be deducted from the cost of damage inflicted. This would mean that a liability would be extinguished where a compensating benefit was conferred, even though the benefit might have been conferred accidentally or otherwise than as compensation for damage inflicted. This would not be the result as far as liability under existing English law is concerned. In the case of a breach of duty by the directors of the dependent company, for example, unless a benefit conferred on the company was strictly referable to the breach it would, in the absence of ratification, remain actionable and similarly the liability of the dominant enterprise where it satisfied the requirements for liability. It seems unlikely that the policy of the Directive will be to facilitate damaging intra-group transactions in the absence of a control contract and so the "set-off" principle will probably be restricted to the new remedy provided by the Directive.(63) In addition to the payment of compensation, the Directive will probably provide for the court to be given a wide range of discretionary remedies,(64) enabling it, for example, to order the removal of directors from the board of the dependent company or the discontinuance of damaging transactions.

In addition to the measures considered under the last two headings, it is likely that the Directive will provide that minority shareholders (both within and outside the formal structure) shall be entitled to require the majority to purchase their shares at any time, where the majority holds at least 90% of the company's capital for a price to be fixed by the court in the absence of agreement. Section 209 of the Companies Act 1948 confers a similar right, but it may only be exercised within a fixed period of the acquisition of 90 per cent of the share capital of the company by a single corporate shareholder.

These proposals go some way towards dealing with the deficiencies of the present English law, but there appears to be no justification for restricting their operation to public companies. The legal recognition of the group enterprise may lead to a more efficient use of group resources, which a concentration on the company as a distinct unit inhibits in some cases, without at the same time providing adequate protection for the interests of minorities and creditors in less scrupulous organisations. The existing remedies are defective, and because in the case of minority protection they are dependent on shareholder action they will only rarely be invoked. The formal group structure has the attraction, therefore, that barriers to group transactions are removed, and the status of minority shareholders who do not dispose of their shares, whilst being significantly changed, is put on a secure footing.

It may be hoped that by the time the Directive is required to be incorporated into English law, some principle of mutual liability for group debts will have been introduced, which may be wider than the proposals in the Directive and which would probably not be restricted to the formal group structure. Should this be the case, the main contribution of the Directive would be to create a choice as to how the problem of minority shareholders is to be dealt with, either by institutionalising minority safeguards where the company enters a control contract, or by the retention of the present restrictions on intercompany transactions, supplemented by the improved remedies which the Directive provides.

FOOTNOTES

(1) Bull Supp 8/75 p 7.

(2) Art 58 para 1.

(3) See eg the Companies (Disclosure of Directors' Nationalities)(Exemption) Order 1974 which exempted EEC nationals who were directors of UK companies from the obligation to state their nationality on the company notepaper under CA 1948 s 201(1)(c)(since repealed by CA 1981 s 119 and Schedule 3 para 11 (1)).

(4) [1962] JO 32-46. This General Programme was issued by the Council pursuant to Art 54 (1) of the Treaty. The English language version is contained in the Special Edition of the Official Journal (Second Series) published in January 1974 at pp 7-15.

(5) Ibid Title I.

(6) cf the United States where the State of Delaware has proved by far the most popular State for the incorporation of companies.

(7) At one time the Commission took the view that the United Kingdom had not fully implemented the first Directive (68/151/EEC-OJ 1969 L65/8). See the Question to and Answer by the Commission OJ 1977 C289/1. It is understood that the Commission now take the view that the United Kingdom has done all it can to implement the first Directive and neither further legislation nor a review of the European Communities Act 1972 s 9 is planned.

(8) In such a case the Commission could take proceedings under Art 169 of the Treaty.

(9) "The Harmonization of European Company Law" (ed Schmitthoff) pp 66-67.

(10) See particularly Stein, "Harmonization of European Company Laws" pp 162-171.

(11) "The Harmonization of European Company Law" (ed Schmitthoff) pp 68-69.

(12) Ibid p 70.

(13) Newby v Colt's Patent Firearms Manufacturing Company and Van Oppen (1872) LR 7 QB 293. Similarly an English court will recognise a Scottish partnership because in Scotland a partnership has legal personality: Partnership Act 1890 s 4(2).

(14) Lazard Bros v Midland Bank Ltd [1933] AC 289.

(15) Income and Corporation Taxes Act 1970 s 482(7).

(16) Risdon Iron & Locomotive Works v Furness [1906] 1 KB 49; Spiller v Turner [1897] 1 Ch 911.

(17) Rabel, "The Conflict of Laws - A Comparative Study" (2nd edn) II pp 51-52. But cf Conard in "The Harmonization of European Company Law" (ed Schmitthoff) p 56.

(18) The Convention on Mutual Recognition of Companies and Legal Persons signed on behalf of the original Member States on February 29th 1968. The Convention only comes into force, however, when ratified by all the signatories, which now include the new Member States: Art 14. As the Convention was not Community legislation but analogous to a Treaty between the Member States it was not originally subject to the jurisdiction of the Court of Justice. It was, however, made subject to the Court's jurisdiction by a Protocol signed on June 3rd 1971.

(19) Arts 1 and 2 of the Convention.

(20) Ibid Art 8.

(21) Supra p150.

(22) See Kay [1975] JBL 88.

(23) Bull Supp 13/73.

(24) Bull Supp 4/75. Some doubt has been expressed whether this is a legitimate use of Art 235. See Hood (1973) 22 ICLQ 434, 441-443.

(25) The idea comes from the French Groupement d'Interet Economique. The intention is to introduce it via a Regulation under Art 235. For the latest draft of the Regulation, see OJ 1978 C103/4.

(26) No formal draft of the ninth Directive has yet been issued so our comments are based on what is thought likely to be contained in the Directive. It is understood that two drafts have been privately circulated to Member State governments for their comments and that a third draft is currently being prepared.

(27) Sections 150-153 CA 1948, as amended, provide that companies with subsidiaries must prepare group accounts, which will normally be consolidated into one account covering the whole group. Various other provisions provide for disclosure on a group basis, eg s 196 CA 1948 (disclosure of emoluments of directors and s 27 CA 1967 (notification of directors' interests in shares and debentures). The existence of groups is also recognised in those provisions of the Companies Acts which require a parent company to disclose details of its holdings in its subsidiaries and a subsidiary to disclose the name and place of incorporation of its holding company (ss 3 and 5 CA 1967 respectively). The 1967 Act also requires disclosure of similar information with regards to companies in which a company holds at least ten per cent of the issued shares of any class of the equity share capital, or ten per cent of the issued share capital, or where the shares which it holds exceed one tenth of the value of the assets of the company in which the shares are held (s 4).

(28) See Re Lee, Behrens & Co [1932] 2 Ch 46 and Re Roith [1967] 1 WLR 432.

(29) See Re Introductions [1970] Ch 199.

(30) Re Horsley & Weight [1982] 3 WLR 431.

(31) [1970] Ch 62.

(32) There is also the possibility of prejudice to third parties, since ultra vires transactions are void. Such transactions being void, there is, however, the advantage as far as minorities and creditors are concerned, that they are not ratifiable.

(33) ie has "profits available for the purpose"; see ss 39, 40 and 45(2) CA 1980.

(34) Directors must normally give active consideration to whether a transaction is in the company's interest (see Re Roith, above and SCWS v Meyer [1959] AC 324) but it has been suggested that where they do not, and instead look to the group interest, they will have discharged their duty if "an intelligent and honest man in the position of a director of the company concerned, could, in the whole of the existing circumstances, have reasonably believed that the transaction [was] for the benefit of the company" (per Pennycuick J in Charterbridge Corporation v Lloyds Bank, above, at p 74).

His lordship rejected a test based on benefit to the group as a whole. On either test, therefore, benefit to the company is central.

(35) Lonrho v Shell [1980] 1 WLR 627.

(36) But SCWS v Meyer, above.

(37) See eg IDC v Cooley [1972] 1 WLR 443and cl 44(2) Companies Bill 1978.

(38) Barnes v Addy (1874) LR 9 Ch App 244; Belmont Finance v Williams Furniture (No2) [1980] 1 All ER 393.

(39) Belmont Finance v Williams Furniture (No 2), above. There may also be criminal liability: see s 22 Theft Act 1968.

(40) Re Smith & Fawcett [1942] Ch 304.

(41) An inspection under s 164 or s 165 CA 1948 might unearth them, but this is an unwieldy process. See also s 109 CA 1967.

(42) The Rule in Foss v Harbottle (1843) 2 Hare 461.

(43) So long as the requirement that the wrongdoers be in control is satisfied. cf Pavlides v Jensen [1956] Ch 565; Prudential Assurance v Newman Industries (No2) [1980] 2 All ER 841 (Vinelott J).

(44) For signs of a "duty to creditors" see Lord Diplock in Lonrho v Shell, above, at p 634 and Pennycuick J in Charterbridge Corporation v Lloyds Bank, above, at p 74. For dicta in support of the non-ratifiability of breaches of duty which prejudice creditors see Cumming-Bruce LJ and Templeman LJ in Re Horsley & Weight Ltd [1982] 3 WLR 431.

(45) The duty is enforceable "in the same way as other fiduciary duties".

(46) Cook v Deeks [1916] 1 AC 554.

(47) On the, perhaps challengeable, assumption that ratification could only be upset where there is a "fraud on the minority"; this is not possible where there is no minority. But see Re Horsley & Weight above.

(48) See the line of cases, the latest in which is Cane v Jones [1981] 1 All ER 533.

(49) For an illustration of the type of situation in which the section might be used, see SCWS v Meyer (above), a decision on section 210 C A 1948, which is the predecessor of s 75.

(50) cf Canadian Business Code, s 234.

(51) See, eg Chapter 51 of the Cork Committee Report on Insolvency Law and Practice.

(52) See Re Patrick & Lyon [1933] Ch 786. The Cork Committee has suggested that so far as s 332 provides a civil remedy, it should be replaced by a section imposing liability for "wrongful trading" under which in order to found liability it would not be necessary to establish fraud or dishonesty.

(53) Bull Supp 4/75.

(54) cf draft Statute for European Company, Art 228(2) & 231.

(55) Under existing English law a minority interest may be compulsorily acquired by the majority pursuant to an appropriate article; where this power does not already exist a change in the company's constitution will be necessary. The validity of the alteration and the degree to which such a power could be relied on is uncertain, being dependent on the rather vague concept of "fraud on the minority"; see, eg Brown v British Abrasive Wheel Co [1919] 1 Ch 290 Sidebottom v Kershaw, Leese & Co [1920] 1 Ch 154. A minority interest might also be acquired under a scheme of arrangement governed by s 206 CA 1948, but the acquisition must be sanctioned by the court and the holders of three-quarters in value of the class of shares affected. Shares held by the would-be acquirer or its nominees will not be treated as part of the class: Re Hellenic & General Trust [1975] 3 All ER 382. A further method is s 209 CA 1948, which empowers an offeror which has received acceptances in respect of 90% of the offeree shares compulsorily to acquire the remainder at the offer price. However, in its application to a majority buying out a minority, the offer must be accepted by 90% of the minority, representing three-quarters in value: proviso to s 209(1).

(56) cf Aktiengesetz, Art 304(5).

(57) Under German law the directors of the dominant enterprise would be liable to the dependent company in these circumstances; see Aktg Art 309.

(58) On termination of the contract it is likely that the Directive will require the dominant enterprise to make good any loss which has resulted from its conduct of the company's affairs. This is essential since the past conduct of the dominant enterprise may affect the company's future profitability, and hence the interests of minority shareholders and creditors.

(59) cf s 154 CA 1948.

(60) OJ 1979 C14/2 Art 2.2.

(61) Ibid Art 2.2.

(62) As would be the case under s 75 CA 1980.

(63) Whether German law in this situation permits such transactions is controversial; see Wooldridge, "Groups of Companies" pp69-71.

(64) cf s 75 CA 1980.

FREEDOM OF MOVEMENT AND
UNITED KINGDOM IMMIGRATION LAW

B E Sufrin

I

Freedom of movement is an area in which Community membership has impinged on a basic and sacrosanct aspect of the Member States' sovereign rights: the control of aliens. The relevant provisions of the Treaty of Rome cover the free movement of workers (Arts. 48-51), freedom of establishment (Arts. 52-58) and the freedom to supply services (Arts. 59-66). The subject is central to the concept of the Community for free movement of labour and the freedom to provide services are two of the "four freedoms" which characterise the Common Market. The idea that the nationals of the Member States may freely cross national frontiers in order to work without disadvantage or discrimination is fundamental[1] and is for the personal advantage of the individual as well as for the benefit of the Community's objectives.[2]

Community law provides restrictions on how far Member States may apply against those within the free movement provisions their immigration and deportation rules, or maintain against them discriminatory measures. In R v Home Secretary ex p. Sandhu[3] Comyn J described the relationship between domestic and Community rules in this area:
> "... it is plain and entirely clear that our rules must
> be read in the light of the EEC law which is the
> foundation stone of all the law in this matter",
and he reversed the decision of an Adjudicator on the grounds that it was "contrary to the letter and the spirit of the EEC law".

UK immigration law is preoccupied with controlling the movement of certain groups of people perceived by successive Governments as eager to enter and settle in the UK, i.e. those from the New Commonwealth and the Indian sub-continent.[4] It is a defensive law whose fallout affects all others wishing to

enter the UK. No British Government has been similarly
concerned with the entry of Community nationals, as they are
not seen as the same kind of threat;(5) and little attention has
been devoted to amending the law to accommodate the special
treatment which must be accorded to them. Council Directive
64/221(6),   for   example,   has   never   been   specifically
implemented, but is applied by the immigration authorities and
by the courts all the same.

The Immigration Act 1971 came into force on the 1st
January 1973, the day of Britain's entry into the European
Community but contains no reference to the position of EEC
nationals.(7) It has not been amended in any relevant way.
The practices to be followed in the administration of the 1971
Act are contained in the Immigration Rules which are of
uncertain status. They are made by the Secretary of State
under s. 3(2) of the Act and are required to be laid before
Parliament and subjected to a disapproval procedure. It
appears that they are not strictly delegated legislation. Lord
Denning MR described them in R v Secretary of State ex p.
Hosenball(8) as:
    "rules of practice laid down for the guidance of
    immigration officers and tribunals who are entrusted
    with the administration of the Act",
although he admitted that s. 19 makes them for some purposes
more than a guide.(9) It is these Rules which contain
references to the position of EEC nationals. Immigration
officers   are   issued   with   detailed   formal   instructions
("Instructions to Immigration Officers") which elaborate on the
Rules themselves, and in particular upon the criteria to be
followed in exercising the considerable discretion which
certain of the Rules give the Officers. The Instructions are
issued pursuant to para 1(3) Sched. 2 of the 1971 Act(10) but
are unpublished, secret and confidential.

The Community provisions on free movement are not only
incomplete as a body of law but are also replete with
difficulties   and   uncertainties   which   raise   problems   in
themselves, quite apart from those caused by their interaction with domestic provisions. The relevant Treaty Articles

"use language more suited to a programme of action than a charter of rights."(11) They contemplate the Community Institutions and the Member States taking action to achieve the ends and objectives set out in the Treaty, although this plan has been short-circuited by the Court of Justice which declared first Art. 48 and then Art. 52 and Art. 59 to produce direct effects.(12) The decisions on Art. 52 and Art. 59 in particular were taken despite the lack of liberalising measures from the Community Institutions, the Court declaring such measures unnecessary to the exercise of the basic rights given to individuals by the Treaty itself. That is not to gainsay the importance of the implementing legisation which has been enacted, which specifies in detail the rights of those exercising their freedom of movement,(13) and which has been the subject of much interpretation by the Court of Justice.

II

Art. 48 talks about freedom of movement for "workers of the Member States". What does this mean? It could mean anyone of whatever nationality who is part of the workforce of a Member State. Such an interpretation leaves all Member States at the mercy of each other's immigration policies. Arts. 52 & 59, however, accord freedom of establishment and provision of services to "nationals of" Member States. Art. 48 has been interpreted as encompassing only workers who are nationals of a Member State and the implementing legislation on workers adopts that terminology.(14) This criteria presents a problem for the UK which has no idea of "nationality" as such. At common law, the concept used was "British Subject" but the British Nationality Act 1948 overlaid this with different categories of citizenship, the primary one being citizenship of the United Kingdom and Colonies.(15) The Commonwealth Immigrants Acts 1962 and 1968 applied immigration restrictions to some British subjects for the first time, and the Immigration Act 1971 introduced the refinement of "patriality". The reasons for these developments were the increasing number of colonies gaining their independence and then concern about the number of inhabitants of these former colonies exercising their right to emigrate to this country.

Under the 1971 Act only "patrials" have the "right of abode" in the UK.(16) Having the right of abode means being free from all immigration controls and liability to deportation.

At Accession the British Government defined a United Kingdom national for the purposes of Community law by way of unilateral declaration annexed to the Treaty of Accession. This produced a further refined category - nationals for Community law purposes. These are patrial citizens of the United Kingdom and Colonies, patrial British subjects without the citizenship of any other Commonwealth country or territory and Gibraltarians.(17) Gibraltarians were not patrials under the Immigration Act.

It has been suggested(18) that the Declaration is invalid as amounting to a unilateral amendment of the Treaty. The most persuasive of the various arguments against this view(19) is that as English law did not recognise anyone as being a "national" of the UK, some definition had to be made.(20)

British immigration and nationality legislation is controversial and subject to charges of racism. One effect of Britain's almost contemporaneous Accession to the Community was the the "grand-patriality" idea. Under the Immigration Rules(21) a Commonwealth citizen who had a grandparent with citizenship of the United Kingdom and Colonies acquired through birth in the UK or the Islands is allowed to enter the UK to work with entry clearance only and without a work permit being required of him. This concession (with millions of potential beneficiaries) obviously favours those from the old "white" Commonwealth, but was given as a result of pressure from certain Members of Parliament who were particularly concerned about the restrictions to be imposed upon "old Commonwealth" citizens when contrasted with the free movement advantages suddenly to be given to European "foreigners".(22)

On the 1st January 1983 the British Nationality Act 1981 comes into force. This replaces the old categories of citizenship and the concept of partriality with three new classes of citizenship: British Citizenship, British Dependent Territories Citizenship and British Overseas Citizenship. S.39 provides a new s.2 for the 1971 Immigration Act and gives the right of abode in the UK to all British citizens and to Commonwealth citizens who were partrials immediately before the coming into force of the 1981 Act.(23). The main amendment to the 1971 Act is that "British citizen(s)" replaces "patrial(s)" throughout. The provisions as to who acquires British Citizenship at the commencement of the Act are complex(24) but the basic provision is that a person who immediately before commencement was a citizen of the United Kingdom and Colonies and had the right of abode under the 1971 Act becomes a British citizen. The other categories do not carry the right of abode.(25)

Charges of racism were levelled at the Bill throughout its passage. It was the subject of a debate in the European Parliament(26) when the Legal Affairs Committee presented a report on the Bill, at which the Commissioner for the Internal Market gave the Commission's views. Parliament's concern was mainly over the new provisions on acquisition of British Citizenship at birth. The new law abandons the complete application of both the jus soli (nationality depends on place of birth) and the jus sanguinis (nationality depends on descent). By s.1 a person acquires British Citizenship at birth only if the birth is in the UK and at least one parent is a British Citizen or settled in the UK.(27) By s.2 a person born outside the UK will be a British citizen only if at least one parent is a British citizen otherwise than by descent, unless the parent is in certain types of official employment. The concern expressed in the Parliament was that these two provisions would lead to an increase in statelessness(28), which is obviously undesirable, and the provisions could also be disadvantageous to those exercising their freedom of movement.(29) The Act does contain provisions to safeguard the position of the descendants of British Citizens working abroad in Government service.(30) It was pointed out both in the European Parliament and at Westminster that no similar protection was being given to the children of those working for European Community Institutions and the Government therefore moved a late amendment to the

Bill which extended the provisions about Government service to those working in the Community Institutions, provided recruitment was in a country which was a Member State at the time.(31) This means that a child of a parent working for the Community who is a British Citizen but only by descent will still acquire British Citizenship at birth.

During the debate in the European Parliament the Commissioner for the Internal Market said that the UK's definition of nationality made in the Declaration at the time of Accession would have to be changed. He noted that the Bill did not deal with this. Neither does the Act as finally passed. The Green Paper on British Nationality Law did advert to the Declaration in passing (32) but the subject of the Declaration's amendment was not followed up in the White Paper and does not feature in the Act. Amendments would seem necessary since the Declaration is couched in terms of classifications which will no longer exist (unless one takes the view that the Declaration is an "instrument" for the purposes of s.51(3) of the 1981 Act).(33) The Government has accepted the need for Community consultation on its amendment.(34)

The Declaration does however feature in the Act, albeit in a curious way. Throughout the Bill's passage concern was expressed about the position of Gibraltarians. The Government submitted to this pressure and the result is s.5 which reads: "A British Dependent Territories Citizen who falls to be treated as a national of the UK for the purpose of the Community Treaties shall be entitled to be registered as a British citizen if an application is made for his registration as such a citizen". This section does not expressly mention Gibraltarians, but they are the only people designated as UK nationals for Community purposes who become British Dependent Territories Citizens under the Act. It seems that the anomalous position of Gibraltarians under the Declaration was used as a device for giving them the valuable right to be registered as British citizens without the embarrassment of singling out Gibraltar by name. It is confusing that the Act makes this reference to a Declaration which in turn refers to categories of citizenship and rights of abode which the Act itself changes. The position of Gibraltarians seems, anyway, still to be contrary to Community law as the right to registration is not the same as giving them the right of abode in the UK. By British nationality law therefore they are subject to immigration control although under the Declaration they are beneficiaries of free movement.

III

It was hardly foreseen, when Britain entered the EEC, that membership would have any repercussions on our nationality law, or that changes in that law might one day be considered a legitimate subject for debate and criticism in Strasbourg and Brussels. Nationality laws and the free movement provisions are in the end inseparable, however, because both are concerned with who does or does not have rights of entry and residence in a Member State. Also, the Community has shown a growing concern with human rights, with the Court of Justice developing a considerable jurisprudence on that subject, and nationality and immigration law is an area in which human rights issues are much involved.(35) In the Rutili case(36) the Court stated that the limitations placed on the powers of Member States in their control of aliens by Art. 48(3) of the Treaty are a "specific manifestation" of the principle enshrined in Arts. 8, 9, 10 and 11 of the European Convention on Human Rights. In the recent Levin case(37) the Court has once again referred to free movement as "one of the fundamental freedoms guaranteed by the Treaty" and said that the terms used in determining its area of application must on that basis not be interpreted restrictively. On the contrary, it is derogations from free movement which have to be strictly construed.(38)

This is a completely different attitude to that adopted by UK immigration law. Community provisions favour the immigrant and his rights and the law leans in his favour as the Court time and again gives the provisions a generous and expansive interpretation; whereas in domestic law it is often a mockery to speak of "rights" at all. Immigration law is an area noted for the exercise of wide discretionary powers.

When the Bill which became the Immigration Act 1971 was passing through Parliament the relevance of the UK's contemplated Accession was discussed(39) partly because some MPs (of rather opposite sympathies to those concerned with the grand-patriality idea) contrasted the position to be given to EEC nationals with that to be accorded to other (coloured) immigrants. One notices, when reading the debates, the blithe complacency of the Government benches, the Secretary of State declaring that "joining the European Economic Community would not call for any amendment to the Bill",(40) and one MP confidently proclaiming that there was "nothing in the Treaty of Rome which would oblige us to exempt people from immigration control".(41)

IV

In fact Community law has undermined basic principles of UK immigration law in so far as they are applied to EEC nationals, in particular the idea of "leave to enter".

UK immigration law, as explained above, is based on the right of abode, given under the 1971 Act to patrials and under the amendments in the 1981 Act, to British Citizens. Anyone not having the right of abode is subject to immigration control and requires leave to enter.(42) The application of this principle to nationals of other Member States seeking to work, establish themselves or provide services in the UK is inconsistent with Community law. This was finally established in R v Pieck.(43) Pieck was a Dutch national employed as a printer in Taff Wells. His passport was endorsed "given leave to enter the UK for six months"(44) each time he returned to the UK from visits to Holland. Ten months after the last endorsement the expiry of his leave was discovered and he was charged with remaining in the UK beyond the time of his leave, under s.24(1)(b)(i) 1971 Act. This made him liable to a maximum penalty of £200 or 6 months imprisonment and to deportation under s.3(b) of the Act. Pieck claimed that as he was within Art. 48 both the initial grant of 6 months' leave and the requirement that he had to apply for an extension if he wished to remain were incompatible with Community law, in particular with Art. 48 and Directive 68/360.

Directive 68/360 spells out what freedom of movement means in terms of permissible entry formalities, residence permits and other documentation and clarifies what is meant by the right to remain. (Council Directive 73/148 covers the same points as regards those establishing themselves or providing services.) Art. 3 provides that the worker must be admitted to the host state simply on production of a valid identity card or passport and that no entry visa or similar document may be required.(45) Art. 4 provides that the host state "shall grant the right of residence to a worker able to produce the document with which he entered that state, and proof of employment and that as proof of the right of residence the state shall issue a "Residence Permit for a National of a Member State of the EEC". Art. 6 provides for the permit's automatic renewal.

The UK has made some amendments to its immigration laws and procedures to comply with Community law, by putting into the Immigration Rules paragraphs applicable to EEC nationals alone. At the time of Pieck these were contained in the H.C. 79-81. Para. 51, under which Pieck's passport was endorsed, read "when an EEC national is given leave to enter no condition is to be imposed restricting his employment or occupation in the UK. Admission should normally be for a period of 6 months."(46) When Pieck raised his Community law defence, the Magistrates referred to Luxembourg questions, inter alia, as to the meaning of "entry visa or equivalent document" in Art. 3(2) Directive 68/360 and as to whether the grant of 6 months initial leave was consistent with an EEC national's rights under Community law. The Court held that Art. 3(2), providing that "no entry visa or equivalent document" be demanded from a qualifying EEC national covered any formality for the purpose of granting leave to enter a Member State which is coupled with a passport or identity check at the frontier.(47) It also held, referring to its judgment in Sagulo, (48) that Art. 4 of 68/360 provides that Member States shall grant the right of residence.

By thus establishing that "leave to enter" is not a privilege which a Member State may grant or withold, and that misleading endorsements on the passports or identity cards of EEC nationals which disguise the source of the right to enter are incompatible with Community law, the Court struck at the whole concept that every non-patrial/non-British Citizen without a right of abode needs "leave to enter" the UK.

There is a proviso, contained in Art 48 (3), providing that the rights therein are subject to limitations justified on public policy, public security or public health. The UK submitted that Member States did have a discretion over the admittance of EEC nationals as the right to enter was limited to workers(49) who were not objectionable on the proviso grounds, and so "leave to enter" was recognition that the person concerned fulfilled both criteria. Warner A-G admitted there were inherent difficulties over how it is possible, consistent with the Community legislation on entry requirements, to ascertain whether or not an immigrant is within the free movement provisions as being a worker etc. at all. He considered the preferable solution to be that Community law allows all EEC nationals to enter another Member State simply upon proof of nationality, and that any question of their right to do so should be examined after entry. The Court adverted specifically only to the proviso problems and repeated what it said in Royer,(50) that this did not provide a condition precedent to the acquisition of the right of entry and residence, merely the possibility of restricting someone's Treaty-derived rights if individual circumstances justified it. But in Pieck the Court stated categorically that "it [ie. the proviso] does not therefore justify administrative measures requiring in a general way formalities at the frontier other than simply the production of a valid identity card or passport."(51)

The implications for UK immigration procedures are profound, since they depend heavily on port of entry control rather than on measures aimed at those already in the country, as in many other Member States. The reason is partly geographical; port of entry controls are easier to maintain on an island than in a country with long land borders with several other states. The UK has stringent controls which can be applied at ports of entry - its checks on those who have entered the country are by comparison haphazard.(52)

The Court of Justice has shown itself more tolerant of Continental methods of control. In Watson and Belmann(53) it considered Italian regulations requiring foreign nations to report to the authorities within three days of entering Italy, and requiring anyone providing a foreign national or stateless person with employment or board and lodging to report the matter within three days. The Court held this did not conflict with Community law provided the regulations were not so onerous as to detract from the right of free movement and did not impose disproportionate penalties or those such as deportation which were inconsistent with Community rights. Likewise in Sagulo it was held permissible for a Member State to demand that other Member States' nationals hold valid identity cards and to impose penalties for non-compliance more severe than those imposed on the State's own nationals for identity card offences, provided the penalties were not so severe as to detract from free movement. The Court clearly considers that excessive entry formalities are an impediment to free movement whereas formalities after entry are not, an attitude which is a blow to UK immigration procedures.

It was in fact no longer the practice of the immigration authorities to apply strict entry controls to EEC nationals even prior to Pieck. There are special channels for EEC nationals at the ports of entry where examination is less stringent than for other non-citizens. The central purpose of immigration control according to the Home Office(54) is to prevent people coming in, settling and taking employment without authorisation and with EEC nationals,"if they have the right to take employment anyway there is not a great deal of purpose in stringently operating the other provisions of immigration control." The majority of EEC nationals excluded (in 1979 the figure was 1,347 out of 5,100,000 aspiring entrants) are kept out because they were believed to be coming in to live on public funds(55).

This does not diminish the importance of Pieck, far from it. It is one thing for the Home Office, as a matter of grace, to relax its controls on EEC nationals, quite another to be told that it must do so as a matter of Community law. In the first situation the immigration authorities remain in control. Speaking before the House of Lords Select Committee on the proposals in the draft Directive on Residence, the Home Office representative recognised this distinction when admitting that the present practice was already to admit people who would come under this draft Directive, but "the difficulty arises from a formal Directive which goes all the way up to the European Court and is interpreted as a piece of law."(56) So, for the Home Office, its discretion is one thing, but people having rights under laws to be interpreted in Luxembourg it is a different matter.

It appears from Pieck that the extent to which an EEC national can be examined at the point of entry with a view to the application of the public policy proviso is limited. It cannot be done as a matter of course - that much is clear from the words disapproving "administrative measures requiring in a general way formalities at the frontier...". Does this imply that an Immigration Officer whose suspicions are aroused(57) or who has good prima facie reasons for thinking the proviso might apply may not interrogate that person to discover whether that is so? It surely cannot do so without rendering the caveat in Pieck, that restrictions are allowed "in individual cases where there is sufficient justification" meaningless. So far the Immigration Rules remain unchanged, but it may be that the UK will wish to adopt some kind of systematic check upon EEC nationals once they are in the country, if it cannot continue its former practices.

V

Royer,(58) Watson and Belmann and Sagulo had already established, prior to Pieck, that the rights of EEC nationals to enter another Member State and to reside there for the purposes of the Treaty are conferred directly by the Treaty itself and the implementing provisions, and that the Residence Permit has a merely evidentiary function. Pieck made it clear that the right to reside flows from the Treaty and not from a grant by the Member State. In <u>Royer</u> the Court said that the grant of the permit was not "a measure giving rise to rights but a measure by a Member State serving to prove the individual position of a national of another Member State with regard to the provisions of Community law." None of this is totally consistent with the actual wording of Directive 68/360 itself (or likewise with 73/148) which tends to describe the rights of those concerned in terms of whether or not they hold a valid the holding of a valid Permit.(59)   It is therefore necessary to regard the Directives as merely using shorthand when they appear to describe substantive rights as flowing form anything other than the provisions of Community law itself.

The Immigration Rules, paras. 127 and 128, obedient to the Directives, provide for the granting of residence permits to employed and self-employed EEC nationals.   Para. 127 provides for a worker entering for employment of less than a year to have a temporary permit limited to the expected length of employment (following Art. 6 of Directive 68/360), "otherwise the permit should normally be for 5 years." The word "normally" is questionable as the Directive only makes an exception to the five year permit for temporary and seasonal workers. If the cautious "normally" covers anything but the other reservation allowed - the ubiquitous public policy proviso - then it is incompatible with Community law.

Para. 129 provides for the curtailment of a residence permit or leave to enter if it becomes evident that the person concerned is "living on public funds although capable of maintaining himself." It appears from Art. 7 of 68/360 that an EEC national becoming <u>voluntarily</u> unemployed does cease to be a beneficiary of the Treaty provisions and presumably para. 129 is referring to such a situation: if it is any wider it has no basis in Community law.

There is no provision in the Immigration Rules for renewal of the Residence Permit. The EEC national who has been here for four years in employment or self-employment should have the time-limit removed; if there are grounds for non-renewal, the matter is reviewed on actual expiry. Reference is made to para. 88(60) for examples of reasons for non-renewal after four years, but para. 88 contains many grounds which could not possibly be applied to an EEC national if there was any question of denial of further residence after five years. After five years an EEC national can only be denied residence on unemployment or public policy etc. grounds.

VI

The major derogation from the free movement provisions is the public policy, public security or public health proviso in Art. 48(3).(61)   The extent of the proviso is spelt out in Directive 64/221, Art. 2(1) of which says it relates to "all measures concerning entry into [the Member States'] territory, issue or renewal of residence permits, or explusion ... taken by Member States on grounds of public policy, public security or public health." Arts. 2(2), 3 and 4 limit the type of situations in which the proviso can be applied, whereas Arts. 5-9 contain procedural safeguards.(62)   The proviso and the Directive provisions have been the subject of many preliminary rulings in Luxembourg.(63) Time and again the Court has stressed how strictly the proviso must be construed as it derogates from such a fundamental right, while interpreting the Directive's procedural provisions in a way advantageous to the immigrant.

As the Court of Justice pointed out in the Santillo case(64), the UK has not introduced any specific legislation to implement Directive 64/221.   The 1971 Act contains no recognition of the fact that a qualifying EEC national may be excluded or deported only on the proviso grounds, and the Immigration Rules, amended twice since then and most recently in 1980, likewise ignore the proviso, the Directive and the relevant caselaw. What happens is that in practice the judges apply Community law, either ignoring the discrepancy or else impliedly construing the phrase which does appear in the English legislation "not conducive to the public good" as contrary to public policy or public security in the Community law sense.(65)

Refusal of leave to enter the UK on grounds of personal unacceptability ie. the person is in a general category qualifying for admission but is denied entry for some specific individual reason is dealt with in the 1971 Act, Sched. 2 and Part VIII of the Rules, which apply to all those without a right of abode, including EEC nationals.

There are provisions about exclusion on medical grounds(66) which give a wide discretion to the immigration authorities and which clearly cannot be applied to EEC nationals exercising their right of free movement except in accordance with the Annex to Directive 64/21 which lays down specific conditions and diseases alone justifying refusal of entry or of a first residence permit.(67) Rule 74 provides for refusal of entry to a person convicted of a crime covered by the Extradition Act 1967, which is clearly at variance with Art. 3(2) of the Directive which provides that previous criminal convictions shall not in themselves constitute grounds for applying such measures. A person may also be excluded because he is "currently subject to a deportation order"(68) or because his exclusion is "conducive to the public good". One's exclusion can be conducive to the public good either where the Secretary of State has personally directed this to be so or "it seems right to the Immigration Officer" to refuse on that ground". The significance of the personal discretion of the Secretary of State is that the person concerned then has no right of appeal.(69) In the Van Duyn case(70) a Dutch scientologist was excluded pursuant to the policy of keeping out aliens wishing to work for the cult, as announced in the Commons. When she challenged this in an action in the High Court for a declaration, the Vice-Chancellor dealt with the case on the basis that the exclusion had to be justified under the public policy proviso.

The grounds for deportation are laid down in the 1971 Act s.3(5) & (6), and reproduced in the Rules, para. 33. A person may be deported:

1) for breach of immigration control
2) because he is a member of the family of a person subject to a deportation order

3) if a Court recommends his deportation on conviction for an offence punishable by imprisonment and he is over 17
4) if the Secretary of State deems his deportation conducive to the public good.

If one considers this in the light of Community law, it is clear that ground (1) cannot be applied to qualifying EEC nationals. That was held to be so in Pieck when one of the questions asked of the Court by the Magistrates was whether an EEC national could be deported or imprisoned for overstaying. The answer of course was no. This should have already been obvious from the decisions in Watson and Balmann and Sagulo and it is perhaps surprising that the question was referred. The Royer case held that offences against immigration laws cannot be considered "against public policy" so as to justify deportation under the proviso.

The "family members" deportation provisions of English law are sexually discriminatory for the family of a male primary deportee is his wife and children under 18, but that of a female being deported includes only the children.(71) The Secretary of State does have a discretion over the deportation of the wife and children(72) but that has no bearing on the fact that if the wife or children are themselves EEC nationals who come under Arts. 48, 52 or 59 in their own right they cannot be deported unless the proviso can be applied to them personally: even if the wife alone is so protected, the children can stay as her dependants.(73)

In order to justify deportation after conviction or on the conducive to the public good grounds, the behaviour must come within the Community concept of public policy or public security. In the case of Bouchereau(74) the Court, expanding on what it had said earlier in Rutili, (75) held that conduct justifying use of the public policy proviso must involve a genuine and sufficiently serious threat to the requirements of public policy affecting one of the fundamental interests of society. Adoui and Cornuaille (76) has recently added the gloss that it is not possible to use the proviso on account of behaviour not subject to repressive or "real and effective" measures designed to combat it.

The first English case on deportation of an EEC national was <u>Secchi</u>(76a) where the Marylebone Magistrate recommended deportation of a Sardinian convicted of shoplifting and indecent exposure after deciding he was not a worker within <u>Art. 48</u>. The Magistrate said he would still have made the recommendation had he been a worker as "public policy requires the removal of a national of a Member State who has shown by his conduct 1) considerable lack of honesty and propriety, which has resulted in the commission of crimes which of their kind are bad ones 2) an attitude to personal behaviour which is completely alien to what is acceptable in this country and, I am sure, in any other Member State and 3) general irresponsibility." It is clear from <u>Bouchereau</u> that the defendant's behaviour in <u>Secchi</u> would not be caught by the proviso.   In <u>Bouchereau</u> itself the Magistrate declined to recommend deportation, after considering the Court of Justice's ruling, for the offence concerned was possession of small quantities of soft drugs.   This was clearly a correct application of Community law, contrary to the previous practice of the courts in deporting non-patrials in such circumstances.   The third English case on deportation, <u>Santillo</u>, was fought on procedural grounds, but there the offences involved were violent sexual and other assaults and a major issue was the medical evidence that he was likely to re-offend.

VII

The Articles of Directive 64/221 on procedural safeguards for EEC nationals faced with deportation or expulsion have been considered in Luxembourg in several cases.   English immigration law provides a system of appeals to an Adjudicator, the Immigration Appeal Tribunal, and in some cases, straight through the normal court system.(77)

There are two situations worth particular consideration in the light of the Community provisions.   The first is where deportation is because the Secretary of State considers it conducive to the public good as being in the interests of national security or of the relations between the UK and any other country or for other reasons of a political nature; when there is no appeal.(78) The second is deportation pursuant to a court's recommendation which was the subject of the Santillo case. In the "national security" situation the lack of appeal is questionable in the light of Art. 9 of the Directive. In such circumstances that Article provides that the deportation decision (the Article does not apply to refusal of entry) should not be taken by the administrative authority "save in cases of urgency, until an opinion has been obtained from a competent authority of the host country before which the person concerned enjoys such rights of defence and of assistance and representation as the domestic law of that country provides for". In the UK, compensating for the lack of appeal, the non-statutory "three adviser" procedure is used. Under this procedure, now referred to in para. 135 of the Rules, the case is reconsidered by "three advisers" who make a recommendation to the Secretary of State. Para. 135 provides for the appellant to be informed as far as possible of the allegations against him. In Hosenball (79) certiorari was sought on the grounds that the appellant had not given details of the charges, the sources of evidence had been protected and he was unable to cross-examine witnesses. The Court of Appeal held this did not offend the principles of natural justice since their application was properly restricted in cases involving national security.

Would the application of this procedure to an EEC national be contrary to Directive 64/221? Art. 6 thereof specifically provides an exception such as that allowed in Hosenball, saying that the person concerned "shall be informed of the grounds of public policy, public security or public health upon which the decision.....is based unless this is contrary to the interests of the security of the State involved". The possibility of concealing the grounds for decision must surely include that of denying both knowledge of the evidence and the opportunity to cross-examine witnesses. The proviso to Art. 6 leaves open the question of who should judge the involvement of state security. Could a Member State be left to decide such issues were present or must that ultimately be a question for Community law too? It is submitted that it must be the latter.

Para. 135 is silent on legal representation but when the Secretary of State announced in the Commons the introduction of the non-statutory procedure he said "[the appellant] will not be entitled to legal representation but he may arrange for a third party to testify on his behalf".(80) In Hosenball the appellant was in fact represented by a solicitor at the hearing in issue.   Art. 6 contains no exception about legal representation and the lack of such entitlement is incompatible with Art. 9. In Adoui and Cornuaille it was said that the appellant must be entitled to put forward his defence and to be assisted or represented under conditions no less favourable than those applicable to proceedings before other national authorities of the same type. It is difficult, however, to think of such "other national authorities" in the UK although this same procedure is used over civil servants suspected of security leaks - where there is no entitlement to legal representation.(81)

More fundamental is the objection that the "three advisers" are not a "competent authority" within Art. 9 at all and that nothing about the procedure therefore accords with Community Law. What is meant by an "opinion of a competent authority" was considered by the Court of Justice in Santillo when it decided that an English Criminal Court was such an authority as it was "independent of the administration". In Pecastaing(82) Caportorti A-G assumed that "competent authority" referred to an administrative body. In Santillo the Court said the phrase "refers to an authority which must be independent of the administration but it gives member states a margin of discretion in regard to the nature of the authority". The "three advisers" or "three wise men" cannot be properly described as an "authority" or an "administrative body" and a panel of civil servants advising the Minister is difficult to see as "independent" especially when they owe their function to a statement of the House of Commons and a reference in the Immigration Rules. Adoui and Cornuaille did allow that the members of the authority need not be appointed for a specified period and that they could be paid from the budget of the administrative department whose decision they were reviewing, so the ad hoc nature of the "three advisers" might not be fatal to compliance with Art. 9. However, in Pecastaing the Court emphasized that the appeal to a "competent authority" should precede the decision ordering expulsion "save in cases of urgency". This order of events is plainly not the case when the non-statutory procedure is used, and involvement of security does not necessarily denote urgency.

Santillo concerned the compatibility with Art. 9 of English procedures involving the implementation of a court's recommendation for deportation after completion of a prison sentence.Santillo was sentenced to eight years' imprisonment with a recommendation for deportation and as the date of his release grew near the Secretary of State made the order, having taken into account such matters as the police believing him guilty of yet further offences other than those for which he was convicted and the fact that he had been refused parole or release on licence. One ground of Santillo's claim for certiorari was that Community law had been infringed as the Secretary of State had not obtained "an opinion from a competent authority" before he made the order.

The Court of Justice said that Art 9(1) produced direct effects and that as the UK's criminal courts are independent of the administration which is responsible for the actual making of the deportation order, and as the person concerned enjoys the rights to be represented and to exercise his rights of defence before such courts, a recommendation by a criminal court was capable of constituting an opinion within the meaning of Art. 9.(83) The crucial point was the lapse of time between the recommendation and the Secretary of State's decision. The Court said that a "lapse of time amounting to several years" between these two events "is liable to deprive the recommendation of its function as an opinion within the meaning of Art. 9", and that "it is indeed essential that the social danger resulting from a foreigner's presence should be assessed at the very time when the decision ordering expulsion is made". The Court pointed out that the provisions about representation and defence could only be a real safeguard if the "opinion" and the final decision to deport were sufficiently proximate in time to ensure there were no new factors to take into account and if both the administrative authority and the person concerned are in a position to take cognizance of the reasons which led the competent authority to give its opinion.

Consideration of this ruling must raise grave doubts as to whether the deportation procedure, as correctly followed in Santillo does fulfil the requirements of the Directive . The "social danger resulting from a foreigner's presence" was assessed at the time when the decision ordering expulsion was made by the Secretary of State but it was an assessment purely by the administration, with no reference back to the "competent authority" and took into account factors upon which Santillo could not make representations.(84) If the sufficient proximity in time between opinion and decision is to ensure the absence of new factors, how can a lapse of time due to imprisonment, during which matters of possible parole and licence have raised further discussion of the person's behaviour not be "liable" to deprive the Court's recommendation of its nature as an opinion within the formulation of the Court of Justice?

None of the English Judges thought that Art. 9(1) as interpreted was not satisfied. Those who fully considered the matter were Donaldson LJ in the Divisional Court and Lord Denning MR and Templeman LJ in the Court of Appeal. (85) All made the same point: that with Santillo there were no new factors (favourable to him) to be taken into account and so the lapse of time did not invalidate the recommendation as an opinion. That, with respect, seems to view the matter from the wrong end of the telescope. The English judges ask whether the lapse of time did in fact make any difference. The answer is no. The Court of Justice says that an approximation in time is necessary to ensure there are no new factors arising which is a different matter. Lord Denning considered that if the word "until" halfway through Art. 9(1) was read as if it said "except after" then "that is necessary to effect the reconcilation" - which suggests that a reconciliation is needed because otherwise English law and Community law diverge. Yet he emphasised that UK deportation procedures are in conformity with Community law and that it was a good thing for the proceedings to have been brought and for that fact to have been established! The only English judge to consider what would be the position in a case in which the lapse of time was too long - a situation which Lord Denning MR ignored and Templeman L J declined to consider - was Donaldson L J. He discussed the possibility of a "competent authority", either the original court or an Adjudicator under the Immigration Act, being charged with considering whether, given that the recommendation was justified when made, circumstances have so changed that it can no longer be treated as effective. Donaldson L J considered this as being "the question of how a procedure can be devised which will give the Secretary of State the benefit of an "opinion"...from a competent authority", in cases in which the convicted person has been imprisoned for such term as, in the circumstances of the case, has deprived the trial court's recommendation for deportation of its status as such an opinion".

Again, with respect, this is not the question. For who is to decide the initial point of whether the recommendation has been to deprived of its status? What is needed in English law to ensure compliance with Community law, is, at the very least, a procedure by which all recommendations for deportation of Community nationals sentenced to terms of imprisonment are reviewed by somebody to see whether the recommendation has lost its "opinion" status when the sentence is nearing completion. That body could either be the original sentencing court or another "competent authority". This would not be an undue burden since it would be a procedure applicable only to Community nationals and the number of those deported each year after serving terms of imprisonment is low.(86) The matter is said at the moment to be under "active consideration" by the Home Office. It is to be hoped that they do not share the judicial complacency, and that if new Immigration Rules are issued in consequence of the British Nationality Act coming into force, they will reflect this.

VIII

The position of the EEC national who comes within the Treaty provisions is obviously a favoured one and particularly since Pieck, with its attack on controls on entry, the UK immigration authorities may find it essential to know exactly who is within the provisions. Oddly enough, what is referred to as the "personal scope" of the provisions is not at all clear. There are problems over how much of what kind of work makes a person a worker, and as to whether those looking for work are covered.(87)

The Court uses the criteria of whether the activities concerned are of an "economic nature", whether they are in the nature of gainful employment or remunerated service, which brings professional and semi-professional sport within the provisions.(88) Whether it also includes prostitution is something which could have been considered in Adoui and Cornuaille but that case (like Pecastaing before it) was fought and decided on other grounds.

The application of this criteria is not easy. In the Secchi case already referred to, the Magistrate refused to agree that casual washing-up, done only when earning some money became an unavoidable necessity, classified Secchi as a worker. The Magistrate considered the aims of the Treaty in Art. 2 and said that Secchi's activities could not "reasonably be regarded as forming part of the economic life of one or more of the Member States." In Levin(89) the Court declined to say that any minimum amount of work earning a minimum amount of money was necessary before a person became a beneficiary of the Treaty (so long as there was no living on public funds involved) but stressed that part-time workers are covered. However the provisions do apply only to the performance of "real and actual work, to the exclusion of work of such small degree that it appears merely minimal and subsidiary." In practice the task of the national judge in applying the distinction between part-time work and the merely "minimal and subsidiary" may be difficult. It may be that the Court would agree with the Magistrate's views of Secchi and his washing-up.

There is a long standing controversy in Community law as to whether freedom of movement covers those merely looking for work.(90) Levin strongly suggests that it does because the Court said there that "the rights to enter the territory of a Member State and to remain there are thus connected with status as a worker or else as a person who works or wishes to take up work in paid employment....." (emphasis added). Later in the judgment a gloss was added in a reference to "persons actually working in paid employment or who seriously wish to do so."(emphasis added).

The "looking for work" uncertainty has not thrown up problems for the UK because of paras. 60 and 61 of the Rules which provide that when any EEC national is given leave to enter "admission should normally be for six months" and that "an EEC national who wishes to enter the UK in order to take or seek employment, set up in business or work as a self-employed person, is to be admitted without a work permit or other prior consent". As already explained, this liberality arises from the Home Office view that since EEC nationals are free to take any employment they like, stringent controls are pointless. Since Pieck showed how far the immigration authorities are constrained in their dealings with qualified EEC nationals, it may become more necessary to know whether or not those looking for work are really covered by Community law. The qualification in Levin that one must seriously wish to work could cause problems: how is seriousness to be ascertained? Where a person's entry is concerned it would surely have to entail the kind of interrogation at the frontier of which the Court seems to diapprove.

The UK's practice of 6 months leave to enter also masks the problem over the provision of services. Art. 59 provides "restrictions on freedom to provide services in the Community shall be progressively abolished." Directive 73/148 directs Member States, in Art. 1(1)(b) to abolish restrictions on the movement and residence of "nationals of Member States wishing to go to another Member State as recipients of services" which goes beyond Art. 59 but seems a sensible complement to it. But who qualifies as a "recipient of services" is unclear. The matter was raised, but not disposed of by the Court in <u>Watson and Belmann</u> in the context of whether tourists are recipients of services . The Commission argued that an EEC national going to another Member State as a tourist is a recipient of services - he will pay for accommodation and refreshment. Trabucchi AG thought such an interpretation would extend the right of free movement to all EEC nationals - since all are potentially receivers of services on entering another Member State. He preferred to confine the right of recipients of services to situations in which they are indivisibly linked with the rights of movement of those who have to provide these services.

English law is silent on the issue. Nowhere is the right to provide services, let alone receive them, specifically mentioned. Para. 61 of the Rules refers only to the admittance of "an EEC national who wishes to enter the UK in order to take or seek employment, set up in business or work as a self-employed person." The latter phrase can be construed to cover the provider of services but nothing is said about recipients. Again, the matter is of greater significance since <u>Pieck</u>. The position could be that tourists from other Member States enter the UK as of right without any question of leave arising. While it cannot be expected that the Immigration Rules deal with this point while it is unclear in Community law the Rules might usefully say something about recipients of more specific services in line with the Directive.

IX

Art. 10. Reg. 1612/68 provides that the worker can install in the host state his spouse, descendants who are under 21 or dependent and dependent relatives in the ascending line of himself and his spouse. Member States are enjoined to "facilitate the admission" of other family members either dependent on the worker, or living under his roof "in the country whence he comes".(91) There is a proviso in Art. 10(3) that the worker should have normal standard housing available for his family.

The Immigration Rules do not mention the position of relations other than spouses, children under 21, their other children and grandchildren if still dependent and their dependent parents and grandparents, who "should be given leave to enter" according to paras. 62 and 63. There are even small differences of wording between the Rules and Art. 10 Reg. 1612/68, which uses the words ascendants and descendants - a non-dependent grandchild comes under the Article but not the Rules, for example. The general part of the Rules (not dealing specifically with EEC nationals) contains complex provisions in paras. 48 and 49 about the admission of dependent relatives other than spouses and children. The Rules do not mention the housing proviso at all.

The nationality of the spouse or dependant of the EEC national is irrelevant and non-EEC nationals therefore have rights of entry and residence in the UK under Commuinity law by virtue of their connection with the person exercising his right of free movement, which may contrast favourably with a non-national trying to enter a Member State by virtue of a connection with the State's own national. This can lead to ridiculous situations, particularly if the Member State's immigration laws are sexually discriminatory and raises issues as to whether a Member State may discriminate against its own nationals. In 1972 a German Court, denying a residence permit to the Egyptian husband of a German citizen, admitted that the Egyptian husband of a citizen of any other Member State working in the FDR would seem entitled to residence.(92)

It may certainly be preferable to seek entry to the UK through an EEC national. For example, under para. 50 of the Rules the foreign husband of a woman who is a British citizen has the right to live with her in the UK only if she, or one of her parents, was born in the UK. The rule does not apply to the foreign wives of British men. The Government announced, in October 1982, its intention to change this rule when the British Nationality Act comes into force, so that all British citizens may bring in their foreign husbands.(93)

The favoured position of these non-EEC nationals makes the Home Office interested in the duration of such position. In R v Immigration Adjudicator ex parte Sandhu(94) Comyn J considered the case of an Indian citizen married in the Federal Republic to a German citizen. The German wife came to the UK as a worker and the husband entered with her. The wife returned temporarily to Germany but the parting became permanent and she was probably now contemplating divorce. The Home Office requested the husband to leave the UK as he was no longer living with his EEC spouse, who was not even in the country.

In Grewal (95) the Immigration Appeal Tribunal upheld a decision to deport a non-EEC national separated from his EEC spouse on the basis that the separation ipso facto put an end to the former's rights. Comyn J in Sandhu disapproved this, holding that the non-EEC national will not automatically lose the right to remain merely because the EEC spouse separates, divorces, or leaves the UK, but that all the relevant circumstances must be considered. Sandhu won his appeal because he had been here since 1975 and was "a man who has been of impeccable conduct and who has a good work record..." and his matrimonial history was different from a case where a brief cohabitation had followed a marriage of convenience. The judge thought that the Grewal idea of automatic loss of rights was undesirable and would add "a new terror to marriage". He considered that "the Treaty of Rome is also based on the foundation of the family, and any wide provisions about freedom of people to move, freedom of workers, must recognise the family which in all civilised states is the basic unit", and that while Regulation 1612/68(96) did not throw a permanent cloak around the non-EEC partner it did give him "a status of which, in my judgment, the other party by a unilateral act cannot deprive him. It gives him a status to have the circumstances of his continued stay....judged objectively and fairly on all the circumstances and not on alleged rules of law such as were promulgated in....Grewal".

Community legislation does not deal with the position of the non-EEC national after a matrimonial breakdown but Reg.

1251/70 Art. 3(2) (97) provides a right to remain for the family of a deceased worker. Comyn J's sympathetic and liberal approach in Sandhu is to be commended but at the time of writing the Home Office, concerned at its implications are believed to be appealing.

It is interesting to consider the concern over dependants after the Levin case, from which it appears that a woman doing a modest amount of part-time work and thereby earning a small amount of money is a worker within the Treaty provisions, and therefore has the right to have her spouse with her. That spouse may be a non-EEC national, but under Reg. 1612/68 Art. 11 the spouse of the EEC national has the right to take up any activity as an employed person in the host State. The spouse may therefore earn the family's main income, which is why the worker (for the purposes of Art. 48) is not fatally thrown onto public funds to supplement her meagre wage. This seems to have been what was going on in Levin. In that case the Court rejected the contention that one's motive for working could be relevant to one's status as a worker. There is no reason why a woman who is an EEC national should not take a part-time job in the host State in order to gain rights of entry for a non-EEC husband who can then work in that State, her children, her parents-in-law, and other dependent relatives, even though nobody except her has the nationality of a Member State. It is interesting to reflect on such a scenario in the light of the paranoia of the Home Office over arranged marriages, husbands, fiances, male immigration and dependent relatives which is reflected in the Immigration Rules and badly affects non-EEC immigrants.

X

Under the Immigration Rules para. 38 a person of "independent means" may be admitted to the UK for an initial period of twelve months. To obtain the necessary entry clearance he must demonstrate that he can support himself and his dependants indefinitely without working: the Rules specify a minimum requirement of £100,000. disposable capital under his control in the UK or £10,000. p.a. income. The applicant has to show a close connection with the UK or that his admission would be in the UK's "general interests". Persons of independent means are prohibited from taking employment.

The present Community provisions do not cover an EEC national wishing to enter the UK to live here as a person of independent means without working although no EEC national who is admitted may be prohibited from taking employment. There are, however, Community proposals to change this; on the 31 July 1979 the Commission submitted to the Council a proposal (subsequently twice amended) "for a Directive on the right of residence for nationals of Member States in the territory of another Member State".(98). This proposes to give to EEC nationals able to support themselves without any type of employment the right to reside permanently in another Member State. It is a departure from previous Community provisions on free movement which have been part of the economic concept of the Common Market in providing for the mobility of labour and services. This Directive is a social measure promoting the idea of a "European citizenship", and there is some doubt about its vires.(99)

The draft provides for the abolition of restrictions on the movement and residence of EEC nationals not already covered by the free movement provisions who can show they have sufficient resources to provide for the needs of themselves and their accompanying dependants. "Sufficient resources" is explained by Art. 4(2) laying down that Member States may not require such resources to be greater than the minimum subsistence level applicable under their law in respect of their own nationals. "Minimum subsistence level" is a far cry from the £100,000. or £10,000. p.a. of para. 38 and has anyway no real meaning in English law or in any administrative provision. The nearest thing would be supplementary benefit rates, but these are not absolute because of complications of the rent element, "single payments" (previously exxceptional needs payments), and deductions for capital and other income.

The House of Lords Select Committee on the European Communities(1) had reservations about the draft which centred around two issues: firstly, the possibility that the persons concerned might in fact prove unable to support themselves, and so become a charge on public funds, and secondly the categories of dependants able to come in. Some Committee Members seemed to envisage the UK being flooded by hoards of EEC nationals intending to live off supplementary benefit. It was in this context that the Home Office admitted that the present practice was already to admit the people who would come under this Directive but that a formal directive was a different matter.(2)

As for dependants, the concern of the Committee was largely over exactly whose admission Member States were required to favour. The original draft referred to members of the family "when that member is dependent on them or was living under the same roof in the country of origin". This was later changed to "any person whom the holder of the right of residence has an obligation to support or who is in practice dependent on the holder". The Committee, sought clarification from the Chairman of the European Parliament's Legal Affairs Committee about the nature of the obligation (legal or moral) (3) and whether living under the same roof was still necessary. His answers were that it must be a legal obligation and that living under the same roof was still implied. He explained Art. 1(2)(c) in terms of the Italian concept of "a carico" which has a French equivalent and means "somebody who is financially dependent on somebody else and lives under the same roof". The legal obligation can "come either by the law or by a tribunal". In English law the legal obligation to support extends only to spouses and children.(4) In other States there may be liability to maintain ascendants and parents-in-law as well, and social security may be withheld until liable relatives have been called upon for assistance. This could mean British migrants were unable to take with them certain relatives because of the lack of legal obligation. The Committee did not take this point; they worried about people coming in, not the rights of British citizens going. It is difficult to see how there can be uniformity without a Community concept of dependence.

The categories of dependants featuring in the draft Directive are very similar to those in existing secondary legislation (5) and some of the points made by the Committee are equally applicable to Reg. 1612/68, Directive 73/148 etc. However, this time the Select Committee has the opportunity of considering the legislation prior to its enactment.(6)

The Committee recommended in its Report that the principle behind the proposal was acceptable and noted that it "raises important questions of policy and principle". As indeed it does, in extending rights of movement and residence to those EEC citizens (of sufficient resources) who just fancy living in another Member State without the justification of economic activity. The way is open for mass retirement in the South of France or Italy, a more likely consequence of the Directive perhaps, than retirement by EEC nationals in the UK!

XI

The last few years have witnessed such developments in the law on free movement that one can but smile at the naivety of those Immigration Bill debates in 1971. The most striking thing however, is that when the Immigration Rules were revised in 1980 so little attention was paid to bringing them into line with Community law. Years after the English courts dealt with Miss Van Duyn and Mr. Bouchereau in accordance with the public proviso, that proviso remains unrecognised by the Rules, and even where the Rules appear to be implementing Community law, they diverge on points of detail. With the coming into force of the British Nationality Act the British Government will have to make some amendments to the Rules and it may be that they will take the opportunity to make the Rules reflect the real position of EEC nationals and their families. That would be a constructive and overdue move.

Meanwhile, the judges do apply Community law, albeit with the odd hiccup. In Santillo lip-service was paid to the Court's ruling while its spirit was ignored: the hard lesson to learn is that Community law must be adhered to even when dealing with rapists. It is also hard to recognise Community provisions and the judgments of the Court as holding sway over matters as bound up with the identity and integrity of the State as the control of aliens. It is easier to accept Community diktats over free movement of goods than over that of people.

Community law is concerned with the rights of the migrant because the Community is seeking to promote freedom of movement; to remove obstacles and barriers to the movement of persons is to advance the objectives of the Treaty. Such an attitude is irreconcilable with that of a Member State whose immigration law is designed to keep people out rather than let them in. In the UK therefore one sees an enormous gap between the position of EEC and non-EEC immigrants, which is a matter of more than the procedures to which they are subject: it is a difference in the philosophy which lies behind those procedures.

Footnotes

(1) The Court of Justice has stressed this many times, most recently in Case 53/81 Levin v Secretary of State for Justice [1982] 2 CMLR 454.

(2) See the preamble to Council Regulation 1612/68, O J Spec Ed 1968 (II) 475 and Levi-Sandri, V P of the Commission in [1969] E C Bull No 11: "free movement of persons represents something more immportant and more exciting than the free movement of a factor of production. It represents rather an incipient form - still embryonic and imperfect - of European citizenship."

(3) [1982] 2 CMLR 553.

(4) And anomalous cases from former colonies, such as East African Asians with British passports.

(5) Although Lord Denning in De Falco v Crawley B C [1980] 1 All ER 913 at p922 spoke emotionally in terms of "advancing tides" (of EEC immigrants this time).

(6) O J Spec Ed [1963-4] p117.

(7) It was assumed at the time that no amendment to the Bill in the light of the forthcoming Accession was necessary; see HC Off Report vol 819 col 575 - 585 and below.

(8) [1977] 2 All ER 452, disapproving Roskill L J in R v Chief Immigration Offices ex p Salamat Bibi [1976] 2 All ER 845 at 848.

(9) See R v Immigration Appeal Tribuanl ex p Yau, The Times 25 February 1982. The current Immigration Rules are the Statement of Changes in Immigration Rules HC 394. They were laid before Parliament of 20 February 1980 and replaced those of 25 January 1973, HC 79-81 which were the current version at the time of the Pieck and Santillo decisions, discussed below.

(10) "In the exercise of their functions under this Act, immigration officials shall act in accordance with such instructions (not inconsistent with the immigration rules) as may be given them by the Secretary of State."

(11) Hartley: EEC Immigration Law p6.

(12) Art 48 in Case 167/78 Commission v France Re Merchant Seamen [1974] ECR 359; [1974] 2 CMLR 216 and Case 41/74 Van Duyn v Home Office [1974] ECR 1337; [1975] 1 CMLR 472: Art 52 in Case 2/74 Jean Reyners v Belgian State [1974] ECR 631; [1974] 2 CMLR 305 and Art 59 and Art 60(3) in Case 33/74 Van Binsbergen [1974] ECR 1299; [1975] 1 CMLR 298. If a provision has direct effect an individual may rely on it in a national court.

(13) The main legislation discussed in this essay is: Council Regulation 1612/68 on freedom of movement for workers within the Community O J Sp Ed, 1968 (II) p475, as amended by Reg 312/76, O J 1976, L 39/2; Council Directive 68/360 on the abolition of restrictions on movement and residence within the Community for workers of Member States and their families O J Sp Ed, 1968 (II) p485; Council Directive 64/221 on the co ordination of special measures concerning the movement and residence of foreign nationals which are justified on grounds of public policy, public security or public health O J Sp Ed, 1963-4 p117 and Council Directive 73/148 on the abolition

of restrictions on movement and residence within the Community for nationals of Member States with regard to establishment and the provision of services, O J 1973 L 172/14. There are also important harmonisation Directives concerning the mutual recognition of professional qualifications, vital to the proper operation of the freedom of establishment and provision of services.

(14) eg Reg 1612/68 Art 1: "Any national of a Member State shall, irrespective of his place of residence, have the right to take up an activity as an employed person..." As part of the terms upon which Greece entered the Community freedom of movement for workers is not to apply to Greece until 1 January 1988: Greek nationals will not have a right of movement until then and EEC nationals will not have free movement in Greece: (Treaty of Greek Accession, Arts 44-46).

(15) The idea being broadly to distinguish those "belonging" to the UK and her remaining colonies and those belonging to independent Commonwealth countries.

(16) Immigration Act 1971 s2.

(17) The exact text of the definition defines a UK national for Community law purposes as: "(a) persons who are citizens of the UK and Colonies or British subjects not possessing that citizenship or the citizenship of any other Commonwealth country or territory, who, in either case, have the right of abode in the UK and are therefore exempt from UK immigration control; (b) persons who are citizens of the UK and Colonies by birth or by registration or naturalisation in Gibraltar, or whose father was so born, registered or naturalised."

(18) Chiefly by Bohning (1973) 10 C M L Rev 81.

(19) See Hartley: EEC Immigration Law p73.

(20) Other Member States have nationality definition problems. The Federal Republic of Germany also produced a Declaration for the purposes of Community law, as the result of the Grundgesetz Art 116 (1) is that most of the population of East Germany have citizenship of the Federal Republic.

(21) Now H C 394 para 29.

(22) This concession was originally in the Bill itself.

(23) The Commonwealth citizens who acquired the right of abode by s2 (1)(d) of the 1971 Act.

(24) British Nationality Act 1981 s11.

(25) The most significant result of this is that people from Hong Kong have no right of abode, the British Government having an eye to the future - the lease on Hong Kong expires in 1997. Similarly, the Act's provisions give the Falkland Islanders no right to enter the UK a matter much commented upon when the Falklands crisis arose so soon after the passing of the Act. On 22 June 1982, however, the Falkland Islands (British Citizenship) Bill, which would enable Falkland Islanders to acquire British Citizenship, had its first reading.

(26) On 17 September 1981.

(27) "Settled", according to s50 (2), means a person ordinarily resident in the UK without being subject under the immigration laws to any restriction on the period for which he may remain.

(28) As a child born in the UK of foreign parents might not obtain their nationality by descent under the foreign law and a child born abroad to persons British by descent only might not obtain that country's nationality unless the jus solis applied there.

(29) There are, however, provisions for acquisition of British citizenship through registration. 1981 Act ss3 - 5, 7 - 10.

(30) Either in Crown service under the government of the UK, or service which is designated by the Secretary of State as being closely associated with the UK Government's activities outside the UK. Recruitment to such service must have been in the UK s2 (1)(b); s2 (2), (3) and (4).

(31) The amendment was agreed to on 6 October 1981. It now appears as s2 (1)(c).

(32) Cmnd 6795 April 1977 para 30.

(33) s51 concerns the "meaning of certain expressions relating to nationality in other Acts and Instruments." It is unlikely that the Declaration, or anything in the Treaty of Accession could be considered an "instrument".

(34) See Official Report, Standing Committee, British Nationality Bill, 26 March 1981.

(35) For example, the UK was taken before the European Commission on Human Rights in 1971 over the exclusion of East African Asians with British passports.

(36) Case 36/75. Rutili v French Minister of the Interior [1975] ECR 1219; [1976] 1 CMLR 140.

(37) Case 53/81 Levin v Secretary of State for Justice [1982] 2 CMLR 454.

(38) See eg Case 67/74 Bonsignore v Oberstadt Direktors Koln [1975] ECR 297; [1975] 1 CMLR 472; case 30/77 R v Bouchereau [1977] ECR 1999; [1977] 2 CMLR 800.

(39) H C Official Report 819.

(40) Ibid col 584.

(41) Ibid col 583.

(42) British Nationality Act 1981 s39 replacing Immigration Act 1971 s2; Immigration Rules H C 394 para 4.

(43) Case 157/79 [1980] ECR 2171; [1980] 3 CMLR 220.

(44) In accordance with para 51 of the Rules then in force (H C 81)

(45) Art 3 actually refers to Art 1 which in turn refers to those whom Reg 1612/68 applies. Reg 1612/68 applies to workers who are nationals of Member States and their families. Art 3(2) does allow for entry visas or equivalent documents to be required of family members who are not themselves EEC nationals.

(46) The corresponding provision of the Rules currently in force H C 394, is para 60 which is identical except that the clause beginning "no condition" and the second sentence are transposed.

(47) The matter was confused by the translation of the English text which rendered the French words "obligation" and "impose" as "document" and "demanded" rather than "requirement" and "imposed".

(48) Case 8/77 The State v Sagulo [1977] ECR 1495, [1997] 2 CMLR 585.

(49) And the self-employed and providers of services.
(50) Case 48/75[1976] ECR 497; [1976] 2 CMLR 619.
(51) Even before the Pieck judgment, EEC nationals were being given a notice on entry, instead of a passport endorsement:
"Immigration Act 1971. Notice of Leave to Enter the United Kingdom for nationals of EEC countries:
You are hereby given leave to enter the United Kingdom for 6 months."
The notice continues the instruction (or is it a warning) that "if you wish to remain longer than the period permitted" you should contact the Home Office.
(52) H C 394, para 122 provides for foreign nationals to register with the police.
(53) Case 118/75[1976] ECR 1185; [1977] 2 CMLR 552.
(54) See the evidence given by Home Office officials to the House of Lords Select Committee on the European Communities, Session 1980-81, 9th Report, p3.
(55) Ibid p7.
(56) Ibid p3.
(57) Wyatt in [1980] 5 EL Rev 380 at 386 suggests a case of a person who is clearly exhibiting signs of mental disturbance (and would therefore come under the Annex to Directive 64/221).
(58) Case 48/75[1976] ECR 497; [1976] 2 CMLR 619.
(59) Particularly Arts 6 & 7. Art 4 states "Member States shall grant the right of residence" to those who fulfill certain criteria - wording which sits oddly with the Pieck decision.
(60) Which applies to all applications from non-patrials for leave to remain.
(61) The proviso applies to the matter dealt with in Art 48(3). It does not qualify Art 48(2).
(62) It seems that in fact the procedural matters in this Directive mainly apply on whatever grounds the authorities are purporting to act. See Hartley: EEC Immigration Law p185 n32. This is an argument a contrario from Act 6 where it specifically states that reasons must be given for decisions taken on the proviso grounds.
(63) The provisions have been held to produce direct effects.
(64) Case 131/79 R v Secretary of State for Home Affairs ex parte Santillo[1980] ECR 1585; [1980] 2 CMLR 308.
(65) The application of Community law by Immigration officers where entry is concerned is obviously more difficult to assess, unless the person concerned exercises his rights of appeal.
(66) H C 394 paras 70-72.
(67) The fact that a first residence permit may be refused on medical grounds must mean that Community law sanctions deportation for medical reasons until the issue of the permit.
(68) H C 394 para 75. In Cases 115 and 116/81 Adoui and Cornuaille v Belgian State (judgment of 18th May 1982. 1982 O J C 148/3) however, the Court said that a national of one Member State wishing to work in another who was already the subject of previous measures expelling him, could re-

apply for a residence permit after a "reasonable period" and have the matter re-examined by the host state who should consider evidence as to change of circumstance.

(69) Immigration Act 1971, s13(5).

(70) Case 4/74 Van Duyn v Home Office[1974] ECR 1337; [1975] 1 CMLR 1.

(71) Immigration Act 1971 s5(4).

(72) H C 394 paras 145-149.

(73) Reg 1612/68 Art 10; Directive 73/148 Art 1.

(74) Case 30/77 R v Bouchereau[1977] ECR 1999; [1977] 2 CMLR 800.

(75) Case 36/75 Rutili v French Minister of the Interior[1975] ECR 1219; [1976] 1 CMLR 140.

(76) See n. 68 above.

(76a) R v Secchi[1975] 1 CMLR 383.

(77) Immigration Act 1971 Part II deals with the Immigration Appeals system.

(78) 1971 Act, s15(3).

(79) [1977] 2 All ER 452.

(80) 16th June 1971 H C Official Report (5th Series) col 376.

(81) The procedure is modelled on that used under the Defence (General) Regulations 1939 (SR & O No. 927), reg 18. Mr Driberg asked the Secretary of State why there should be no right of representation and the reply was that "This procedure has worked well with civil servants..." The Secretary of State stated that these were "executive, political decisions" subject to Parliament and not "justiciable, legal decisions", subject to the courts.

(82) Case 98/79 Pecastaing v Belgian State [1980] ECR 691 [1980] 3 CMLR 685.

(83) It is notable that the right to representation and rights of defence were part of the reason for recognising the court as a "competent authority".

(84) He was not able to make representations about the police evidence of other offences, about prison medical reports on his mental state and the likelihood of re-offending, or about the significance of the refusal to release him on parole or licence. The other ground for his certiorari application was breach of the rules of natural justice.

(85) [1980] 3 CMLR 212 and [1981] 1 CMLR 569.

(86) The Home Office evidence in Luxembourg revealed that in 1977, 1978 and 1979 there were respectively 73, 60 and 72 EEC nationals recommended for deportation by English criminal courts. About half received non-custodial sentences, a third under six months, and only a dozen or so a year received more than six months: see [1980] ECR 1985 at 1615 (Warner A-G). Even assuming that all these people were within the free movement provisions and that the lapse of time might become relevant in as little as six month, the problem is not huge.

(87) It is also difficult sometimes to tell whether a person comes within Art 48, Art 52 or Art 59. See eg case 36/74 Walrave & Koch v Association Union Cyclists [1974] ECR 1405; [1975] 1 CMLR 30. Case 39/45 Coenen v Sociaal Economische Raad [1975] 1 CMLR 30 shows how narrow can be the distinction between establishing oneself and providing services.

(88) Walrave & Koch n 87 above; Case 13/76 Dona v Mantero [1976] ECR 1333; [1976] 2 CMLR 578.

(89) Case 23/81 [1982] 2 CMLR.

(90) Art 48(3) does not specifically mention entry to look for work as being entailed in freedom of movement. It is known however that at the Council meeting which passed Directive 68/360 it was agreed that EEC nationals should have three months to find work in another Member State, so long as they did not become a charge on public funds (see H Ter Heide (1969) 6 CML Rev 466 and the reference to the Council minutes by Slynn A G in Levin). Directive 68/360 does not require proof of employment until a Residence Permit is issued. Directive 73/148 Art 1 specifically covers those "who wish to establish themselves in another Member State" or "who wish to provide services in that State."

(91) cf Directive 73/148. These are seemingly pointless small differences in the exact wording of different pieces of Community legislation on dependants.

(92) Re Residence Permit for an Egyptian National [1975] 2 CMLR 402.

(93) H C 394 para 50. This Rule is currently (August 1982) the subject of challenge before the European Commission on Human Rights as being contrary to the European Convention.

(94) [1982] 2 CMLR.

(95) [1979-80] Imm A R 119.

(96) And Directives 68/360 and 73/148 also. Comyn J put much emphasis on the preambles to the secondary legislation, and construes "wishing to establish themselves" in the Preamble to 73/148 as "plainly and clearly" connoting a family!

(97) Directive 75/34 for the self-employed.

(98) 1979 O J C 207/14 amended, 1980 O J C 188/7 and 1980 O J C 292/3.

(99) It is expressed to be based upon Arts 56(2) and 235 but the former is mentioned only because of the necessary extension to Directive 64/221. Its sole basis is really Art 235. Part of the Directive's preamble reads: "Whereas, however, freedom of movement of persons is by virtue of Art 3(c) of the Treaty one of the foundations of the Community and can be fully attained only if a right of permanent residence os granted to those Community nationals in whom such a right does not already vest under the Community law in force and to the members of their family" which is an attempt to show the Directive is a necessity such as is referred to in Art 235. The Legal Affairs Committee of the European Parliament considers it is intra virus (EP Working Document 1-40/80).

(1) Session 1980-91, 9th Report.

(2) See above.

(3) One peer's example of a moral obligation to support was the one owed to "the nursemaid of your childhood". (9th Report p14).

(4) The exact extent of the obligation is different in matrimonial law from the rules for social security.

(5) But not identical. For example, the age below which children enter without dependence being necessary is 18 rather than 21.

(6) The draft Directive also contains the provision (Art 2(2)) found in Directives 68/360 and 73/148 that Member States shall issue passports or identity cards to their nationals "acting in accordance with their laws". In the UK passport facilities are part of the prerogative of the Crown and nobody is entitled to the grant or renewed of a passport. This seems to be contrary to Community law therefore.

POLICY CONSIDERATIONS IN THE COURTS
IN MATTERS OF JURISDICTION IN CONFLICT OF LAWS:
THE TRADITIONAL ENGLISH APPROACH
COMPARED WITH THE APPROACH ADOPTED BY
THE COURT OF JUSTICE OF THE EUROPEAN COMMUNITIES

J J Fawcett

The Civil Jurisdiction and Judgments Act 1982 introduces new bases of jurisdiction in English conflict of laws in cases where the defendant is domiciled within the EEC. The Act gives effect to the Convention on Jurisdiction and the Enforcement of Judgments in Civil and Commercial Matters of 27 September 1968 (Brussels Convention), to which the United Kingdom acceded by the Convention of Accession of 9 October 1978.(1) There have already been a number of decisions by the Court of Justice interpreting the Brussels Convention. Nonetheless the English courts will still have an important role to play in interpreting this Convention where there is no previous Court of Justice decision and there is no referral to that Court in the instant case.To achieve harmonisation of the law on jurisdiction in the EEC it is vital that national courts should interpret it in the same spirit as the Court of Justice. It is necessary therefore for English courts to apply the techniques and adopt the objectives sought by the Court of Justice when interpreting the Brussels Convention.(2) It would be naive to believe that English attitudes can be changed overnight. The greatest impact of the Brussels Convention on English Law may well turn out to be not the introduction of different bases of jurisdiction but the changes in approach needed to interpret those consistently with the spirit adopted by the Court of Justice. To appreciate the difficulties with which the English courts are likely to be faced it is vital to study the Court of Justice decisions on the Convention and to compare these with decisions of the English courts on the bases of jurisdiction prior to the Civil Jurisdiction and Judgments Act.

I LITERAL INTERPRETATION OR POLICY

A Teleological Interpretation of the Brussels Convention

A literal interpretation considers the rule to be interpreted in isolation and does so according to a rigid principle. It is both mechanical and inward looking. A policy interpretation means that a court is looking outwards to achieve some wide ulterior objective(s). The first difference to be noticed between interpretation of the Brussels Convention and English law on jurisdiction is that the former has consistently been subjected to a policy interpretation and the latter has often been subjected to a literal interpretation. The Court of Justice has frequently adopted a teleological interpretation of Community law.(3) It is not surprising therefore to find it using this technique in respect of the Brussels Convention. According to the Court of Justice: "the Convention must be interpreted having regard both to its principles and objectives and to its relationship within the Treaty."(4) The result is that the interpretation of the bases of jurisdiction contained in the Brussels Convention has been sophisticated and policy orientated rather than mechanical and literal. A good example is the interpretation of Art. 5(3) by the Court of Justice in the Reinwater case.(5) Art. 5(3) gives jurisdiction in the place where the harmful event occurred in actions involving non-contractual obligations. A literal view would say a single clear definition must be given to the word place. A definition in terms of alternatives of act or injury means looking at more than one place. But this wide definition was justified by the Court of Justice by looking at the purpose of Art. 5(3).

Literal Interpretation under English Law

A distinction has to be made between two aspects of a jurisdiction case. First, there are the bases of jurisdiction i.e. residence, submission and, for these purposes, the heads of Ord. 11 Rules of the Supreme Court. Second, there is the discretionary element ie. the discretion to allow service out of the jurisdiction under Ord. 11 and the question of whether an action already commenced here will be stayed for injustice to the defendant or because of a foreign choice of jurisdiction clause. The English courts' attitude towards bases of jurisdiction is particularly important since the Brussels Convention has no discretionary element within it. Their attitude is very different from that towards the discretionary element. It is marked by a love of technical distinctions and a literal interpretation. A good illustration is one of the leading cases on Ord. 11 R S C, George Monro v American Cyanamid Corporation.(6) Here, the Court of Appeal had to define the phrase "a tort committed within the jurisdiction." The English court, unlike the Court of Justice in Reinwater, decided that the essence of a tort was the negligent act rather than the injury and so the tort was committed in the United States where the product was manufactured and not in England where injury was suffered. The result was that jurisdiction could not be taken in England but the court did not consider whether this head of Ord. 11 would ever be of any use if interpreted in this way. The phrase is sufficiently ambiguous to leave it open to a court to take a wider policy orientated viewpoint. The decision was a bad one because it drastically restricted the width of English jurisdiction in all cases involving products liability. A plaintiff will usually be injured by a defective product in his place of residence and this is where he will want to bring his action. Yet he is unable to do so. The subsequent cases of Distillers Co Ltd(7) v Thompson and Castree v Squibb(8) are to be welcomed because they give English courts jurisdiction in this area but the method by which this was achieved was very unsatisfactory. Instead of meeting the problem head on and saying that George Monro was wrong and should be overruled, the courts in both cases side-stepped the problem by simply redefining the negligent act. In both it was said to be a failure to warn persons likely to be injured by the product and not faulty manufacture. This gives the law an extremely mechanical appearance, all the attention is focused on the abstract question of the nature of the wrongful act in a tort case; is it faulty manufacture or failure to warn and if the latter where should the warning be given? This ignores the ultimate question of whether there ought to be a trial in England where a foreign manufacturer knows his goods are to be distributed in the forum and these injure someone there. Instead, the concern for precedent dictated that the means for avoiding that case had to be found within it by an examination of the concept of the negligent act. Furthermore, the fact that the heads of Ord. 11 are treated as being statutory inevitably means they are given a literal interpretation.

This does not mean that the courts disregard policy objectives when deciding a case. The failure openly to espouse a policy orientated approach makes it more difficult to identify these than is the case with decisions of the Court of Justice but they are still there. Distillers and Castree undoubtedly expanded the use of Ord. 11 in recent years. A technique of literal interpretation was adopted which masked the fact that expansion was deliberate. In Distillers v Thompson the negligent act was said to be a failure to give a warning to pregnant mothers that the use of the drug containing thalidomide might be dangerous to the unborn child. It was not faulty manufacture. This meant that the New South Wales forum had jurisdiction which it would not have had if the negligent act had been regarded as defective manufacture. This decision was followed in Castree v Squibb where a weighing machine, manufactured in West Germany but sold in this country, blew up in England. The negligent act was again failure to warn. There was some case for arguing that there was a failure to warn in Distillers because women, apart from pregnant ones, would be unaffected by the drug. But in Castree it is hard to see how the court came to the conclusion that the machine could have been used in such a way that it would not blow up. This examination of the key concept of the wrongful act was followed by a suspect twisting of the facts, resulting in jurisdiction being available in the forum, and would suggest that the new idea of a failure to warn was deliberately introduced to give the forum jurisdiction.

II COMPARISON OF THE POLICIES

1 Policy Considerations in Interpreting an International Convention

Some of the policies adopted when interpreting the Brussels Convention have no counterpart under the traditional English law on jurisdiction. Uniformity of interpretation is one such objective. This will be important when interpreting any International Convention, whatever its subject matter, whether it be jurisdiction or carriage of goods. Another objective, avoiding overlapping jurisdiction, will arise because this is an International Convention which harmonises rules on jurisdiction and which does this as part of an overall scheme of facilitating enforcement of judgments throughout the EEC.

(i) Uniformity of Interpretation

Harmonisation of the law on jurisdiction requires not only shared bases but also a uniform interpretation. It would defeat the whole purpose of the Convention if its operation depended on the place of trial, with each Contracting State defining words and phrases differently. The Convention is based on trust between the Contracting States. This is primarily an enforcement of judgments Convention, the jurisdiction rules being subordinate to this and semi-automatic enforcement is only possible with trust. To prevent a lack of uniformity of interpretation the Court of Justice has frequently adopted an independent Community meaning for the terms used in the Brussels Convention rather than referring the words back to national courts to define. The leading authority is L T U v Eurocontrol(9) where the Court of Justice said that:

> "as Art. 1 serves to indicate the scope of the Convention it is necessary, in order to ensure, as far as possible, that the rights and obligations which derive from it for the Contracting State and the persons to whom it applies are equal and uniform, that the terms of that provision should not be interpreted as a mere reference to the internal law of one or other of the States concerned."

It was natural to give an independent Community meaning to something as fundamental as the scope of the Convention, but the same has happened with bases of jurisdiction. In Galeries Segoura v Firma Rahim(10) the Court of Justice had to interpret the requirement under Art. 17 that an agreement on jurisdiction be in writing or confirmed in writing. A Community meaning was given to this phrase and also to the question of when an oral agreement assigning jurisdiction is created. Similarly in <u>Somafer</u> v <u>Saar-Ferngas</u> the Court of Justice had to interpret "a dispute arising out of the operations of a branch, agency or other establishment" under Art. 5(5). The phrase was given a Community meaning.Once it has been decided that the Court of Justice will define a word or phrase the desire for uniformity can operate at the next stage of fixing upon this definition. The Advocate-General in <u>Reinwater</u> said that the definition of the place of the harmful event occurring under Art. 5(3) should be clear, precise and objective.(11) He rejected defining this in terms of the proper law of the tort since the imprecise nature of this concept would inevitably lead to different definitions being applied by different Contracting States.

(ii) Avoidance of overlapping jurisdiction

The Jenard Report which preceeded the Brussels Convention was concerned that the courts of two Contracting States should not have jurisdiction in respect of the same action(12) and introduced exclusive jurisdiction under Art. 17. In <u>Establissements A De Bloos</u> v <u>Bouyer S A</u>, the Court of Justice said that the objectives of the Convention imply the need to avoid, so far as possible, a situation in which a number of courts have jurisdiction in respect of one and the same contract.(13) The Convention allocates jurisdiction amongst the Contracting States. By its very nature a division presupposes fairly watertight compartments. To take an extreme position, if each Contracting State had jurisdiction in respect of any dispute of a civil and commercial nature, this could not be called a true division. Avoiding overlapping jurisdiction is desirable for other reasons. It fits in with the theory of territorial sovereignty which will be considered shortly. It gives the plaintiff an opportunity to "forum shop" which is regarded as undesirable in Europe. It can also lead to problems not only of two courts having jurisdiction but of two judgments being given. Such <u>lis alibi pendens</u> problems, if unsolved, could negate the main objective of facilitating recognition and enforcement of judgments within the EEC. Finally, overlapping jurisdiction can lead to injustice, particularly where there is more than one plaintiff. It can lead to one plaintiff suing in one country and getting a judgment in his favour and another plaintiff suing elsewhere with a contrary result.

These considerations have affected the interpretation of the Convention. According to the Advocate-General in Reinwater(14) one of the disadvantages of applying a place of injury definition under Art. 5(3) was that it might produce unfairness to the parties. Avoiding an overlap also leads to a Community definition being adopted. If a phrase is defined by national laws, according to De Bloos(15), two different interpretations may be given in different Contracting States, giving jurisdiction to both. Avoiding an overlap helps to explain the narrow interpretation given to Art. 5 of the Convention. In De Bloos the Court of Justice had to decide whether the term "obligation" in Art. 5(1) of the Convention was to be interpreted widely, as applying without distinction to any obligation arising out of the outline contract granting an exclusive sales concession, or narrowly, as referring exclusively to the obligation forming the basis of the legal proceedings. The Court adopted this latter interpretation because it wanted to see jurisdiction concentrated in a single country wherever possible. For the same reason a narrow interpretation was given to Art. 5(5) in De Bloos. The Court held that as an "establishment" had the same essential characteristics as a branch or agency, it had to be subject to the direction and control of the parent.(16) It was impossible to extend Art. 5(5) to the grantee of an exclusive sales concession which was not under the control and supervision of the grantor but was an independent economic operator. If it had been desired to extend the law beyond the branch or agency it would have been quite possible under a literal interpretation to do so using the "other establishment" terminology but the Court did not do this.

2   A National or International Interpretation

An international spirit - taking into account the reaction of other States to the exercise of jurisdiction - has been adopted when interpreting the Brussels Convention. The Court of Justice is thus giving full recognition to the fact that a jurisdiction case in conflict of laws not only involves a plaintiff and defendant, it also involves two different States. One of the principles of interpretation of International Conventions in public international law is not to take away sovereignty unless it is clear that this is intended.(17) The Court of Justice has been influenced by this in two ways.(18) First, it does not want to appear to be taking away national rights by seeking to define everything. There is a danger of antagonising Contracting States by taking away the role of their courts. This is a consideration which only exists for the Court of Justice and would not be relevant for an English court. Second, neither does it want to define bases of jurisdiction so widely that one Contracting State feels another is encroaching on the position of its citizens when it applies these rules. Here the concern is with one State's relations with another which is crucial where a convention is passed for liberal enforcement of judgments based on mutual trust. This is a consideration which an English court could take into account when interpreting the Convention.

(i) Is the Court of Justice or a national Court to define the term?

A clash of policies faces the Court of Justice when deciding whether to give a Community meaning to a concept in the Convention or to leave it to national courts to define. The urgent need for uniformity dictates that a Community meaning be adopted. On the other hand, the desire to respect Contracting States' sovereignty dictates that the definition should be left to the courts in those States,(19) with the Court of Justice telling the judge in the court seised of the matter which municipal law to apply. The clash comes out clearly in cases on the scope of the Convention under Art. 1 where the sophisticated nature of the arguments used in these cases contrasts strongly with the mechanical line of reasoning adopted in English cases on jurisdiction. Not surprisingly, the Court of Justice as a body given a political role in achieving European integration(20) has favoured the Community meaning at the expense of national sovereignty.(21) In exceptional cases it is not possible to adopt a Community meaning. One example is where the term being defined presupposes the application of the choice of law rules of Contracting States.

In Industrie Tessili Italiana Como v Dunlop A G, the first case on the Brussels Convention to be interpreted by the Court of Justice, the Court emphasised the importance of a national definition for Art. 5(1).(22) The place of performance of the obligation in question was to be determined by the forum in accordance with its rules of choice of law. This place would also depend on the contractual context so that it was impossible to give an abstract Community meaning to it. In Reinwater, Industrie Tesseli was referred to by the Advocate-General but he said that the provision now in question, Art. 5(3), was not linked with any contractual dispute or influenced in any way by various types of contract, the concept in question was much more homogeneous in its nature than that of a contactual obligation and the differences between the national systems of tort or delict ruled out an independent definition.(23)

(ii) Defining the term by the Court of Justice

Giving a Community meaning to terms used in the Convention, as in Reinwater, takes away the sovereign rights of Contracting States, but the way that the Community definition is arrived at shows how the Court of Justice realises that it is treading on thin ice. The Court of Justice, when interpreting the Brussels Convention, has used the same technique as that used when filling any gap in Community law. It has looked for the common core of the concept as used in individual Contracting States. This principle was enunciated in cases on the scope of the Convention under Art. 1.(24) It may well be possible to ascertain the common core from earlier bilateral treaties between the various Contracting States. In Reinwater the Court could not find a common core, when defining the place of the harmful event occurring, because of the variety of different definitions used in the Contracting States. Yet the Court did not take the same approach as in Industrie Tessili and leave the definition to national courts. Instead, it took into account all the different national definitions and added to the existing bases being used rather than detracting from them. The Court of Justice said that this would avoid upheaval in the systems already adopted. It also meant a new independent meaning was given, rather than just adopting one used in an individual State and was therefore less likely to annoy Contracting States.The desire to respect the sovereign rights of Contracting States has also led to the narrow interpretation, already mentioned, of Art. 5 bases of jurisdiction thus avoiding multiplication of bases of jurisdiction. It was pointed out in <u>Somafer</u> that if States are given a wide power to take jurisdiction there is a danger they will act in a parochial way and benefit their nationals.(25) This is what happened in France and the Convention seeks to avoid this. If a parochial attitude were to be adopted by the forum this would be to the detriment of foreign defendants and would destroy the essential trust amongst Contracting States.

English Law

English courts will be faced with a similar dilemma to that facing the Court of Justice but will be looking at the problem from a different angle. Should they assert their own sovereignty and define terms under the Convention or should they refer them to the Court of Justice for a Community definition in all cases where a referral to that Court is allowed? The importance of terms being given a Community meaning requires that the English courts make full use of their powers of referral.(26) English courts are not well equipped to search for the common core of laws and so could not accurately assess what Community meaning might be given to the term, unlike the Court of Justice which has the expertise to make such a judgment. When it comes to English courts actually interpreting the provisions of the Convention there is a heritage of internationalism to fall back on. With English rules on jurisdiction it is interesting that despite their purely national source they nonetheless have traditionally been interpreted in a way that takes into account the reaction of other States to our exercise of jurisdiction. Although in recent years a more nationalistic interpretation has emerged.

(i) The traditional policy of respecting the territorial sovereignty of other States.

A sharp distinction has been made by the Courts between where jurisdiction in personam is based on residence or submission on the one hand and service of a writ out of the jurisdiction under Ord. 11 R S C on the other. Parliament undoubtedly has municipal authority to pass a statute which gives the courts a discretionary power to serve a defendant abroad and thereby subject him to our jurisdiction. There is no enforceable rule of international law which prevents this. Nonetheless, it has been said that the exercise of this power represents an infringement of the exclusive jurisdiction of the sovereignty of other States. For this reason Ord. 11 has come to be regarded by the courts as an exceptional form of jursidiction only to be used with reluctance. This has taken the form of, firstly, giving a restrictive interpretation to the heads of Ord. 11 and, secondly, where the courts have jurisdiction, in the sense that a head of Ord. 11 is satisfied, to exercise their discretion against actually taking jurisdiction.

A good example of the first technique is provided by the recent decision of the House of Lords in The Siskina.(27) Here a "Mareva" injunction was sought by the plaintiff cargo-owners to prevent defendant shipowners from disposing of their assets within the jurisdiction. Damages were also claimed by the cargo-owners "for breach of duty and/or contract." The plaintiffs sought to base jurisdiction on Ord. 11 r 1(I)(i) which says that service out of the jurisdiction is possible "if in the action begun by the writ an injunction is sought ordering the defendant to do or refrain from doing anything within the jurisdiction ..." It was argued that the "Mareva" injunction would constitute the necessary injunction for the purposes of r1(I)(i). Their Lordships rejected this argument and held that the injunction in question must be part of the substantive relief to which the plaintiffs' cause of action entitled them and enforceable by a final judgment. The relief sought here was merely of an interim nature. The law Lords decision was not compelled by the wording of the provision and was undoubtedly a narrow interpretation which denied jurisdiction to the plaintiff. Lord Diplock acknowledged this, pointing out that Ord. 11 was an exorbitant form of jurisdiction which was contrary to normal rules amongst civilised nations and so any doubt as to its meaning was to be construed against taking jurisdiction. The theory of territorial sovereignty may sound very abstract but underlying the courts' desire to comply with it is a practical concern about foreign courts' reactions to our use of an exorbitant form of jurisdiction. In one of the leading Ord. 11 cases, George Monro Ltd v American Cyanamid and Chemical Corp. Scott L J said that "service out of the jurisdiction at the instance of our courts is necessarily prima facie an interference with the exclusive jurisdiction of the sovereignty of the foreign country where service is to be effected. I have known many continental lawyers of different nations in the past criticise very strongly our law about service out of the jurisdiction. As a matter of international comity it seems to be important to make sure that no such service shall be allowed unless it is clearly within both the letter and the spirit of Ord. 11."(28) The result was to give a very narrow interpretation to the head of Ord. 11 in question and to use the discretion against allowing service abroad. Defining the place where the tort was committed as being where the wrongful act occurred rather than the injury denied jurisdiction to this plaintiff and deprived this head of Ord. 11 of any real effect.

When it comes to residence or submission by the defendant to the English court the position is very different. These bases of jurisdiction are entirely consistent with the theory of territorial sovereignty and it was assumed that foreign courts would accordingly recognise our judgments where jurisdiction was so taken.(29) The result was that the basic rule was actor sequitur forum rei. Residence and submission do not present the difficult problems of interpretation that the heads of Ord. 11 do, so it is much harder to provide cases showing that the courts' attitude in construing the former has been more liberal (ie. more likely to result in jurisdiction being taken) than in Ord. 11 cases. The main area of difficulty is that of jurisdiction against foreign incorporated companies. These are subject to jurisdiction if they establish a place of business in England. In one of the leading cases, Dunlop Pneumatic Tyre Co.Ltd v A/G Cudell and Co,(30) there is evidence of a willingness to take jurisdiction which is in marked contrast to the attitude in Ord. 11 cases. The Court was faced with a foreign incorporated company which carried on business in

England at a stand at a motor show for a mere nine days. The question was whether the business was carried on for a substantial length of time and from a fixed place. The first requirement was satisfied because the Court of Appeal equated volume of business with length of time for which the business was carried on. As to the second requirement a stand at a motor show was regarded as a sufficiently fixed place of business. The result was that jurisdiction was available against the foreign incorporated company. Equally revealing is the different attitude towards Ord. 11 where its use does not infringe the territorial sovereignty of other countries. Ord. 11 r 2 allows jurisdiction to be taken where there is an English choice of jurisdiction clause in a contract. The principle of territorial sovereignty is not infringed because there is submission to trial and in this situation the court is inclined to exercise its discretion towards taking jurisdiction. A recent example is the Chaparral.(31) The dispute in question had no apparent connection with England but the contract between the parties provided that "any dispute arising must be treated before the London Court of Justice." Service of notice of a writ out of the jurisdiction was willingly given.

(ii) The modern policy of promoting England as a place for trial
(a) The condonation of "forum shopping."

The desire to promote England as a place for trial can be seen in cases involving the courts' discretionary power to stay actions for injustice to the defendant. These arise generally where jurisdiction has been founded on presence or residence of the defendant in England. It has frequently been argued by defendants who wish to obtain a stay of the English proceedings that the plaintiff is "forum shopping." This is an argument that would be available to courts if they were unwilling to take jurisdiction but it has met with no success. The House of Lords in the Atlantic Star(32) made it easier for a defendant to obtain a stay by looking at extreme incovenience as amounting to injustice to the defendant. This being enough for a stay rather than having to show the narrow traditional idea of vexation or oppression. However, where a plaintiff can show some real advantage in coming to England the action is unlikely to be stayed. The facts of the Atlantic Star were unusual in that the plaintiff could show no real advantage in coming to England only the negative advantage of a report adverse to it, which was available in Belgian proceedings, not being available here. The number of times a stay is actually granted is unlikely therefore to increase dramatically. As Lord Wilberforce said in the subsequent case of Camilla Cotton v Grandex, in this context it had to be born in mind that in principle the English courts are open to all.(33) In the later case of MacShannon v Rockware Glass Ltd,(34) where a stay was granted, the House of Lords was unconvinced that the plaintiff could point to a real advantage in coming here.

(b) The international dispute.

An attitude has developed in the Court of Appeal that if a dispute is of an international nature which could be tried either in England or abroad it might as well be tried here. This shows a more positive desire for trial to take place in England than the rather negative attitude that it will not count against trial if the plaintiff is "forum shopping". The leading case is Baroda v Wildenstein.(35) The dispute concerned the authenticity of a painting sold in Paris by the defendant, an art dealer of international repute, to the plaintiff. Both were French residents. The defendant had a writ served on him whilst fleetingly in England. The Court of Appeal refused to stay the action. Lord Denning, after agreeing that he would stay an action which was wholly foreign, said that the "art world is so international in character today that this issue has itself something of an international character. The parties on either side are citizens of the world."(36) The action might as well be tried here as in France. This device can also be found in cases involving the exercise of the courts' discretion to serve writs out of the jurisdiction under Ord. 11 R S C.(37) Where e.g. all the elements of the tort are committed in this country there is a substantial connection with England which justifies taking jurisdiction. In Baroda v Wildenstein however, the claim to jurisdiction was based on the presence of the defendant, a ground which other countries may well object to. To take jurisdiction in such a case shows a strongly nationalistic spirit and the strength of the desire to promote England as a place for trial.

3 Pro-Plaintiff or Pro-Defendant Rules

Interpretation of the Brussels Convention to favour the Defendant.

(i) Protection of the defendant and enforcement of judgments.

Protection of the defendant has been a traditional policy under civil law systems.(38)   A narrow interpretation of the Convention inevitably favours the defendant.   Protection of the defendant has been regarded by the Court of Justice as an essential pre-requisite for liberal enforcement of judgments throughout the EEC.(39)   Trust between the Contracting States is based on the avoidance of infringements of the territorial sovereignty of others and the provision of adequate safeguards for the defendant. If the defendant were exposed to jurisdiction in any Contracting State the plaintiff chose, he would have a justifiable complaint. The defendant would have increased problems of having to defend himself.   Any subsequent judgment would be capable of enforcement throughout the EEC. Contracting States would be reluctant to enter into a multilateral Convention which exposed their citizens to this danger or which lacked adequate procedural safeguards for the defendant. It is for this reason that ex parte proceedings, such as the English "Mareva" injunction and its continental equivalents, have been held to be outside the scope of the Brussels Convention. Stressing the inconvenience to the defendant of having to defend away from home shows a pro-defendant attitude because one could equally well talk of the inconvenience to the plaintiff of having to pursue the defendant abroad.

This pro-defendant tendency is also clear from the interpretation adopted in some Art.5 cases. This article is designed, inter alia, to help the plaintiff. He is given the option of invoking it and the defendant can not demand that trial take place in his domicile instead. The grounds of jurisdiction used in Art.5 are based on a connection with the forum but again it is the plaintiff who invokes them and if he choses to sue the defendant in the latter's domicile the defendant cannot prevent this. Yet, as has been seen, the narrow interpretation of Art.5 has tended to minimise any advantage to the plaintiff. In Somafer, the Court went as far as denying that Art.5 was designed to help the plaintiff. The justification for Art.5 was said to be solely in the interests of justice.(40) The Court agreed that the sort of exceptions found in Art. 5 were often used in national laws to help the plaintiff in a parochial way but that this was inappropriate in a Community Convention so some other justification for Art.5(5) would have to be found. Looking for substantial contacts with the forum that lead to the efficacious conduct of the proceedings leads to Art.5(5) being interpreted narrowly to require the foreign company to have a permanent place of business in the forum. The desire to protect the defendant is not taken to the extreme of depriving Art.5 of any effect. In Reinwater the wide definition of the place of the harmful event was adopted because to apply the place of acting as the sole definition would, in most cases, add nothing to the basic idea of suing the defendant in his domicile.(41) The Court of Justice did not fall into the trap of depriving this concept of any meaning. This contrasts with applying a limited mechanical view as the English Court did in George Monro.

(ii) Protection of the defendant from "forum shopping".

There was considerable academic criticism of the potentialities for "forum shopping" within Europe under the pre-Brussels Convention law.(42) Its avoidance is an objective which is even more important in the context of a multilateral Convention.(43) "Forum shopping" is objectionable because it is unfair to the defendant and so deterring it is part of the policy of protecting the defendant and ensuring mutual trust amongst Contracting States. The overlapping bases of jurisdiction under the Convention do allow some scope for abuse by the plaintiff but the narrow interpretation of Art.5 limits this. In De Bloos the United Kingdom government made representations for a narrow interpretation of Art.5(1) for this very reason(44) and the Court of Justice adopted this course. Where there is a contractual agreement on jurisdiction it is a moot point whether this comprises a form of pre-dispute "forum shopping" by the party whose standard form contains the choice of jurisdiction clause.(45) There is nothing wrong where the other party willingly and knowingly agrees to the clause. The conduct is more questionable and is more likely to be termed "forum shopping" where there is no notice of and consent to the clause by one of the parties. Interpretation of Art.17 which makes the evidential requirement of writing difficult to satisfy, is designed to protect the defendant and can therefore be seen as an attempt to exclude this type of behaviour.

The pursuit by the Court of Justice of policies which favour neither party.

(i) Equality of treatment of the parties regardless of the forum.

One of the arguments used by the Court of Justice for giving an independent Community meaning to bases of jurisdiction is equality of treatment of the parties.(46) If Contracting States were to define terms themselves, different interpretations would mean that a defendant would be favoured in one country because of the definition adopted there whereas in another country, under a different definition, the effect would be to favour the plaintiff. This can lead to "forum shopping". Moreover, it is not in the interests of either party that there should be a disparity in the way that they are treated in different States. In one case this may favour the plaintiff, in another it may happen to favour the defendant. The principle of equality of treatment should also apply vis a vis two plaintiffs or two defendants and not just between plaintiff and defendant. It there are two defendants from different States who injure one plaintiff, defining Art. 5(3) in terms of the place of injury would result in uniform treatment for both defendants. On the other hand, if there are two plaintiffs injured by different defendants this would point to the place of acting. To deal with these problems of equality of treatment in multi-plaintiff and multi-defendant cases the Court of Justice in Reinwater adopted a flexible definition of the place of the harmful event in terms of the place of acting or injury.(47)

(ii) Protection of the weaker party.

Although it has on several occasions interpreted the Brussels Convention to protect the weaker party, the Court of Justice has not made any attempt at an overall definition of who the weaker party is. Instead it has adopted an ad hoc approach with the identity of the weaker party depending on the provision of the Convention. In a tort case where Art. 5(3) is used the weaker party is the plaintiff who has been injured. A desire to help him was one of the factors leading to the wide interpretation in Reinwater.(48) Also, looking at the place of injury, as their definition does, would protect the weaker party, presupposing that the plaintiff lives where he is injured and will want to sue there. The Advocate-General expressly said that the flexible interpretation of Art. 5(3) would fit in with the principle of protection underlying other provisions of the Convention. In cases involving the evidential requirement of writing under Art. 17 the weaker party is the one who is subject to the standard form of contract used by the stronger party. The stereotype here will be the defendant who is the weaker party and is now arguing against jurisdiction being taken under Art. 17. This is what happened in Galeries Segoura where a narrow interpretation was taken of Art. 17 with jurisdiction being unavailable under it.(49) The plaintiff could, of course, use Arts. 2 or 5 - which he could not do if Art. 17 applied - but since Art. 5 is itself narrowly construed the result is to push the plaintiff towards suing in the defendant's domicile. The upshot is that although both Reinwater and Galeries Segoura adopted the same underlying policy, its application led to entirely different results. The identification of this policy is particularly helpful in explaining those difficult cases where a liberal interpretation has been taken. It can also help one predict how certain provisions in the Convention will be interpreted. The special provisions dealing with maintenance payments (Art. 5(2)), insurance contracts (Art. 7) and consumer contracts (Art. 14) are all designed to protect the weaker party and should be interpreted liberally where this achieves that objective.(50) In contracts of employment the weaker party is the employee. The obligation referred to under Art. 5(1) has very recently been interpreted as being that which is characteristic of the contract, in effect giving jurisdiction to the country of employment. Thereby helping the plaintiff and giving jurisdiction to the country whose law would be applicable under the Contractual Obligations Convention.(50a)

(iii) The desire to help the European business community.

The ultimate aim of the Brussels Convention is to remove legal obstacles to trade within the EEC in order to help the European business community. This is why simplification of enforcement procedures was required.(51) This aim arises as a policy in a number of cases. It is wider than other policies in that it looks not just at the parties to this dispute but at the class of persons the Convention is aimed to help. In Colzani Estasi Solatti v Ruwa(52) the Court of Justice was inclined to take a strict interpretation of the requirements set out in Art. 17 but it was clear that the desire to help the business community meant that there was a limit to how strict this interpretation should be. Art. 17 did not require the choice of jurisdiction to be expressly and specifically agreed upon. This consideration led to a more liberal attitude towards Art. 17 in Case 23/78 Meeth v Glacetal.(53) There, the Court of Justice had to decide whether Art. 17 prevented a court, before which proceedings had started pursuant to a choice of jurisdiction clause, taking into account a claim for a set off connected with the legal relationship. The Court noted the policy objective of avoiding superfluous procedure under the Convention and held that it did not. It shows the Court of Justice typically taking a teleological viewpoint.

The switch in emphasis under English Law

The effect of the traditional narrow interpretation of Ord. 11 has been to favour the defendant. This has been quite deliberately sought. In Ord. 11 cases the emphasis has been on protecting the defendant and putting obstacles in the way of the plaintiff. In the Hagen(54) Farewell L J said any ambiguties in the wording of the heads of Ord. 11 or doubts about the exercise of the discretion are to be construed in favour of the defendant.(55) The court also sees if the plaintiff has a probable cause of action(56) and requires a full and frank disclosure of all relevant facts when the plaintiff

makes his ex parte application for service out of the
jurisdiction. When it exercises its discretion to take
jurisdiction, the court regards the defendant's convenience as
a special consideration(57) and if trial in England is
incovenient to him this will weigh against taking
jurisdiction.(58) A double standard is applied and the present
writer can find no case where it was said that it would be
inconvenient for the plaintiff to go abroad and therefore the
discretion should be exercised in favour of taking jurisdiction.
There have been reported cases where it is clear from the
facts that this was the situation.(59) This double standard also
applies in relation to the significance of the plaintiff's
residence. A plaintiff's residing in England is not a factor to
be used in favour of using the discretion to take
jurisdiction.(60) On the other hand, the discretion to allow
service abroad has been refused, taking into account that the
plaintiff's residence is abroad.(61)

In cases where jurisdiction has been expanded there is
always the suspicion that this was done to help the plaintiff.
In the World Harmony(62) a liberal interpretation of corporate
presence was taken to protect plaintiffs who face particular
difficulties when wishing to sue foreign incorporated
shipowners. Hewson J referred to the common practice of
shipowners forming companies which are incorporated in
Liberia or Panama and registering their ships there under a
flag of convenience and then operating these ships through
entirely independent operating companies positioned across
the globe. This exposes plaintiffs to the tremendous
incovenience of having to sue in Liberia or Panama, countries
with which the dispute has no real connection. The problem
was surmounted by taking jurisdiction because of the presence
of an operating company here. The case is a good illustration
of how the desire to help the plaintiff is not dictated merely
by a crude principle that plaintiffs are better than defendants
but by a realisation that in the modern commercial world the
plaintiff can be quite vulnerable. The clearest evidence of
this policy comes from Castanho v Brown. The House of
Lords(63) stressed that the advantage to the plaintiff in
obtaining higher damages in Texas outweighed any possible

disadvantage to the defendant in trial abroad and discharged an injunction restraining the plaintiff from proceeding in Texas.

4 Certainty or Flexibility
The Brussels Convention and the pursuit of certainty

(i) Certainty

In civil law systems certainty and predictability are regarded as vital jurisprudential virtues.(64) They are virtues which are particularly important in the context of the Brussels Convention. Certainty in the law of jurisdiction is clearly desirable from the parties' point of view. Particularly if they are businessmen since the ultimate objective of the Convention is to remove obstacles to business within the EEC. Certainty is also vital from the Contracting States' point of view when it comes to enforcement of judgments. In De Cavel v De Cavel the Advocate-General pointed out that semi-automatic enforcement requires that a court be able to tell virtually at a glance whether a judgment is one to which the Convention applies.(65) Uncertainty would jeopardise the trust on which liberal enforcement is based. Too much flexibility in interpretation of the jurisdictional bases could lead to States taking an excessively wide jurisdiction and thus endangering good relations between States, which was one of the dangers under the old law. Narrow bases of jurisdiction were introduced to avoid this and so interpretation had to be narrow.

The desire for certainty has been used as a reason for giving a Community meaning to words used in the Convention. If the phrase in question is unknown under national legal systems a Community meaning will provide more certainty. In Industrial Diamond Supplies v Riva(66) the Court of Justice gave a Community meaning to "ordinary appeal" under Arts. 30 and 36, which deal with stays pending appeal. The Court of Justice was faced with widely differing interpretations of this phrase under national legal systems and in some the phrase was completely unknown.Moving to the second stage, the Court of Justice defining a word or phrase with a Community meaning, certainty is again important. Certainty requires that there should not be a multiplication of the bases of jurisdiction. In Somafer(67) the Court of Justice held that the general basis of jurisdiction under the Convention is domicile and Art. 5 is an exception and only to be used as such. This meant that Art. 5 is to be narrowly construed. The Court applied this principle to Art. 5(5). It required an "agency, branch or other establishment" to have a permanent place of business and have a management which can negotiate with third parties so that they will know there is a legal link with the parent body. The extension of the parent body must be under its control and will not be so if it is an independent body which is free to organise its own work and hours, is free to represent rival firms, and merely transmits orders but does not participate in their completion and execution.(68) When it comes to the requirement under Art. 5(5) that the dispute arise out of the operations of the branch, agency or other establishment the Court took an equally narrow construction. This covers the agency's contractual or tortious obligations concerning the management, and undertakings entered into by the agency on behalf of the parent and non-contractual obligations arising from the activities of the branch.(69) But if the agency sells a defective product manufactured by the parent and the essence of the claim is defective manufacture the dispute does not seem to come within these criteria. Certainty dictated that a narrow interpretation be given to Art. 17 in Galeries Segoura.(70) There, the Court of Justice excluded a unilateral declaration in writing confirming the choice of jurisdiction clause, although the wording of Art. 17 could be interpreted literally to cover this. The Court of Justice looked at the rationale of the provision and then applied this to its interpretation. Being certain as to the legal relationship between the parties was the reason for the evidential requirement under Art. 17 and its interpretation had to help achieve this objective.

(ii) Trial in the most appropriate forum

Other jurisprudential objectives are sometimes pursued, even at the cost of certainty. The Court of Justice has shown a concern that trial be held in the most appropriate forum. It can lead to flexibility of interpretation and to that extent has a jurisprudential element within it. Appropriate is being used here in the same sense as it is used under the English courts' discretion under Ord. 11 R S C. A place of trial can be regarded as being appropriate if there is a particularly close connection between the facts of the case and that country and if it is convenient from a litigational point of view that trial should take place there. Art. 5 is justified as an exception to Art. 2 because of "the existence, in certain clearly defined situations of a paricularly close connecting factor between a dispute and the court which may be called upon to hear it, with a view to the efficacious conduct of the proceeding."(71) In Reinwater the Court said that under Art. 5(3) both the place of acting and of injury can be helpful from the point of view of the evidence and the conduct of the proceedings. Therefore both concepts were used in tandem.(72) The place of injury as a single definition would exclude the place of acting -except where this also happened to be the domicile - but that place was closely related to the cause of action and so should be reflected somewhere in the definition. Similarly, when interpreting Art. 5(1) in De Bloos the Court looked at the specific obligation forming the basis of the legal proceedings and not at any obligation.(73) This has the effect of closely linking the particular dispute to the forum. Also the Court looked at the question of litigational convenience and interpreted Art. 5(1) so that the governing law was likely to be the same as the place of performance of the obligation in question. This would produce the desirable result of the forum applying its own law.

The English values

(i) The desire for certainty
The bases of jurisdiction in English law remained constant for many years. Only recently have the heads of Ord. 11 been given a wider interpretation. Residence and submission have usually been given a narrow interpretation. Where flexibility is most apparent is in the exercise of the courts' discretion to allow service out of the jurisdiction or to stay actions for injustice to the defendant. These discretionary powers, like

any discretion, inevitably cause uncertainty in the law but it is not as to whether we have jurisdiction. The discretion operates in a negative way. Actions already commenced may subsequently be stayed, permission to allow service out of the jurisdiction may be refused although one of the heads of Ord. 11 is satisfied. The discretionary powers cannot operate to give jurisdiction where no basis is satisfied. Furthermore, discretionary powers are exercised on the basis of well understood criteria which have not changed radically over the years. More uncertainty has been created by the twisting of facts so as to bring them within Ord. 11 in Distillers v Thompson and Castree v Squibb. None the less, these cases follow earlier authorities in confining the head of Ord. 11 in question to wrongful acts in the forum. They only allow a limited degree of flexibility by giving a wide view to the concept of a wrongful act.

(ii) The policy of not usurping Parliament's role

The leading case is the Siskina(74) where the wide interpretation of Ord. 11 r 1(I)(i) adopted by the Court of Appeal was rejected by the House of Lords because it offended against this policy. The Court of Appeal introduced an entirely new basis of jurisdiction into English law, founded on the presence of assets belonging to the defendant, a basis of jurisdiction found in many other countries. A "Mareva" injunction requires, inter alia, the presence in England of assets belonging to the defendant. If an injunction is interpreted to include a "Mareva" injunction for the purposes of the head of Ord. 11 in question, jurisdiction would be available simply on the basis of assets here. The House of Lords were alarmed by this and Lord Hailsham said that changes in rules of practice were a matter for the Rules Committee which is a legislative body entrusted by Parliament with a particular task and it would be wrong for judges deciding an individual case to usurp its functions. Lord Diplock went further and said that it might even require legislation by Parliament to enact such a fundamental change. The heads of Ord. 11 are regarded as being statutory and are to be interpreted like a statute.(75)

5 Expansion and Restraint

The result of pursuing the policies set out above has usually been to give a restrictive interpretation to the bases of jurisdiction under the Brussels Convention, with jurisdiction being unavailable in the forum. Restraint seems to be deliberately sought and in this sense one can call it a policy but if it is such it is not an independent policy. It is sought because it achieves the objectives and fulfils the policy considerations adopted by the Court of Justice.

The traditional English position has been one of restraint, particularly in the use of Ord. 11. However, there has been a deliberate desire to expand jurisdiction in recent years. In some cases expansion may have been sought because the courts wished to promote England as a place for trial, as happened in Buttes v Hammer where the international dispute device was adopted, or because they wished to help plaintiffs. These two motives form separate policy objectives. One emphasises the interests of the forum and the other the interests of the plaintiff. Distillers v Thompson involved a deliberate desire to expand jurisdiction but why was this? The case cannot be explained on the grounds of promoting England as the best place for trial since the Privy Council was deciding if New South Wales would have jurisdiction, although an expansion of the definition in that case would help English courts when faced with similar facts. The result helps the plaintiff yet Lord Pearson seemed to be solely interested in the defendant and whether the result was fair to him.(76) There are other cases where the decision was even more clearly influenced by a desire to expand jurisdiction. The most remarkable is Evans Marshall and Co. v Bertola SA(77) where jurisdiction was taken under Ord. 11 despite the fact that there was a Spanish choice of jurisdiction clause in the contract, and thus the plaintiff was going against the parties agreement in seeking trial here and the issue was whether under Spanish law the contract was properly terminated. The Court of Appeal said that the case was exceptional. Despite the fact that it involved the marketing of sherry in England and thus had a strong connection with this country it is hard to see how one could use Ord. 11 if one really regards it as a basis of jurisdiction only to be used exceptionally. Had the defendant been properly served, e.g. by being resident here, prima facie the action would have been stayed as being in breach of the foreign choice of jurisdiction clause. This was a case where the defendant was not so served but instead was seeking to use Ord. 11 which places an even heavier burden upon him. Yet trial was allowed here.

6. Inter-relationship of the policies

The Brussels Convention is of recent origin and all the Court of Justice decisions on it have occurred since 1973. It is natural therefore that although a large number of policy considerations have been adopted by the Court of Justice these all appear to be consistent with each other. The major policies of seeking uniformity, taking account of the reaction of other States, protecting the defendant and promoting certainty have all led to a narrow interpretation of the bases of jurisdiction. There are other less important policies; promoting trial in the most appropriate forum, protecting the weaker party and achieving equality of treatment of the parties, regardless of the forum. But these are not necessarily inconsistent with the major policies. Protecting the weaker party will sometimes favour the plaintiff but may equally well favour the defendant. Equally, the policy of promoting trial in the most appropriate forum has led to a narrow interpretation in some cases and a wide one in others.

The position is different under English law. Some of the major policy considerations flatly contradict each other. The traditional policies of respecting the territorial sovereignty of others and protecting the defendant lead to a narrow interpretation of Ord. 11. The more recent desire to expand Ord. 11 is directly contrary to this and the policies of helping the plaintiff and promoting England as a place for trial lead to expansion of jurisdiction in areas other than Ord. 11. It is not surprising that the English policies lack consistency since they are the product of over a century of case law. The desire to expand is only in the process of evolving and a tension exists between the traditional policy of restraint in using Ord.11, and this more modern policy.

III ADOPTION BY AN ENGLISH COURT OF THE POLICIES OF THE COURT OF JUSTICE

The Adoption of a Teleological Approach

It will require a major change in technique for English courts to reject a literal interpretation of bases of jurisdiction in favour of a teleological approach. There are no great practical problems in this given that these new bases stem from an International Convention. This sort of approach has already been used by English courts when interpreting statutes based on other International Conventions and our rules of statutory interpretation allow recourse to aids such as reports preceeding such Conventions in order to discover their purpose. S.3(3) of the Civil Jurisdiction and Judgments Act 1982 goes further by providing that reports preceding the Conventions "may be considered in ascertaining the meaning or effect of any provisions of the Conventions and shall be given such weight as is appropriate in the circumstances".

The Adoption of New Policies

It will need a change in attitude before English courts openly admit they are adopting policy considerations when interpreting bases of jurisdiction. There should be no great problems in actually adopting these policies where they stem from the origin of the rules being an International Convention. The desire to achieve uniformity of interpretation throughout the EEC and to avoid overlapping jurisdiction are policies which are obviously absent from traditional English law on jurisdiction but are central to a multilateral Convention seeking to harmonise jurisdiction rules. Where a phrase has to be defined, a new independent meaning should be attempted rather than the English courts using national concepts and definitions. In the case of jurisdiction against foreign companies under Art. 5(5) there may be a temptation for English courts to define the concept of a "branch, agency or other establishment" by looking at the copious English case law on corporate residence through an agent. This temptation should be resisted. One cannot imagine the English courts searching for the common core of the national legal systems of Contracting States to find the sort of definition that the Court of Justice would give. The best solution is therefore to refer interpretation of the Convention to that Court whenever possible.

The adoption of new policies is going to be more difficult where these run counter to our existing policies. The desire for certainty in the law which is important for a multilateral Convention should not on the face of it cause too many problems for English courts. It is true that the existing English law on jurisdiction has a strong element of uncertainty and can be said to show a policy of seeking flexibility in the law. But this flexibility is most evident when the English courts are exercising their discretionary powers. The absence of flexibility in the jurisdiction rules and in their interpretation makes it clear that this would be a completely wrong policy to pursue in this new context. The policy of discouraging "forum shopping is understandable in the context of the Brussels Convention. But it is impossible to reconcile with the modern English policies of expanding jurisdiction, helping the plaintiff and promoting England as a place for trial. The adoption of this new policy therefore needs to be coupled with a reassertion of the traditional policy of taking a narrow jurisdiction and an abandonment of the modern expansionist policies.

The Reassertion of Traditional Policies

The concern with not infringing the territorial sovereignty of other States expressed by the Court of Justice is matched by the traditional concern for the comity of nations in English law. If the English courts adopt their long-standing attitude towards Ord.11, that it should be used sparingly, and then equate this with Art. 5 there will be few problems. Some provisions of Art. 5 should be equated with Ord. 11 even if they are not the equivalent under non-EEC law. Think of the case of jurisdiction against foreign incorporated companies. This has traditionally been dealt with under presence and not under Ord. 11. However, it comes under Art. 5(5) of the Brussels Convention. It is essential that Art. 5(5) be narrowly interpreted, whereas under our traditional law the interpretation of this form of jurisdiction has been more liberal than with Ord. 11 cases. It is also important to remember that the traditional pro-defendant bias in Ord. 11 cases fits in well with the pro-defendant policy of the Court of Justice. We should also equate the discretionary element in Ord. 11 with Art. 5. One of the policies underlying interpretation of the latter has been to look for the most appropriate forum. This has not influenced the interpretation of the heads of Ord. 11 but it is an important consideration under the English discretion. The jurisprudential policy of not usurping Parliament's role is one that is applicable to the Civil Jurisdiction and Judgments Act. It is a policy which leads to a restrained interpretation and this is essential if one is to achieve the objectives of the Brussels Convention.

The Abandonment of Recent Expansionist Policies

What must be prevented is any attempt to widen the interpretation of Art. 5 by pursuing the recent policies of expanding jurisdiction, favouring the plaintiff and promoting England as a place for trial. The clearest manifestations of the last policy have occurred in cases involving the courts' discretionary powers to stay actions for injustice to the defendant, since no such discretion exists under the Brussels Convention this policy may not arise in such a naked form when interpreting the Convention. However, a desire to expand jurisdiction and to help the plaintiff are policies which have influenced interpretation of bases of jurisdiction under English law and are the direct opposite of the new pro-defendant policy of restraint required by the Court of Justice. Abandonment of the existing pro-forum policy will also affect the law on jurisdiction agreements. The present law encourages trial here if there is an English choice of law clause whereas the Court of Justice has adopted a policy of protecting the weaker party and has given a narrow interpretation to Art. 17 thereby precluding exclusive jurisdiction in the forum.

CONCLUSION

The policies pursued by the Court of Justice are different from those of the English courts, particularly the recent pro-plaintiff, pro-forum English policies. Provided the context in which the new rules have evolved is always born in mind there should be no insurmountable problems in our courts adopting the policy considerations expoused by the Court of Justice. It should not be forgotten that the Brussels Convention is a multilateral Convention, which seeks to harmonise the rules on jurisdiction within the EEC and that it is more concerned with enforcement than the reform of bases of jurisdiction. Accordingly it uses bases which look to the past and to the common core of civil law systems and which have therefore been interpreted in a conservative and narrow way. The unfortunate thing is that it has taken so long for bases of jurisdiction for the most part agreed in a 1968 Convention to become part of English law. For it is in the period since then that the modern pro-plaintiff, pro-forum policies have evolved in England. We must think of the new law as being rooted in the past and forget about the most recent English policies and rely upon our traditional attitudes towards jurisdiction. If this is done the Convention will be interpreted in the spirit and manner intended by the Court of Justice.

FOOTNOTES

(1) For both Conventions see [1978] O J L 304/1 and [1978] O J L 304/77. The latter is a version of the Brussels Convention amended in the light of the Convention of Accession. From now on in this article whenever reference is made to the Brussels Convention this is referring to this amended version. S.2 of The Civil Jurisdiction and Judgments Act 1982 gives the Brussels Convention (set out in Schedule 1 of the Act) the force of law.

(2) See S. 3(1) of the Civil Jurisdiction and Judgments Act 1982.

(3) Brown and Jacobs, "The Court of Justice of the European Community", ch 12 (1977); Machenzie Stuart, "The EEC Court of Justice and the Rule of Law", pp76-77; Marsh, "Interpretation in a National and International Context" (1973), pp82-90; Court of Justice of the European Communities, Judicial and Academic Conference of 27-28 Sept 1976, papers by Kutscher and Dumon; Bredimas, "Methods of Interpretation and Community Law" (1977).

(4) Case 33/78 Somafer S A v Saar-Ferngas A G [1978] ECR 2183, 2190; [1979] 1 CMLR 490, 501.

(5) Case 21/76 [1976] ECR 1735; [1977] 1 CMLR 284.

(6) [1944] K B 432.

(7) [1971] A C 458.

(8) [1980] 1 W L R 1248.

(9) Case 29/76 [1976] ECR 1541; [1977] 1 CMLR 68. See also Case 133/78 Gourdain v Nadler [1978] ECR 733, 749; [1979] 3 CMLR 180, 195 - 196 and in Case 814/79 State of Netherlands v Ruffer [1981] 3 CMLR 293.

(10) Case 25/76 [1976] ECR 1851; [1977] 1 CMLR 361.

(11) [1976] ECR 1735; [1977] 1 CMLR 284.

(12) EEC Bull Supp 12/78 p29.

(13) Case 14/76 [1976] ECR 1497, 1508; [1977] 1 CMLR 60, 81.

(14) [1976] ECR 1735, 1756; [1977] 1 CMLR 284, 295.

(15) [1976] ECR 1497, 1516 - 1517; [1977] 1 CMLR 60, 76.

(16) [1976] ECR 1497, 1510; [1977] 1 CMLR 60, 82. See also Case 139/80 Blanckaert and Willems P V B A v Luise Trost [1981] ECR 819; [1982] 2 CMLR 1.

(17) See O'Connell, "International Law", Vol I 2nd ed 1970, pp256 - 257.

(18) See L T U v Eurocontrol, op cit (footnote 9), p1559, pp97 - 98.

(19) See Giardina, 27 I C L Q 263 (1978).

(20) See generally Schermers, 22 Am J Comp Law 444 (1974).

(21) See the cases listed in Somafer [1978] ECR 2183, 2196-97; [1979] 1 CMLR 490, 496 - 497. See generally Kohler, 1982 European L Rev 3; Kloss in "The Law of the Common Market" (ed Wortley 1974) p189; Rasmussen 15 CMLR 249 (1978).

(22) Case 12/76 [1976] ECR 1473; [1977] 1 CMLR 26. See also Case 14/76 Establissments A de Bloos SPRL v Bouyer SA [1976] ECR 1497, 1511; [1977] 1 CMLR 60.

(23) [1976] ECR 1735, 1750 - 1751; [1977] 1 CMLR 284, 288.

(24) LTU v Eurocontrol, op cit footnote 9; Gourdain v Nadler, op cit footnote 9.

(25) [1978] ECR 2183, 2191; [1979] 1 CMLR 490, 502.

(26) See amended protocol on interpretation of the Brussels Convention [1978] L 304/987, Arts. 2 and 3.

(27) [1979] AC 210, 254.

(28) [1944] 1 K B 432, 437.

(29) Employers Liability Assurance Corp v Sedgwick Collins and Co [1927] A C 114, 115.

(30) [1902] 1 K B 342 (C A).

(31) [1968] 2 Lloyds Reps 158. For United States proceedings arising from the same facts see The Bremen 407 U S 1 (1972).

(32) [1974] A C 436.

(33) [1976] 2 Lloyds Reps 10, 14.

(34) [1978] A C 795.

(35) [1972] 2 Q B 283.

(36) Ibid, pp292 - 293.

(37) Buttes Gas and Oil Co v Hammer[1971] 3 All ER 1025.

(38) See Smit, 21 ICLQ 335 (1972).

(39) See the Advocate-General's opinion in Case 125/79 Denilauler v SNC Couchet Freres [1980] ECR 1553, 1579; [1981] 1 CMLR 62, 71.

(40) [1979] ECR 2183, 2191; [1979] 1 CMLR 490, 502.

(41) 1976] ECR 1735, 1747 - 1747; [1977] 1 CMLR 284, 300. See also Colzani where a narrow independent meaning was given to Art. 17, otherwise the plaintiff would be deprived of using Arts. 2 and 5. See also Effer v Kantner (not yet reported) 1982 European L Rev 235.

(42) Droz, "Competence Judiciare et Effets Des Judgements Dans le Marche Commun" (1972) para 7.

(43) Weser, "Convention Communautaire sur la Competence Judiciare et L'Execution Des Decisions" (1975) para 28.

(44) [1976] ECR 1497, 1503; [1977] 1 CMLR 60, 66.

(45) Compare Lord Reid in The Atlantic Star with Grainger, Ottowa L Rev 416, 417 (1974).

(46) Somafer op cit footnote 4, p2191, p503. See also Case 24/76 Estasis Salotti Colzani v Ruwa [1976] ECR 1831, 1845; [1977] 1 CMLR 345, 349.

(47) See the Advocate-General's opinion in Reinwater [1976] ECR 1735, 1756; [1977] 1 CMLR 284, 295 - 296.

(48) See the opinion of the Advocate-General [1976] ECR 1735, 1758; [1977] 1 CMLR 284, 297, 298.

(49) Op cit (footnote 10); a narrow interpretation was also applied in Colzani op cit (footnote 46).

(50) See Art. 1 of the Protocol and Case 784/79 Porta-Leasing GMBH v Prestige International SA [1980] ECR 1517; [1981] 1 CMLR 135.

(50a) See Ivenel v Schwab (not yet reported) 1982 European L Rev 328.

(51) Jenard Report, p350.

(52) Case 24/76[1976] ECR 1831; [1977] 1 CMLR 345.

(53) Case 23/78 [1978] ECR 2133; [1979] 1 CMLR 520.

(54) [1908] P189.

(55) Ibid p201. See more recently the Siskina [1978] 1 Lloyds Reps 1, 4.

(56) John Russell and Co Ltd v Cayzer Irvine and Co Ltd [1916] 2 A C 298.

(57) Williams v Cartwright [1895] 1 Q B 142, 149.

(58) See e g Coast Lines v Hudig and Veder [1972] 2 Q B 34.

(59) See e g Mauroux v Pereira [1972] 1 W L R 962.

(60) Mackender v Feldia [1967] 2 Q B 590.

(61) Rosler v Hilbery [1625] Ch 250. But it has not always told against him, see Buttes v Hammer [1971] 3 All E R 1025.

(62) [1967] P341.

(63) [1981] A C 557, Per Lord Scarman at p576.

(64) Merryman, "The Civil Law System" (1969) p51; Cappalletti et al, "The Italian Legal System" (1967) pp191 -195; See also De Winter, 17 ICLQ 706 (1968) who was writing about the pre-Brussels Convention Continental rules on jurisdiction.

(65) Case 143/78 [1979] ECR 1055, 1073; [1979] 2 CMLR 547, 554 -555. This meant on the facts that Art. 1 of the Convention was interpreted widely so that a freezing of assets of a couple in the process of a divorce was outside the scope of the Convention unless it was clear the matrimonial relationship played no part in the distribution of the property.

(66) Case 43/77 [1977] ECR 2175; [1978] 1 CMLR 349.

(67) [1978] ECR 2183, 2191; [1979] 1 CMLR 490, 502.

(68) Blanckaert and Willems PVBA v Trost [1981] ECR 819; [1982] 1 CMLR 1

(69) Op cit (footnote 67), pp2192 - 1293; pp503, 504.

(70) [1976] ECR 1851, 1863; [1977] 1 CMLR 361, 373.

(71) Somafer op cit (footnote 4) p2191 p502. See also Kohler, 1982 European L Rev 3, 16 and 17.

(72) [1976] ECR 1735, 1746; [1977] 1 CMLR 284, 299.

(73) [1976] ECR 1497, 1511; [1977] 1 CMLR 60, 83.

(74) Op cit (footnote 27).

(75) See Lawton L J in the C A; [1979] A C 225, 236.

(76) [1971] A C 458, 468.

(77) [1973] 1 W L R 349.

INCORPORATION OF THE EUROPEAN CONVENTION ON HUMAN RIGHTS INTO UNITED KINGDOM DOMESTIC LAW

Roger Kerridge

I

The United Kingdom was, on 4th November 1950, one of the first thirteen Member States of the Council of Europe to sign the Convention for the Protection of Human Rights and Fundamental Freedoms, usually called the European Convention on Human Rights. She was, on 8th March 1951, the first country to ratify the Convention which came into force on 3rd September 1953, when it had been ratified by ten states. Since this latter date the United Kingdom has been bound, in International Law, by the provisions of the Convention.

"To ensure the observance of the engagements undertaken by the High Contracting Parties in the ...Convention,"[1] it was provided that there should be set up a European Commission of Human Rights and a European Court of Human Rights. It was further provided - and this was the really revolutionary aspect of the Convention - that the Commission could receive petitions from individuals who claimed to be the victims of violations of the Convention. Nevertheless, this right of individual petition depended on there being a declaration under Art 25 of the Convention by the relevant respondent State. In other words it was for each State which ratified the Convention to decide whether or not it would go on to grant the right of individual petition. It was also for each State to decide whether it would recognise as compulsory the jurisdiction of the European Court of Human Rights.

Although the United Kingdom had been very quick to ratify the Convention, she was much slower to grant the right of individual petition. The right of individual petition became effective on 5th July 1955 when it had been recognized by six High Contracting Parties.[2] The United Kingdom did not recognize the right of individual petition until 14th January 1966 when she recognized it for three years. This was extended for a further period of three years in 1969, for two years in 1972, two years in 1974, five years in 1976 and then for five years in 1981.

It seems that most people in the United Kingdom know almost nothing about the Convention. Even lawyers and politicians, who really ought to know better, often seem to assume either that the Convention is a meaningless set of principles without any provisions for enforcement and/or that it is something to do with the Common Market. In a debate in the House of Lords in 1976 a former Lord Chancellor referred more than once to the fact that the European Court of Human Rights sits in Brussels.(3) It does not, it sits in Strasbourg and the reference to Brussels would seem to indicate that the speaker thought it was a Common Market institution. No one corrected him.

Very slowly, things are changing. The publicity surrounding cases where the United Kingdom has appeared as respondent before the Commission or the Court in Strasbourg does have an effect and a number of cases have recently hit the newspaper headlines.(4)

II

English lawyers have, traditionally, been educated to despise both declarations of rights and written constitutions. But it is also part of the English legal tradition that abstract discussion should be avoided and that emphasis should be placed on the concrete.

An enormous amount has been written about the European Convention on Human Rights(5) and in the past ten years or so there has been a growing debate about whether the Convention should, in some way, be incorporated into English domestic law. The debate is now affected by political prejudice, even though many of the participants deny this. It is submitted that an attempt should be made to clarify the political bias at the outset because that makes the debate easier to follow. The point is that the political bias has changed. The Convention was originally signed and ratified when a Labour Government was in power. It was also a Labour Government which originally granted the right of individual petition in 1966. It was a Conservative Government which only extended that right for two years, rather than three, in 1972 and again in 1974 (this seems to have been quite deliberate) and a Labour one which extended it for five years in 1976. Up to that point it seems clear that it was Labour which was broadly in favour of the Convention and the Conservatives who lacked enthusiasm. Actually, there may have been some difference of approach as between governments, of whatever political persuasion, on the one hand and their supporters, on the other. Governments are advised by civil servants and civil servants as a group, especially those in the Home Office, are reputed to feel only muted enthusiasm for the Convention. The civil service bias against the Convention may actually infect any government, of whatever persuasion, while such government is in power.

Nevertheless, the change in the general political bias is shown by the attitudes taken in the House of Lords to an attempt by Lord Wade to incorporate the European Convention into English law. His Bill of Rights Bill was actually given a third reading in the House of Lords in December 1979.(6) After the second and before the third reading a Select Committee had produced a Report on the Bill and in the voting on that Report fifty six members of the House of Lords were in favour of incorporation while thirty were against.(7) The voting was not along strict party political lines but the bias was clear. Lord Wade is a Liberal and he carried with him all the Liberals except one. The significant thing is that most Conservatives also voted for the Bill while most Labour peers voted against. Actually, the group most clearly in favour consisted of the hereditary peers. Only two hereditary peers voted against, one a Labour peer and the other a first generation Conservative. So why the sudden, but apparent, switch in political support?

"Human Rights" is neither an attractive nor an accurate term. There are two types of "rights" which can be designated Human Rights (though few are strictly "rights" in the Hohfeldian sense). On the one hand there are Civil and Political rights and on the other hand there are Social and Economic rights. Those whose political bias is to the Right will generally show little interest in the latter. Those on the Left may say that there is no point in having Civil and Political rights unless the citizen also has Social and Economic rights. Social and Economic rights are difficult, if not impossible, to guarantee so the ultimate reaction of the Left may be that there is no point in guaranteeing any rights at all. Someone on the Right may feel that it is perfectly proper to guarantee only Civil and Political rights.

The European Convention on Human Rights covers Civil and Political rights. It should therefore appeal to the Right and to the Centre. Not only does the Convention exclude Social and Economic Rights but it includes at least one right to which some politicians on the Left may take exception in principle. Article 1 of the First Protocol to the Convention states that

> "Every natural or legal person is entitled to the peaceful enjoyment of his possessions. No one shall be deprived of his possessions except in the public interest and subject to the conditions provided for by law and by the general principles of international law".(8)

The voting in the House of Lords on the third reading of Lord Wade's Bill is easier to understand than is the previous history of support, or lack of it, for the Convention.

III

There are really two questions relating to the incorporating of the European Convention on Human Rights into English domestic law. Firstly, can the Convention be incorporated? Secondly, if it can, what would be the effect of incorporation? To some extent the two questions must overlap. The form of incorporation, if it is possible, may have a bearing on the effect of incorporation. At this point there is a temptation for those who are opposed to incorporation to make everything sound horribly complicated and then suggest that there is no point in proceeding further. It is submitted that this is wrong.

The Convention can be incorporated. There may be difficulties about entrenchment but there are no fundamental difficulties about incorporation. This point will be dealt with in greater detail later. The real question relates to the effect of incorporation.

Most discussions about the possibility of incorporating the European Convention on Human Rights into United Kingdom domestic law start by asking whether the United Kingdom needs a Bill or Rights(9) and then go on to suggest, as a semi afterthought, that if it is to have one it would probably be best to incorporate the Convention. The bias is basically insular. The European Convention on Human Rights was ratified by the Government of the United Kingdom more than thirty years ago. Its provisions are binding on the United Kingdom in International Law. It is submitted that the basic question should not be whether we incorporate but by what right, or what logic, we do not incorporate. It has been suggested from time to time that certain provisions of the Convention itself, in particular Articles 1 and 13, oblige ratifying states to incorporate.(10) The present writer would not go as far as to argue this - the point verges on the pedantic - but he would say that once a state has ratified then the logic of its position demands incorporation or some very clear explanation of why incorporation is unnecessary or impossible. In fact the European Convention may not be the only treaty to which this argument applies but that in no way invalidates it. Those who think it is an invasion of the Sovereignty of the United Kingdom to demand that the Convention be incorporated into domestic law should ask themselves by what logic the Convention was ratified in the first place. If we are, and were, incapable of incorporating it, then the United Kingdom should not have become a party. In that case the honest and logical course would now be to denounce the Convention under

Article 65. Such denunciation would be effective -for the future - after six months.

At the moment there are, in relation to any Member State of the Council of Europe, five different options as regards the European Convention on Human Rights.

(i)   a State can simply not ratify the Convention, this was the position of France and Switzerland before 1974. Such an option is quite logical, though it may be politically embarrassing either at home or abroad;

(ii) a State can ratify the Convention but neither incorporate it into its domestic law nor grant the right of individual petition under Art 25. This was the position of the United Kingdom before 1966;

(iii) a State can ratify the Convention and incorporate it into its domestic law but not grant the right of individual petition. This approach is suspect. The suspicion must be that a State which has incorporated the Convention into its own domestic law but is unwilling to grant the right of individual petition to Strasbourg is one which keeps a relatively close rein on its own courts and tribunals;

(iv) a State can ratify the Convention and grant the right of individual petition to Strasbourg but not incorporate it into its domestic law. This has been the position of the United Kingdom since 1966;

(v) a State can ratify, grant the right of individual petition and incorporate, this is the most complete possible protection.(11)

The question now being discussed is whether the United Kingdom should move from category (iv) to category (v). What is the real reason for the State to prefer to be in category (iv) when it seems that category (v) is so much more logical? It is submitted that the real reason why some States originally chose to grant the right of individual petition but not to incorporate the Convention into their domestic law was not that they were afraid of getting into trouble for committing wholesale violations of the Convention. If they feared this they would, according to taste, have put themselves into categories (i), (ii), or (iii); in other words they would not grant the right of individual petition. States which granted the right of individual petition but which did not incorporate the Convention into their domestic law were States which were basically smug. The West Germans, with little in their recent history to be smug about, were naturally among the first both to incorporate the Convention into their domestic law and to grant the right of individual petition. The States which have granted the right of individual petition but which have not incorporated are the Scandinavians, Ireland and the United Kingdom.

When the Convention was ratified by the United Kingdom in 1951, it is almost certain that those who were responsible for the ratification had been advised that there would be no question of the United Kingdom authorities' violating any of its provisions.(12) The smugness survived until about two years after the United Kingdom had granted the right of individual petition in 1966. Since then it has been much less widespread.

IV

So what are now the substantive arguments against incorporation? Those who oppose incorporation nearly always begin by saying that the position in the United Kingdom is fine, that United Kingdom law already complies fully with the Convention and that incorporation is therefore unnecessary.(13) This is the old smug line. It is a line which requires a certain amount of wilfull blindness or special pleading. Those who take this approach skim quickly over, or around, all the decisions from Strasbourg to the effect that there have been violations of the Convention by the United Kingdom authorities. Anyway, the position is basically unsound because if the United Kingdom is fully complying with the Convention there can be no possible harm in incorporation. It would have no effect. Every time a litigant was rash enough to suggest to one of Her Majesty's judges that the authorities were involved in a violation of one or other of the rights guaranteed by the Convention, the judge would merely have to explain to the litigant that they were not. Why should anyone be worried by this? It is precisely because they do not think that this would happen that some people oppose incorporation. And those who oppose incorporation show this by the other reasons they give for their opposition. These, of necessity, often contradict the idea that the United Kingdom is incapable of violating the Convention. The arguments are, in what the present writer thinks is their reverse order of seriousness:

(i)   that it would increase the number of lawyers until we had as many as the Americans;

(ii)   that it would encourage crackpots to invade the courts;(14)

(iii)   that there would be difficulties about remedies;

(iv)   that there would be confusion as to whether individuals (and bodies which have nothing to do with the state) could be held responsible for violations of the Convention in litigation before the domestic courts;(15)

(v)   that it would waste litigants' time while they exhausted domestic remedies in the United Kingdom before taking their complaints to Strasbourg;

(vi)   that it would be of no real use if, for example, a dictator tried to take over;(16)

(vii) that it would bring the United Kingdom judges into politics;(17)

(viii)   that incorporation would throw the domestic law of the United Kingdom into confusion.(18)

(i) This point was made by Lord Lloyd in the House of Lords debate on the Select Committee Report on Lord Wade's Bill of Rights Bill.(19) It is a red herring. The Americans have got nothing to do with the European Convention on Human Rights. It is true that America seems to be a good place for a lawyer to make a living and that this may have some slight connection with the fact that the American Constitution contains entrenched rights but it is almost certainly much more significant that the United States has a Federal Legal System, that many of the judges are elected, that there is the widespread use of juries, that there is lots of divorce, that there is limited state medical care and that American lawyers are allowed to operate a contingency fee system whereby they may receive a percentage of the damages in civil actions. If it is to be suggested that the incorporation of the European Convention on Human Rights into domestic law causes an unreasonable increase in the number of lawyers who practice in the countries where such incorporation has taken place, then statistics should be called for from Germany, Austria, Belgium, Italy and so on. Any such statistics would then have to be examined with some care. All kinds of things affect the number of lawyers who practice in a particular country. The United Kingdom does not have a high proportion of lawyers per head of the population but this is partly because English lawyers are afraid to do sums and so are self disqualified from being too much involved in business, which is left to the accountants.(20) It is also partly because lawyers do not run the Civil Service in the United Kingdom as, for example, German lawyers run the German Civil Service. But anyway, no one who opposes the incorporation of the European Convention on Human Rights into English domestic law has produced any statistics, or even any argument, that Germany, Austria, Belgium, Italy and so on are over inhabited by lawyers. This point can now be left.

(ii) If the European Convention on Human Rights were to become part of the domestic law of the United Kingdom it is true that a certain number of crackpots would start making absurd applications to the Courts in the United Kingdom and that this would be a nuisance. But surely the Courts could cope! The Registry of the European Commission of Human Rights has always been full of would be applications from people whose grasp of reality has been somewhat less than total and at one time the vast majority of even the most absurd applications were actually registered and put before the Commission so that they could be formally declared inadmissable. This is one reason why the statistics for cases registered by the Commission's Secretariat may be rather misleading. But the position was tightened up in 1977(21) and fewer of the really crazy cases are now registered. The present writer may not be alone in thinking that the registration of absurd cases by the Commission in Strasbourg might in the past have had some indirect effect on its decisions. If you spend too much time in the examination of the completely mad you may get to the stage where the half mad seems sane. But this has nothing at all to do with the United Kingdom courts. The number of cases going to Strasbourg has always been very small. There have never been more than two hundred cases registered against the United Kingdom in any one year and at the present time there are about one hundred each year.(22) Just suppose that one third of these applications are from crackpots and that this number is multiplied by ten, or even twenty, when the crackpots get a chance to litigate on their own doorstep. The effect on the caseload of English courts would not be worth considering. Measures can be taken to declare crazy litigants vexatious and anyway the problem is tiny. If they are not pestering the courts they will be bothering someone else so the increase in real work that will be generated will be, virtually, nil.

(iii) If the European Convention on Human Rights were incorporated into English Domestic Law there would in many cases be no need for a complainant to seek a direct remedy because his use of the Convention would be defensive. To take a simple example, someone who alleged a violation of Art 7 of the Convention - which says that penal laws shall not be retrospective - could plead the Article as a defence when proceedings were brought against him. He would not need to take the offensive. In many other cases the complainant would have a prima facie right of action in tort. For example, if a statute were passed giving the police the right to pull suspects' fingernails out while questioning them, then this would contravene Art 3 of the Convention -which prohibits (inter alia) torture. The statutory provision would be void and the nail pulling would be tortious. It would also be criminal; the intentional infliction of grevious bodily harm.

There might be some cases where a complainant would need to take the offensive to protect some right granted under the Convention e.g. the right of privacy (Art 8). Wallington & McBride suggest that all violations of the Convention should be prima facie tortious but not necessarily criminal.(23) This seems reasonable. There are a number of points here that could be discussed at some length. Should some violations of the provisions of the Convention be made criminal? Should some violations which are tortious result in the award of exemplary damages? Who should be able to bring proceedings in respect of violations which have occurred? Should there be some sort of machinary to prevent the passing of legislation which conflicts with the Convention? There is insufficient space in this paper for the further discussion of these matters and there is certainly room for disagreement on some or all of them. But these points are relatively peripheral to the much more important question as to whether the Convention should be incorporated. The main point should be discussed and decided first. If it is decided, in principle, that the Convention should be incorporated, then these points can then be dealt with later. It is a Civil Service device to suggest that a particular form of legislation is impossible because of some technical problem in a peripheral area.

(iv) The problem usually referred to as that of the "Drittwirkung der Grundrechte" involves a discussion as to whether not only the state and its agencies, but also private individuals and non state bodies, can be held responsible before domestic courts for violations of the European Convention. The problem is to some extent linked with the question of remedies discussed immediately above. The problem is limited. Basically it arises in relation to Art 8 of the Convention which protects the right to privacy. There are arguments both for and against the view that Art 8, as drafted, was intended to be capable of invocation against acts done by private individuals. Anyway, this point can be clarified if and when the Convention is incorporated. The preferred view seems to be that remedies should be provided against violations by private individuals.

(v) One of the points made in the debates in the House of Lords on Lord Wade's Bill of Rights Bill was that it takes an awfully long time for a case to pass through the Strasbourg machinery and that an applicant will waste even more time if he has to go through the English courts first. Golder(24) it was said, took five years to work his way through the various stages in Strasbourg and that was more than enough.

This argument begs one question. It assumes that the complainant would obtain no redress in the United Kingdom and would then have to go to Strasbourg. It is to be hoped that, where there has been a violation of the Convention, this assumption would generally be wrong. If Golder had been able to plead the Convention before the United Kingdom courts he should have been able to get his complaints sorted out much more quickly and without needing to complain to Strasbourg at all. Anyway, even without the incorporation of the Convention into United Kingdom law, many complainants do have to go through the United Kingdom Courts before complaining to Strasbourg. They have to do this in order to exhaust their domestic remedies.(25) It is true that they cannot plead the Convention direct before the United Kingdom courts but they must still do everything that they reasonably can to obtain relief. This means that they must try to obtain redress in the United Kingdom without actually relying directly on the Convention and then, if they fail, they go on to Strasbourg.

But there is another point. If the Convention were to become part of the domestic law of the United Kingdom, and if a complainant were to fail to obtain redress in the United Kingdom and were then to take his case to Strasbourg, the case would be likely to proceed more quickly in Strasbourg.

This would happen for two reasons. First, assuming that the complaint raised a point which seemed worthy of real discussion, the application could be expedited in Strasbourg. There is usually a serious backlog of cases before the Human Rights Commission and the big danger is that the relatively small number of cases which raise real issues get delayed along with the run of the mill nonsense cases and so are not spotted until they are put before the Commission some years after their original registration. This happens partly because cases are usually introduced by the applicants themselves, without legal representation, in a relatively incoherent form. Applicants to Strasbourg often introduce technically serious complaints sandwiched between numerous other complaints which are quite unworthy of consideration -at least from the Commission's point of view. Second, the complaint would be presented coherently with arguments already made out. The case would not really start from scratch twice. In fact, it is suggested that if complaints were dealt with in the United Kingdom either instead of, or before, going to Strasbourg they would generally be dealt with more quickly than under the present system.

(vi)If the United Kingdom were to incorporate the European Convention on Human Rights into its domestic law and if a dictator were to take over in, say, a sudden military coup then such incorporation would probably be of little effect. The dictator would promulgate a new constitution, scrap the incorporation of the Convention, denounce the Convention at Strasbourg (as the Greek Colonels did) and give his secret police whatever instructions he thought necessary to preserve public order.

Nevertheless, this scenario is a bit far fetched. If a totalitarian regime were going to take over in England, it is more likely that it would do so gradually. Even Hitler was originally elected to power. An incorporated Human Rights Convention would stand in the way of a gradual take over. It might not be a big obstacle but it would be some sort of hindrance. Its abrogation, in whole or part, would be one of the, presumably numerous, warnings that things were moving in an unfortunate direction.

The people who drafted the European Convention on Human Rights were anxious to preserve Democracy. The history of Western Europe since 1945 has been, from that point of view, reasonably encouraging. Only one state has ratified the Convention and then had to denounce it and that state, Greece, has since returned to the democratic fold and is again bound by the provisions of the Convention. It is not suggested that ratification of the Convention is proof against dictators, nor that the grant of the right of individual petition or the incorporation of the Convention into domestic law are complete guarantees against totalitarian take overs. But it is submitted that they are all steps in the right direction.

(vii) It has been suggested that if the European Convention on Human Rights were made part of the domestic law of the United Kingdom then the judges would be dragged into politics. For this reason, some judges do not want incorporation. In the debates on Lord Wade's Bill, Lords Morris, Diplock and Denning all spoke at varying times against incorporation. The view is not unanimous. Lords Scarman and Salmon were in favour. Lord Scarman is one of the leading protagonists of some form of Bill of Rights. His main reservation about the incorporation of the Convention is that it would not be enough. In a sense, the surprise in all this is to find Lord Denning in the camp of those opposed to incorporation. As one who has often been accused of being both innovative and political he might have been expected to take the opposite line. Maybe Lord Denning is really more fundamentally traditional that is generally realised. Or possibly he feels that the incorporation of the Convention would be just too much temptation. In a debate on the Second Reading of Lord Wade's Bill in the House of Lords on 25th March 1976(26) Lord Denning implied that he thought that the European Convention on Human Rights granted rights which were wider than those granted to the citizen under Common Law. This is not the general line taken by those who oppose incorporation. Lord Denning may have thought that he would be embarrassed by his own interpretation.

So would the judges be dragged into politics? Professor Griffith(27) thinks that they are already in politics up to their eyebrows. And there is no doubt that there are occasions when, quite apart from the interpretation of the Convention, judges will be accused of political involvement. The only way to prevent this is to take certain fields - say industrial relations - away from them. This does not work perfectly because the judges still have to decide what has been taken away and what they are not allowed to touch. Lord Scarman(28) thinks that the judges ought to be more robust. It can be shown that the doctrine of Parliamentary Sovereignty, whereby judges always interpret the will of parliament as being absolute is relatively modern. It can be argued that the judges should not give parliament such a free hand.(29)

In fact the judges are in politics whether they like it or not. The law and politics are inextricably interwoven. In any Constitution the judges have to decide whom they will obey. That is a political decision. In a state with a written Constitution, the written Constitution may tell them, but they have to decide whether they will obey the written Constitution. In time of revolution the judges must decide whether, or at what point, they will take orders from the new government rather than the old. The Glorious Revolution of 1668 became legally effective when the judges showed that they would regard acts passed by the new King and Queen in "Parliament" as being good law.(30)

The real question is whether the judges are now prepared to be more adventurous than they have been for the past 200 years or so. Professor Griffith would say that they already suffer from a political and a class bias; they are too conservative. Yet, in spite of what he says, their conservatism may actually make them unwilling to strike down legislation passed by the House of Commons however unreasonable it may appear.(31) The politics of this issue may actually be inverted. It has been suggested that politicians from the best families are those most reluctant to fight a class war.(32) May not the same be true of the judges? Still, this becomes a digression and the solution is simple. If it is thought that the incorporation of the European Convention on Human Rights into United Kingdom domestic law would bring the judges too much into politics then it is always possible to have a separate court (call it a "Constitutional Court" if you like) to deal with questions which relate to the Convention and its incorporation. It is submitted that this solution is clumsy and unnecessary. It would mean that a litigant might have to go to two separate courts in relation to the same matter, and that would really be turning the clock back. An ordinary judge would have to decide the case without paying any attention to its Human Rights aspects even though the knew perfectly well that it might raise a point under the Convention. That would be for someone else. He could not move into "politics". Still, the difficulty could be to some extent avoided by getting the "Constitutional Court" to take the case first or to give some sort of declaratory judgement on the point before it came before the ordinary courts. Either way, the whole procedure would be a lot less clumsy than having to take the case to Strasbourg.

(viii) So we finally return to the charge that the incorporation of the European Convention on Human Rights into United Kingdom domestic law would throw the whole of such domestic law into confusion. This is in flat contradiction of the theory that United Kingdom law already complies with the Convention (or is in some way superior to or in advance of the Convention). If the law of the United Kingdom is already in a state of compliance there is no room for the slightest confusion. The people who were responsible for the ratification of the Convention in 1951, and who presumably thought that United Kingdom law did in all respects comply with its provisions, would not have thought that its incorporation would have caused any confusion. It would have been simply pointless. There was, for example, no point in enacting a provision to the effect that no one was to be tortured when United Kingdom law did not permit torture anyway. And so on and so forth.

So where is the confusion? Someone who makes a speech in the House of Lords and who says at the same time that English law is in advance of the Convention and that its incorporation would cause confusion is himself surely guilty of causing confusion.(33)

If the incorporation of the European Convention into English law is going to cause confusion it must be because English law does not measure up to the requirements of the Convention. So the simplest course would be for those who allege the shortfall to explain, as clearly as is reasonably possible, where it lies. This they do not do. The confusion allegation is made in very general terms. The point of wanting to identify the areas of confusion is certainly not pedantic. The European Convention may conflict with United Kingdom law either because the Convention grants the subject too many rights or because United Kingdom law grants him too few. If the areas of conflict can be approximately identified then the argument can be narrowed. It might be possible for everyone then to agree that the Convention is defective (too wide) and it would then be true that incorporation would be a bad thing. But nobody really seems to say this. The people who have looked closely at the Convention and at the possible areas of difficulty seem nearly always to agree that United Kingdom law, about which United Kingdom lawyers are usually so smug, is defective.

In fact the present writer does not think that the areas of conflict would be large, or terribly important. The idea that incorporation would throw United Kingdom law into wholesale confusion is almost certainly nonsense. The people who ratified the Convention in 1951 and who thought that United Kingdom law already measured up to its standards were wrong, but they were not very wrong. Incorporation of the Convention would be a step in the right direction. It would not be a step of enormous significance.

V

There is one difficulty about incorporation which is seldom referred to directly by its opponents but which probably does influence them. This concerns the relationship between decisions taken by national courts on the one hand and the Commission and Court in Strasbourg on the other. What happens if the national courts interpret the Convention differently from the bodies in Strasbourg? Theoretically this should be no great problem. The Court in Strasbourg should have the last word. But in practice there may be some embarrassment about letting a court which is staffed largely by foreign law professors overule the House of Lords.

All cases which go to Strasbourg are dealt with first by the Commission. When the Commission was originally set up, it was envisaged that its members would not necessarily be lawyers and there is nothing in the Convention to say that members of the Commission shall be lawyers.(34) By contrast, Article 39 (3) of the Convention states that members of the European Court of Human Rights "must either possess the qualifications required for appointment to high judicial office or be jurisconsults of recognised competence." So it seems that the original idea behind the setting up of the Commission was that it was to be a body that did not necessarily consist of lawyers and whose main task, if it thought that there might be a violation of the Convention, was to effect a "friendly settlement" under Art 28 (b).

Things did not work out quite as planned. The Commission has tended to act more like a Court than the Convention would imply. Since the Commission was set up, only one non-lawyer has served as a member.(35) There has, in general, been no distinction of substance between the kind of person who has been appointed to serve as a member of the Commission and the kind who has been appointed to serve as a member of the Court. Some members of the Commission have later been promoted to the Court.(36) The effect has been that the Commission has tended to operate as if it were a court and the Court has tended to operate as if it were a higher court - a court of appeal from the Commission. This does actually make sense. Articles 26 and 27 of the Convention set out various grounds on which the Commission must declare applications to it to be inadmissable. For example, the Commission may not deal with an application unless domestic remedies have been exhausted.(37) And it may not deal with an individual application if it considers it to be "incompatible with the provisions of the ......Convention, manifestly ill founded, or an abuse of the right of petition." (38) These provisions are badly drafted. "Incompatible with the ......Convention" is taken to mean "outside the scope of the Convention" which is quite different and "manifestly ill founded" seems to have been taken to mean "unproved as a matter of fact." But the point is that the task of deciding for example, whether an application is outside the scope of the Convention is clearly one which should be undertaken by lawyers. So the decisions of the Commission on, for example, questions of "compatibility" are clearly questions which require it to interpret the Convention.(39) This being so, such decisions may conflict with decisions taken by domestic courts. Is it probable that there will be such conflict here?

When the Convention was originally drafted, and when it was first ratified, it seems probable that the representatives of the ratifying states thought that these states would not violate the Convention. This point has already been made above in relation to the United Kingdom but it applies generally. If someone represents the government of a state which regularly tortures its citizens he would be ill advised to agree to the ratification of a Convention which forbids torture - especially if the Convention has enforcement procedures. So juicy violations by ratifying governments are unlikely. Wholesale violations are most probable where a government changes and the government which originally ratified is replaced by one made of sterner stuff. This happened in Greece when the Colonels took over. This was, it is to be hoped, an exception that proved the rule. It is even clearer that a state will not grant the right of individual petition under Art 25 unless it thinks it is going to behave itself. The granting of the right of individual petition is a mark of self confidence.

Therein lies a catch. If every state which had granted the right of individual petition had then proceeded to comply with the provisions of the Convention, the Commission and Court in Strasbourg would have had nothing to do. The Commission would merely have had to churn out a string of decisions explaining how every application to it was inadmissable. Applications would have continued to come in from cranks and from prisoners who had no better way of spending their time but most people would soon have forgotten that the Strasbourg machinery existed.

Life is not like that: lawyers are not like that. How could a body of highly qualified lawyers spend all its time declaring all applications to it to be inadmissable? Some cases had to be declared admissable. They were.

It is not being suggested that all decisions coming from Strasbourg which decide that there have been violations of the Convention are wrong. Nevertheless the bias should be watched. There will be a temptation for the Commission, and for the Court, when in doubt to find that there have been violations of the Convention. To this extent it is probable that the interpretation of the Convention by the bodies in Strasbourg will be more generous than its interpretation by domestic tribunals, especially if such domestic tribunals have other work to do. It has been suggested above that if the Convention is incorporated into United Kingdom law then it could either be interpreted by the ordinary courts or by a special "Constitutional" court. A special court would probably fall into the temptation to interpret generously. The ordinary courts would be less likely to do so. That is an argument for having the Convention interpreted by the ordinary courts. But that leads to the likelihood of conflicts about interpretation between, say, the House of Lords and the bodies in Strasbourg.

The problem may not be as serious as all that. The Court in Strasbourg is marginally less likely to be biased towards a generous interpretation than the Commission.(40) And it would be the decisions of the Court which would matter.

That still leaves the point that a foreign court, staffed largely by law professors will, in effect, be able to tell the highest United Kingdom courts that they are wrong. The problem does not arise at the present time because United Kingdom courts are not called on to interpret the Convention, but it could arise as soon as they are. Suppose that someone alleges a violation of the Convention by the United Kingdom authorities and takes his complaint to the United Kingdom courts. He fails. He goes to Strasbourg. He succeeds. The Strasbourg Court may say that the House of Lords interpreted the Convention too narrowly - incorrectly. There are some United Kingdom lawyers who would greet such a result with apoplexy. But why? The Strasbourg Court is, in effect, a supra national court. It is perfectly logical that it should be an ultimate court of appeal. Its place in the Human Rights heirarchy is equivalent to that held in matters of Community Law by the Court of Justice of the European Communities in Luxembourg. No one can say that a decision taken by foreigners is prima facie less authoratative than one taken by true born Britons. So does it matter that the Human Rights Court is manned by judges who are part time and who, when they are not in Strasbourg, are usually law professors?

In the United Kingdom legal system top ranking judges are all recruited from the practising bar. It is a good system. At least, practising barristers think it is a good system. So there may be some unhappiness about allowing decisions to be taken in Strasbourg by a Commission or a Court which is largely staffed by academics. Are such misgivings well founded? The point is that most Continental legal systems rank the academic lawyer higher than he is ranked in the United Kingdom. It is not odd that Human Rights judges are academics if most other judges are recruited from the academic world. Maybe the British are wrong to be frightened at the idea of academics as judges. But if it is really thought that academics should not be judges in the United Kingdom then the United Kingdom authorities should think twice about sending them to be members of the European Commission of Human Rights or to be judges of the European Court of Human Rights. That is the oddity. There would be something wrong with sending someone who would not be qualified to hold high judicial office in the United Kingdom to become a member of a body which would, in effect, hear appeals from the highest United Kingdom courts. The remedy is to send someone of sufficient rank. Either academics, ex civil servants and so on should be entitled to hold judicial office in the United Kingdom or someone who is so entitled should be sent to Strasbourg.

There is another oddity about the recruitment of members of the European Commission of Human Rights and the European Court of Human Rights which has nothing specifically to do with the United Kingdom. Members of the Commission and of the Court are, in effect, nominated by governments but it should be noted that every state which is a member of the Council of Europe can nominate one member of the Court(41) while every state which has ratified the Human Rights Convention can nominate one member of the Commission.(42) It is strange that a state can choose a member of the Court when it has not even ratified the Convention let alone recognised as compulsory the Court's jurisdiction. Yet a French judge sat in the Court from the outset, long before France ratified the Convention in 1974. But in practical terms, because far more cases go to the Commission than go to the Court, it is the composition of the Commission which is really odd. There is one member of the Commission for every state which has ratified the Convention. No distinction is drawn between states which have granted the right of individual petition and those which have not. So a member of the Commission from state X, which has not recognised this right, will (in effect) sit in judgement on state Y when an individual application is brought against state Y (state Y having recognised the right). That seems unfair. If state X is unwilling or unable to grant the right of individual petition it should not be entitled to choose a member of the Commission to sit in proceedings to which it itself could not be subject. And this is not just a question of abstract justice. It could affect the care with which members of the Commission and Court are chosen.

One possible justification for allowing a state which has not granted the right of individual petition to supply a member of the Commission to sit in individual petition cases is that such state might later grant the right and its member would have gained experience by the time that cases against that state started to come in. This argument might justify the member sitting for, say, three years before the state which had chosen him granted the right of individual petition but it does not explain or justify cases where members sit for longer

with no sign that the states which choose them will ever ↳
the right.   Anyway, if members really want to pre̲↲e
themselves and gain experience they could do so without
speaking and without voting.

The point could be pursued in greater detail. Suffice it to
say that the Strasbourg machinery might appear to be more
fair if only countries which had granted the right of individual
petition were to supply speaking and voting members of the
Commission or Court when individual petition cases were
being considered.(43)   A reduction in the size of the
Commission would be no bad thing.   It is clear from the
Travaux Preparatoires that when the Convention was being
drafted, worries were expressed about the Commission being
too big.(44) Furthermore, members both of the Commission
and of the Court should be people who are competent practical
lawyers.   This does not mean that they should not be
academics.   But those who interpret the Convention in
Strasbourg   must   resist   the   temptation   to   become   so
accustomed to crazy applications that any application which
has been introduced by a sane applicant seems to have merit
and they must also resist the temptation to seek out violations
of the Convention because so many cases are being, and have
been, declared inadmissable.   If these temptations can be
resisted, the interpretation of the Convention in Strasbourg
and in the domestic courts should not be very different.

VI

So, in concrete terms, what effect would it have if the
European   Convention   on   Human   Rights   were   to   be
incorporated into United Kingdom domestic law? Would there
be more or fewer decisions to the effect that there had been
violations   of   the   Convention   by   the   United   Kingdom
authorities.   Clearly there would be more decisions by the
United Kingdom domestic courts. Without incorporation there
are none. With incorporation there would certainly be some.
What about the position in Strasbourg? Would incorporation in
the United Kingdom be likely to increase or decrease the

number of decisions by the Commission and by the Court to the effect that the Convention had been violated?

The incorporation of the Convention into the domestic law of the United Kingdom would receive publicity. More people would know about their "rights"; more people would demand them; more violations of the Convention would come to light. But why not? The traditional English feeling of distaste for bills of rights is based not so much on there being anything wrong with the rights as on the feeling that setting them out in bills is a meaningless charade. Dicey thought that the Habeas Corpus Acts had "done for the liberty of Englishmen more than could have been done by any declaration of rights."(45) But the clear implication of his objection to declarations of rights was their lack of remedies. If the European Convention was worth ratifying it is worth broadcasting and worth enforcing -easily and cheaply. It is logically indefensible for a state to become a party to an instrument of this sort and then to hope that most of those who are affected will never find out and never ask for their entitlement.

There are some provisions in the Convention which are unsatisfactory. For example, the provisos to Articles 8, 9 and 10 of the Convention are all difficult to construe and must raise difficulties of interpretation.(46) The difficulties can be overcome. The enforcement of the Convention has, on the whole, worked quite well. Any government which is alleged to have violated the Convention and which is then summoned to appear in proceedings in Strasbourg tends to feel that it has been accused of something monstrous but this is to over-react. Touchiness is, in this respect, the converse of smugness.

The United Kingdom Home Office, in particular, seems to have taken the whole thing too seriously. At one time it seems that the Home Office was so worried about complaints by prisoners in United Kingdom prisons to the Human Rights Commission in Strasbourg that orders were given that all letters written by prisoners to the Commission should be photocopied and copies kept. Most of the complaints were a complete waste of time. The prisoners generally knew this. They seem also to have known that the photocopying was going on. A prisoner who wanted to draw the attention of the Home Office to his grievances would often think that it was easier to do so by writing to the Commission than by making a complaint direct. The Commission would, in due course, declare his application inadmissable but meanwhile someone in the Home Office would have made a note about the poor quality of the breakfasts in H.M. Prison Z.

To return to the point - would the incorporation of the Convention into United Kingdom domestic law lead to more or fewer findings in Strasbourg that there had been violations of the Convention? That is a point of national pride. It should not be but it is. If the people in the Home Office could be convinced that incorporation would lead to fewer findings in Strasbourg that there had been violations then they might back incorporation.

The answer here is not straightforward. If the Convention were incorporated more people would know about it. More people would start to make complaints. More people would write to Strasbourg. But many applications to Strasbourg would fail because the applicants had not exhausted their domestic remedies in the United Kingdom and it would be easier for the authorities, at least in some cases, to point to non exhaustion. Yet in another completely different way, incorporation might make it easier for applicants to bring successful applications to Strasbourg.

All applications to the Commission in Strasbourg are, initially, made in writing. If an applicant fails to produce written or documentary proof of the subject matter of his complaint, then the chances are that it will almost certainly be declared in-admissable. Even if the complaint is inside the scope of the Convention and the domestic remedies have been exhausted, the application will be declared manifestly ill founded for want of proof. And that will be so even if written proof is very difficult to come by. So the applications which have been declared admissable by the Commission have nearly always been ones where written proof of the basic complaint has been easily obtained. Take the Golder case,(47) the authorities stopped Golder, a prisoner, from contacting a solicitor. It was easy for him to prove the facts, he had correspondence with the authorities to prove them. The same point can be made about nearly all the applications against the United Kingdom so far declared admissable by the Commission. There was no difficulty about the East African Asians(48) producing written evidence that they had been denied admission to the United Kingdom, no difficulty about Tyrer(49) proving that birching was a punishment administered in the Isle of Man, about Mrs. Amekrane(50) proving that her husband had been returned to Morocco, about "The Sunday Times"(51) proving that a court order had been made preventing it from publishing an article, about Handyside(52) proving that the United Kingdom provided legislation to cover obscenity, about Mrs. Campbell and Mrs. Cosans(53) proving that corporal punishment was administered in Scottish schools and so on and so forth.

But there are types of cases where it is extremely difficult for an applicant to produce written or documentary proof to substantiate his allegations. It is even more difficult if the applicant is not particularly literate. Suppose, for example, that an applicant has been convicted of a criminal offence but alleges that his trial was unfair and that what happened at the trial constituted a violation of Article 6 of the Convention. How can the applicant prove his allegations? It is very difficult. The Commission in Strasbourg has done what it can to remove any theoretical difficulty by devising a special formula designed to declare in-admissable any complaints under Article 6 about an unfair trial. This is the so called "fourth instance formula." (54)

If the domestic courts in the United Kingdom could investigate alleged violations of the Human Rights Convention, they would not be hamstrung by an incapacity to deal with cases unless there was clear written and documentary proof of the complainants' allegations. They would be able to deal with cases where written proof was difficult to come by. They would not be tempted, as the Commission and Court in Strasbourg are almost certainly - if subconsciously - tempted, to lean towards an extended interpretation of the Convention whenever they are dealing with cases where the facts are well documented. They would not, for example, be tempted to find a violation of the Convention because a child might be subjected to corporal punishment in a Scottish state school only to be told that before they reached their decision his parents had already decided voluntarily to send him to an independent school which administered equivalent punishment.(55)

They would almost certainly not insist on proceeding with cases after the people involved had specifically asked to withdraw their complaints. Theoretically the Commission in Strasbourg will not allow an applicant to withdraw his complaint if there is a matter of "general interest" involved. But this must lead to the suspicion that the Commission is trying to make work for itself even when an applicant has lost interest.(56)

Ultimately, then, it is suggested that incorporation of the European Convention on Human Rights into the domestic law of the United Kingdom would not greatly affect the Strasbourg statistics. Some cases which would have proceeded in Strasbourg if there had been no incorporation would instead be dealt with, and hopefully sorted out, in the United Kingdom. Other applications which would have proceeded in Strasbourg in the days before incorporation would not proceed after it because of failure to exhaust the new domestic remedies. But some applications which would have failed in the days before incorporation because of lack of written or documentary evidence might subsequently succeed on the basis that domestic proceedings might produce the evidence. It is submitted that the system as a whole would be much healthier. If the bodies in Strasbourg are determined to look round for cases to get their teeth into, then it is only sensible that they should be sent a fair cross section of different kinds of cases and not be obliged to deal only with cases where documentary proof can be provided without the need for instituting proceedings in the United Kingdom based specifically on a violation of the Convention.

VII

There are now two final questions:

1. It is possible for United Kingdom judges to interpret a document like the European Convention on Human Rights which consists of a number of outline propositions rather than a detailed statutory code?

2. Is it technically possible to incorporate the Convention into the United Kingdom legal system?

Some opponents of incorporation have suggested that United Kingdom judges might have difficulty with a Convention which is drafted less precisely than a United Kingdom statute. It has been suggested that lawyers trained in Civil Law systems feel more at home with a document like the Convention. For example, Anthony Lester(57) says "it might take years to get the English Bench to interpret a Bill of Rights as a living document rather than as an Income Tax Act." The present writer is not clear what this is supposed to mean. If it is being suggested that English judges are only at home with legislation which goes into great detail and which they can interpret quite literally, then the choice of the Income Tax Acts as a point of comparison is both inappropriate and somewhat offensive to Tax Lawyers. For example, in the tax case of Colquhoun v Brooks(58) the House of Lords effectively deleted two words from a statutory provision because they thought it made more sense that way.(59) That is not literal interpretation. One of the reasons why the legislature in the United Kingdom may have adopted the approach of spelling provisions out in great detail may have been to hamstring the judges. This does not imply that they, the judges, lacked imagination.

Mr. Lester's reference to the interpretation of a Bill of Rights as a "living document" is also open to question. If the suggestion is that the interpretation should change (presumably in favour of the citizen) as time passes then this might not be greeted by universal enthusiasm. It is only fair to Parliament that if it is asked to enact a Bill of Rights it should be told at the outset that it is intended that the interpretation of such a Bill will change and be extended, in some way, with the passing of time. But is it intended? The present writer is not sure that a Bill of Rights should be "alive" in some extra special sense. All statutes must be interpreted in the light of circumstances as they exist at the time of interpretation but Mr. Lester seems to want something more. It is true that the Commission and the Court in Strasbourg may have modified their own interpretation of the Convention in favour of the citizen as time has gone by. But the point has been made above that this may be due to a conscious or subconscious need to show that they are doing something useful. It is difficult for them to dismiss every complaint that comes before them. This is nothing whatsoever to do with the distinction between Common Lawyers and Civilians.(60)

Anyway, United Kingdom judges interpret not only statutes but the Common Law itself. Any one who can interpret the Common Law must be able to handle outline principles. There is no reason why United Kingdom judges should be baffled in any attempt to interpret the Convention. United Kingdom lawyers who have argued cases before the Commission and the Court have never, to the present writer's knowledge, been known to say that the interpretation of the Convention presents them with any special kind of difficulty. In the Human Rights field it is submitted that there is no divergence of approach between people whose training is based on Common Law and those whose training is based on Roman Law - the distinction is between good and bad lawyers. Neither the good nor the bad all come from one camp.(61)

So can the Convention be incorporated? Is there any technical difficulty?

There is no technical difficulty in drafting a provision which states that the substantive parts of the European

Convention on Human Rights shall become part of United Kingdom Law and that where there is any conflict between the provisions of the Convention on the one hand, and Common Law or previously enacted Statute Law on the other, then the Convention shall prevail.But what about subsequently enacted Statute Law?   Can a provision be enacted whereby the Convention takes precedence over subsequently enacted Statute Law? This is the problem of entrenchment.

There seem to be five theoretical possibilities.

(i)to provide that the Convention should take precedence over all subsequent United Kingdom legislation, with no provision of any kind whereby a subsequent Act of the United Kingdom Parliament might prevail over it;

(ii) to provide that the Convention should take precedence but subject to a procedure whereby subsequent United Kingdom legislation might prevail if enacted by some special parliamentary majority;

(iii) to provide that the Convention should take precedence unless a subsequent Act (passed in the ordinary way) specifically stated that it was to prevail;

(iv) to provide that subsequent legislation should take precedence unless it contained some formula indicating that it was subject to the Convention;

(v) to provide that the Convention should not take precedence if there were any express or implied conflict with any later Statute.

Possibility (i) is unlikely to be adopted and can, for the purposes of the present discussion, be ignored.

Possibility (ii) would require a new Constitutional Settlement in the United Kingdom.   Nevertheless, such a possibility is by no means as far fetched as it might have seemed, say, ten years ago.   The requirement of a special parliamentary majority would, actually, not be very suitable under the two party system which exists at the moment because even the requirement of say a 60% majority, let alone a 66% or 75% majority, would mean that the main opposition party could, by itself, block all change.(62) A special majority works better in the context of a multi party system. So possibility (ii) is unlikely to be adopted at the moment but might well be thought attractive in the future.

Possibilities (iii) and (iv) are very similar in effect. It is the technicalities which are different. Whether the supporters of incorporation would prefer to adopt the clumsier solution (iv) rather than the neater solution (iii) would depend on whether they thought that the judges would be willing to proceed on the basis of solution (iii). A judge brought up in the traditions of "pure" parliamentary sovereignty and who follows the rules as laid down by Dicey might have some difficulty with solution (iii) so the choice between solutions (iii) and (iv) depends on how the judges are likely to react. Solution (iii) would obviously be neater. If the judges found that their consciences troubled them they could regard it as an exercise in statutory interpretation. Nevertheless this is not really a question of statutory interpretation, it is more fundamental. As Professor Wade puts it(63)

> "in every legal system there must be a basic rule or rules for identifying a valid piece of legislation, whether we call it the grundnorm, like Kelsen, or the ultimate legal principle, like Salmond, or the rule of recognition, like Professor Hart.... This grundnorm ... lies in the keeping of the judges."

Solution (iii) (like solutions (i) and (ii)) requires a change in the grundnorm. It requires what amounts to a (technical) revolution. No statute can effect the change because "for this one purpose Parliament's powers of giving orders to judges are ineffective...it is the judges who are sovereign."(64)

Professor Wade's solution for effecting any change in the grundnorm is to make a change in the judge's oath.(65) There is no way of telling whether this would work until it has been tried, but the present writer thinks that it is certainly worth a try.

If solution (iii) were adopted it would mean that Parliament would be perfectly free to enact legislation in conflict with the Convention but only if it expressly said that it was doing this. The political safeguards would then be substantial.It would not be easy for elected politicians to enact legislation which specifically stated that it contravened a Human Rights Convention which had by that time been specifically incorporated into United Kingdom domestic law.

That is why the opponents of incorporation do not want it in the first place. Those who originally advocated the ratification of the Human Rights Convention, and then the granting of the right of individual petition, should now pursue the logic of their own reasoning to the point where the Convention is incorporated.

FOOTNOTES

(1) Art 19.

(2) Art 25 (4)

(3) 369 HL Deb (1976) 775 at 781 ff.

(4) At the time of writing, there is considerable publicity about cases concerning trades unions, corporal punishment in schools and immigration.

(5) It has been claimed that more has been written about the European Convention on Human Rights than about any other international treaty except for the UN Charter and the Treaty of Rome.

(6) 403 HL Deb (1979) 911.

(7) 396 HL Deb (1978) 1301 at 1395.

(8) It has been suggested that the expropriation of the rights of freeholders under the provisions of the Leasehold Reform Act 1967 might amount to a violation of this Article - see The Law of Real Property, Megarry and Wade, 4th ed p 1149 and see discussion by Kidd in Vol 249 of Estates Gazette at p 31. It is understood that (at the time of writing) there are cases on this point pending before the Commission.

(9) See eg Do we need a Bill of Rights, ed Campbell, 1980 and Wallington & McBride, Civil Liberties and a Bill of Rights, 1976.

(10) See Golsong (1957) 33 BYIL 317; Buergenthal ICLQ Supplement 11 (1975) 79; Golsong (1962) 38 BYIL 445.

(11) It is not as easy as might be supposed to list the states which have incorporated the Convention into their domestic law because incorporation may take different forms. But two states which have not granted the right of individual petition, but have, at least to some extent, incorporated the Convention are Greece and Turkey.

(12) See Report of the Select Committee on the Bill of Rights: House of Lords Paper 176 (1978) Para 25.

(13) See Do we need a Bill of Rights, ed Campbell, 1980 Chpt by Lord Boston "The record of the United Kingdom on Human Rights is ... exemplary." Or Lord Lloyd in a debate in the House of Lords - 369 HL Deb (1976) 775 at 795 "Human Rights have fared a good deal better in this country than in most others, even in those which have ..... Bills of Rights."

(14) See 396 HL Deb (1978) p 1301 at 1366.

(15) This problem is usually referred to as that of the "Drittwirkung der Grundrechte".

(16) See 396 HL Deb (1978) p 1301 at 1329 ff.

(17) See Lloyd (1976) 39 MLR 121 at 126.

(18) See House of Lords debate on Bill of Rights Select Committee Report 396 HL Deb (1978) p 1301 at 1325.

(19) See 396 HL Deb (1978) p 1301 at 1326

(20) There are many more practicing accountants than practicing lawyers in the United Kingdom and the accountants do much of the work which lawyers would do in other countries (especially in the USA). It is high time that the lawyers fought back, but this is not the place to discuss this topic.

(21) See European Commission's Stocktaking 1979 p 4.

(22) The number of cases registered against the UK actually fell each year from 1975 to 1978. This was partly because numbers used to be swelled by the East African Asians and partly because the Secretariat in Strasbourg tightened up on registration generally.

(23) Wallington and McBride, Civil Liberties and a Bill of Rights 1976, Chpt 5.

(24) Application No. 4451/70 - Golder v UK.

(25) Art 26 of the Convention.

(26) 369 HL Deb 775 at 797.

(27) The Politics of the Judiciary - Manchester UP 1977.

(28) English law - The New Dimension - Hamlyn Lecture 1974.

(29) See Scarman, English law - The New Dimension - at page 16 and authorities cited there.

(30) See Wade 1955 CLJ 172 at 188.

(31) Does this - in part - account for Lord Denning's lack of enthusiasm for incorporation? - see 369 HL Deb 775 at 797.

(32) It has been suggested that the Conservative politicians who went to the best schools and who come from the best families are not generally as right wing (in the presently accepted sense of the expression) or "dry" as their less privileged colleagues. The "union bashers" are not the old Etonians.

(33) See 369 HL Deb 1978 p 1301 at pp 1322 and 1325 where Lord Lloyd of Hampstead said ".... we in this country are far in advance of the European Convention" and "...to introduce a Bill or Rights .... would throw practically the whole of our law into a state of total uncertainty."

(34) See Collected Edition of Travaux Preparatoires -Nijhoff 1976 Vol III p 212 - when drafting the Convention the Committee of Experts' drafting sub-committee queried whether members of the Commission needed formal qualifications (presumably legal).

(35) Mr. N. Klecker - the Luxembourg member of the Commission from 1975 - 1981.

(36) The first United Kingdom member of the Commission, Sir Humphrey Waldock, later sat on the Court. Two Irishmen, Messrs Maquire and O'Donoghue, went from the Commission to the Court. The real difference between the people who sit on the Commission and those who sit in the Court is that members of the Commission are worked harder and so need more time for the job.

(37) Art 26.

(38) Art 27 (2).

(39) The Court of Appeal in Guilfoyle v Home Office 1981 1 All ER 943 seems to have decided that proceedings before the European Commission of Human Rights were not "legal proceedings". (though the ratio of the case would be that the applicant was not "a party to legal proceedings"). The case relates to the construction of the Prison Rules 1964 and is not directly related to the construction of the Convention. But the present writer thinks that, in the ordinary sense of the word, proceedings before the Commission are legal proceedings and that applicants are parties to them.

(40) See Morrisson The Dynamics of Development in the European Human Rights Convention System - Nijhoff 1981 - . Morrisson notes that the

Commission is more "activist" that the Court (p 8ff) and that it has been more likely to rule in favour of applicants (p 30).

(41) Arts 38 and 39.

(42) Arts 20 and 21.

(43) The change could probably be effected by a change in the Rules of Procedure.

(44) See Collected Edition of Travaux Preparatoires -Nijhoff 1976 - Vol II p 184.

(45) AV Dicey An Introduction to the Study of the Law of the Constitution 10th ed p 221.

(46) Arts 8, 9 and 10 of the Convention protect the rights to respect for private and family life, home and correspondence; the right to freedom of thought, conscience and religion; and the right to freedom of expression. Each of these Articles has a proviso (8(2), 9(2), 10(2)) but the provisos are rather restricted. Even without a generous interpretation of 8(1), 9(1) and 10(1), a literal reading of the provisos may cause serious problems for the High Contracting Parties.

(47) See footnote 24.

(48) Application Nos 4403/70 - 4419 et al.

(49) Application No 5856/72.

(50) Application No 5961/72.

(51) Application No 6538/74.

(52) Application No 5493/72.

(53) Application Nos 7511/76 and 7743/76.

(54) For what the present writer thinks was a very unfortunate refusal by the Commission to investigate an alleged unfair trial see the Stock case referred to in the 24th Annual Report of Justice at p21 - then constrast this with Golder - where was the greater injustice?

(55) On 25th February 1982 the European Court of Human Rights held that the United Kingdom was in breach of Art 2 of the first Protocol to the Convention because it had failed to respect the right of Mrs Grace Campbell to ensure that the education and teaching of her son Gordon was in conformity with her religious and philosophical convictions in that corporal punishment was used for disciplinary purposes in a state primary school which had been attended by her son. Gordon Campbell had been a pupil at Glasgow Academy, an independent school, since 1979. Corporal punishment is a sanction used in Glasgow Academy.

(56) In Tyrer v UK, application no: 5856/72, the applicant complained about the punishment of birching imposed by a Manx Court. In 1976 the applicant said he wanted to withdraw his application though his lawyers wanted to continue with it. The Commission refused to accede to the applicant's request "given the questions of general interest" (see 1979 Stocktaking p 30). But what questions of general interest were involved? If anyone else on the Isle of Man was sentenced to be birched such other person would have -if he so wished - and he might not -an opportunity to complain to Strasbourg.

(57) Democracy and Individual Rights - Fabian Tract No. 390 at p 15.

(58) 1889 14 App Cas 493.

(59)   What is now s.109 of the Taxes Act 1970 taxes (inter alia) "any trade carried on in the United Kingdom or elsewhere." The House of Lords thought that it was unreasonable to tax a trade carried on elsewhere.

(60)   Lester may want the Convention to be interpreted in the (generous) way in which the US Supreme Court has interpreted the American Constitution - but American judges are, of course, Common Lawyers.

(61)   And, of course, not all United Kingdom lawyers are Common Lawyers. There are the Scots too.

(62)   See Jaconelli - Enacting a Bill of Rights. OUP at p 72 ff.

(63)   HWR Wade Constitutional Fundamentals (Hamlyn Lecture) at p. 26.

(64)   Wade (supra) at pp 26 and 27.

(65)   Wade (supra) at pp 37.

THE CLOSED SHOP AND THE EUROPEAN CONVENTION ON HUMAN RIGHTS

A M Dugdale and H F Rawlings

(1) Introduction

In this essay we analyse the consequences for the operation of the "closed shop"(1) in Britain of the decision of the European Court of Human Rights in Young, James and Webster v United Kingdom(2)(hereinafter the British Rail Case). We shall be principally(3) concerned with ArtII of the Convention, which, so far as relevant, provides:-

"1.   Everyone has the right to freedom of peaceful assembly and to freedom of association with others, including the right to form and to join trade unions for the protection of his interests.

2.   No restrictions shall be placed on the exercise of these rights other than such as are prescribed by law and are necessary in a democratic society....for protection of the rights and freedoms of others."

(2) The Legislative History

The origin of this provision, as with other Articles of the Convention, is to be found in the Universal Declaration of Human Rights, adopted by the General Assembly of the United Nations in 1948.(4)   It is to be noted that the Universal Declaration contains separate Articles on Freedom of Association (Art 20) and the Right to Form and Join Trade Unions (Art 23(4)), and further, that Art 20 not only protects "freedom of association" but also insists that "No-one may be compelled to belong to an association." (Art 20(2)).   Early drafts of the European Convention, promulgated by the Consultative Assembly, followed the pattern of the Universal Declaration, in particular separating "freedom of association" (and dissociation) from the right to form and join trade unions. A number of countries, including the United Kingdom, felt

that the "mere listing" (5) of rights provided by the draft
Convention was insufficiently specific to enable signatory
governments to be clear as to their obligations. An
alternative draft was proposed, based on a more precise
definition of the rights to be protected. In this British draft,
"freedom of association" was retained, but the right to form
and join trade unions was omitted, on the basis that this was
an element in "freedom of association" and did not need
independent protection.

To achieve a compromise, an ad-hoc drafting committee of
the Conference of Senior Officials was constituted. This
committee produced a form of words based on the British
proposals, but which incorporated elements from the Universal
Declaration.(6) One of the elements incorporated made it
explicit that the right to form and join trade unions was
encompassed within freedom of association. This compromise
necessitated, however, that the "freedom to dissociate" (Art
20(2) of the Universal Declaration) had to be excluded from
the Convention. The Conference of Senior Officials reported
that "On account of the difficulties raised by the 'closed shop
system' in certain countries, the Conference in this connection
considered that it was undesirable to introduce into the
Convention a rule under which 'no-one may be compelled to
belong to an association' which features in the United Nations
Universal Declaration."(7) It was in this form that Art II(i) of
the Convention was adopted.

In view of this legislative history, it may occasion surprise
that Art II has been prayed in aid by opponents of the closed
shop. Are not the Travaux Preparatoires conclusive evidence
that Art II was not intended to be inconsistent with the closed
shop? The answer is that the Travaux Preparatoires may be
used as an aid to construction of the Convention only in very
limited circumstances. The reasons for this are twofold.
First, the Convention, as a treaty, must be interpreted in
accordance with the Vienna Convention on the Law of
Treaties, which permits recourse to the "preparatory work of
the treaty" in three circumstances only: to confirm the
interpretation reached by application of the "General rule of

interpretation" in Art 31 of the Vienna Convention; to assist where application of the general rule leaves the meaning of the provision ambiguous or obscure; and to correct where application of the general rule leads to a manifestly absurd or unreasonable result.(8)

The second reason for the limited use of the Travaux Preparatoires is one of principle, "that the interpretation of the Convention must be 'dynamic', in the sense that it must be interpreted in the light of developments in social and political attitudes. Its effects cannot be confined to the conceptions of the period when it was drafted or entered into force....(The Contracting States) did not intend solely to protect the individual against the threats to human rights which were then prevalent, with the result that, as the nature of the threats changed, the protection gradually fell away. Their intention was to protect the individual against the threats of the future, as well as the threats of the past. It follows that....(the Travaux Preparatoires) should be invoked, if at all, as a guide to the general intentions of the Parties....rather than to delimit strictly the scope of the Articles."(9)

Consistently with this general tendency to play down the relevance of Travaux Preparatoires , that element of the majority in the British Rail Case which appeared to hold the closed shop inconsistent with Art II dismissed Travaux Preparatoires in general as "not conclusive" on the meaning of Convention articles, and in any case pointed out that the preparatory works referred only to the "undesirability" of incorporating a right to dissociate, and "and so do not enable one to conclude that the negative aspect of trade union freedom was intended to be excluded from the ambit of Art II."(10) That element of the majority which sidestepped the question of the consistency of the closed shop with Art II did not consider it necessary to deal with the evidence of the Travaux Preparatoires.(11)

(3) The Closed Shop and the Convention

Prior to the British Rail Case, the case-law on the Convention and the closed shop was scanty. In R v Greater

London Council, ex p. Burgess (12), there was an optimistic attempt to challenge a post-entry closed shop agreement entered into by the G.L.C. with a number of unions. One of the grounds of challenge was that the Council, by omitting to have incorporated into the agreement an exemption clause for individuals who had a conscientious objection to membership, had thereby acted in violation of Art 9 of the Convention (guaranteeing freedom of thought, conscience and religion) and that the agreement was void. This argument was dismissed on the short ground that the agreement as it stood was perfectly compatible with the then existing domestic legislation (the Trade Union and Labour Relations Act 1974), and that in any question of conflict between domestic legislation and the Convention, "the statute must prevail because the Convention is no more than an unadopted convention persuasive in its purpose only."(13)

In X against Belgium(14) the applicant alleged that he had been dismissed because of his refusal to join either a Socialist or a Catholic trade union. In the event, because of his failures both to adduce evidence in support of the allegation and to exhaust domestic remedies, the Commission declared the application inadmissable - but the Commission observed that "the very concept of freedom of association with others also implies freedom not to associate with others or not to join trade unions."(15) This statement, being (in English legal terminology) obiter, is of limited persuasive force, and it played no part in the decisions of either Commission or Court in the British Rail Case. Further, in Le Compte, Van Leuven and De Meyere v Belgium,(16) both Commission and Court were able to sidestep an argument that the right to associate implied a right to dissociate by pointing out that the organisation, membership of which was compulsory for the applicants to be able to practise medicine, was a creature of public statutory law, rather than one deriving its existence from the voluntary agreement of private individuals. As such, it was not an "association" within the meaning of Art II to which any freedom to associate (and, hence, any attendant right to dissociate) could apply.

Therefore, both Commission and Court were effectively unencumbered with authority in their respective approaches to the British Rail Case.(17) This absence of case-law can be easily explained, in that in many of the larger countries signatory to the Convention the closed shop is already unlawful under domestic law.(18) Thus, Kahn-Freund (19) noted that "the closed shop has been banned in France (20), in Western Germany (21), in Italy, in Switzerland, in Belgium, but not in the Netherlands or in Sweden." Additionally, neither Austria nor Ireland (22) permit closed shops any legal status. There is no simple or straightforward explanation for the varying legal provisions in these countries, but Forde has drawn attention to the different organisational principles of the national trade union movements, and the implications which these may have for legal provisions. "In some countries it is accepted as axiomatic that freedom of association in trade unions entails freedom not to join....What perhaps explains this attitude....is that the labour movements in those countries are divided along ideological and sometimes confessional lines, so that the very idea of, say, a devout Catholic and supporter of right-wing parties having no legal protection against compulsion to join a Communist trade union is unthinkable."(23) It is interesting to note that this was the position in X against Belgium, the applicant in that case being faced with a choice of a Catholic or a Socialist trade union. This may explain the Commission's apparently greater willingness in that case to infer a right to dissociate, and, given the relevant trade unions' apparent political affiliations and philosophies as expressed in their rule-books, was also a factor in the Commission's (if not the Court's) decision in the British Rail Case.

(4) The British Rail Case

(a) The Background.

The British Rail Case stemmed from the closed shop agreement made in 1975 between British Rail and three railway unions, the NUR, the TSSA, and the ASLEF. That agreement provided that every employee of British Rail had to join one of these unions unless he genuinely objected on grounds of religious belief to being a member of any trade union. At the time that the agreement was made the three applicants were already British Rail employees, but none were members of any union. Subsequent to the agreement they refused to join any of the specified unions for reasons which were primarily political in nature. As a result of their refusal to join, all three were dismissed. Under domestic law no remedy was available in respect of the dismissals, as the then subsisting legislation(24) provided that such dismissals were only to be regarded as unfair if the individuals objected to union membership on grounds of religious belief.(25)

Shortly after their dismissals, the three applied to the European Commission of Human Rights, alleging that the United Kingdom, by enacting legislation which permitted an employer to dismiss employees in such circumstances without remedy, was in breach of Articles 9 (freedom of thought, conscience, and religion), 10 (freedom of expression) and 11 (freedom of association with others). In 1979 the Commission, having earlier found the applications admissible, gave its opinion that the United Kingdom was in breach of Art II, and it accordingly referred the matter to the Court. In August 1981 the Court gave judgement, holding that there had indeed been a breach of Art II. Neither Commission nor Court found it necessary to determine whether there had additionally been breaches of Arts. 9 or 10.

(b) The Basis of the Decision

(i)   The Applicants' Argument - The Negative Right

The applicants' main argument to establish breach was that Art II, by expressly conferring a positive right to freedom of association, also impliedly conferred a right to dissociate - in other words, a negative right not to be compelled to join an association. Neither Commission nor Court found it necessary to reach any decision on this argument, each preferring to base its decision on narrower grounds. By this tactic both bodies avoided any detailed consideration of the Travaux

Preparatoires, which the United Kingdom government invoked to show that no negative right should be implied. In all probability, each body also thereby avoided the risk of a wide division of opinion on the matter. As it was, three members of the Commission and three judges of the Court took the view that no negative right could be implied, arguing that the positive right of association was collective in nature, designed to protect associations, and that neither by logic nor by necessary implication did it give rise to a negative right designed to protect individuals. On the other hand, six judges of the Court gave a separate opinion to the effect that the negative right was "necessarily complementary to, a correlative of, and inseparable from, its positive aspect." In view of these divisions it is not surprising that the majority in each body preferred narrower bases for their decisions.

(ii) The Commission Decision - The Plural Right

The majority of the Commission took the view that the text of Art II, by referring to the freedom to join unions (in the plural) and by stating that the purpose of the freedom was to protect the individual's interests, implied that "the worker must be able to choose the union which in his opinion best serves his interests." On this basis they concluded that the British Rail closed shop agreement interfered with the applicants' freedom to form or join a union of their own choice, and that by enacting legislation which permitted this the United Kingdom government was in breach of Art II.

Before the Court, the government sought to counter this argument by contending that as in law the applicants would still have been free to form or join a union of their choice in addition to joining one of the unions specified in the closed shop agreement, it followed that there was no interference with their plural right of choice.(26) The applicants responded by arguing that whatever the position in law, in practice the operation of the Bridlington Principles (27) would have severely limited the applicants' choice of union, and that in any case, joining and taking part in the activities of a competing union would have led to expulsion from one of the specified unions (and so, loss of employment). The Court avoided reaching any conclusion on these arguments.(28) Indeed, it would have been difficult for it to do so in the absence of clear evidence as to the effect of the Bridlington Principles.(29)

(iii) The Court Decision - The Nature of the Compulsion

Unlike the Commission, the Court did not analyse the nature of the right conferred by the Article. Rather, it based its decision on the nature of the compulsion involved. In the key paragraph of its judgement the Court stated that "a threat of dismissal involving loss of livelihood is a most serious form of compulsion and, in the present instance, it was directed against persons engaged by British Rail before the introduction of any obligation to join a particular trade union. In the Court's opinion, such a form of compulsion, in the circumstances of the case, strikes at the very substance of the freedom guaranteed by Art II. For this reason alone there has been an interference with that freedom as regards each of the three applicants."(30) The Commission had also referred to the nature of the compulsion, but as a supporting reason to show a particularly clear infringement of the Convention, and had commented that lesser forms of compulsion might still constitute an infringement. The essence of the Commission's decision, however, was the identification of the plural right. In contrast, the Court concentrated on compulsion - "For that reason alone" it found a breach of Art II.

(iv) The Unused Defence - Justification.

Art II(2) permits restriction of the rights conferred by Art II(1) if it can be justified as "necessary in a democratic society....for the protection of the interests and freedoms of others." Before both Commission and Court the British government stated that if an infringement of Art II(1) was found, they would not seek to argue that it was justified under Art II(2).(31) The Court, nevertheless, decided of its own motion to consider the justification argument (32), which it then firmly rejected. The rejection was based on two considerations: first, that a democratic society requires fair protection of minorities, and secondly that any restriction must be proportionate to the aim pursued, and such evidence as there was on United Kingdom industrial relations suggested that protection of the closed shop system did not require that existing non-union employees join a specified union. Judge Evrigenis dissented from this conclusion, arguing that the Court could not properly assess the political issues involved in a justification argument in the absence of evidence from the state concerned.

(5) The Consequences of the Decision.

As has already been noted, the basis of the Court's decision was that the nature of the compulsion involved (a threat of dismissal involving loss of livelihood) was sufficient to constitute in itself a breach of Art II rights. However, the Court conceded that not every form of compulsion to join a particular trade union could be regarded as a breach of the Convention. The question therefore arises as to what forms of compulsion, exerted to what degree, are incompatible with Art II such that the United Kingdom government must provide a legal remedy for them. Is, for example, the requirement to join a union as a condition of obtaining (rather than retaining) a job an improper compulsion under the Convention? If the consequence of refusing to be a member is not dismissal but some form of action short of dismissal, is that a sufficient compulsion to be held a breach of Art II? We attempt to answer such questions in the following pages, and consider also whether the present legislative scheme satisfies the United Kingdom government's responsibility under the Convention.(33)

A preliminary point must be made. As the Court made clear in its judgement, the British Rail Case was ultimately concerned not with the closed shop system as such, but with compulsion on individuals to join trade unions. While this will most often occur where closed shop agreements are in operation, it is quite possible to conceive of situations outside the closed shop context in which pressure is brought upon an employee to become a union member. The British Rail Case may be relevant in such a context, notwithstanding that no question of a closed shop is in issue. Therefore, we must consider the possible consequences of the decision in areas outside the operation of the closed shop as such.

(6) Dismissal

The obvious case of dismissal for non-union membership arises where the employee has always refused to join the closed shop union. In this context, although there is some uncertainty as to the effect of both domestic legislation and the Convention, it would seem that there is a broad conformity between them. A more complex situation is raised by the case of an employee who has ceased to be a member of a closed shop union. Here again there is uncertainty as to the effects of domestic legislation and the Convention, but in this context it seems likely that domestic legislation does not fully conform to the requirements of the Convention. We consider these in turn.

(a) Refusal to Join a Union

(i) Existing Non-Members

The British Rail Case establishes that dismissal of an employee for refusal to join a closed shop union where the closed shop arrangement was introduced after the employee's engagement by his employer constitutes an unjustified infringement of his Art II rights. During the period from 1974 to 1980, United Kingdom legislation provided that such a dismissal was fair unless the employee had religious objections to membership of any trade union (or, for the 1974 to 1976 period, he objected to membership of any trade union or of a particular trade union "on any reasonable grounds".(34) Consequently, for the period until 1980 it was clear that United Kingdom Legislation did not provide the protection required by the Convention, and the U.K. government was in breach of the Convention.

The Employment Act 1980 (35) rectified the situation for the future by providing that any dismissal of a non-union

member engaged before the introduction of the closed shop
was unfair, provided that the employee had not been a member
of the union subsequent to the introduction of the closed shop.
Thus, dismissal of employees in circumstances similar to those
in the British Rail Case would now be unfair. The Employment
Act 1982, s.2, provides a retrospective rectification by
enabling existing non-members who were fairly dismissed
between 1974 and 1980 in circumstances which would now be
unfair to claim compensation from a special fund. The
position of existing non-members is then clear - they are
protected under the Convention, and United Kingdom
legislation now conforms with the Convention by providing
that their dismissal is unfair.

(ii) Existing Closed Shop

The Court in the British Rail Case did not consider whether
dismissal of a newly-engaged employee who refused to join a
closed shop union would amount to an unjustifiable
interference with his Art II rights. The Commission did
comment that the situation "might be different (from that of
the British Rail Case) where the worker is entering into a
contract of employment with an enterprise where a closed
shop agreement already exists. In such a case it might perhaps
be said that he has consented to join a specific union when
taking up employment." Indeed, the Court may have had this
in mind when it commented that "compulsion to join a
particular trade union may not always be contrary to the
Convention." However, this comment was expressly made
subject to the assumption that "Article II does not guarantee
the negative aspect of the freedom". Thus, even if dismissal
of a new employee for refusal to join a closed shop union was
not found to be a breach of Art II on grounds of unjustifiable
compulsion, it would still be open to the Court to hold that Art
II creates a negative right, which would almost certainly be
infringed by such a dismissal. Furthermore, even if the Court
was not prepared to go so far as to uphold the full negative
right, it could still find that Art II created a plural right, a
right to choose one's own union, for there is nothing in the
opinion of the majority expressing disapproval of such a
view.(36) On this basis, dismissal of a new employee who

refused to join one of the unions specified in the closed shop agreement because he wished to join (or was already a member of) a union not so specified would amount to an infringement of his plural right to choose whichever union he wished.

The 1980 Employment Act, s 7(3), provides that dismissal of a new employee who refuses to join an existing closed shop will be unfair if the closed shop was introduced subsequent to the Act without the approval of 80% of affected employees expressed in a ballot. The 1982 Act (37) extends this by providing that, whenever the closed shop was introduced, the dismissal will be unfair unless the closed shop agreement has been approved by a ballot (38) within five years prior to the dismissal. Where the closed shop has received the required approval by ballot, then under both provisions the dismissal will be fair unless the employee has "grounds of conscience or other deeply held personal conviction" (39) for refusing to join the closed shop union. To date there has been no case-law interpreting this latter provision, but it would seem wide enough to include political convictions. Thus it would seem that new employees who object to the political views of the closed shop union and refuse to join it on this ground may well be protected from dismissal. It could be argued that such an employee has waived his right to object if he accepted employment knowing of the existence of the closed shop. This argument would, however, render the "convictions" provision largely otiose, because it would then only be open to employees engaged before the introduction of the closed shop, and such employees are protected anyway as existing non-members. Thus it is suggested that the "convictions" provision will be interpreted as open to new employees refusing to join a specified union, although some uncertainty must remain as to whether the protection afforded by this provision will fully meet the requirements of the Convention.

(b) Ceasing to be a Member of a Union.
In the case of employees who cease to be members of a closed shop union there are greater doubts as to whether U.K. legislation meets the requirements of the Convention. Three circumstances must be examined. The first is where the

employee resigns from, and then refuses to rejoin, a closed shop union; the second is where the employee resigns from one closed shop union with the intention of transferring to another,and then finds that he is refused membership as a result of the Bridlington Principles; the third is where the employee is expelled by his union.

(i) Resignation

Under the current legislation, dismissal of an employee who resigns from his union will be unfair if the closed shop has not been approved by the required ballot. If it has been so approved, dismissal will only be unfair if the employee resigned before the introduction of the closed shop (or on the day of the ballot approving its introduction), or resigned subsequently for reasons of deeply-held personal conviction. Whilst it has been suggested that an employee who has never been a member of the closed shop union may be able to prove such conviction, it would seem that an employee resigning from the closed shop will face a much harder task. In 1968 the Donovan Commission suggested that such an employee should not be protected from dismissal as it would have remained "open to him to remain a member of the union and take every opportunity of securing the reversal of policies repugnant to him."(41) More recently it has been said that before a resigning member could invoke the "conviction" provision there would need to be "a change of policy on the part of the union, for example the frequent use of overtly political strikes."(42) Thus it is concluded that dismissal of an employee who resigns after the introduction of the closed shop may well be fair under the present legislative scheme.

In this respect it may well be that United Kingdom legislation still falls short of the requirements of the Convention. True, the Commission suggested that a new employee refusing to join an existing closed shop could be taken as consenting to union membership when he accepted employment. It could equally be argued that an employee who is a member of a closed shop union has consented to the operation of the closed shop and, as Donovan put it, if he resigns he "is presumed to have done so with his eyes open."(43) The Court may well accept this type of argument as showing a less onerous compulsion in some situations, but not, it is submitted, in all. What of the employee who joined the union before the introduction of the closed shop and subsequently found that he did not approve of its operation? Under U.K. legislation he is only clearly protected from dismissal if he resigns on the day that the closed shop is approved by ballot. But can it really be said that he is consenting to its operation if he delays his resignation for a short time to give it a trial period? It would seem that dismissal of such an employee would infringe his Art II rights, but would still be likely to be fair under domestic legislation.

(ii)   The Bridlington Principles.

The   Bridlington   Principles   are   designed   to   settle membership disputes arising between TUC-affiliated trade unions. They provide that a member may not transfer from one affiliated union to another without the consent of the former. The rules of affiliated unions normally permit them to refuse admission to, or expel, an employee who is attempting to transfer in breach of the Bridlington Principles. As a result an employee who resigns from one closed shop union in order to transfer to another may well find himself a member of neither, and liable to be dismissed for that reason. Whether such a dismissal will be unfair depends upon the restraints placed upon the operation of the Bridlington Principles by both common law and legislation.

Common law restraints have recently been expressed by Lord Denning in Cheall v APEX(44) There the employee's dissatisfaction with a local official of his union, the TGWU, led him to resign and apply to APEX He was admitted, but following a ruling in favour of the TGWU by the TUC's Bridlington disputes committee, APEX terminated his membership under the model rule permitting termination in order to comply with a decision of the disputes committee. There was no closed shop, and hence no risk of dismissal, but the employee was determined to remain a member of APEX and he sought a declaration that his expulsion was invalid. Giving the leading judgement in the Court of Appeal, Lord

Denning upheld this claim on the ground that APEX had failed to abide by the principles of natural justice, in that the decision to terminate Cheall's membership was taken without first giving him the opportunity of preventing his case. A further restraint was that the model termination rule "must be confined to cases where there was a reasonable case for expulsion or termination." Where the employee obtains a declaration that his expulsion was invalid, it will not then be open to his employer to dismiss him fairly on grounds of non-membership.

The legislative restraints are contained in s 4 of the Employment Act 1980, which provides that an employee has a right not to be unreasonably expelled from a union or unreasonably excluded from it. Section 3(1) of the Employment Act 1982 further provides that a dismissal will be unfair if the employee has complained to an Industrial Tribunal of unreasonable exclusion under s 4 of the 1980 Act, and either the Tribunal has declared in his favour or proceedings are still pending.(45) Under this provision then, the fairness of the dismissal will depend on whether the union's operation of the Bridlington Principles is regarded as reasonable under s 4.

There is as yet no case-law on s 4, but evidence from other contexts suggests some judicial disagreement as to what amounts to reasonable conduct by the union. In Cheall, Lord Denning took the view that the common law requirement of reasonableness had to be considered in the light of the fundamental principle of "the freedom of the individual to join a trade union of his choice", and that this principle should prevail over the fear of industrial chaos which might result from holding that union rules implementing the Bridlington Principles were invalid. A different view had been suggested at first instance by Bingham J. He refused to hold the Bridlington Principles contrary to public policy, commenting that although, "the policy of English law is in general to lean in favour of the liberty of the individual", this was "whittled down somewhat by the countervailing consideration that the law also, in general, leans in favour of upholding contracts, and the plaintiff became a member of APEX on terms which included rule 14" (46) (the Bridlington termination rule). Bingham J. further commented that although one could not predict how the reasonableness test of s 4 would be applied in any given case, the Donovan Commission "was inclined to regard refusal of membership to an applicant in compliance with the Bridlington Principles as a good reason for refusal, and termination of an existing membership for the same reason would not seem very different in kind."(47) Further support for this approach can be found in Remington v NUPE, (48) a case decided under s 65(4) of the Industrial Relations Act, which conferred a similar right on employees not to be unreasonably refused admission. In Remington the claimant resigned from the TGWU and applied to join NUPE. He was refused admission because a sphere of influence agreement between the unions designated the TGWU as the appropriate one for him. The Tribunal found the exclusion reasonable, as the agreement itself promoted good industrial relations by preventing interunion membership disputes. This is exactly the purpose of the Bridlington agreement, and there seems no reason why tribunals should not take a similar view of the reasonableness of that agreement.

Although there is, then, considerable doubt as to whether Lord Denning's approach would be followed under U.K. legislation, it seems much more likely that it would be adopted under the Convention, which is expressed in terms of individuals' rights rather than the reasonableness of union actions. Clearly the Human Rights Court could take the view that dismissal of an employee who was a non-member as a result of the operation of the Bridlington Principles amounted to an infringement of his Art II rights, as it would be compelling him to rejoin his original union to preserve his job. It could be argued that such compulsion was justified on the basis that the Principles promoted good industrial relations and therefore the broader public interest. Counsel for APEX in the Cheall case argued along these lines, citing the opinion of Judge Evrigenis in the British Rail Case that "account has to be taken of the welfare of the public and of the collective interests of the trade union organisation that are at stake as well as of the individual's freedom of association." On this issue Judge Evrigenis was in the minority. The majority argued that "pluralism, tolerance and broadmindedness are hallmarks of a democratic society." Thus, it would seem that whilst dismissal following the operation of the Bridlington Principles could well be found fair under domestic legislation, under the provisions of the Convention the opposite is the case, and in this respect the U.K. government could still be in breach of the Convention. Whether strict compliance with the requirements of the Convention in this area would be in the best interests of British industrial relations is, of course, another matter.

(c) Expulsion from the Union.
Under the Employment Act 1980 an employee who ceased to be a member of a closed shop union as a result of expulsion was treated in the same way as one who had refused to join: his dismissal would only have been unfair if he could have shown that his non-membership resulted from grounds of conscience or other deeply-held personal conviction. It would seem difficult to prove such a ground - arguably, resignation from the union rather than breach of its rules leading to expulsion would be the only proper way of demonstrating such a conviction. Under the 1980 Act it made no difference to the fairness of the dismissal whether the union acted reasonably or not in expelling its member. An unreasonably expelled member could complain under s 4 of the Act, but that would only result in compensation from the union, not re-instatement as a member, and consequently it would not affect the fairness of his dismissal for non-membership. The 1982 Act remedies this by providing that dismissal will be unfair if the expelled employee has made a complaint against his union under s 4, and either the tribunal has found in his favour or proceedings were still pending. Thus the position under the 1982 legislation is that an employee may only be fairly dismissed following his expulsion from a union if that expulsion was itself reasonable.(49)

Would dismissal of an employee reasonably expelled by his union amount to an infringement of his rights under the Convention? It is suggested that on the basis of the "compulsion" approach of the Court, it would not constitute an infringement. The purposee of such a dismissal would not be to compel the employee to join a union, but rather to support the union's disciplinary control of the workforce. If the "plural" approach of the Commission were to be taken, there would again seem to be no infringement unless the reason for the expulsion was the employee's membership of another union. Only on the basis of the wide negative right would such a dismissal be likely to constitute an infringement, and even then it could be justified in the light of the employee's conduct which led to his reasonable expulsion.

(d) Redundancy Dismissals
Before leaving the subject of dismissal there is one further situation to consider, albeit that it does not arise directly out of the operation of the closed shop system as such. Arrangements are occasionally made which provide for discriminatory redundancy selection practices on grounds of uniion membership or non-membership. By virtue of s 59(a) of the 1978 Act, selection of an individual for redundancy on the grounds of his membership of, or participation at an appropriate time in the activities of, an independent trade union, is automatically unfair. What of the converse position, where selection for redundancy is based on non-membership of the union?

This situation is likely to arise only as the result of an agreement to that effect with a union. By virtue of s 59[b] of the 1978 Act an employer who selects an individual for redundancy by reference to criteria other than those provided for in any agreed procedure will be guilty of unfair dismissal unless there are "special reasons" justifying this departure. It would follow that an employer who succumbed to union pressure for an agreement that non-unionists be dismissed first could not subsequently do other than select such individuals for redundancy.

If individuals so selected were to complain of unfair dismissal, they would in effect be challenging the reasonableness of the employer in entering into such an agreement in the first place. Clearly this would raise considerable difficulties for any tribunal, and both at Employment Appeal Tribunal and Industrial Tribunal level applicants selected for redundancy on grounds of non-membership in accordance with such agreed procedures have been held fairly dismissed.(50) But is a structure of law which, by refusing a remedy to those dismissed in such circumstances, permits discriminatory action of this kind consistent with the Convention? The British Rail Case establishes that certain forms of compulsion to join a trade union are a breach of Art II rights, and while it is true that these will most often arise in a closed shop context, there seems no reason why compulsion such as an increased threat of dismissal based on an increased liability to selection for redundancy should not be incompatible with the Convention, regardless of the non-existence of a closed shop.

Let us take the position of the existing employee,(51) a non-unionist in an employment for which a trade union has been recognised. The union negotiates a redundancy agreement specifying that non-unionists be first in line for dismissal in any future redundancy situation. The employee, knowing of the situation, refuses to join the union and is subsequently made redundant. Under present domestic law the dismissal is fair, for the employer is merely complying with the terms of his collective agreement with the union. Whether this is compatible with the Convention might depend on why the individual refused to join the union. If it is as a result of a deeply-held personal conviction that membership is incompatible with his religious, moral or political beliefs, it is possible that the failure of domestic law to provide a remedy is a breach of the Convention, because underlying the British Rail Case, in particular in the Commission's approach to the matter, is a strong antipathy to compelling individuals to join associations which are committed to objectives of which they disapprove. If, on the other hand, the employee has merely taken his chance and remained a free-rider because of unwillingness, say, to pay the membership subscription, then it would be quite unreasonable to argue that his subsequent dismissal was in breach of the Convention.

(7) Action Short of Dismissal.

For our purposes, compulsions to join a trade union taking forms other than that of dismissal fall into two categories - refusal to employ non-unionists, and discriminatory treatment of non-unionists once employed. We consider each in turn.

(a) Refusal to employ non-unionists.

The British Rail Case was concerned exclusively with the operation of a post-entry closed shop agreement. There are, however, industries where unions have established that job applicants must already be union members before being considered for employment.(53) The Industrial Relations Act 1971, s 7, attempted to make pre-entry closed shop agreements void, but present domestic legislation does not appear to deal with the matter. The employer is therefore free to discriminate against an applicant on the ground that he does not hold a union card. The position is equivalent to that appertaining to the active trade unionist - the employer can refuse to employ on the ground that the applicant is a trade union member.(54)

If no domestic remedy is available to the disappointed applicant as against the employer,(55) can he argue that the refusal to employ is effectively an attempt by the employer to coerce him into membership of the union, and that the state, by permitting such action without remedy, is thereby in breach of its Art I obligations to secure Art II rights for individual citizens? This, of course, is dependent upon whether Art II rights have been breached in this situation. It is submitted that they have not. Take the compulsion rationale for the for the British Rail decision. The degree of compulsion to join a union in a pre-entry closed shop situation cannot be so great as that imposed in the British Rail Case, for in the latter the individuals were having taken away form them jobs which they already held and had enjoyed for some years. In a pre-entry closed shop situation the individual, far from being under pain of forfeiture of a benefit already enjoyed, is in the position only of an applicant with a hope of benefit. The denial of that hope is, it is submitted, of significantly less coercive force - and it is clear from the British Rail case that some degrees of compulsion do not amount to a breach of Art II rights.

The same result will usually be reached if Art II is given a "plural right" interpretation. The situation under consideration is of an individual, qualified for employment in a given industry, being denied work in that industry by reason of non-membership of the appropriate union. However, such an individual will very rarely be a non-member of the particular union by reason of conscience, but will almost certainly have had a history of membership in the past, which membership has now been lost.(56) This is because, given the types of employment in respect of which pre-entry closed shops operate, had the individual not had some history of membership of the union, and so proper training, it is extremely unlikely that he would be qualified for employment in the industry anyway. In the vast majority of cases, therefore, the individual's main concern will not be to secure employment without union membership, or while retaining membership of another union, but will be to recover membership of the particular union as a prelude to obtaining a job in th industry - and ss 4-5 of the Employment Act 1980 provide for the possibility of complaint to an Industrial Tribunal in the event of the union refusing to re-admit. Therefore, the absence of any possible legal action against the employer will be irrelevant.

Finally, it should in any case be pointed out that any application by a disappointed non-union job-seeker would amount effectively to a claim that his "right to work" had been infringed by the employer. If this is so, then the application would have to be declared inadmissable ratione materiae, since the Convention does not protect the "right to work".(57) The result would appear to be that the British Rail Case will probably be regarded as irrelevant to the pre-entry closed shop situation.

(b) Discriminatory Treatment in Employment.
Under this heading we are concerned with the denial of

benefits, such as pay increases and promotion opportunities, and the imposition of burdens, such as transfers to less desirable work. Again the issue is whether such discriminatory treatment on grounds of non-membership may be remedied under domestic legislation and, if not, whether its domestic legality is consistent with the requirements of Art II.

We first consider discriminatory pay agreements. It must immediately be pointed out that the common practice is for unions to bargain on pay for all employees within the bargaining units for which they are recognised, regardless of whether or not they are union members.(58) Nevertheless, there may be some aspects of pay determination which discriminate against non-unionists -for example, where the employer allows the union shop steward to allocate overtime work among the workforce, and the steward gives preference to union members, perhaps to the extent of excluding non-unionists altogether.(59)   What is the legal significance of this?   Section 23(1) of the Employment Protection (Consolidation) Act 1978, as amended by s.15(1) of the Employment Act 1980 and s.10 of the 1982 Act provides:-

> "Subject to the following provisions of this section, every employee shall have the right not to have action (short of dismissal) taken against him as an individual by his employer for the purpose of
> (a)......
> (b)......
> (c) compelling him to become a member of any trade union or of a particular trade union or of one of a number of particular trade unions."

The right conferred by s 23(1)[c] is taken away if, inter alia, there is a closed shop agreement in existence which satisfies the requirements of the revised s 58 of the 1978 Act (as provided by s 3 of the 1982 Act), that is to say one approved by the appropriate percentage in a secret ballot under the new s58A.

It is submitted that s 23(1)[c] would not be applicable to the position of the non-unionist denied overtime work, because the denial would not be <u>for the purpose</u> of compelling him to become a union member, but would be for the purpose of allowing union members to earn more - at best an indirect attempt at compulsion of the non-unionist. The contention that the compulsion must be direct if it is to amount to a breach of s 23(1)[c] is reinforced by the fact that the action complained of must be taken "against (the non-unionist) as an individual", that is, directed at him personally rather than merely having coincidental consequences for him.

If, therefore, there is no domestic remedy, we must turn our attention to the Convention. So far as the denial of overtime is concerned, it can hardly be doubted that this is a quite inadequate compulsion to constitute a breach of Art II rights under the <u>British Rail</u> Case. If, however, we widen our inquiry to consider more extensive discriminatory pay arrangements, rather more serious questions might be raised. This is not a wholly academic exercise, for it is quite possible that, as a result of the Employment Acts 1980 and 1982, the traditional British union practice of bargaining for all employees regardless of membership will come into question. The effect of those Acts will be severely to limit the negotiation of new closed shop agreements, and possibly to undermine long-established union membership arrangements. If unions find themselves with increasing numbers of free-riders, whom they cannot, as a result of the legislation, compel into membership, they may well be tempted to seek to negotiate pay increases only for those who have accepted the obligations of membership. Thus, in West Germany, for example, where the closed shop is unconstitutional, there have been a number of attempts by unions to negotiate "differential clauses" in collective agreements, entitling union members only to pay and holiday benefits, but these have been held to be a "socially inadequate" way of compelling individuals to join unions.(60) Whether such differentiation clauses would amount to improper compulsion of non-unionists contrary to the Convention is by no means clear. In <u>Schmidt and Dahlstrom v Sweden</u> (61) it was argued that the Swedish National Collective Bargaining Office, by insisting that individual members of a trade union confederation which had taken industrial action should be denied retroactive pay rises, was attempting to induce them to join another union or to cease to be a member of any union. (On the facts this intention was not established). This is the converse of the situation where the employer seeks to induce the non-unionist into membership by paying pay increases to union members only, but the Court gave no guidance as to whether the action of the Office would have been a breach of the Convention had the appropriate intention been established. Thus the issue remains entirely open, but it may be suggested that if any indirect action short of dismissal constitutes improper compulsion contrary to Art II, then the denial to non-unionists of equal treatment in terms of pay would seem to fall within that category.

Turning now to discriminatory action in respect of promotion opportunities, the same point may be made with respect to EP(C)A s 23(1)[c] as was made with regard to matters of pay - promotion advantages given to union members cannot be construed as action taken against non-unionists as individuals in order to compel them into union membership.(62)

Again, this is no purely academic consideration. There is in a number of industries, notably the steel industry, a particular form of closed shop, termed by McCarthy the "promotion veto shop". Thus, for process workers in iron and steel manufacture, "promotion depends, in the main, on seniority, with one important proviso: promotion opportunities will be vetoed by the union if the candidate for promotion is not, at the time the vacancy arises, a fully paid-up member. In this case promotion will normally go to the next senior man who is in compliance.(63) The latest survey of the extent of closed shop arrangements in Britain provides a figure of 127,000 workers employed in activities in respect of which the "promotion veto" shop operates.(64) Does this type of promotion preference for unionists amount to improper compulsion against non-unionists, contrary to the Convention?

Can any action short of dismissal based on denial of benefits to non-unionists be regarded as inconsistent with

Art II? No guidance is offered by the British Rail Case, but the Swedish Engine Drivers Case tells us that "What the Convention requires is that under national law trade unions should be enabled, in conditions not at variance with Art II to strive for the protection of their members' interests.(65) On the other hand, the Convention does not require public authorities to treat all trade unions absolutely equally as both the Engine Drivers and the Belgian Police (66) cases show. If, within the general framework of freedom of trade unions, the Convention permits public authorities to discriminate between different unions, why should it not permit employers to discriminate between members of different unions in the allocation of benefits? If this is accepted, it would seem that a "plural right" interpretation of Art II would permit employers to deny promotion opportunities to members of particular unions in favour of members of other unions. So far as the compulsion rationale is concerned, it would be a considerable step to take to decide that discrimination against an individual could be equated with dismissal as a form of compulsion, especially as the type of discrimination was to offer benefits, rather than to impose detriments on non-unionists. It would seem that only adoption of a full "negative right" interpretation of Art II could have implications for the operation of "promotion veto" closed shops.(67)

Our second category of action short of dismissal, the imposition of less desirable work or working conditions on non-unionists, might seem to provide a stronger case for a breach of Art II rights on the compulsion rationale. Provided that the employer, in reallocating the individual, stays within the terms of the employment contract and so does not entitle the individual employee to claim to have been constructively dismissed, the only possible domestic remedy is once again s 23(1)[c] of the 1978 Act. In deciding whether this affords a remedy, it must be remembered that the action taken by the employer must, to be actionable, be "for the purpose of compelling" the individual to become a trade union member. In cases of re-allocation of non-unionists to other work, it will nearly always be the case that management's primary purpose will be to prevent industrial action by those union members

who refuse to work with a non-unionist.(68)   Therefore,
s 23(1)[c] will be inapplicable, as the action is not being taken
against the non-unionist "as an individual" for the requisite
purposes.   Equally, it is submitted, the Convention will not
assist either, for the compulsion is both significantly less
forceful than dismissal, and the Court would, if it were to find
a breach of Art II, effectively be saying that the individual had
not only a right to work (which is excluded from the list of
rights protected by the Convention), but a right to work at a
particular job without interference.   Under the current
framework of the Convention this is a wholly untenable
proposition.

(8) Some Final Reflections

Our   discussion   thus   far   has   concentrated   on   the
compatibility of domestic legislation with the requirements of
Art II, and has necessarily proceeded at a somewhat technical
level. The British Rail Case may have considerable impact on
the structure and operation of the wider industrial relations
system, however, and we consider these briefly.

The Court's decision leaves many matters obscure.(69) This
obscurity is accentuated by the fact that the situation dealt
with in the British Rail Case was somewhat unusual, in that
the collective agreement at issue provided no exemption from
membership for existing employees.(70) If it is the case that
the decision is applicable only to this type of fact situation,
we may assume that little will come of the litigation which
will affect the operation of the closed shop in general.
However, the way is still open for the Court either to follow
the Commission's "plural right" approach, or to adopt a full
"negative right" position.   How might adoption of either of
these affect the closed shop?

The major problems which would be thrown up by adoption
of the plural right are those of inter-union membership
disputes and fragmentation of collective bargaining structures.
If Cheall v APEX is followed, this will have the most serious
impact on the working of the Bridlington Principles.   The

Principles are a direct negation of the plural right to choose between unions. They necessarily require unions to be able to expel, or refuse to admit, employees who have recently been members of other TUC-affiliated unions unless permission to accept them into membership has been given. The proposition in Cheall, per Lord Denning, is that expulsion and admission rules are valid only in so far that they are "reasonable", and the reasonableness of their exercise is to be tested having regard to the individual's fundamental freedom of choice of union. Such unfettered freedom of choice will inevitably lead to inter-union competition for membership and inter-union disputes,(71) with the possible consequential breakdown of multi-union joint negotiating committees.(72)

This raises the possibility of great problems for management. Hart has argued that the recent expansion of the closed shop into industries where it had never previously penetrated has been due in part to management recognition of the advantages to them of stable bargaining relationships.(73) As Kalis has observed (in a comment originally made with reference to the Bridlington Disputes Committee, but which is generally applicable to the Bridlington arrangements as a whole), "Removing the Committee....would licence breakaway unionism and indiscriminate transfers of members from union to union, both of which would have a profoundly unsettling effect on patterns of union organisation and hence on collective bargaining.(74) The introduction of a plural right of free choice of union could raise inter-union and collective bargaining difficulties of the most intractable nature.(75)

While the "plural right" has severe disadvantages for both management and unions, the "negative right" is a weapon directed principally at trade unions, for the "discipline function" of the closed shop is thereby undermined. McCarthy pointed out that the closed shop enabled the union to retain a degree of control over its members, especially in situations of industrial conflict.(76) As Dunn comments, this discipline function becomes of considerable importance where the closed shop has spread into areas where employees may have weaker traditional feelings of solidarity, and where "the closed shop's discipline function may be vital in strengthening the resolve of workers with little experience of striking when a dispute drags and enthusiasm wanes."(77) In this situation the adoption of the "negative right", by lessening the trade union's control over the whole workforce, weakens union industrial and bargaining power, and redounds to the advantage of management.

It is a well-established feature of the closed shop that management may benefit from the availability to the union of coercive powers, in that the union can enforce unpopular agreements on their unwilling members on pain of expulsion and hence loss of job.(78) Recognition of the "negative right" would eradicate this direct sanction, and raise again the issue of fragmentation of existing collective bargaining structures, or lead to unions attempting to bargain exclusively for the benefit of their own members.

In sum, the proposition is that in recent years the closed shop has been a force for stability in British collective bargaining, and that its undermining will lead to a consequential destabilisation of that system. If this transpires, however, it would be naive to attribute it wholly, or even mainly, to the British Rail decision. Domestic political developments had already resulted in a legislative attack on the closed shop in the Employment Act 1980, and the Conservative government had made it clear that a step-by-step reform of labour law, involving further legsislation, was in train. The decision, therefore, did not lead to the enactment of the 1982 Act. Further, apart from the introduction of s 2, providing for compensation in certain circumstances to be paid to those dismissed from closed shops during the period 1974-80, the British Rail Case has had no direct effect on the content of the 1982 Act.(79)

What the decision may well have done is to provide a political justification (as against a reason) for further attacks on the closed shop by the 1982 Act, encouraged by a political rhetoric of "meeting our international obligations."

As has been seen, the precise extent of these obligations is quite unclear. Future cases may succeed in clarifying them, but if the clarification is achieved by adoption either of the "plural right" or the "negative right", we may expect to see a weakened trade union movement in conflict with the law, and a destabilised collective bargaining structure. The Human Rights Court's intervention into the operation of the closed shop system will be judged worthwhile only and insofar that its future decisions on the closed shop avoid that outcome. As Wedderburn has said, "the duty of a labour law system is <u>first</u> to the individuals in the collective majority; and only <u>second</u> -not to be forgotten, but <u>second</u> - to individuals who wish to opt out of collective labour relations."(80) Will the European Court of Human Rights heed that warning?

FOOTNOTES

(1) The "closed shop" takes a variety of forms. The generally accepted definition is McCarthy's: "a situation in which employees come to realise that a particular job is only to be obtained or retained if they become and remain members of one of a specified number of trade unions." W E J McCarthy, "The Closed Shop in Britain", p3. See also Trade Union and Labour Relations Act 1974, s30 (definition of a "union membership agreement"). Gennard et al estimate that in 1978 at least five million British workers were employed in jobs in respect of which the closed shop operated -see "The Extent of Closed Shop Arrangements in British Industry", [1980] D E Gaz 16-22.

(2) Publications of the Court, series A, vol 44; also reported [1981] IRLR 408.

(3) Although Art 9 may also be relevant - see below, discussion of R v Greater London Council, ex p Burgess, [1978] IRLR 261.

(4) The text may be found in Brownlie, "Basic Documents on Human Rights" (2nd ed), pp21-27. Staines notes that "It was the original intention of the Council of Europe that the European Convention should include all 'the rights and fundamental freedoms referred to in the Universal Declaration'." "Constitutional Protection and the European Convention on Human Rights - An Irish Joke?"(1981) 44 MLR 149,150.

(5) Observation of Mr Hoare, the British Representative, in Travaux Preparatoires (TP), vol iv, p170.

(6) TP vol iv, p176 et seq.

(7) TP vol iv, p262.

(8) Vienna Convention on the Law of Treaties, Art 32. In the Golder Case the Commission noted that it is permissible to use the Travaux Preparatoires to correct a manifestly absurd or unreasonable result, but not to depart from the result of the application of the general rule of interpretation in other cases. Report of the Commission in the Golder Case, para 46.

(9) Jacobs, "The European Convention on Human Rights", p18. For a similar argument, predicated on the distinction between "concepts" of fairness and (historically-specific) "conceptions" of fairness, see Dworkin, "Constitutional Cases" in his "Taking Rights Seriously". Dworkin argues that the American constitution contains "concepts" rather than "conceptions", and that such "concepts" must be given meaning in constitutional cases without regard to the framers "conceptions" of what, for example, "cruel and unusual punishment" might comprise. It would follow that the "Travaux Preparatoires" of the Constitution would be of minimal relevance, being evidence only of historically-specific "conceptions".

(10) Concurring Opinions of Judges Ganshof Van Der Meersch, Bundschneider-Robert, Liesch, Matscher, Pinheiro Farinha, and Pettiti, [1981] IRLR 408, 419.

(11) [1981] IRLR 408,416.

(12) [1978] IRLR 261 DC.

(13) At 263 - "unadopted", presumably, because it has not been incorporated into English domestic law.

(14) Application No 4072/69, (1971) 13 YB 708.

(15) (1971) 13 YB 708, 718.

(16) Publications of the Court, Series A, vol 43.

(17) The major cases under Art II, the Belgian Police case (Series A, vol 19), the Swedish Train Drivers case (Series A, vol 20) and Schmidt and Dahlstrom v Sweden (Series A, vol 21) are concerned with the scope of the "positive " right to associate, with whether the Convention requires signatory states to take positive action (or refrain from action) in order to encourage union membership. As such they shed little light on the question of the rights of non-members.

(18) Which is, of course, not to say that closed shops do not operate in practice in such countries - see, for example, for West Germany, Hanson, Jackson and Miller's "The Closed Shop" at pp218-229, and Kahn-Freund's often-quoted statement doubting "whether it is very advisable to look for a job in a coal mine in the Ruhr...without carrying a union card." (Labour and the Law, First ed, p210).

(19) Labour and the Law, Second ed, pp194-5.

(20) "In France the closed shop was banned in 1956, partly to protect minority unions against the powerful Confederation Generale du Travail. (Kahn-Freund, op cit, p196). The CGT is a Communist-dominated confederation.

(21) See Hanson, Jackson and Miller, n18 supra, at pp201-5.

(22) For the Irish position, see Staines (1981) 44 MLR 149, and Whyte's reply, (1981) 44 MLR 541.

(23) M Forde, "The 'Closed Shop' Case", (1982) 11 ILJ 1,5. See Wedderburn, "Discrimination in the Right to Organise and the Right to be a Non-Unionist" in F Schmidt (ed) "Discrimination in Employment", especially at pp461 et seq.

(24) Trade Union and Labour Relations Act 1974, Sched 1, para 6(5), as amended by s 1(e) of the Trade Union and Labour Relations (Amendment) Act 1976.

(25) Cf Saggers v British Railways [1977] IRLR 266 and (No2) [1978] IRLR 435, arising out of the same closed shop agreement.

(26) Section 53(1) of the Employment Protection Act 1975 gave employees the right not to have action short of dismissal taken against them by their employers for the purpose of preventing or deterring them from becoming members of, or taking part in the activities of, independent trade unions. Where a closed shop agreement was operative, s 53(3) and (4) limited activity rights to participation in the affairs of one of the closed shop unions, but these subsections did not similarly limit membership rights, so that in law an individual was free to be a member of another independent union as well as the closed shop union although he could only participate in the affairs of the latter. See now EP(C)A 1978,s 23, as amended by the 1980 and 1982 Employment Acts.

(27) "TUC Principles Governing Relations Between Unions". The relevance for the Principles of the decision in the British Rail Case is discussed below.

(28) But see the separate concurring opinion: "The possibility of choice, an indispensable component of freedom of association, is in reality non-existent where there is a trade union monopoly of the kind encountered in the present case." [1981] IRLR at 419.

(29) "Whether the Bridlington principles ...are on balance beneficial or detrimental to British industry and industrial relations is a very large question, the resolution of which would involve much factual research and comparative study. It would be naive to suppose that a reliable view could be formed on the basis of a couple of hours' evidence, from sources however eminent." Cheall v APEX [1982] ICR at 255, per Bingham J.

(30) [1981] IRLR at 417.

(31) Prior to the General Election of May 1979, the Labour government had been preparing a justification defence under Art II(2). This defence was dropped by the incoming Conservative government which actually argued the case before the Court.

(32) As the dissenting British member of the Commission had done. He suggested that justification could be established as a means of making collective bargaining effective and preventing non-unionists from "free-riding" (taking the benefits of collective bargaining without paying union subscriptions). He further argued that the democratic principle that the interests of the majority should prevail, assuming fair and equal treatment for minorities, supported a justification defence.

(33) Art 1 of the Convention imposes an obligation on each Contracting State to "secure to everyone within (its) jurisdiction the rights and freedoms defined in Section I of (the) Convention", and a failure to do this engages the liability of the State (as was the case in the British Rail Case itself). The corollary of this is that by virtue of Art 26 and Art 27(3) the Commission is required to reject any petition as inadmissable if the petitioner has failed to exhaust domestic remedies. Thus, the availability of a domestic remedy precludes consideration by the Commission (or Court) as to whether the Convention has been breached.

(34) TULRA 1974, Sched 1, para 6(5).

(35) Section 7(2), providing for the insertion of a new sub-section (3B) in s 58 of the 1978 Act. See now the Employment Act 1982, s 3(i), re-enacting this provision.

(36) See [1981] IRLR at 417, and for a much stronger formulation compare the separate concurring opinion, n 28 supra.

(37) Section 3(i), providing inter alia for a new sub-section 58(3)[c] of the 1978 Act. This provision is not yet in force.

(38) Such approval may be expressed either by 80% of those actually voting - s 3(i) of the 1982 Act, providing a new s 58A of the 1978 Act.

(39) Employment Act 1982, s 3(i), re-enacting s 58(3A) of the 1978 Act, which was provided by s 7(2) of the Employment Act 1980.

(40) "In every contract of membership of a trade union, whether made before or after the passing of this Act, there shall be implied a term conferring a right on the member, on giving reasonable notice and complying with any reasonable conditions, to terminate his membership of the union." Trade Union and Labour Relation Act 1974, s 7, as provided by s 3(i) of the 1976 Amendment Act.

(41) Royal Commission on Trade Unions and Employers' Associations ("The Donovan Commission") Report, Cmnd 3623, para 616.

(42) Hanson, Jackson and Miller, n 18 supra, at p91.

(43) Para 616.

(44) [1982] IRLR 362 CA.

(45) Employment Act 1982, s 3

(46) [1982] ICR at 253-4.

(47) [1982] ICR at 254. The reference is to para 624 of the Donovan Report.

(48) [1973] IRLR 273(IT)

(49) See n 45, supra.

(50) For example, Evans and Morgan v AB Electronics [1981] IRLR III (EAT), and Bygott v Woodall-Duckham [1976] IRLR 168 (IT)

(51) The probem is unlikely to arise otherwise, because in the case of a new non-unionist employee entering a situation in which a discriminatory redundancy agreement applies, he will be vulnerable to selection for redundancy anyway as a result of the operation of "last-in first-out" schemes.

(52) If he is not made aware of it, Keepin v Hurn Bros, [1975] IRLR 141(IT) suggests that a subsequent dismissal might be unfair.

(53) See Gennard et al, n 1 supra. The researchers estimate that over 800,000 employees work in pre-entry closed shop shops, that this number is either static or declining, and that pre-entry closed shops are to be found most frequently in the printing, paper and publishing industry.

(54) See City of Birmingham v Beyer [1977] IRLR 211(EAT), noted (1977) 6 ILJ 246 (Lewis). Cf the legislation on sex and race discrimination, by which the employer is specifically enjoined from discriminatory action in considering job applications - Sex Discrimination Act 1975, s 6(i) [c], Race Relations Act 1976, s 4(i)[c].

(55) Remedies for unreasonable exclusion from membership lie against the union, both by way of statute (Employment Act 1980, ss 4-5) and, more dubiously, at common law (the "right to work" cases, such as Nagle v Fielden [1966] 2Q.B. 633). Success here, however, could only have the effect at best of obtaining union membership, and ex hypothesi the individual is seeking the employment without the necessity of union membership.

(56) Cases such as Edwards v SOGAT [1971] Ch354 and Kirkham v NATSOPA [1981] IRLR 244 (IT) exemplify this. (It is noteworthy that both cases are concerned with the printing industry - see n 53, supra.)

(57) Cf Art I of the European Social Charter (1961).

(58) An early discussion of this feature of British industrial relations is to be found in S and B Webb, "Industrial Democracy", pp209 et seq.

(59) Smith v Deputy Master, Royal Mint [1973] IRLR 267 (IT) (Unfair discrimination against non-unionist, breach of s 5(2)[b] Industrial Relations Act 1971.

(60) Hanson, Jackson and Miller, op cit n 18 supra, at pp203-4, 210-214. The connection between unions bargaining for all employees and the possibility of enforcing closed shops is impliedly observed by the Webbs, n 58 supra.

(61) Note 17, supra (Human Rights Court).

(62) But sce the proceedings on the Employment Bill 1982, Standing Committee G, 22nd April 1982, col 1155, where the Government spokesman,

Mr David Waddington MP, clearly envisaged that discriminatory promotion procedures would be caught by the subsection.

(63) McCarthy, n 1 supra, p49.

(64) Gennard et al, n 1 supra. The figure of 127,000 represents a significant decline from the 193,000 estimated by McCarthy in 1965. This, as Gennard et al observe, is no doubt due to the declining numbers of workers employed in the industries principally involved (iron and steel, and textiles).

(65) Note 17, supra.

(66) (1975) Series A, No19 (Human Rights Court).

(67) Cf s 5(2)[b], Industrial Relations Act 1971.

(68) See, for example, Langston v AUEW [1974] 1 WLR 185 (CA) and Ross v NCB [1973] IRLR 37(IT)

(69) The uncertainties may be clarified by future litigation. Recent cases are Applications 8476-81/79 (applicants complain of dismissal for having refused to join a trade union) and Application 9520/81 (complaint of dismissal for refusal to remain a trade union member.) Applications 8476-81/79 have been found admissible by the Commission, and Application 9520/81 has been referred to the UK government for comment.

(70) It has been estimated that about two-thirds of closed shop agreements place no obligation upon existing non-union employees to join the union. See Gennard et al, "The content of British closed shop agreements" [1979] D E Gaz 1088-1092, and R Benedictus, "Closed shop exemptions and their wording" (1979) 8 ILJ 160.

(71) In this context the limitation on immunity in tort brought about by the 1982 Act's redefining of "trade dispute" to apply only to disputes between employers and workers (not workers and workers) may be of fundamental importance, as Cory Lighterage v TGWU [1973] ICR 339 (CA) shows.

(72) See W Brown (ed), "The Changing Contours of British Industrial Relations", pp59-61, 67.

(73) M Hart, "Why Bosses Love the Closed Shop", New Society, 15 February, pp352-4.

(74) P Kalis, "The Effectiveness and Utility of the Disputes Committee of the TUC", (1978) 16 BJIR 41, 49.

(75) "As everyone in industry knows, it is very undesirable to have a large number of small unions negotiating on behalf of small groups of men." R v Post Office, ex p ASTMS[1981] 1AER 139,140.

(76) McCarthy, op cit n 1 supra, p114 et seq.

(77) S Dunn, "The Growth of the Post-Entry Closed Shop in Britain Since the 1960's: Some Theoretical Considerations", (1981) 19 BJIR 275, 278.

(78) For a notorious example, see T Lane and K Roberts, "Strike at Pilkingtons". This aspect of trade union disciplinary powers has been judicially recognised - see Evans v NUPBPW [1938] 4 All ER 51,54 (per Goddard LJ).

(79) Compare the provisions of the Act with those of the Trade Union (Freedom of Association) Bill, introduced by Mr Ivan Lawrence QC, MP, on 22nd July 1981, providing (inter alia) that "every person shall have the right to join a trade union and the right not to join a trade union."

(80) K W Wedderburn, "Labour Law and Labour Relations in Britain", (1972) 10 BJIR 270, 290 (emphasis in original).

THE ENGLISH LAW OF CONTEMPT OF COURT AND ARTICLE 10 OF THE EUROPEAN CONVENTION ON HUMAN RIGHTS

N V Lowe

This essay will consider first what obligations were put upon the United Kingdom to reform the law of contempt of court by the decision of the European Court of Human Rights in Sunday Times v United Kingdom(1) and secondly whether the legislative response, the Contempt of Court Act 1981, complies with the requirements.

I Preliminary Observations

A Contempt of Court

The phrase "contempt of court" may lead some to conclude that the law is concerned to uphold the personal dignity of the judiciary. This is not so. The object of the contempt laws is to protect the due administration of justice.   As Lord President Clyde said in Johnson v Grant:(2)

> "The phrase 'contempt of court' does not in the least describe the true nature of the class of offence with which we are here concerned, ... The offence consists in interfering with the administration of the law; in impeding and preventing the course of justice.... It is not the dignity of the Court which is offended - a petty and misleading view of the issues involved - it is the fundamental supremacy of the law which is challenged."

Contempts are classified as being either criminal or civil. Civil contempts comprise disobedience to court orders. Our concern is with criminal contempts which take a variety of forms though as Lord Diplock said in A-G v Leveller Magazine, Ltd.:(3)

> "they all share a common characteristic: they involve an interference with the due administration of justice

either in a particular case or more generally as a continuing process."

Criminal contempts commonly comprise misconduct committed in connexion with particular legal proceedings. One example relevant to our discussion, is publications that are liable to interfere with the course of justice in a particular case. Traditionally,(4) publications are thought liable to interfere if they create a real risk of jeopardising the court's impartiality, of contaminating the evidence or of unduly pressurising a party to the proceedings. Individual litigants benefit from the protection afforded by this aspect of the law of contempt but its purpose is not to protect the private rights of litigants but rather to protect the due administration of justice by protecting litigants' rights as a whole.(5) Hence, in restricting comment on a particular case there is an element of protecting the administration of justice as a continuing process. There are, however, contempt laws that are purely concerned with the administration of justice as a continuing process. One example is that known as "scandalising the court" which is usually thought of(6) as comprising publications that are scurrilously abusive of a judge or which impugn a judge's impartiality. Again the object of the law is not to preserve the personal dignity of the judiciary but to maintain public confidence both in the administration of justice and those who administer it.

The effect of the above laws is that freedom to comment on current litigation and to a lesser extent the judiciary is restricted. It seems fair to add that though similar restrictions exist in a number of common law jurisdictions there is no true counterpart to the contempt laws in European legal systems.(7)

B   Article 10 of the European Convention on Human Rights
Article 10(1) enshrines the basic right to freedom of expression which includes the "freedom to hold opinions and to receive and impart information and ideas without interference by public authority". This freedom is qualified by Art. 10(2) which states:

"The exercise of these freedoms, since it carries with it duties and responsibilities, may be subject to such formalities, conditions, restrictions or penalties as are prescribed by law and are necessary in a democratic society in the interests of national security, territorial integrity or public safety, for the prevention of disorder or crime, for the protection of health or morals, for the protection of the reputation or rights of others, for preventing the disclosure of information received in confidence, or for maintaining the authority and impartiality of the judiciary."

Under the Convention any restriction of freedom of expression must be justified by reference to the exceptions laid down by Art. 10(2). As the contempt laws restrict freedom of expression they must be justified and the most appropriate exception within Art. 10 (2) is that relating to the authority and impartiality of the judiciary. Indeed this phrase was first drafted by the British Delegation,(8) specifically, it is said,(9) to cover contempt of court. However, since contempt operates to protect litigants' rights to a fair trial (a right enshrined by Art. 6) the exception relating to the "rights of others" might also be appropriate.

II The Sunday Times Litigation(10)

A The Facts
The Sunday Times litigation is set against the background of the thalidomide tragedy. Thalidomide was a drug used in a sedative that was marketed as being safe for pregnant women. Tragically, it was not safe. In England thalidomide was thought to be responsible for the birth of some 451 deformed babies. The question arose as to whether Distillers (Biochemicals) Ltd. who had marketed the drug in England, were legally liable to pay damages to the deformed children. Liability hinged on two difficult points whether (i) under English law, at that time,(11) there was legal liability at all for causing damage to a foetus and (ii) Distillers had been negligent. Faced with these formidable difficulties a first batch of claims was settled in 1968, Distillers agreeing

(without admitting negligence) to pay £1 million to some 58 children. More claims followed. Distillers were minded to set up a fund of some £3.25 million for the benefit of those children not covered by the 1968 settlement but only if all the parents agreed to drop their claims against the company. Not all of them did agree and an attempt to remove the objecting parents as next friends of the children and replace them by the Official Solicitor (who would have agreed to the settlement) failed.(12) It was at this stage, i.e. autumn 1972, that the Sunday Times took up the children's cause and began a campaign urging Distillers to pay more and to do so promptly. The timing of the campaign is to be noted. It was some eleven years after the withdrawal of the drug from the market and many of the children involved, then aged ten, had received no compensation from Distillers. Furthermore, though the matter was moving towards a settlement (which would require court approval) there was little prospect of the legal issues of liability coming before the courts.

On September 24 1972 the newspaper published a powerful article entitled: "OUR THALIDOMIDE CHILDREN: A CAUSE FOR NATIONAL SHAME" which discussed whether those who put drugs on the market ought to be absolutely liable for damage done by them and whether the currently accepted method of assessing damages is inadequate. The sting of the article lay in the following:

"....the thalidomide children shame Distillers .... there are times when to insist on the letter of the law is as exposed to criticism as infringement of another's legal rights. The figure in the proposed settlement is to be £3.25 million spread over 10 years. This does not shine as a beacon against pre-tax profits last year of £64.8 million and company assets worth £421 million. Without in anyway surrendering on negligence, Distillers could and should think again."

Distillers complained to the Attorney General suggesting that the article constituted a contempt. No action was taken but in the course of discussing the complaint the Sunday Times showed the Attorney General a copy of a further article they intended to publish. It was in respect of this proposed article that, the Attorney General decided to act when he sought an injunction restricting its publication.

It is generally agreed that the proposed article was different to those which preceded it. Although written in temperate terms it contained a detailed and well researched analysis of the evidence against Distillers marshalling forcibly the arguments for saying Distillers did not measure up to their responsibilities. The article concluded inter alia that "it could be argued" that: 1. (Distillers) should have found all the scientific literature about drugs related to thalidomide. It did not. 2. It should have done further tests when it discovered that the drug had anti-thyroid activity and unsuspected toxicity. It did not. 3. It should have had proof before advertising the drug as safe for pregnant women that this was in fact so. It did not.

However, the article stopped short of saying that Distillers were actually negligent and attempted to marshall the arguments on the company's side concluding that in the end, "There appears to be no neat set of answers."

B   The English Decisions

(i) The Divisional Court and the Court of Appeal(13)
The Queen's Bench Divisional Court granted the injunction. In its view the article created a serious risk of interfering with the course of justice in the particular case because it put pressure upon Distillers to settle on worse terms than they wished. Lord Widgery C.J. concluded:

"In the end this appears to us a very simple case in which a newspaper is deliberately seeking to influence the settlement of pending proceedings by bringing pressure to bear on one party. Not only is the interference intended, but, having regard to the power of public opinion we have no hesitation in saying that publication of the article complained of would create a

serious risk of interference with Distillers' freedom of
action in the litigation."

The Court of Appeal unanimously reversed the Divisional
Court's decision, principally because it considered the
proceedings had gone to sleep. Phillimore L J commented:

"The litigation is dormant and has been now for several
years. Both sides have displayed a masterly inactivity
in its pursuit. Neither wishes to bring one of these
claims into court. Delay exerts pressure on the parents
rather than on Distillers. The whole problem is
inevitably of public interest and rightly so. Is no one
ever to be free to comment on such matters as the
delay, the size of Distillers' offer or the question of
their legal and moral responsibility? If it is true that
Distillers are putting pressure on the parents is no one
to be permitted to say so and to give reasons for
suggesting that pressure should be put on Distillers?"

Another reason for allowing the publication, pursued by
Lord Denning M.R. was that the competing public interest in
informing the public outweighed in this unique case the private
interest of the party in a fair trial.(14)

(ii) The House of Lords(15)
The House of Lords held that the article should not be
published. It was unanimously agreed that the Court of Appeal
was wrong to regard the proceedings between the parents and
Distillers as "dormant." It was emphasised that in civil cases
contempt was as much concerned to protect pre-trial
negotiations as the trial itself. Lord Diplock said:

"Parties to litigation are entitled to the same freedom
from interference in negotiating the settlement of a
civil action as they are from interference in the trial of
it."

All were agreed that the negotiations for a settlement
were being actively pursued. Lord Cross said the settlement
of the original actions was necessarily, in view of the

complexities and legal difficulties, a lengthy process and Lord Reid thought that so long "as there is not undue procrastination in negotiations for a settlement proceedings cannot be said to be dormant."(16)

None of their Lordships thought the case merited special treatment, but instead considered it governed by general principle. It can be taken, therefore, that none of them approved of Lord Denning M.R.'s proposition that in exceptional cases such as this, the public interest in being informed outweighed the private interest of the parties in having a fair trial, although it was only adverted to and rejected by Lords Reid and Cross. Lord Reid said that the proposition rested on the false premise that contempt existed to protect the private interests of particular litigants, whereas in reality it protected the public interest in the due administration of justice. The real question therefore was how the balance should be drawn between two ultimately competing public interests.

Lord Reid, with whom Lord Cross agreed, started from the premise that:

"Freedom of speech should not be limited to any greater extent than is necessary but it cannot be allowed where there would be real prejudice to the administration of justice."

Applying this he thought that a distinction should be made between conduct influencing the tribunal hearing the case - which had to be absolutely prohibited - and conduct influencing litigants - where a balance with freedom of speech could and should be drawn so as to allow fair and temperate criticism of a litigant. It was upon this basis that he thought the article published on September 24th was permissible. The proposed article was different because it contained detailed discussion of the very issue (i.e. negligence) that might come before the court, amounting, in effect, to a prejudgment. Lord Reid accepted that the proposed article would not have added much to the pressure upon Distillers but in his view a wider issue was at stake, namely, the protection of administration of justice as a whole. To allow public prejudgments was tantamount to allowing "trial by newspaper" which, in Lord Reid's view, was intrinsically objectionable. He said:

"I think that anything in the nature of a prejudgment of a case or of specific issues in it is objectionable not only because of its possible effect on that particular case but also because of its side effects which may be far reaching. Responsible "mass media" will do their best to be fair, but there will also be ill-informed, slapdash or prejudiced attempts to influence the public. If people are led to think that it is easy to find the truth, disrespect for the processes of the law could follow, and, if mass media are allowed to judge, unpopular people and unpopular causes will fare very badly."

Lord Cross was of a similar view. He said:

"It is easy enough to see that any publication which prejudges an issue in pending proceedings ought to be forbidden if there is any real risk that it may influence the tribunal...... But why, it may be said, should a publication be prohibited when there is no such risk? The reason is that one cannot deal with one particular publication in isolation. A publication prejudging an issue in pending litigation which is itself innocuous enough may provoke replies which are far from innocuous but which, as they are replies, it would seem unfair to restrain. So gradually the public would become habituated to, look forward to, and resent the absence of, preliminary discussions in the "media" of any case which aroused widespread interest. An absolute rule, though it may seem to be unreasonable if one looks only to the particular case, is necessary in order to prevent a gradual slide towards trial by newspaper or television."

Both Lords Reid and Cross considered it was therefore a necessary general rule to allow no prejudgments upon a pending case. Lord Morris must also be taken to agree with that conclusion. He too, was concerned to prevent "trial by newspaper" though unlike Lords Reid and Cross he also linked his objections to it, the protection of particular litigants. He said:

> "the courts, I think, owe it to the parties to protect them either from the prejudices of pre-judgment or from the necessity of having themselves to participate in the flurries of pre-trial publicity."

Lord Morris agreed that the article published on September 24th was unobjectionable saying that he saw no reason why a "temperate and reasoned" appeal might not have been expressed inviting Distillers, regardless of their legal position, to make generous payments.

Lord Diplock's judgment was expressed differently. In his view the due administration required inter alia "that all citizens should have unhindered access to the constitutionally established courts .... for the determination of disputes as to their legal rights and liabilities" and "once the dispute has been submitted to a court of law, they should be able to rely on there being no usurpation by any other person of that court to decide it according to law." In his view conduct calculated to prejudice either of these requirements or to undermine public confidence that they will be observed amounts to a contempt because:

> "If to have recourse to civil litigation were to expose a litigant to the risk of public obloquy or to public and prejudicial discussion of the facts or merits of the case before they have been determined by the court, potential suitors would be inhibited from availing themselves of courts of law for the purpose for which they are established."

His objection to the proposed article was that in discussing the merits of the dispute between the parents and Distillers it was calculated to prejudice the second of the above requirements. He also objected to the article published on September 24th because he consdered that it held up Distillers to public obloquy and as such was calculated to prejudice the first of the above requirements of the administration of justice. In this respect it was the public persuasion by the Sunday Times that Distillers should not rely upon their strict legal rights that Lord Diplock objected to. His Lordship was prepared to countenance private persuasion.

Lord Simon generally agreed with Lord Diplock and he too objected both to the proposed article and the one published on September 24th (which he described as holding Distillers to execration).(17) However, he went further than Lord Diplock for he was not prepared to draw a simple distinction between public and private pressure upon litigants. In his view even private pressure was acceptable only within narrow limits, namely, where there was a common interest such that fair, reasonable and moderate personal representations would be appropriate.

Although more restrictive than their colleagues both Lords Diplock and Simon did contemplate some freedom for comment during the pendency of legal proceedings. Like the majority they approved the proposition first expressed in the Australian case of Ex parte Dawson:(18)

> "The discussion of public affairs .... cannot be required
> to be suspended merely because the discussion .... may,
> as an incidental but not intended by-product, cause
> some likelihood of prejudice to a person who happens at
> the time to be a litigant."

It is difficult to summarise with precision the collective judgments of their Lordships but what seems to have been established was that there was an objection to and a rule against publications (no matter how well researched or temperately expressed) which prejudge issues pending before the courts. Lords Reid and Cross and to a lesser extent Morris were openly prepared to apply this prohibition regardless of whether a publication created a risk of prejudice to a particular case. This is usually referred to as the "prejudgment test." It is less clear whether Lords Diplock and Simon were saying the same thing (though their underlying concern was the same, namely, to prevent "trial by newspaper") since they linked their objections to the effects upon litigants and in this respect both objected to public criticism of litigants. This is commonly referred to as the "pressure principle."

(iii)   Commentary on and Reactions to the Decision
    The prejudgment test in as much as it was not linked to the risk of prejudice to a particular case broke new ground but it was not entirely unprecedented. In A-G v Butterworth(19) the Court of Appeal held that punishing a witness for giving evidence in a case which had since been concluded amounted to contempt because the act was calculated to prejudice the course of justice by deterring witnesses in future cases from giving evidence.

    Whether it was necessary to expand the law, however, has been doubted. The House of Lords' decision was generally criticised as an over-reaction to an imagined threat of "trial by newspaper." As one commentator said "Thus far we have managed to avoid the spectre of trial by newspaper without the rule".(20)   Doubt has also been cast on the alleged certainty of the prohibition - a claim made by Lord Reid(21) - for it has rightly been said that it is by no means clear what "prejudgment" means.(22)   It may also be thought that the price of this alleged certainty, namely, the curb on freedom to comment, is too high.(23)

    These criticisms were later endorsed by a highly respected report of a Committee originally chaired by Lord Justice Phillimore,(24) which had been set up to consider whether any changes were required in the law relating to contempt of court.   The Committee recommended(25) that the "prejudgment test" be replaced by a test relating to a risk that the course of justice will be seriously impeded or prejudiced." This recommendation was impliedly endorsed by a Government Green Paper.(26)

C. The European Decisions

(i) The Commision's Decision(27)

The Sunday Times' main(28) claim was that the injunction granted by the English Courts violated Art. 10 of the Convention because it restricted the applicant's freedom of expression. By a majority of 8 to 5 the Commission upheld the claim.

There was no doubt that the injunction infringed Art. 10 (1), the whole argument centred on whether it be justified within the terms of Art. 10 (2). The majority ruled that restrictions on freedom of expression cannot be implied by the interpretation of other provisions of the Convention independently of Art. 10.(29) This ruling undermined a major plank of the Government's case, namely, that freedom of expression is subject to an inherent limitation imposed by Art. 6, which requires a fair trial and a fair administration of justice, and that in cases of conflict between Arts. 6 and 10 the latter has to give way. The Commision ruled that the provisions of Art. 6 can only provide arguments for the interpretation of Art. 10 (2) but not substitute the criteria there laid down.(30)

Proceeding on the assumption that the restriction was "prescribed by law"(31) the Commission accepted that the law of contempt in general and the restraint in particular had the legitimate object within the terms of Art. 10 (2) of maintaining the authority and impartiality of the judiciary. The remaining question was whether the particular restriction was "necessary" for this purpose. The Commission did not think that it was, commenting:(32)

> "given the fact that the litigation involved was civil in character, that the contents of the draft article need not necessarily be understood as passing legal judgment on the issues involved in the actions and was not aimed at directly influencing the opinion of the judge, and that at the time of the granting of the injunction the thalidomide proceedings were at the stage of settlement and not court action apart from the

approval of the settlement because of the involvement
of minors was likely to be forthcoming in the
immediate future, the Commission finds that the
authority of the judiciary was not directly put in
question by the publication of the draft article of that
time."

The Government also sought to justify the injunction by
reference in Art. 10 (2) to the protection of the "rights of
others" - in this case, the right of Distillers to a fair trial.
The Commission did not think that it had to consider this as a
separate issue primarily because in their view the aim of
protecting the authority of the judiciary comprehended the
protection of particular litigants' rights.

The dissenters, relying on a point strangely not adverted to
by the majority, maintained that the U.K had acted within its
"margin of appreciation" (discussed below) vested in each
Contracting State to determine the "necessity" and application
of the restrictions as appropriate to that State. They stressed
that it was important to recognise the discretion in this case
because although covered by Art. 10 (2) the particular
restriction is unique to common law jurisdictions and it could
not therefore be said that there was a "European" standard or
concept of what kind of protection the functioning of the
judiciary requires.(33)

(ii) The Court's Decision
The Court ruled by 11 to 9 that the injunction violated Art
10.

It was unanimously agreed that at least one purpose of the
contempt laws is to maintain the authority and impartiality of
the judiciary and that the injunction was specifically aimed at
maintaining the judiciary's "authority".(34)   Hence, the
restriction had a legitimate aim within Art. 10 (2). Like the
Commission, the majority ruled that it was unnecessary to
consider as a separate issue whether the contempt laws had
the further purpose of safeguarding the "rights of others"
because that purpose was included in the notion of protecting
the judiciary's "authority".

It was generally agreed that the injunction was a restriction "prescribed by law" for the purposes of Art. 10 (2).(35) The argument that it might not be stemmed from the alleged novelty of the "prejudgment test" which the Court took to be established by the majority of the House of Lords. As the Court ruled that "prescribed by law" requires first, that "the citizen must be able to have an indication that is adequate in the circumstances of the legal rules applicable to a given case" and that "he must be able-if need be with appropriate advice - to foresee, to a degree that is reasonable in the circumstances, the consequences which a given action may ·entail", it was perhaps surprising that the "prejudgment test" passed this hurdle.

Given these findings the key issue became whether the restriction was "necessary in a democratic society." To determine this, regard had first to be had to the "margin of appreciation" that should be accorded to the UK courts. That a Contracting State has some discretion to decide for itself the "necessity" of the restriction in a particular case stems from the principle that intitial responsibility for securing the rights and freedoms under the Convention lies with the individual Contracting States.(36) The width of this margin of appreciation has been a recurring problem of Convention law, the dilemma being that if it is too wide the Commission and the Court would be reduced to a state of vitual impotence but if it is ignored those bodies would become in effect supranational appeal courts and thereby override Contracting States' sovereign rights and democratic duties.(37)

The scope of the margin of appreciation had been previously considered by the Court in Handyside v United Kingdom.(38) There, a wide "margin of appreciation" had been accorded to the U.K. with regard to the protection of morals because, there being no uniform European conception of morals the State authorities by "reason of their direct and continuous contact with the vital forces of their countries" were "in principle in a better position than the international judge to give an opinion on the exact content of the requirements as well as on the "necessity of a restriction"---

intended to meet them". The majority in the Sunday Times case distinguished Handyside on the basis that unlike morals, the notion of the "authority" of the judicary is far more objective, the domestic law and practice of the Contracting States revealing a "fairly substantial measure of common ground in this area". Hence, "a more extensive European supervision corresponds to a less discretionary power of appreciation". The majority accepted that it was not the Court's task simply to take the place of a competent national court, nevertheless that did not mean that its role was limited to judging whether a State had exercised its discretion reasonably, carefully and in good faith. As they said:

"Even a Contracting State so acting remains subject to the Court's control as regards the compatiblity of its conduct with the engagements it has undertaken under the Convention".

In particular this meant that the generally legitimate aims of the contempt laws did not ipso facto make the particular restriction "necessary".

It remained to consider the "necessity" of the particular restriction. Following Handyside, "necessity" was ruled to mean something between "indispensable" and "reasonable", "useful" or "desirable" and implied the existence of a "pressing social need". The question therefore pursued by the majority was whether the "interference" complained of corresponded to a "pressing social need", whether it was "proportionate" to the legitimate aim pursued" and whether the reasons given by the national authorities to justify it were "relevant and sufficient under Article 10 (2)". With regard to the latter inquiry the majority noted that the Law Lords had emphasised the concern that the processes of the law may be brought into disrespect and the functions of the court usurped inter alia if litigants had to undergo "trial by newspaper." Though certainly "relevant" to the maintenance of the authority of the judiciary it was doubted whether the particular article would have had that effect. However, it was acknowledged that the fear that publication of the proposed article might have provoked replies was also a "relevant" concern but the question then was whether in all the circumstances this was "sufficient" reason so as to make the restriction "necessary". In the majority's view it was not. Working from the principle that the:

"Court is faced not with a choice between two conflicting principles but with a principle of freedom of expression that is subject to a number of exceptions which must be narrowly interpreted."

The majority were not so much concerned with the timing of the proposed article (for they accepted(39) that preventing interference with negotiations towards the settlement of a pending suit was a "legitimate" aim) but more with the public interest in the case. In their view a court cannot operate in a vacuum so there cannot be a total embargo against prior discussion of disputes outside the courts, indeed, it was incumbent on the mass media to impart information and ideas concerning matters that come before the court just as in other areas of public interest. In this case the thalidomide disaster was a matter of "undisputed" public concern and that concern extended to the question of where responsibility for the tragedy actually lay. This public concern was not outweighed by any demonstrative need on the facts to maintain "the authority of the judiciary". Accordingly, the majority ruled that Art. 10 had been violated.

(iii)   Commentary on and Reactions to the Decision

The crucial part of the majority's judgment was their dismissal of the claim that the UK courts had acted within their "margin of appreciation". Ironically, in view of the serious inquiry as to whether the "prejudgment test" was "prescribed by law", the majority's distinction of Handyside, namely, that the breadth of the appreciation depended upon the character of the right or restriction involved, was itself unprecedented. Furthermore, the application of the alleged distinction, namely, that unlike morals there is in effect a common European concept of "authority of the judicary", seems questionable. As the minority said,(40) given the uniqueness of the contempt laws to common law jurisdictions, which restriction is specifically safeguarded by the concluding words of Art. 10 (2), it is difficult to accept the majority's contention that "the domestic law and practice of the Contracting States reveal a fairly broad measure of common ground" as to the notion of "authority of the judiciary". Nevertheless it is the majority decision which sets the precedent and in Convention terms it is an important one since it amounts to a significant expansion of jurisdiction. Indeed one commentator has suggested(41) that this was the majority's real motive and that they were attempting to accomplish a break generally from the traditionally accepted concept of the margin of appreciation. Hence, the necessity to circumscribe rather narrowly the findings of Handyside so as not to embarrass the Court as a precedent for any other area save public morals and obscenity. Time will tell whether the Court will generally choose to follow the Sunday Times rather than Handyside,(42) but so far as the particular restriction is concerned, the Court is perhaps unlikely to depart from its now established stance. Whether this is a desirable stance is another matter.

Commentaries on the Sunday Times decision from the domestic law point of view have varied from outright condemnation(43) to evident pleasure.(44) However, one's views of the merits of the particular decision of the European Court are likely to be coloured by the opinion held of the House of Lords' decision. In this respect it is worth remembering that the emotionally charged facts of the Sunday Times case presented in an extreme form the ultimately inevitable clash between freedom of speech and the right to a fair trial. It may well be that the English law of contempt deserved in the instant case the jolt that the European Court gave it. However, to have a European ruling on one outstandingly difficult case is one thing but quite another to have constant interference and potential clash of opinion which is what the European decision could herald.

Two other criticisms of the European Court's decision might be ventured. First, it may be thought that the majority were too dismissive of the point (which weighed heavily with the minority) that the injunction was neither a total nor a permanent ban on what could be said about the thalidomide tragedy. In fact, as Lord Morris pointed out,(45) the scope for comment was quite wide and it is matter of debate whether the majority were right in considering it "artificial" to attempt to divide the "wider issues" and the negligence issue. There was certainly no justification, as the minority pointed out, for insinuating that because of the contempt laws the English courts acted in a vacuum. Secondly, it may be wondered how the Court can reconcile its decision under Art. 10 with the rights guaranteed under Art. 6. Whatever the technical merits may have been for ruling that the exception relating to the "rights of others" did not constitute a separate issue the fact remains that whether it is its direct objective or not the law of contempt does protect a litigant's right to a fair trial and that right is guaranteed by Art. 6. Is the European Court therefore, as the majority maintained, free of the need to balance the ultimately conflicting principles? It is suggested that it is not. Indeed if its "isolationist" approach is pursued to its logical conclusion it is possible to imagine that an individual litigant might justifiably claim a breach of Art. 6 in respect of a publication the restraint of which the Court could rule to be in breach of Art. 10!

(III) The Changes to the Domestic Law Required by the
        European Court's Decision.
  Whatever criticism may be made of the European Court's decision the fact remains that by being found to have violated Art. 10 the UK was obliged, by reason of Art. 53, to amend the laws to conform with its ruling. What then was required of the UK? No- one disputes the need to reverse the prejudgment test as laid down by the majority in the House of Lords. The majority in the European Court expressly concluded(46) that they had to weigh the balance in each case between freedom of expression and the maintenance of the authority of judicary. The prejudgment test amounted to an absolute prohibtion irrespective of the risks of prejudice to an individual case and as such was inconsistent with the European Court's decision.

  What further reform, if any, was required by the European Court's decision? There has been heated dispute about this. Lord Hailsham (who, as Lord Chancellor, introduced the Contempt of Court Bill before Parliament) has always maintained(47) that the sole issue before the European Court was the "prejudgment test" and therefore reform of this test was all that the ruling required. Hence, he saw no necessity to implement the Phillimore Committee's recommendation that:(48)

"Bringing influence or pressure to bear upon a party to proceedings should not be held to be a contempt unless it amounts to intimidation or unlawful threats to his person, property or reputation".

In any event he argued that there was no need to reform the law in this respect since the Sunday Times had won that point before the House of Lords. Finally, and more controversially, he does not see the European decision as establishing precedence of freedom of speech over the administration of justice. As he said when introuducing the Contempt Bill for its second reading:(49)

"The Strasbourg Court was divided in its opinion on the result of the Sunday Times case, but the members were all agreed on the principles to be applied when the two sets of rights [ie. the right to a fair trial and the right of freedom of expression] came potentially into conflict. Justice, they said, comes first, but only to the extent - and here I quote -"necessary in a free society" and when seeking an explanation of the word "necessary" in this context, the Court explained that they intended it to carry a meaning somewhere between "desirable" and "indispensable". Whatever my opinion may be regarding the semantics of this, I venture to adopt the principle".

Antony Whitaker, the Legal Manager of Times Newspapers Ltd., sees the European Court's decision in markedly different terms. In his view(50) the decision represented a wider condemnation of the law of contempt than simply the "prejudgment test" and in general amounted to a victory for freedom of expression over the right to a fair trial. He therefore disputes Lord Hailsham's conclusions. In particular, he considers him to be wrong in maintaining that Art. 6 takes precedence over Art. 10 citing in support the European Court's statement that it:

"is not faced with a choice of two conflicting
principles, but with a principle of free expression that
is subject to a number of exceptions which must be
narrowly defined".

Secondly, he believes the Lord Chancellor's interpretation of
"necessary" erroneous in that it omitted to say that the Court
said that restriction on free expression could only be justified
by a sufficiently pressing social need. Finally, he takes issue
with the belief that the "pressure test" was not a "live" issue
before the European Court adding that in any event the House
of Lords did not clearly establish that pressure upon litigants
was permissible.

It is submitted that it would be misleading simply to assert
that one of the above views is "right" and the other "wrong"
because the European decision is sufficiently open-ended to
allow a difference of view. Indeed, to some extent it is
possible to find in the decision what one is seeking to find.
What characterises Lord Hailsham's approach is that he is
looking to respond more to the letter of the judgment whereas
Whitaker urges a response to what he conceives to be the
spirit of the decision. For example, though one would search
the European Court's judgment in vain for express support for
the argument that Art. 6 takes precedence over Art. 10,(51) it
could be argued(52) that the Lord Chancellor is in fact
technically correct in that Art. 10 (2) permits restrictions on
freedom of expression inter alia to protect a fair trial, which
is a right guaranteed by Art. 6. To that extent Art. 6 might be
said to have precedence over Art. 10. But to regard the
European Court's decision in this light is perhaps to miss the
spirit of the decision. The Court did, as Whitaker maintains,
start from the basic premise that freedom of expression is the
master value, though whether it was free to do so is
debatable.(53) Lord Hailsham starts from the premise that the
administration of justice is the master value. Such conflicting
view points will produce opposite results in at least border line
cases and while that does not necessarily mean that the
ensuing legislation fails to meet the obligations to reform the
law, it does prompt different attitudes as to what reform is
required. It is in this context that the dispute as to the

meaning of "necessary" becomes understandable. Lord Hailsham, perhaps not seeing it as crucial, was content to paraphrase it by reference to the Court's statement that it meant something between "desirable" and "indispensable". Whitaker, conceiving the definition to be important and keen to curb the courts' contempt powers, thought the European Court's subsequent reference to the restraint having to be justified by a sufficiently pressing social need, much more relevant. The latter's views probably more accurately reflect the spirit of the Court's decision. As one commentator pointed out,(54) Lord Hailsham's interpretation gives the impression that the European concept of "necessary" was more woolly than it really is.

Lord Hailsham was probably wrong to say that the "pressure test" was not a "live issue" before the European Court. Although it was not its major concern the majority did advert to the "pressure test" and held it insufficient to justify the restraint imposed upon the Sunday Times.(55) However, Lord Hailsham was technically right when he said the newspaper had won its fight on this point(56) in the House of Lords and although the law would have been clearer had the point been enshrined by statute there was in principle no need to change the law to comply with the European Court's ruling.

Although Whitaker's views probably more accurately reflect the spirit of the European Court's decision that does not mean that a narrow construction of what reform is required cannot be justified. It is not to be forgotten that the European decision was reached only by the narrowest of margins. Furthermore, the majority's approach to the issue of the "margin of appreciation" was novel and controversial nor is their approach to the relevance of Art. 6 beyond criticism. That in itself might justify caution on the issue of reform. Secondly, it cannot be said that the European decision represented a wholesale condemnation of the law of contempt. On the contrary, it was accepted that the domestic law had a legitimate aim within the terms of Art. 10(2). This does not support the view that radical reform of contempt was required. Further, the Court was only concerned with that aspect of contempt aimed at protecting the "authority" of the Judiciary.(57) It did not pass comment, nor therefore criticise, the application of contempt when concerned to protect the "impartiality" of the judiciary. This would seem to confine the decision to the application of contempt with respect to freedom of comment upon civil proceedings. Lastly, it may be said that the particular facts of the litigation were unique to the extent that one might be justifiably wary of drawing too many conclusions from the European Court's decision as to the validity of the general application of the law of contempt.

The above factors, it is submitted, justify a narrow construction of the European Court's decision. On this basis all that can be said to be unequivocally demanded was the abolition of the prejudgment test and its replacement by a test to be applied in each case approximating to what the European Court conceived to be "necessary". It is submitted that in essence this is what Lord Hailsham set out to achieve so that it might be said that he was justified in claiming that his Bill complied with the European Court's ruling. In fact, soon after the Bill's introduction to Parliament, the Committee of Ministers (which under Art. 54 is charged with the duty of supervising the execution of the judgments of the European Court) declared themselves satisfied that the obligation had been met.(58) However, as Zellick(59) pointed out this was hardly a credible exercise since the Committee did not even see a copy of the Bill and could not take into account any subsequent amendments.

IV Does the Contempt of Court Act 1981 in fact comply with the European Court's decision?

A Do the provisions implement the requirements of the European Court's Decision?
The relevant part of the Contempt of Court Act 1981 is that dealing with what is termed the "strict liability rule". This is defined by s.1 as

"the rule of law whereby conduct may be treated as a contempt of court as tending to interfere with the course of justice in particular legal proceedings regardless of intent to do so".

S.2(1) confines the application of the rule to "publications" while s.2(2) provides:

"The strict liability rule applies only to a publication which creates a substantial risk that the course of justice in the proceedings in question will be seriously impeded or prejudiced".

In deciding whether the Act complies with the European Court's ruling s.2(2) is crucial for it is by this provision that it is intended(60) to replace the prejudgment test, as laid down by the majority in the House of Lords, with a more flexible test that is in accordance with the criterion of "necessity" permitted under Art. 10(2). These objectives, as we have seen, are the minimum requirements demanded by the European Court. The question remains as to whether the Act achieves these objectives.

Some(61) have argued that despite its intention the Act may not abolish the prejudgment test as applied in the Sunday Times case. One argument is that as the Act does not apply to intentional contempts it does not apply to intentional prejudgments. Hence, it is argued that as the Sunday Times intended to interfere with the proceedings against Distillers, the Act will not reverse the decision. At first sight, the argument appears meritorious especially as some of the Law Lords adverted(62) to the purpose and object of the proposed article. However, the decision did not turn on intent nor is it so certain that the defendants were guilty of a deliberate contempt. The editor might have conceded that he intended to influence Distillers against relying upon their strict legal rights but he would undoubtedly have contested the claim that he intended to interfere with the course of justice against Distillers.

A second argument is more formidable. It is said - rightly - that the majority of the Law Lords conceived the prejudgment test to protect the administration of justice as a whole and not necessarily to protect the individual litigant. Since by s.1 the Act is only concerned to control publications interfering with the course of justice "in particular legal proceedings", it is said that the Act fails completely to deal with the Sunday Times decision. This is a tenable interpretation. However, were it to be adopted it could arguably mean that no publication was caught by the Act since they could be said to constitute contempt upon the wide basis of interfering with the administration of justice generally. For this reason alone it is unlikely that the courts would adopt such an interpretation.(63) Indeed it is suggested that it is incumbent upon the courts not to interpret the Act so as to preserve the prejudgment test for not only would that thwart Parliament's intention but it would fly in the face of the European Court's ruling. With regard to the latter Lord Scarman has said in A-G v B.B.C.(64) that though the European Court's decision in the Sunday Times case is not part of English law yet "there is a presumption, albeit rebuttable, that our municipal law will be consistent with our international obligations". Bearing these points in mind it is suggested that the courts should interpret s.1 as referring to publications that relate in some way to particular legal proceedings.

A further problem with s.2(2) is whether it overturns the prejudgment test as conceived by the minority of the Law Lords in the Sunday Times case. It will be recalled that the minority's objection to prejudgments was inter alia because of the pressure it put upon litigants. Moreover, it was because of such pressure that they objected to an article already published by the newspaper. It could be argued that such pressure constitutes a substantial risk of serious prejudice to particular proceedings within the meaning of s.2(2). It would have been preferable had the statute expressly stated that a publication cannot be a contempt merely because a litigant is brought into the pressure of public argument to settle the action or forego his legal rights.(65) However, it cannot be said that s.2(2) creates the possibility of such publications being held to be contempt. On the contrary, the convoluted s.6(b) is intended to prevent any publication being a contempt under the strict liability rule that was not formerly so under the common law. On this basis the minority's viewpoint should not represent the current law and in any event it should not do so in view of the European Court's decision. In theory, therefore, publications constituting a fair and temperate criticism of litigants do not constitute contempt. There may, however, be legitimate fears among publishers that the judiciary, especially in view of the minority's attitude, will not readily regard a publication as constituting "fair and temperate criticism". It is to be hoped that the courts, mindful of their international obligations, will allay such fears.

Assuming that the prejudgment test in its various guises has been replaced, the question remains as to whether the new test under s.2(2) corresponds to the concept of "necessity" under Art.10(2). Whitaker doubts(6) whether it accords with what he maintains is a higher standard of freedom envisaged by the European Court. There is perhaps room for doubt on this. Whitaker has been proved right in maintaining that the requirement of a substantial risk of serious prejudice is only cosmetically different to the pre-Sunday Times test of a "real risk of prejudice". Lord Diplock virtually said as much in A-G v English.(67) On the other hand, Lord Scarman has said(68) that he understands the test of "pressing social need" as referring to a substantial risk of grave injustice which is essentially what s.2(2) provides. What matters of course, is not so much the words used in the Act (though some would say that s.2(2) is a fair synonym for "pressing social need") but how the judiciary will apply them. Potentially, given the elimination of the prejudgment test and the recognition of the legitimacy of criticising litigants, s.2(2) allows considerable latitude for comment on civil proceedings. Since it is accepted(69) that professionally trained judges are not susceptible to the deleterious effect of newspaper comment the only risk of prejudice is the possible effect on witnesses. Such a risk, though recognised as a reason for holding a publication to be contempt,(70) was not adverted to in the Sunday Times case and has not been frequently used as the basis for upholding a prosecution. It is possible that restrictions on what can be said about civil litigation will be developed under this head but it is to be hoped that mindful of the UK's international obligations the courts will not too readily refer to this risk as a reason for holding a publication to be a contempt.

With these reservations the new test does, it is submitted, approximate to the "necessity" criterion under Art.10(2). In any event it will be difficult in any future case for the European Court to interfere since to do so will entirely eliminate the "margin of appreciation" accorded to Contracting States.

Ironically, one provision which overrules the Sunday Times decision was not a reform demanded by the European Court's decision. Under s.2(3) the strict liability rule only applies to "active" proceedings. By Sched 1 para. 13 civil proceedings become "active" either (in the case of the High Court) when the case is set down for trial or when a date for the hearing is fixed. This, therefore, leaves pre-trial negotiations unprotected at least from unintentional interference with the course of justice thereby overruling the Sunday Times decision.(71)

The new timing provisions implement the Phillimore Committee's recommendation(72) in this respect and effectively uphold Court of Appeal view in the Sunday Times case that the proceedings in question were "dormant". The European Court referred to the fact that the case had been in a "legal cocoon" for several years when examining the circumstances to determine whether there was a pressing social need for the restraint but it also commented that preventing interference with negotiations towards the settlement of a pending suit was a legitimate aim under Art.10(2).(73) Although it is submitted that the new provision represents a fair compromise between the respective claims of freedom of expression and the right to a fair trial nevertheless it does give rise to the intriguing possibility of a litigant claiming that by not protecting pre-trial negotiations the UK is in breach of Art.6!

During the passage of the Bill the Attorney-General claimed(74) that compliance with the European Court's ruling was made "doubly sure" by what is now s.5. That provides:

"A publication made as or as part of a discussion in good faith of public affairs or other matters of general public interest is not to be treated as a contempt of court under the strict liability rule if the risk of impediment or prejudice to particular legal proceedings is merely incidental to the discussion".

To the extent that s.5 permits greater freedom of expression it is in line with the spirit of the European Court's decision, but it is in fact only statutory confirmation of what the Law Lords unanimously took to be the position prior to the Act. Furthermore it was not thought to help the Sunday Times since the risk of prejudice was not "incidental" to the discussion.

B   Do Other Provisions Infringe the European Court's Ruling?

Hitherto our concern has been whether the Act implements the changes demanded by the European Court but do other provisions infringe the ruling?   It is suggested that one provision might.(75) Under s.8 there is now an absolute ban on publication of "statements made, opinions expressed, arguments advanced or votes cast by members of a jury in the course of their deliberations in any legal proceedings".(76) In Convention terms this blanket prohibition can be said in general to have the legitimate aim of protecting the "authority of the judiciary". In individual cases, however, it may be difficult to justify the restraint. As an example one can cite A-G v New Statesman and Nation Publishing Co. Ltd.(77) where the defendants were prosecuted, prior to the Act, for publishing an unsolicited and unpaid for account by unnamed jurors in the Thorpe trial, saying, inter alia, that the jury could not accept the uncorroborated word of a prosecution witness who had agreed to accept money from a newspaper. On the facts of the case the Divisional Court could find no particular risks to the administration of justice to justify a finding of contempt. The prosecution failed. Had the circumstances occurred after the Act the prosecution would have succeeded, but would not that run counter to Art.10 following the European Court's ruling in the <u>Sunday Times</u> Case since the revelations might properly be thought to be a matter of public interest and concern?

V   Conclusions

On October 3 1982 the <u>Sunday Times</u> complained that the Contempt of Court Act 1981 "has palpably failed in its purpose of bringing English law into line with the European Convention on Human Rights".   It announced its intention of taking its complaint back to Europe.   Even if some procedure for taking the complaint back can be found(78) it is submitted that it should be dismissed.   As this essay has sought to demonstrate, on a narrow construction (which was arguably justified) of the European Court of Human Rights' ruling in the <u>Sunday Times</u> v <u>United Kingdom</u> the only reform of contempt that was required was the replacement of the "prejudgment test" by a test approximating to the concept of "necessity" and on a (possibly) liberal construction of the Contempt of Court Act 1981 the UK has complied with these obligations though another provision of the Act, namely s.8, might be thought to have potentially violated Art. 10.

It is submitted that there is no evidence yet that the courts will interpret the Act in a way which will infringe the European Court's ruling.   The media have seized on a comment made by Lord Diplock in <u>A-G</u> v <u>English</u>(79) in which he said that an article published by the <u>Daily Mail</u> which made no direct reference to any particular case was the "antithesis" of the article written by the <u>Sunday Times</u>.   This has been taken to mean that such an article would still be a contempt under the 1981 Act.   It may be that Lord Diplock was being unnecessarily provocative in referring to the <u>Sunday Times</u> but it cannot be said that he intended to say that the article would still be a contempt. It is submitted, that looked at in context, all he was saying, was that direct discussion of pending cases does not come under s.5 since any resulting prejudice cannot be described as being "merely incidental".   For the reasons already stated in this essay it is submitted that the <u>Sunday Times</u> <u>has</u> been reversed by the Contempt of Court Act 1981.

That contempt needed reform in the light of Art.10 came perhaps as a shock to many. To some this was an unacceptable shock, the European Court's ruling being an example of an International Court interfering in national affairs about which it knew little. On balance it is submitted that international scrutiny of the contempt laws was no bad thing. The Human Rights Court perhaps works best in regard to substantive laws when it is called upon to judge upon a rigid rule of law - such was the prejudgment test. It is another matter to have the Court passing its own value judgments on the application of a fair test that is to be applied according to the facts on each case. In such cases the Court would simply be operating as a supranational appeal court which is not its function.(80) For this reason it will be difficult for the Court to interfere with a decision that a particular publication creates a substantial risk of serious prejudice to the course of justice in a particular case.

The immediate tangible legacy of the Sunday Times litigation is the Contempt of Court Act 1981. To some the legislative response is disappointing though it is not as restrictive as the media claims. The Act is not the only legacy for there is now a wider awareness of the Convention and in particular of its relevance to contempt of court. One consequence is that others, notably Harriet Harman,(81) have decided to follow the Sunday Times' example and take their case to Europe. No doubt more will follow. What effect this will have upon the domestic law of contempt remains to be seen. The irony is that had the recommendations of the Phillimore Committee, which reported in 1974 been speedily implemented, the relevance of Art.10 may not have been appreciated for it is unlikely that the Sunday Times would have pursued its case in Europe and, until it did, scant attention had been paid to the possible implications the Convention had for the domestic law of contempt.(82) This irony is all the more striking for although the European Court's decision finally prompted the Government to legislate, none of the statute's provisions are actually modelled on the Strasbourg decision.

FOOTNOTES

(1) 1979 2 EHRR 245.

(2) 1923 SC 789 cited with approval by Lord Edmund-Davies in A-G v Leveller Magazine Ltd [1979] AC 440, 459 and the Report of the Committee on Contempt of Court ("the Phillimore Report") 1974 Cmnd 5794 p2. For a similar comment see Lord Cross in A-G v Times Newspapers Ltd [1974]AC 273 at p322.

(3) [1979] AC 440, 449.

(4) See Borrie and Lowe: The Law of Contempt (1st Edn,1973 Butterworths) Chs 3 and 4.

(5) See A-G v Butterworth [1963] 1 QB 696, 273 per Donovan LJ. See also A-G v Times Newspapers Ltd [1974] AC 273, 294 per Lord Reid.

(6) See Borrie and Lowe op cit Ch6. In R v Gray [1900] 2 QB 36,40 Lord Russell of Killowen CJ said:
"Any act done or writing published calculated to bring a Court or a judge of the Court into contempt or to lower his authority is a contempt of Court".

(7) For an excellent comparative survey see Murray Rosen: The Sunday Times thalidomide case: Contempt of Court and the Freedom of the Press (1979, Writers and Scholars Educational Trust) Part 4.

(8) According to the Travaux Preparatoires Vol III, these words first appeared as Art 11(2) (see p292) for consideration before the Second meeting of the Committee of Experts 6-10 March 1950 (see p278). Earlier versions (see eg. the Consultative Assembly, Draft Art 6 2(b) at p264 of Vol III of the Travaux Preparatoires) simply referred to "the functioning of administration and justice".

(9) See the Joint Dissenting Opinion in Sunday Times v UK 1979 2 EHRR 245, 285 para 2. Query whether the phrase truly encapsulates the contempt doctrine? It might be argued that the maintenance of the authority and impartiality of the judiciary is narrower than the maintenance of the due administration of justice which is the real objective of the contempt laws.

(10) See generally The Thalidomide Children and the Law (1973 Andre Deutsch) and Murray Rosen: The Sunday Times Case: Contempt of Court and Freedom of the Press

(11) See now the Congenital Disabilities (Civial Liability) Act 1976.

(12) Re Taylor's Application [1972] 2 QB 369.

(13) A-G v Times Newspapers Ltd [1973] 1 QB 710 (Div Ct), 727 (CA)

(14) The Divisional Court had rejected the contention that they were required to balance the public interest in protecting the administration of justice and the right of the public to be informed.

(15) [1974]AC 273.

(16) Lord Reid was said to be hesitant on this point and he concluded his judgment with the comment: "But if things drag on indefinitely so that there is no early prospect either of a settlement or of a trial in court then I think that there will have to be a reassessment of the public interest in a unique situation".

(17) CJ Miller: (Contempt of Court: The Sunday Times Case[1975] Crim LR 132, 138) has suggested that it was "extravagant" to describe the Sept 24

article as holding Distillers up to execration or public obloquy. But is not that exactly what the article did do, even if it was temperately written?

(18) [1961] SR (NSW) 573, 575.

(19) [1963]1 QB 696 - and see Borrie and Lowe op cit at p 213 et seq.

(20) Miller: [1975] Crim LR 132, 135.

(21) [1974]AC at p300 G-H.

(22) Miller: The Sunday Times Case(1974) 37 MLR 94, 98.

(23) Lowe: Freedom of Speech and the Sub Judice Rule(1977) 127 NLJ 676, 678.

(24) The report was published in December 1974 (Cmnd 5794).

(25) See paras 103-114.

(26) "Contempt of Court: A Discussion Paper", (1978) Cmnd 7145.

(27) Application No 6538/74 - Adopted on 18 May 1977.

(28) They also claimed that they had been unfairly discriminated against, contrary to Art 14 (when read in conjunction with Art 10) because although other publications dealt with the thalidomide tragedy it was only their article which was restrained. Both the Commission and the Court unanimously rejected this claim. A further claim that the injunction prevented the applicants from exercising their duties as journalist thereby violating Art 18 (when read in conjunction with Art 10) was rejected by the Commission and not pursued before the Court.

(29) Ibid at para 191. Following De Becker v Belgium Rept of 8 Jan 1960, para 263.

(30) This would seem to contradict Lord Hailsham's views of the case - see below.

(31) Ie. the Commission did not make a ruling on this point -but see paras 200-205. At the hearing before the Court on April 25 1978 the Commission's Principal Delegate considered the restraint was not "prescribed by law" see 1979 2 EHRR at p270 para 46. As to the meaning of "prescribed by law" see below.

(32) At para 235 the majority also commented that as the settlement negotiations took place out of court the "impact of a publication on the process of negotiating itself could therefore not be considered as involving the authority and impartiality of the judiciary". This is an example of the point adverted to in Fn 9 above that the exception in Art 10(2) is narrower than the aim of the domestic law of contempt, namely, to protect the administration of justice. However, the Court ruled (see below) that preventing interference with negotiations towards the settlement of a pending suit is a legitimate aim under Art 10)2).

(33) The Dissenters relied on Handyside v United Kingdom 1980 1 EHRR 737 (discussed below) for authority in according a wide "margin of appreciation" to the UK in the Sunday Times case.

(34) ie it was accepted, that the injunction was not imposed to protect "the impartiality of the judiciary".

(35) Cf the conclusions of Judges Zekia O'Donoghue and Evrigerires.

(36) See eg Handyside v UK 1980 1 EHRR 737, 754 para 48. See also Jacobs: The European Convention on Human Rights (1975 Clarendon Press) pp201-2.

(37) See Rosen: The Sunday Times thalidomide case: etc, op cit para 1.09. Jacobs op cit at p 202.

(38) 1980 1 EHRR 737.

(39) Though the fact that the case had been in a legal "cocoon" was later referred to when examining the circumstances in which the injunction was granted.

(40) Ibid at p289, 290, para 9. A similar point is made by Clovis C Morrison Jnr.: The Dynamics of Development in the European Human Rights Convention System (1981, Nijhoff) pp 110, 111. For a trenchant criticism of this aspect of the decision see FA Mann: Contempt of Court in the House of Lords and the European Court of Human Rights (1979) 95 LQR 348, 351-2.

(41) Clovis C Morrison Jnr op cit at p111.

(42) The trend towards expansion of jurisdiction (see the essay in this volume by R Kerridge) suggests that the Court will follow the Sunday Times' decision.

(43) See FA Mann (1979) 95 LQR 348. See also DJ Harris (1979) 50 BYIL 257 who argues that the Court "made its own assessment of the situation de novo and simply disagreed with the House of Lords".

(44) Apart from the media, which understandibly welcomed decision, see also Lord Denning: The Due Process of Law (1980, Butterworths) pp 45-49 and Murray Rosen: The Sunday Times thalidomide case etc op cit.

(45) [1974] AC at pp306 E-H.

(46) Ibid at p281, para 65.

(47) See Hansard HL Debs Vol 415, Cols 658, 9, Vol 416 Cols 200-201 and The Times Feb 1st 1981 (Interview conducted by Phillip Knightley and Antony Whitaker) and April 30 (letter).

(48) 1974 Cmnd 5794, para 62.

(49) Hansard HL Debs Vol 415 Cols 658-9.

(50) "The Ligature round the neck of the British Press" The Times April 28, 1981. See also The Times Leader on April 28 and Murray Rosen's letter to the Times May 1, 1981.

(51) As we have seen, the Commission expressly ruled to the contrary see: Application No 6538/74 - Report of the Commission May 18 1977 para 191. See Fn 30 above.

(52) This seems to be what SH Bailey believes see (1982) 45 MLR 301, 304.

(53) The American courts, faced with a similar dilemna created by the First and Sixth Amendments to the Constitution, have also favoured freedom of speech but this is because (See Nebraska Press Association v Stuart 1976 96 S Ct 279) it has been concluded that adverse pre-trial publicity does not inevitably lead to an unfair trial.

(54) Murray Rosen in a letter to the Times May 1 1981.

(55) 1979 2 EHRR at p278, paras 62, 63.

(56) As we have seen, the majority ie Lords Reid, Morris and Cross accepted that it was permissible to put some public pressure on litigants to settle. Although Murray Rosen in his letter to the Times May 1 1981 was right to say that Halsbury's Laws of England (4th Edn), Vol 9, para 19 states that it may be a contempt to publish comment which is likely to bring pressure to bear on

one or other of the parties and cites A-G v Times Newspapers Ltd in support, it is submitted that such a proposition is too wide. In any event it is qualified by the statement at the end of the paragraph that "Fair and temperate comment on pending proceedings, made without any oblique motive may be permissible even if its purpose and effect is to urge a party to litigation to forego his legal rights etc".

(57) In fact the "impartiality" ground was not pleaded before the Court and was left out of account see 1979 2 EHRR at p274, para 57.

(58) 1981 3 EHRR 615.

(59) [1981] PL pp145,6.

(60) See Lord Hailsham's comments in Hansard HL Debs Vol 415, Col 660.

(61) Eg AM Tettenborn: The Contempt of Court Bill:Some Problems (1981) 125 Sol Jo 123 with whom ML Pearl agreed 1981 SLT 141 and David Barnard: Contempt of Court Act 1981 (1981) 125 Sol Jo 715.

(62) Eg Lords Morris and Simon at [1974] AC pp307 and 321 respectively.

(63) See also Lowe; Contempt of Court Act 1981 [1981] PL 20, 25.

(64) [1981] AC 303, 354.

(65) See Zellick [1981] PL at p146.

(66) The Times April 28 1981.

(67) [1982] 3 WLR 278, 286.

(68) In A-G v BBC [1981] AC at p362 E-F.

(69) See eg Lord Salmon in A-G v BBC [1981] AC at p 343, Borrie and Lowe op cit at p96 et seq, cf Viscount Dilhorne in the BBC case ibid at p 335. During the debates on the Contmpt of Court Bill Lord Hailsham wass also more cautious see eg Hansard HL Debs Vol 415 Cols 694-5 and Vol 416 Cols 406-9.

(70) See eg Borrie and Lowe op cit p98 et seq. See also Lowe: Contempt of Court Act 1981 : The Strict Liability Rule (1981) 131 NLJ at p1168.

(71) It is assumed that the Sunday Times did not intend to interfere with the course of justice - see the text above. Cf ML Pearl:1981 SLT 141.

(72) 1974 Cmnd 5794 paras 127, 129

(73) 1979 2 EHRR at p281, para 66 and p279, para 64 respectively

(74) Hansard HC Debs Vol 1000 Col 30.

(75) Whitaker (The Times April 28, 1981) has suggested that s 4(2), which allows courts to postpone reports of proceedings, infringes the Sunday Times ruling.

(76) For a critical analysis of this provision see Lowe: The Contempt of Court Act 1981-II (1981) 131 NLJ 1191 and Contempt of Court Act 1981 [1982] PL 20, 21 and McConville and Baldwin: The Effect of the Contempt of Court Act on Research on Juries (1981) 145 JPN 575.

(77) [1980] 2 WLR 246.

(78) There is no obvious route of complaint.

(79) [1982] 3 WLR 278, 288

(80) See Jacobs : The European Convention on Human Rights op cit at p 202.

(81) Following the House of Lords' decision in Home Office v Harman [1982] 2 WLR 338 that it was a contempt for a solicitor to allow a journalist to look at "discovered" documents albeit that they have been read out in open court.

This application promises to be an interesting case. For another unsuccessful application see Weston v United Kingdom 1981 3 EHRR 402.

(82) In his article, The European Convention on Human Rights and English Criminal Law [1966] Crim LR 205 and 266 DJ Harris barely mentions contempt of court while the leading works on contempt eg Borrie and Lowe : The Law of Contempt (1973, Butterworths) and Miller : Contempt of Court (1976, Elek) barely mention the Convention. The only reference to Art 10 was in connection with obliging journalist, on pain of contempt, to divulge their confidential sources of information -see eg Fawcett : Application of the European Convention on Human Rights (1969 Clarendon Press) p221. On this see now s10 of the Contempt of Court Act 1981, a provision introduced by Lord Scarman (Hansard HL Debs Vol 416, Col 210-14) with the Convention specifically in mind.

PRISONERS AND THE EUROPEAN CONVENTION ON HUMAN RIGHTS

Gillian Douglas and Stephen Jones

By the end of 1980, the European Commission of Human Rights had examined nearly 8,700 individual applications brought under Art 25 of the Convention, and about one-third of these came from prisoners or persons deprived of their liberty.(1) The aim of this essay is to examine the extent to which the Convention, as interpreted by the European Commission and European Court of Human Rights, has had an effect on the prison system in the United Kingdom. Concern and interest in 'prisoners' rights' have grown over the last decade.(2) Zellick defines a prison regime which takes full account of prisoners' rights as one which "respects the prisoner's inherent dignity as a person, recognises that he does not surrender the law's protection on being imprisoned, and accords procedures and facilities for ensuring that his treatment is at all times just, fair and humane".(3)

Whether or not one accepts the view that prisoners should have rights, and more of them, it is clear that in Western Europe, concern over what happens to those we detain and imprison is a hallmark of jurisprudence. The European Commission presents separate figures for this category of applicants(4), and a number of cases are being heard in our own domestic courts. Why has there been a growth in awareness on the part of commentators and of prisoners? The European Convention itself was born out of the post-concentration camp desire to ensure that history was not repeated.(5) It is perhaps ironic in view of this that conditions of detention are not of themselves within the ambit of the Convention, being examinable only in so far as they involve a breach of the rights actually guaranteed by the Articles of the Convention (cf Art 10 UN International Covenant on Civil and Political Rights). However, the Standard Minimum Rules for the Treatment of Prisoners, adopted by the Committee of Ministers of the Council of Europe in 1973(6), while not binding on member States, provide a detailed guide for practice, covering registration, allocation, accommodation, hygiene, clothing, discipline etc.

In the field of penology, particularly over the last fifteen years, there has been a shift away from the reformative model of treatment towards that of due process and punishment. In the USA, distrust of indeterminate sentencing and wide powers of parole boards, coupled with the expanding civil rights movement,(7) brought prisons under the focus of those seeking to delineate what rights a person has, rather than what privileges he may hope to have bestowed upon him. The disenchantment with 'treatment' as a penal aim has not been as extreme in the UK. Yet, American views, and radical criminological discussion, have produced an emphasis on the criminal as individual subject rather than as stereotypical object. The over-crowding of our prisons has also made prison conditions a topic for media coverage and political interest. Politicization, as opposed to politicians' interest, has not yet reached the same level here as in the USA, where groups like the Black Muslims saw themselves as victims and enemies of white capitalist imperialism. The IRA hunger-strikes in Northern Ireland however, brought overt political confrontation into the arena of prison conditions, and it may be that the longer the Home Office refuses to liberalise prison regimes on the mainland, the more likely it is that 'domestic' prisoners will perceive their situation in political terms.(8)

The Hull prison riot in 1976 may be seen as the effective starting-point for prisoners' litigation in this country. The final realisation of the Court of Appeal in R v Hull Prison Board of Visitors, ex p St Germain that "the Courts are in general the ultimate custodians of the rights and liberties of the subject whatever his status and however attenuated those rights....may be"(9) was a welcome development. Fears of opening the floodgates to thousands of disgruntled prisoners(10) have proved unwarranted. There have been more cases since St Germain but it is submitted that they have raised important issues of principle which it is right that our courts should discuss. It might be that greater willingness on the part of the courts to hear these issues will produce a decline in the number of applications made to Strasbourg. The requirement under the Convention of prior exhaustion of domestic remedies(11) might mean that more applications may be declared inadmissible if the applicant has not sought certiorari.(12) It is likely that one explanation for the number of cases concerning prisoners before the Commission has been the non-existence of an effective domestic remedy. Also prisoners have been kept uninformed about their 'rights', since standing orders and circular instructions which gloss the Prison Rules have been secret.(13) The government has undertaken to revise and publish standing orders, though not circular instructions, and this may have the effect of either ensuring greater attention to giving prisoners their due 'rights' or of encouraging greater recourse to litigation from prisoners who will theoretically be in a position to check up on whether their 'rights' are being infringed.

The prison grapevine has also played a large part in publicising the availability of the Convention , and one cannot ignore the likelihood of some prisoners using it to air grievances without much wish to go beyond letting off steam. From this point of view, access to the domestic courts cannot serve the same purpose, since the prisoner will usually need legal aid to issue proceedings(14), and vexatious actions will be rejected by the local Legal Aid Committee.

It may be said that the early views of the Commission in prisoner cases were somewhat timid, and a clear change of attitude can be seen emerging as the Commission became more practised in dealing with complaints. Early cases are therefore of limited guidance in assessing what the current approach of the Commission might be to specific applications for it is likely that a more sympathetic attitude towards applicants would now be evinced. We propose to examine those Articles of the Convention which have proved of importance to UK prisoners to date.

Article 3: Inhuman or degrading treatment or punishment

It is proposed first to examine the rulings given by the court on the definition of Art 3 and then to discuss the application of this Article to different aspects of treatment of prisoners.

The two leading cases on the scope of this provision both involve the United Kingdom. In Ireland v United Kingdom(15) it was alleged that the Northern Ireland authorities had inflicted torture on republican prisoners by using a number of interrogation devices known as 'the five techniques': these were wall-standing, hooding, subjection to noise, deprivation of sleep and of food and drink. The Court considered the notion of torture and declared that the difference between this and 'inhuman or degrading treatment' lay in the difference in the intensity of the suffering inflicted.(16)

In the Tyrer Case(17), the Court considered the other elements in Art 3, namely, 'inhuman or degrading' or 'punishment'. Indeed Art 3 by expressly prohibiting 'inhuman' and 'degrading' punishment, implies that there is a distinction between such punishment and punishment in general. In the Court's view, in order for a punishment to be 'degrading', "the humiliation or debasement involved must attain a particular level and must in any event be other than that usual element of humiliation referred to....The assessment is, in the nature of things, relative: it depends on all the circumstances of the case and, in particular, on the nature and context of the punishment itself and the manner and method of its execution". On the facts of the case, the Court considered that the birching amounted to a punishment in which the element of humiliation was sufficient to make it degrading.

One would hardly expect to find official sanction of assaults by prison staff in any country and, indeed, r 44 of our Prison Rules 1964 deals with this situation: "An officer in dealing with a prisoner shall not use force unnecessarily and, when the application of force to a prisoner is necessary, no more force than is necessary shall be used".

Like many of the Prison Rules, r 44 is drafted in broad terms, allowing ample scope for a prison officer to claim, if challenged, that his actions were 'necessary'. As the Prison

Rules themselves have hitherto been held not actionable,(18) the prisoner is left with a criminal or civil action for assault, which can be difficult to prove in practice.

Once the domestic remedies have been exhausted, the way is open for an application to the European Commission. Two such applications against the UK were brought by Hilton in 1972 and Reed in 1976. Hilton(19) complained of having been assaulted by prison staff when held in Leeds and Liverpool prisons. The Commission held that although certain aspects of Hilton's treatment (such as being punished for putting his hands in his pockets) were unsatisfactory, there was no evidence to show that he had actually been physically assaulted. Reed's complaint(20) that he was assaulted after the rioting at Hull Prison was neither confirmed nor denied by the Government which, however, admitted that some prisoners had been kicked and punched by some prison officers. The Commission has decided to admit this part of the application.

The Commission has stated that the use of a certain amount of force by prison officers might be justified. For example, in Kiss,(21) the Commission commented that 'a small push' by an officer would not amount to a breach of Art 3. Such 'small pushes' by prison officers can be found at one end of the spectrum of prison violence. At the other end one finds the Greek Case(22) where the Committee of Ministers upheld the view of the Commission that a large number of political prisoners had been systematically ill-treated or tortured. The average case of prison violence probably falls somewhere between the two.

The Commission has had to consider a number of applications which, although not involving outright physical assault, have concerned some other variety of alleged degrading treatment. In the case brought by Ireland against the UK involving the so-called 'five techniques' of interrogation, the Court held that although the techniques "did not occasion suffering of the particular intensity and cruelty implied by the word torture as so understood", they "undoubtedly" amounted to inhuman and degrading treatment.

In McFeeley v UK,(23) the complaint was made that conditions of detention in the 'H' Blocks of the Maze Prison amounted to an inhuman and degrading system of treatment. The conditions complained of arose from the prisoners' decision not to wear prison uniform or use the toilet and washing facilities provided. The Commission, while making it clear that Art 3 did not become inoperative just because the prisoners were challenging the prison administration, nevertheless considered that because these conditions were self-imposed by the applicants "they....could be eliminated almost immediately". Similarly the Commission did not consider that the element of humiliation involved in strip searches amounted to inhuman and degrading treatment.

The third case involving the United Kingdom(24) was brought by a long-term prisoner who complained that he was being deprived of his conjugal rights and of the exercise of his paternal rights; and that these deprivations amounted to mental cruelty and therefore constituted a degrading punishment. The Commission, however, felt that this kind of situation was not covered by Art 3.

The position regarding cellular confinement in England is governed by r 43 of the Prison Rules 1964 and the disciplinary rules. Rule 43, which is euphemistically entitled "Removal from Association", states that, if such removal appears desirable "for the maintenance of good order and discipline" or in the prisoner's own interests, it can be arranged by the prison governor although not for more than 24 hours without the authority of a member of the board of visitors or the Home Secretary. This authority may be renewed monthly.

In practice, r 43 has two main functions: to protect the prisoner from his fellow inmates where, for example, he has committed a sexual offence, and for use as a disciplinary measure.(25) Efforts involving the use of domestic law to challenge periods of solitary confinement have not to date been successful. A recent example can be seen in Williams v Home Office (No2).(26) The plaintiff claimed damages for false imprisonment against the Home Office in respect of 180 days' confinement in the control unit at Wakefield Prison. Tudor Evans J held that non-compliance with the provisions of r 43 did not affect the lawfulness of his detention, nor could the lawfulness be affected by the conditions of his detention since they were a matter for the Secretary of State. He also ruled that the Bill of Rights 1688 should be interpreted as prohibiting only those punishments which were both cruel and unusual, and he held that there was no evidence that the regime in the control unit had satisfied these criteria. He went on to say that, although conditions of solitary confinement had been held to amount to cruel and unusual punishment under the American and Canadian Bills of Rights,(27) the conditions in those cases had been more extreme than the conditions at Wakefield. Art 3 of the Convention was put to the learned judge and he cited Lord Denning MR who in R v Secretary of State for Home Affairs, ex parte Bhajan Singh said: "The Court can and should take the Convention into account....wherever interpreting a statute which affects the rights and liberties of the individual".(28) Nevertheless, in the view of Tudor Evans J, "Judged by the standards of the English prison system, I do not think that the regime in the unit was cruel."(29)

It seems that Williams would fare no better at Strasbourg. The Commission has yet to find a prison isolation case which violates Art 3. In an early application against the UK(30) de Courcy complained that for ten months he was kept in solitary confinement for twenty hours a day. The Commission was not impressed by this application nor by a later one made against the UK in 1971(31). In this case a Category A prisoner who had spent a large amount of time in solitary confinement (partly at his own request) and had attempted suicide twice claimed that his mental health had been affected by the confinement. However, the Commission noted that he had a background of mental instability and, in any case, had now been re-classified as a Category B prisoner.

In Reed the applicant complained of being held in solitary confinement in Winchester prison. The Commission stated that, as prolonged solitary confinement is undesirable especially for remand prisoners but also for convicted prisoners, it "might thus in certain circumstances raise an issue inter alia under Art 3". The Commission, however, considered that in Reed's case itself, the evidence did not suggest that the segregation was so severe as to amount to an infringement of Art 3.

In a more recent application brought against the UK in 1978,(32) the Commission considered the possibility that particular types of solitary confinement could amount to a breach of Art 3. Although removal from association with other prisoners as such would not amount to a breach, "total social and sensory isolation....can destroy the personality and cause severe mental and physical suffering". The Commission felt that this would constitute "a form of inhuman treatment which cannot be justified by the requirements of security or the maintenance of prison order and discipline". Nevertheless, as in Reed the Commission did not consider that the segregation was severe enough to raise an issue under Art 3.

There is some authority that certain forms of treatment of prisoners, while falling short of physical assault cases, amount to inhuman or degrading treatment under Art 3. A related question to be considered is whether the actual condition of prison itself, such as the level of overcrowding, could amount to a breach of Art 3. In an application against the UK in 1968(33) a prisoner claimed that he was subject to inhuman and degrading treatment in that he had no radio, he had been allowed to write more letters when in other prisons and that he could not participate in a vocational training course but had to sew mailbags. The Commission was unimpressed and stated that "the circumstances in which the applicant was detained in prison can in no way be said to constitute such treatment." In McFeeley the Commission also made it clear that there could be no redress if the conditions were self-imposed.

In a recent case,(34) the 'moors murderer' Ian Brady complained that his conditions of detention as a Category A prisoner,(35) whereby he was held for long periods in solitary confinement, were in breach of Art 3. The Commission, while concluding that the cumulative effect of such conditions could amount to a breach, considered that they had improved sufficiently since 1975 to make Brady's complaint groundless.

Rule 3 of the Prison Rules 1964 deals with the classification of prisoners in England and Wales. It provides, inter alia, that prisoners should be classified with regard to their age, temperament and record and with a view to maintaining good order and facilitating training. As a result of the Mountbatten Report(36) in 1966, a security classification ranging from A to D (lowest) was established. There is no special procedure for a prisoner to appeal against his classification under domestic law but a number of applications against the United Kingdom have been made to the Commission alleging a breach of Art 3.

In a 1969 case,(37) a prisoner complained that, owing to a conviction for murder which was later quashed on appeal, he had been classified as a Category A prisoner and treated accordingly. The Commission, however, did not accept that there had been any violation of Art 3. In 1971 another Category A prisoner applied to the Commission.(38) His complaint concerned the conditions of imprisonment that arose from his classification: no open visits, no evening classes, no access to television and separate exercising. Once again, the Commission declared the application inadmissible. In another 1971 case,(39) the applicant wanted to be sent to Grendon Psychiatric Prison. The Commission declared that it was not a breach of Art 3 to keep a mentally disturbed person in an ordinary prison if he was receiving proper treatment.

The Brady case, also dealt with this problem. Brady complained of his Category A status: he pointed out that his co-defendant had already been removed from Category A, that he had never attempted to escape as she had and that several prison and medical officers thought that he should not be kept in Category A. However, the Commission felt that "this is not a matter which falls within the scope of the rights and freedoms ensured by the Convention".

Article 5: The right to liberty

Article 5 guarantees the right to liberty and security of person. Article 5(2) states that "Everyone who is arrested shall be informed promptly, in a language which he understands, of the reasons for his arrest and of any charge against him". This is a fairly basic procedure under most jurisdictions(40) and has led to few difficulties under the Convention. However, the matter was raised in X,Y and Z v UK.(41) The applicants who were detained under the Prevention of Terrorism (Temporary Provisions) Act 1976, complained that their arrest was in breach of Art 5(2) as no attempt was made to inform them of the reasons for it, save that it was under the 1976 Act. The Commission has declared the application admissible. Of more interest, however, from the point of view of prisoners' rights is Art 5(3): "Everyone arrested or detained ... shall be brought promptly before a judge ... and shall be entitled to trial within a reasonable time or to release pending trial..."

To consider the extent to which English law complies with this provision, it is necessary to look at the law of bail. The problem of bail arises on two occasions(42) for a detained person: at the police station after his arrest and in a court when the question of remand either pending or during trial arises. The law on police bail is contained in section 43 Magistrates Courts Act 1980. Section 43(1) provides "On a person's being taken into custody for an offence without a warrant,(43) [a senior police officer] may, and, if it will not be practicable to bring him before a magistrates' court within 24 hours after his being taken into custody, shall, inquire into the case and unless the offence appears to the officer to be a serious one, release him on his entering into a recognizance..."

The scope of this provision is often misunderstood and it is frequently asserted that a police officer must bring a suspect before a court within 24 hours. However, a close reading of section 43(1) shows that a senior officer does not even have to look at the case if it is practicable to bring the arrested person before a court within 24 hours and even if it is impracticable so to do, the senior officer can still order detention if he thinks it is a serious case. The only other relevant provision is section 43(4) which states "Where a person is taken into custody for an offence without a warrant and is retained in custody he shall be brought before a magistrates' court as soon as is practicable". The interpretation of section 43 favoured by the courts at present can be seen in R v Hudson and Re Sherman and Apps.(44) Hudson appealed against a conviction on the basis that admissions he had made were obtained during a five day period of detention at a police station. In allowing his appeal, the Court of Appeal stated that he had not been brought before a court "as soon as practicable" as required by section 43. Sherman and Apps had been detained for two days when their solicitor applied on their behalf to the Divisional Court for a writ of habeas corpus. There was an adjournment until the following day when the Divisional Court said that they would issue the writ unless the two men were charged within an hour and a half. They were released later that morning.

In each of these two cases the court has considered that 48 hours should represent the limit for which a person can be detained without charge. This period of time has been, as Munro puts it "conjured out of the air"(45) and is certainly not to be found within the provisions of section 43. It seems that, in practice, the police interpret this to mean as soon as practicable after he has been taken into custody.

Despite the apparent latitude given to the police by s.43, it is the general rule that the police have no power of detention apart from genuinely voluntary co-operation or arrest. However, the Prevention of Terrorism (Temporary Provisions) Act 1976 contains an important exception to this. Section 12 allows the police to arrest a person suspected of involvement in terrorism and to detain him for 48 hours without either a warrant or charges. Subsequently, with the written permission of the Home Secretary he may be detained for a further five days. During the period from 1974 to mid-1979 over 4,000 persons were detained under the 1974 and 1976 Acts but charges were brought against only 278 persons.

At present a person who is unlawfully detained by the police appears to have little prospect of obtaining a remedy. One possibility is an application to the Divisional Court for a writ of habeas corpus.(46) The writ can be applied for by the person who has been unlawfully detained or by someone else acting on his behalf. Yet the procedure is unfamiliar to lawyers and the Divisional Court does not easily grant the writ. Subsequently, an accused person may try to argue that proceedings brought against him should be declared null and void. A further possibility is to bring an action for damages for false imprisonment. In most cases this would be of little use as the amount of damages awarded would be purely nominal.

The second occasion when a person may be detained in custody prior to conviction is on remand pending or during trial. Under the Bail Act 1976, there is a statutory presumption in favour of bail for remand cases. The court must grant bail even if the accused has not applied for it unless one of the statutory exceptions applies. If the offence charged is punishable with imprisonment the Court can refuse bail if it considers that, if released, the defendant would fail to appear, commit an offence while on bail or obstruct the course of justice. Moreover, the court might wish the accused to be kept in custody for his own protection or there might have been insufficient time to obtain enough information about the defendant for the court to reach a decision. If the accused has been remanded for reports, bail need not be granted if a court considers that it would hinder inquiries. Where the defendant is charged with an offence not punishable with imprisonment, a defendant can be refused bail if he has previously failed to answer to bail and the court believes, in view of that failure, that he will again fail to surrender to custody if released on bail.

If a defendant is refused bail by magistrates he can apply to a Crown Court judge if he has been committed to the Crown Court. He can also apply through the Crown Office or the Official Solicitor. These last two procedures are also available to a defendant who is refused bail at the Crown Court. They are likely to be used more than ever before following a recent Divisional Court ruling. Section 128 of the Magistrates Courts Act 1980 provides that a magistrates' court should not remand an accused person in custody for a period exceeding eight clear days. In R v Nottingham Justices, ex parte Davies(47) the Divisional Court held that it was permissible for the Nottingham magistrates to adopt a policy whereby on and after the third successive application for bail they would refuse to hear full argument in support of a bail application unless any "new circumstances" existed.

If no domestic remedies for a refusal to grant bail are available, can a defendant invoke Art 5(3)? UK applicants have made relatively little use of this provision. One notable exception is the X,Y and Z case.(48) The applicants complained that their detention was in breach of Art 5(3) as their original arrest had not been justified under Art 5(1). The Commission has declared this application admissible.

Art 5(4) states "Everyone who is deprived of his liberty by arrest or detention shall be entitled to take proceedings by which the lawfulness of his detention shall be decided speedily by a court and his release ordered if the detention is not lawful. "This provision is unlikely to affect a UK prisoner at the sentencing stage as that will be done by a properly constituted court and will clearly be lawful. However an interesting problem could arise in a case involving executive recall. In X v United Kingdom the applicant who was a convicted offender detained under s 65 Mental Health Act 1959 was recalled to a mental hospital some three years after release. The court held that there had been a breach of Art 5(4), notwithstanding the fact that he had unsuccessfully applied for a writ of "habeas corpus" and that his case would be reviewed by a Mental Health Review Tribunal. A parolee who is recalled to prison does not even have the benefit of a tribunal to take his case to and it is perhaps arguable that the lack of any competent review body would mean that he too could challenge his detention under Art 5(4).

Article 6: The right to a fair trial

Several United Kingdom prisoners have applied under this Article, their complaints falling into two categories: first, that they have been denied access to the courts by the prison authorities, and secondly, that decisions taken by prison bodies (e.g. boards of visitors) have been in breach of Art 6.

In the first category, the Commission was initially cautious, rejecting an application on the ground of non-exhaustion of domestic remedies, in that the prisoner had not petitioned the Home Secretary for leave to contact a solicitor.(49) Yet the rule requiring this (r 34(8) Prison Rules 1964) was itself the matter alleged to be in violation of Art 6!

The issue arose again in Knechtl,(50) where the applicant wished to consult a solicitor with a view to starting proceedings in respect of allegedly negligent medical treatment while in prison. The Secretary of State refused permission. Before the Commission could consider the merits of the case a friendly settlement was reached by the Government offering Knechtl compensation, and announcing a change in practice. However, this change applied only to prisoners in Knechtl's situation, alleging medical negligence, and it took a case before the European Court to produce a more wide-ranging change in the Rules, as well as the practice of the Prison Department.

Golder(51) wanted to sue a prison officer for an alleged libel contained in his file, which he thought had damaged his chances of obtaining parole. He was refused permission to consult a solicitor. The Government argued that Art 6 relates only to proceedings already instituted, but this argument was rejected. The Court said "By forbidding Golder to make (contact with a solicitor), the Home Secretary actually impeded the launching of contemplated action. Without formally denying Golder his right to institute proceedings before a court, the Home Secretary did in fact prevent him from commencing an action at that time, 1970. Hindrance in fact can contravene the Convention just like a legal impediment". Art 6(1) does not state expressly that there is a right of access to a court. "It enunciates rights which are distinct but stem from the same basic idea and which, taken together, make up a single right not specifically defined ...

Were Article 6(1) to be understood as concerning exclusively the conduct of an action which had already been initiated before a court, a Contracting State could, without acting in breach of that text, do away with its courts or take away their jurisdiction to determine certain classes of civil actions and entrust it to organs dependent on the Government."(52)

The court accepted the Government's second argument that there are implied limitations on the exercise of the right of access, but refused to delineate these, holding that its only duty was to rule on whether there had been a breach of the Convention in the instant case. Here, since Golder's action would have concerned an incident occuring while he was in prison, against a prison officer acting in the course of his duties and subject to the Home Secretary's authority, he "could justifiably wish to consult a solicitor with a view to instituting legal proceedings. It was not for the Home Secretary himself to appraise the prospects of the action contemplated; it was for an independent and impartial court to rule on any claim that might be brought", a clear reiteration of the principle nemo judex in causa sua.

In the face of this judgement, the Government amended the Prison Rules, inserting r 37A(4) "Subject to any directions of the Secretary of State, a prisoner may correspond with a solicitor for the purpose of obtaining legal advice concerning any course of action in relation to which the prisoner may become a party to civil proceedings or for the purpose of instructing the solicitor to issue such proceedings".(53)

Until the Silver case,(54) practice under r 37A(4) was that an inmate must make a written application to the governor for facilities to seek legal advice so as to have proceedings instituted. Such applications were to be granted, unless the proceedings were to be brought against the Home Office (or a minister or servant thereof) arising out of or in connection with his imprisonment; in which case, he had first to ventilate his complaint through the normal existing internal channels (complaint to the governor, board of visitors or petition to the Home Secretary).

The problem arising from this was that there might be such a delay while the prisoner used internal channels, that his right of access was in fact prevented - a state of affairs condemned by the European Court, and which the Commission later dealt with in Campbell(55) and Reed.(56)

In Campbell, the applicant complained, inter alia, that he was not allowed an independent medical examination nor access to a solicitor in respect of injuries he sustained during a prison demonstration. The Commission considered that the medical examination might well form part of the facilities to be made available to a prisoner in preparing his civil claim under Art 6. They noted that Campbell had failed to co-operate with the internal investigative procedure he was obliged to go through before being given access to a solicitor, and the delay had therefore been protracted (fourteen months). If he had co-operated the delay would only have been of four to five months, but even this was worthy of investigation on the merits.

In Reed, the Government argued that the prisoner's application, alleging breach of Art 3, in respect of alleged assaults at Hull prison, was inadmissible for non-exhaustion of domestic remedies, since Reed had not brought a civil action for damages! The Commission summed up Reed's position: "his access to an effective and adequate remedy was made dependent, first, on his going through a separate preliminary internal procedure and, secondly, on his awaiting the outcome of the public prosecution" of the officers involved. Both procedures, the Commission said, did not constitute in themselves "domestic remedies" under Art 26. Here, Reed was denied access to a lawyer for over two years. "The Commission considers it to be of fundamental importance that an existing remedy for an alleged violation of the Convention is in principle immediately available to every aggrieved person and in particular in cases of alleged maltreatment. The Commission accepts nevertheless that a certain limited period may elapse in a case like the present, where the prison authorities wish to carry out an internal enquiry into the allegations prior to granting the complainant access to legal facilities. It ought to be stressed, on the other hand, that any such enquiry, however justifiable, must not encroach upon the immediacy and effectiveness of the remedy of a civil action for damages ... it cannot be reasonable....to deny, during a period of twenty-seven months, to the alleged victim of a treatment contrary to Art 3, access to the sole remedy capable of providing him immediate, adequate and sufficient redress for his alleged grievances". If there was only one effective remedy, why was the prior ventilation rule justified? In the later case of Silver, in respect of censorship of prisoners' correspondence, the Commission considered that the prior ventilation rule was a breach of the Convention.

An alternative to a prisoner abiding by the prior ventilation rule was for him to institute proceedings himself, as was done in Raymond v Honey.(57) The prisoner was already engaged in legal proceedings. He wrote a letter to his solicitors, which was stopped by the governor. As a consequence, he prepared an application to the High Court for leave to commit the governor for contempt of court. This application was also stopped. The case eventually came to court, and went to the House of Lords. Lords Wilberforce and Bridge with whom the other judges agreed, reasserted the principle that any act done which is calculated to obstruct or interfere with the due course of justice, or the lawful process of the courts, is a contempt of court. Both judges cited Golder for the proposition that access to a court is a right protected by Art 6. Both thought that s 47 Prison Act 1952, under which the Prison Rules are made, is insufficient to authorise hindrance of this right, and they upheld the Divisional Court finding of contempt by the governor as regards stopping the application to the High Court.

From this it would appear that a governor must not stop applications to institute proceedings addressed directly to the court. Ironically, if a prisoner successfully institutes proceedings, he is then a "party to legal proceedings" and would come under the ambit of r 37A which provides for correspondence between a prisoner who is a party to any legal proceedings and his legal adviser.(58) Such a prisoner would, theoretically, be able to consult the solicitor after starting the proceedings first. This might have the effect of wasting the court's time with applications which a solicitor would tell a client were not worth pursuing. This likelihood is now sensibly minimised by the relaxation on restrictions of access to solicitors in the new S O 5 which in any case, gives recognition to the decision in Raymond v Honey.

The most important English domestic decision concerning prisoners' rights is St Germain. It brought to the forefront of public attention the fact that under r 52 of the Prison Rules,(59) the board, which is made up of lay persons and magistrates, may make an award forfeiting a prisoner's remission of any length. In St Germain, two years' remission was lost by one of the appellants - so he in effect would have to serve a two-year sentence, when magistrates themselves may only pass a sentence of imprisonment of up to 12 months. Yet no legal representation is allowed to the prisoner,(60) and until St Germain it was uncertain whether the rules of natural justice applied at all. The large number of offences against discipline - 21 listed in r 47 -puts prisoners at considerable risk of facing 'adjudications' before the governor or, in the most serious cases, before the board of visitors. It is hardly surprising that a number of cases have been dealt with by the Commission in respect of disciplinary proceedings.

In the Engel case,(61) the European Court held that it is open to States to maintain a distinction between disciplinary and criminal law. The former is outside the ambit of Art 6. However, it held that it has jurisdiction to examine whether a charge of a disciplinary character counts as a "criminal charge" or to "satisfy itself that the disciplinary does not improperly encroach upon the criminal". In deciding whether the charge is disciplinary or criminal, the court laid down three criteria. First, "whether the provision(s) defining the offence charged belong, according to the legal system of the respondent State, to criminal law, disciplinary law or both concurrently". Secondly, "the very nature of the offence" and, finally, "the degree of severity of the penalty that the person concerned risks incurring".(62) The issue for the Commission has been to decide whether prison disciplinary bodies are adjudicating on disciplinary or criminal offences.

In Kiss,(63) the prisoner alleged he had been assaulted by a prison officer. He complained to the governor, and was charged under r 47(12) with making a false and malicious allegation against an officer. The board of visitors found him guilty, and he lost eighty days' remission. Before the Commission, Kiss argued that, although the offence had no specific equivalent in English criminal law, it imparted the necessary elements of the traditional notion of crime, and the penalty was the imposition of a serious punishment involving a deprivation of his liberty, being a virtual extension of his sentence. The Commission was unclear whether the charge could also constitute the offence of criminal libel, and did not pursue this line of enquiry. Secondly, the Commission looked at the nature of the charge. It pointed out that making false and malicious allegations can have extremely deleterious effects on the effective functioning of the prison system, while an allegation made outside prison has much less impact. The Commission concluded that the offence "is, prima facie, of a disciplinary nature for which a disciplinary procedure was justified". Finally, the Commission had regard to the degree of severity of the punishment imposed on Kiss - eighty days loss of remission, and a possible loss of a total of 180 days under r 51(4)(f). The Commission found that "loss of remission does not constitute deprivation of liberty. A prisoner....is deprived of his liberty for the whole of his sentence, any remission of that sentence for good behaviour is mere privilege and loss of that privilege does not alter the original basis for detention".(64) The Commission felt that in view of the possible repercussions that allegations may have on a prison officer's career and on prison good order and discipline, the severity of the penalty was justified, and did not of itself bring the offence charged within the criminal sphere. This is an unfortunate decision, because the fear of this rule must obviously deter prisoners from making what may well be justified complaints. After all, if a prisoner made a complaint to the Commission, and was charged with making a false and malicious allegation in it, this would clearly constitute a breach of Art 25 as tending to hinder the effective exercise of the right of individual petition.(65) Why should complaints to other bodies be unprotected?

A more liberal approach to offences against prison discipline was taken in Campbell. The prisoner was charged with "mutiny or incitement to mutiny" and "gross personal violence to an officer" under r 47(1) and (2). Under r 52, the board of visitors awarded 605 days' loss of remission and 90 days' cellular confinement. Applying the Engel criteria, the Commission pointed out that the assault charge was clearly governed concurrently by the criminal law. As regards the 'very nature' of the offences, both were 'disciplinary' in character in so far as they involved the violation of legal rules governing the operation of the prison, but the fact that the assault charge involved a violation of the criminal law was a factor relevant in determining whether the 'disciplinary' improperly encroached on the 'criminal'. The severity of the penalty was also much greater than in Kiss. Here, Campbell could have lost 3 years and 4 months' remission, even though the Commission had to concede, following Kiss, that this did not involve a deprivation of liberty. The Commission concluded that the issue should be determined on the merits. This suggests that the first criterion in Engel is of little importance compared with the latter two, since incitement of prisoners to mutiny is not a criminal offence.

The Commission seemed to be influenced by the severity of the punishment imposed, and this criterion was again of importance in McFeeley v UK where prisoners in Northern Ireland engaged in the 'dirty protest' were regularly charged with breaches of r 30(1) Prison Rules (N I) 1954, "a prisoner who is guilty of any act or omission contrary to the security or good order of the prison shall be guilty of an offence against discipline and on his offence being reported to the governor shall be dealt with as here and after provided in these Rules".(66) They were adjudicated on every 14 and then every 28 days, and received awards of 28 days' loss of remission and privileges (and, at first, also 3 days in cellular confinement).

The prisoners argued that these adjudications by the governor did not involve an independent and impartial tribunal or respect other procedural rights contained in Art 6. They submitted that the constant imposition of periods of solitary confinement and substantial loss of remission constituted a deprivation of liberty. The Government argued that Art 6 is not applicable in the case of disciplinary adjudications by a prison governor, that the offences involved were purely disciplinary matters unrelated to the ordinary criminal law, and that loss of remission cannot be considered a deprivation of liberty since remission is considered a privilege. The Commission adopted the Engel criteria, and held that the offences were governed by disciplinary law and were disciplinary in nature. As regards the severity of the penalty, they noted that the awards of forfeiture of remission and privileges were limited by r 30 to a maximum duration of 28 days. In spite of the cumulative effect of penalties awarded continuously, the Commission felt that it had to regard the punishments as imposed for continuing disciplinary offences. Two of the applicants were also charged with assaults on prison officers or other prisoners. The Commission noted that such offences belong both to disciplinary and criminal law. "However, it is clear, in the context of a prison system, that assaults on prison officers or other prisoners are offences of a disciplinary nature which concern the security and good order of the prison".(67) Yet it would be difficult to imagine an offence more likely to concern security and good order than the mutiny charge against Campbell, which the Commission proposed to examine on its merits.

The severity of the punishment available for an offence, which seems to be significant as regards the Commission, was only one consideration taken by the Court of Appeal in St Germain. The Government cynically relied upon this case to argue that McFeeley had not exhausted domestic remedies under Art 26, because he could have sought an order of certiorari to quash the awards given by the governor! The Commission were unimpressed by this gambit, pointing out that St Germain relates only to judicial review of decisions of boards of visitors, on the basis that the principles of natural

"necessity" (in Art 10 in that case) did not mean indispensable or absolute necessity, but did mean more than being reasonable or desirable. "It considered that the demands of pluralism, tolerance and broadmindedness, essential to a democratic society, required any interference....to be proportionate to the legitimate aim pursued". The Court saw its task as being to examine "whether the reasons given by the national authority to justify the actual measures of 'interference' they take are relevant and sufficient".

The Commission accordingly examined the system of censorship, and the individual letters censored, to see if there had been a breach unjustified by Art 8(2). The practice contained in standing orders whereby prior ventilation of complaints about the prison system was necessary before a prisoner could consult a solicitor was regarded as not "in accordance with the law" because it was not reasonably foreseeable from r 33 or r 34(8). In relation to its necessity, the Commission commented "it is fundamental in a democratic society that people may seek responsible legal advice on any subject in order to protect or enforce their rights or simply to be reasonably informed".(82) The Commission failed to understand how the Government could justify prior ventilation given the unacceptable delays exposed by the cases; for example, a five-month delay in the Home Secretary's reply to a petition from Silver. The prior ventilation rule was therefore regarded by the Commission as a breach of Art 8, and the specific letters censored were interfered with in breach of Art 8. A new standing order gives effect to this criticism, and allows access to solicitors, except in relation to commencing private prosecution so long as the prisoner complains internally at the same time.

The Commission noted in Silver that the Prison Rules contain no specific provision for censorship of letters of complaint to M P 's, where the prisoner has not first used the internal procedure; the practice derived from the standing order. The Commission considered that such a restriction could not reasonably be foreseen by virtue of r 33 and so was not in accordance with the law. It did not feel that the need to enable the prison authorities to provide an immediate remedy and to maintain staff morale by preventing wild allegations against officers justified the priority of an internal enquiry. The practice has now been changed and is eminently desirable; the knowledge that a member of Parliament is appraised of the issue (even more than a solicitor) can be expected to encourage Prison Department officials to pursue their enquiries with somewhat greater diligence and speed than has sometimes been the case in the past.

The general practice of stopping letters of complaint about the penal system was also ruled a breach of Art 8. The Commission appreciated the Government's desire to maintain staff morale but pointed out the "basic human need to express thoughts and feelings including complaints about real or imagined hardships. This need is particularly acute in prison, as prisoners have little choice of social contacts, hence the importance of having access to the outside world by correspondence".(83) The revised standing order now recognises this.

Although the restriction on corresponding with persons other than relatives or friends known prior to sentence is contained in r 34(8), the Commission considered that stopping letters to persons whose character could not be in question (such as the presenter of the Panorama programme, in McMahon's case) could not be foreseen from the rules, and so was not in accordance with the law. The Government argued that the restriction was necessary in view of the difficulty in verifying the identity of all the correspondents for security purposes, since correspondents may visit prisoners. The Commission felt that visiting was a distinct issue, immaterial to the complaints in the present case, and that the Prison Department's practice was an overbroad restriction contrary to Art 8.(84) The new practice will still enable letters to be stopped if they are to or from a person or organisation "whose activities present a genuine and serious threat to the security or good order of the establishment" - this rather vague categorisation presumably excludes communications with PROP, the prisoners' union.

The practice of stopping letters intended for publication could not, according to the Commission, be reasonably foreseen from r 33 and so was not in accordance with the law. The Commission recognised legitimate conflicting interests raised by this issue. "On the one hand, access to the media is an important element in a democratic society. On the other hand, the difficult task of prison administration may be affected by the exploitation of scurrilous material in the 'gutter press' " which might affect staff morale. However, the Commission felt that the blanket restriction, not specifying the kind of material involved, the security risk of the prisoner, the status of the addressee, the contents of the letter or their likely effect on legitimate interests of prison administration, was an overbroad limitation not to be shown to be necessary for the prevention of disorder. The new standing order now allows prisoners to write material for publication or for use by radio or television, so long as they do not write for gain or about their own offences or those of others - unless the publication consists of representations about convictions or sentence or forms part of serious comment about crime, the processes of justice or the penal system.

The Commission went on to condemn various other practices as overbroad and unnecessary, such as stopping letters holding the authorities up to contempt. The new standing order appears to have given effect to the substantive criticisms made by the Commission in Silver. It has therefore gone some way to neutralising any criticism the Court may eventually make, and minimising the further international embarrassment the Government would have to suffer from having the most severe restrictions on freedom of correspondence of prisoners in Western Europe. It is to be hoped that the experiments hitherto restricted to open prisons may now be extended. Under them, domestic mail, that is letters to family and friends, may be handed in for posting already sealed, and incoming mail is opened in the prisoner's presence and not read if found to be "domestic". The much more limited regulations on censorship should now persuade the authorities to save valuable time and manpower by gradually reducing the censorship of letters.

Article 12: The right to marry
Art 12 states that "Men and women of marriageable age have the right to marry and to found a family, according to the national laws governing the exercise of this right". The problem that has arisen concerning prisoners is that the authorities in several of the member states have been reluctant to grant prisoners temporary release for the purpose of getting married and that prisoners are not usually allowed to marry in prison.

In an application against the United Kingdom in 1968,(85) a prisoner, who had been ordered to be deported, complained that he had not been allowed to marry the mother of his son while in prison. The Commission held the application inadmissable as the prisoner had already married in Pakistan and there was no firm evidence to indicate that he was divorced from his first wife. In a later decision,(86) a long-term prisoner complained that he was being deprived of his conjugal rights and the exercise of his paternal rights. The Commission decided, however, that there had been no breach of Art 12: even if the right to found a family applied, it could surely not apply to people who had been lawfully imprisoned.

Both decisions can be explained on their own special facts. In neither of the cases had the straightforward question of a prisoner marrying been faced head-on. However, this situation changed when an English prisoner, Hamer, claimed that a denial of the right to marry was in breach of Art 12.(87) The Commission upheld his complaint, taking the view that deferment of exercise of the right to marry would affect the substance of the right. The rules had recently been changed so that when a prisoner had over twelve months left to serve he could obtain leave of absence to marry whether or not there was a child involved. The Committee of Ministers agreed, but decided to take no action, as the United Kingdom announced that it would prepare legislation to amend the marriage laws to allow prisoners serving a determinate sentence to be married in prison. The legislation is still awaited.

In a 1978 decision,(88) a husband and wife, who were detained in a Swiss prison, invoked Article 12 in relation to the refusal of the authorities to allow them to have sexual relations during their detention. The Commission, noting that the applicants were married and already had a family, considered that they consequently enjoyed the right to respect for their family life as provided by Art 8. If an interference with family life was justified under Art 8(2), it could not at the same time amount to a violation of Art 12.

CONCLUSION

A considerable body of 'case-law' is being built up under the Convention in relation to prisoners' rights. Partly, this is due to the current fashion for prisoners to have resort to Strasbourg in their awareness of, and demand for, their rights.

We have seen that the Commission has become much bolder in its interpretation of the Convention, and in its readiness to uphold complaints, yet it is still the case that the vast majority of applications are declared inadmissible. For example, in 1980, 390 applications were registered, but only 19 cases(89) were declared admissible (and these would have been carried over from previous years, because of the time taken for an application to be dealt with). It seems that for most UK prisoners, who are serving fixed sentences of under four years, taking a case to the Commission will not provide them with a remedy in time to be of much use. For example, in Silver, the applicant died in 1979; in Golder, the applicant was released on parole before the Court reached its decision.

Yet what alternatives does a prisoner have to applying to the Commission? Art 13 of the Convention requires that a domestic remedy be provided for a breach of the Convention. The Commission ruled in Silver that no such remedy existed in relation to censorship of correspondence. Prisoners have had to make use of the Convention because they have found no effective remedy for their grievances in domestic law. It is true that since St Germain, it is possible to challenge the decision of a board of visitors in respect of a disciplinary offence by way of certiorari. It seems, from McFeeley, that this might now, in certain instances, be regarded as an effective remedy to be sought before applying under the Convention, since it is now settled law, and certiorari is effective in quashing the decision taken. From Reed, it would appear that an action for damages for assaults suffered in prison would also be regarded as an adequate remedy by the Commission, provided that the action could be pursued within a reasonable time.

However, actions for example, raising issues under Art 8 and 12 might not be available in the English courts, either because they would be questioning practices made lawful by the Prison Rules, or because breach of these Rules may not, per se, be actionable.(90) In any case, the courts have not exactly welcomed challenges by prisoners to the Prison Department. In St Germain (No 2), the Divisional Court said, in ruling that certain adjudications had been carried out unfairly, "We confess it is with some reluctance that we came to this conclusion, because there is inevitably a feeling that the board of visitors may have reached the right result ultimately in spite of the irregularities. These men were prisoners. Some of them were dangerous. Most of them were difficult. All of them were no doubt to some extent untrustworthy". The Court then more or less invited the authorities to press fresh charges.(91)

It is well recognised that court actions are often too slow to provide effective remedies for people's complaints, but alternative procedures are of little use for prisoners. The Parliamentary Commissioner for Administration seems ineffectual in achieving changes of Prison Department policy.(92) Alternatively, the prisoner may complain to the governor, the board of visitors or the Home Secretary. Only the board is supposed to be objective and independent, but boards are associated with disciplinary matters, and cannot actually order a remedy. The governor is unlikely to change his mind on a decision already taken, and the Home Secretary is similarly judge in his own cause. The prisoner may also complain to his MP (now simultaneously with the internal complaint), but this channel is not set up by the authorities to provide redress.

Prisoners will, then, continue to have recourse to the Convention in a number of situations, and it is the effect that decisions at Strasbourg have on Government practice which is most important. The Court's decision in Golder forced the Government to amend its rules in relation to access to legal advisors. The Commission's view in Silver has led to a considerable change in practice concerning censorship of correspondence and to a commitment to publication of standing orders. A friendly settlement after adverse findings in Hamer has relaxed the rules on the marriage of prisoners. It cannot be said, however, that these changes have been made graciously. Standing orders on r 37A(4) perpetuated difficulties and delays for prisoners trying to initiate legal proceedings, intimating a greater desire on the part of the Home Office to find ways round European decisions than to embrace them in a spirit of goodwill. But change is even less likely where there is no international embarrassment to be suffered. Despite the decision in St Germain and numerous calls for alterations in the functions and powers of boards of visitors, no alterations have been made.

Yet it is only in relation to procedural issues that the Convention has so far challenged the UK prison system. The value of the Convention may be seen as providing a mechanism for prisoners' complaints which is freer from domestic policy considerations than the courts have been. It is clear that, without it, prisoners would have much less access to lawyers and others in order to challenge effectively the system under which they are placed. While it cannot be said that the courts have shown much desire to replace the Commission by providing effective remedies for prisoners, the continuing effect of adverse decisions in an international forum may slowly prod the Government into reforms in selected areas.

384

FOOTNOTES

(1) Human Rights File No 4, 1981 p1.

(2) eg. the development of PROP (Preservation of the Rights of Prisoners) - see M Fitzgerald Prisoners in Revolt (1977). Also, S Cohen and L Taylor Prison Secrets (1978, 1979). G Zellick in Freeman, ed Prisons Past and Future Ch 11 "The Case for Prisoners' Rights" (1978). A M Tettenborn "Prisoners' Rights" (1980) PL 74. P Burkinshaw "The Closed Society" (1981) NILQ 117.

(3) Zellick op cit p105. We are grateful to Prof. Zellick for kindly giving us access to certain unpublished materials of his.

(4) Annual Review 1980, European Commission, Table 2.3. p39.

(5) See Beddard Human Rights and Europe 2nd ed (1980) Ch 2.

(6) Resolution (73) 5.

(7) See G P Alpert Legal Rights of Prisoners (1978) Ch 1.

(8) See Fitzgerald op cit for a description of the development of PROP and the 'failure' of prisoners to look beyond their own immediate living conditions. For American experience, see Hoff in Legal Rights of Prisoners (1980) ed Alpert Ch 2.

(9) Per Shaw L J in R v Hull Prison Board of Visitors, ex p St Germain [1979] 1 All ER 701, 717. Also see Article 10 International Covenant on Civil and Political Rights 1966, Guiding Principle r58, Standard Minimum Rules for the Treatment of Prisoners.

(10) See Lord Denning in Becker v Home Office [1972] 2 QB 407.

(11) Article 26.

(12) Though cf. McFeeley v UK (8317/78).

(13) Though some have been revealed from time to time eg. in Prison Secrets by Cohen & Taylor; In Williams v Home Office (No 2) [1981] 1 All ER 1211, and in the Home Office working party Report on Adjudication Procedures in Prison.(1975).

(14) Though cf Raymond v Honey [1982] 1 All ER 756 (HL).

(15) 5310/71 and 5451/72 Yearbook 21 p602.

(16) European Court of Human Rights, Judgement of 18 January 1978 para 167.

(17) 5856/72 Yearbook 21 p612.

(18) Becker v Home Office [1972] 2 QB 407, Williams v Home Office (No 2) [1982] 2 All ER 564.

(19) 6513/72 DR 4 p177 (1981) EHRR 104.

(20) 7630/76 DR 19 p113.

(21) 6224/73 DR 7 p55.

(22) Yearbook 12. Special Volume The Greek Case.

(23) 8317/78 DR 20 p44 3 EHRR 161.

(24) 6564/74 DR 2 p105.

(25) see H Gruner A Good and Useful Life (1982) Howard League.

(26) [1981] 1 All ER 1211. Dismissed on procedural grounds by Court of Appeal [1982] 2 All ER 564.

(27) Clonce v Richardson (1974) 379 Fed Sup 338; McCann v R (1975) 68 DLR (3d) 661.

(28) [1976] QB 198, 207.
(29) at p1245.
(30) 2749/66 Coll 24 p93.
(31) 5265/71 DR 3 p5.
(32) 8158/78 DR 21 p95.
(33) 3868/68 Coll 34 p10.
(34) 8575/79 3 EHRR 297.
(35) A Category A prisoner is one whose escape would be highly dangerous to the public or the police or to the security of the State.
(36) Home Office, Report of the Inquiry into Prison Escapes and Security Cmnd 3175.
(37) 3973/69 Coll 31 p70.
(38) 5006/71 Coll 39 p91.
(39) 5229/71 Coll 42 p140.
(40) The common law position may be seen in Christie v Leachinsky [1947] AC 553 and Pedro v Diss [1981] 2 All ER 59.
(41) 8022,8025, 8027/77 DR 18 p66. For a domestic case, see ex parte Lynch 1980 NILR 126 and Finnie 45 MLR 215.
(42) It is unusual for bail to be granted pending appeal: R v Watton [1979] Crim LR 246.
(43) A warrant for arrest should specify whether or not bail is to be granted.
(44) (1981) 72 Cr App R 163, (1981) 72 Cr App R 266.
(45) [1981] Crim L R 802 "Detention after Arrest".
(46) See LAG Bulletin August 1979 for a practical guide to making such applications.
(47) [1980] 2 All ER 775.
(48) See note 41 supra.
(49) X v UK 4471/70, Coll 39 p47.
(50) Knechtl v UK 4115/69, Yearbook 13, p730. See Cmnd 4846.
(51) Golder case Publications of the Court, Series A, Vol 18.
(52) p13 para 26, p17-18 para 35.
(53) SI 1976 No 503 rule 4. The Committee of Ministers regarded this amendment to the rules as meeting the issue in Hilton v UK 5613/72 (1981) 3 EHRR 104. Resolution DH (79) 3 24th April 1979.
(54) Silver and others v UK 5947/72 etc.
(55) Campbell v UK 7819/77. Yearbook 22 p256.
(56) Reed v UK 7630/76. supra n20.
(57) Supra n14 see Jones (1982) MLR November.
(58) SI 1972 No 1860 schedule.
(59) as amended by SI 1974 No 713.
(60) The Royal Commission on Legal Services (1979) Cmnd 7648, at para 9.29 recommended that prisoners facing loss of remission of more than seven days should be given the opportunity of being legally represented, unless security grounds required other arrangements.
(61) Publications of the Court Series A, Vol 22.
(62) at para 81, 82 pp34-35.
(63) 6224/73 Yearbook 20, p156.

(64) p176 para 2.
(65) see 1593/62 v Austria Yearbook 7 p163.
(66) c.f. r47(20) in the English Rules - offends against good order and discipline.
(67) para 99 at p210.
(68) 5852/72 CD 46 p136, 144.
(69) [1964] AC 40.
(70) See R v Commission for Racial Equality ex p Cottrell & Rothon [1980] 3 All ER 265 QBD.
(71) [1981] 2 All ER 842.
(72) 95 LQR 393 "Prisoners' Access".
(73) eg. de Courcy v UK 2749/66, Yearbook 10 p388.
(74) op cit p50.
(75) [1981] 1 All ER 943.
(76) [1980] 3 All ER 161.
(77) (1969) Cmnd 4699.
(78) 4133/69 Yearbook 13, p780.
(79) Silver 5947/72.
See also C v UK 7990/77 C(81) 22.14.581.
(80) Sunday Times Case. Publications of the Court Series A, Vol 30.
(81) Publications of the Court Series A Vol 24.
(82) This echoes the view of the Royal Commission on Legal Services (supra n.60).
(83) at para 322.
(86) It remains to be seen whether the rule as it applies to visits is in breach of Art 8. See Fell v UK 7878/77.
(85) 3898/68 Coll 35 p102.
(86) 6564/74 DR 2 p105.
(87) 7114/75 DR 10 p174, see also Draper v UK 8168/78.
(88) 8166/78 DR 13 p241.
(89) Source Annual Review 1980 Table 2.4 p40.
(90) See Arbon v Anderson [1943] KB 252, Becker v HO [1972] 2 All ER676 c.f. Williams v HO (No 2) [1982] 2 All ER 564, Raymond v Honey [1982] 1 All ER 756.
(91) [1979] 3 All ER at p554j and p555j.
(92) eg. Knechtl.

THE EFFECT OF THE EUROPEAN CONVENTION ON HUMAN RIGHTS ON THE PREPARATION AND AMENDMENT OF LEGISLATION, DELEGATED LEGISLATION AND ADMINISTRATIVE RULES IN THE UNITED KINGDOM

Clive Symmons

1. Introduction

Under Art. I of the European Convention on Human Rights (hereafter called the 'Convention'), the United Kingdom has an obligation to secure to everyone within its jurisdiction the rights and freedoms thereby guaranteed.(1) Even if this broadly-worded provision does not have the effect of giving the articles of the Convention automatic application in the individual ratifying States (enforceable by their national courts),(2) a consequential duty may be said to arise whereby each State, by dint of general international law principles, is bound to make such modifications to its legislation as is necessary to implement such obligations.(3) Thus it has been pointed out that as international law does not dictate the means by which municipal law is brought into line with treaty obligations, "individual States are free to secure the conformity of their municipal law with their international obligations in the way that seems to them most appropriate". In other words, Art. I itself does not oblige the United Kingdom systematically to amend apparently non-conforming municipal law by legislative and/or administrative action in this context, and there are no other articles of the Convention which, in the absence of litigation at Strasbourg,(5) have such an effect.(6)

Furthermore, despite the current moves towards a Bill of Rights based on the European Convention, at present the provisions of the Convention have no internal application in the United Kingdom such as to make them directly implementable by United Kingdom courts.(7) Thus the juidiciary are powerless to ensure any changes in the law, and can only apply the Convention insofar as the conventional rule

has been actually put into a statute.(8)   This judicial
impotence to over-ride apparently non-conforming domestic
legislation is well-illustrated in the recent case of Taylor v
Co-operative Retail Services Ltd.(9) where Lord Denning, in
the Court of Appeal took the "unusual step"(10) of advising an
employee, dismissed because of 'closed shop' provisions in
United Kingdom legislation, to apply to the European
Commission, pointing out that in the case of the Three
Railwaymen(11) the United Kingdom Government had been
forced by the European Court to pay compensation in an
analogous situation.

   This general scenario of non-implementation of the
Convention in the United Kingdom(12) except where relevant
statutory or non-statutory rule changes have interposed,
necessarily entails that United Kingdom domestic law is only
consciously made to comply with the Convention in a
haphazard and piecemeal fashion in certain areas.
Articulation of the unsatisfactory nature of such 'ad hoc'
adjustment of United Kingdom law is to be found in the recent
parliamentary debates on the Mental Health Act (Amendment)
Bill, 1982, where one of the many suggested amendments(13)
sought to create machinery in the Bill for awarding
compensation to mental patients wrongly detained, so as to
comply with Art. 5(5) of the Convention. In this context, Lord
Avebury made a general query about the vast number of
matters which might have to be taken into account every time
a new bill was brought before Parliament to see whether it did
not somehow affect the United Kingdom's obligations under
the Convention.(14) A recent example of just such a factor
coming into play can be seen in the case of the Administration
of Justice Bill, 1982, where a last-minute attempt by a
pressure group(15) to amend that part of the Bill dealing with
the 'locking up' (placement in secure accommodation) of
children in care - a move inspired by amendments to the
Mental Health Act (Amendment) Bill in the analogous case of
detained mental patients - has in fact prompted the
Government to make belated provision for this situation.(16) It
will be suggested later that this sort of defect might be
remedied by the setting up of some form of parliamentary

'watch-dog' committee to give systematic scrutiny to pending legislation in respect of its overall conformity with the Convention.(17)

2. What Attention does the United Kingdom Government Give to the European Convention when Preparing new Legislation or Administrative Rules?
(a) What legal briefing by experts on the Convention?
It seems that at least for the past ten years or so, lawyers experienced in human rights matters within relevant government departments(18) (particularly the Home Office) are likely to be consulted on any potential legislation or administrative rules which might conflict with the provisions of the Convention. The progressive build-up of individual petitions against the United Kingdom has seemingly made such legal consultation a political necessity to avoid subsequent publicity at Strasbourg.(19)

None the less, such 'conformity' consultation within (or between) government departments may not always be an automatic process and is shrouded by unnecessary secrecy. A vivid illustration of this can be seen in the history of the preparation of the new British Immigration Rules,(20) where not only was there no reference to the Convention in the 1979 White Paper(21) but also a refusal in the parliamentary debate on the Rules to disclose whether the United Kingdom Government had, in fact, consulted its Law Officers in this connection.(22) If there was no consultation in this matter - which so obviously, in the light of previous proceedings at Strasbourg, had implications for the Convention - it has certainly rebounded on the United Kingdom Government which is now faced with pending litigation at Strasbourg over certain of the rules.(23) By contrast, during the passage of the Contempt of Court Bill in 1980, the Government spokesman admitted that legal advice had been taken from the Law Officers to the effect that the Bill did harmonise with both the European Convention and the Sunday Times case.(24) Such an unfortunate disparity of treatment can only be explained by political motivation.
(b) How far is the influence of the European Convention admitted in the event of legislative or other changes of

domestic law?

The relative lack of research in the United Kingdom into the effect which the Convention has in this important sphere can be explained by the fact that the preparation of new legislative or administrative rules has normally been affected - at least, in the past - without any explicit reference to the European Convention. Thus it has been unusual in United Kingdom practice for there to be any acknowledgment of the influence of the Convention in the 'Explanatory Memorandum' accompanying a new Bill or in the parliamentary debates concerning it, even where the legislative change comes in the immediate aftermath of litigation at Strasbbourg. In this respect the United Kingdom seems to be out of step with its continental partners where the impact of such an international obligation is often freely acknowledged.(25)

Indeed, it is fair to argue that where there has been a statutory change of the law even after adverse litigation at Strasbourg - whether before the Commission or the Court -the government of the day has been reluctant to admit that any such international pressure has instigated the change. Instead it has sought to stress that the amendment of the law has resulted from a purely domestic source without reference to the broader European context; and where such a change might have been introduced in the human rights field by domestic pressure irrespective of such treaty obligations, such an attitude cannot in a technical sense be faulted.

For example, in the earliest instance of individual petitions against the United Kingdom being held admissible by the Commission - the Alam and Khan cases(26) 1967 - involving an allegation that the United Kingdom had failed to provide for a fair and public hearing before an independent and impartial tribunal (Art.6(1)) in the context of immigration law, there is no hint on the public record that the subsequent Immigration Appeals legislation (27) was influenced by these cases. Indeed, the Government spokesman(28) then emphasised that this legislation was in substance based on the earlier Wilson Report of 1967.(29) Strangely, this Report in turn made little reference to international obligations in this area, and none to the European Convention(30).

Another more recent example can be seen in the case of the Contempt of Court Act, 1981 which is based essentially on the 1974 Phillimore Report.(31) Here it is arguable that even if the Sunday Times case(32) had never proceeded to the European Court, this legislation might still have been enacted in similar form and that at most it was expedited by the Strasbourg litigation.(33) But as the Lord Chancellor conceded during debate in the House of Lords on the Bill, the Report had "remained lying on the shelf unimplemented" since 1974, and might have gone on lying there were it not for the "Strasbourg decision".(34) Thus at least in this instance the Convention was admitted to be a spur towards harmonisation of domestic law with the international obligations thereunder, and conformity of United Kingdom contempt law with the requirements of the Convention was actually stated to be one of the three aims of the Bill.(35)

With the unprecedented build-up of cases against the United Kingdom in the European Court in the 1980's - all of which have gone against the United Kingdom - this past attitude of emphasising the 'domestic influence' has inevitably undergone a change, as will be seen below where some of these recent cases are discussed in detail.

It may be asked why the past United Kingdom official practice has been to play down the ostensible influence of Strasbourg on domestic legal change. One possible reason may lie in the 'domestic consumption' idea - namely that too open an acknowledgement of the dictates of a body outside the United Kingdom in instigating legislative activity may prove to be unpopular in the public mind (and indeed among a significant number of MPs - as in the case of the announcement in 1982 of an amendment to the new immigration rules - see infra section 8(d)). For as in the case of the EEC, such an alien influence is likely to be viewed by many as an unjustifiable encroachment on parliamentary sovereignty. A more speculative reason (though this writer doubts it) may be that too open an acknowledgement of the 'Strasbourg influence' may be officially seen as showing a green light to the European Commission and Court to make yet wider interpretations of the obligations under the Convention.

3. What Part does Parliament Play in Ensuring that the European Convention is Reflected in Domestic Legislation?

Reference by members of Parliament to obligations under the European Convention when any proposed legislation affecting human rights is under discussion tends inevitably to be spasmodic(36) and unpredictable. This is because many members of Parliament in the United Kingdom tend to evaluate legal changes from a domestic viewpoint.(37) Furthermore, in some instances active hostility to or open disregard of the Convention has been displayed.(38) It is, for example, surprising in the light of the Tyrer case(39) (on judicial punishment in the Isle of Mann), and more recently, the Campbell and Cosans case(40) (on corporal punishment in Scottish schools) - both of which have resulted in findings against the United Kingdom in the European Court - there should have been a recent attempt by an MP actually to re-introduce corporal punishment for youths convicted of crimes of violence(41) in clear defiance of the European Convention (42). Both inside(43) and outside Parliament(44) the proposed amendment was castigated as being in contravention of Art.3 of the Convention.

Party political manifestos and discussion papers in the United Kingdom can share the same sort of approach to the Convention. For example, the recently proclaimed Labour party's plans to abolish private education (in a document entitled 'A Plan for Private Schools', approved by the party's national executive committee)(45) may well be in conflict with Art.2 of the First Protocol(46) although it professes not to be. (47)

Perhaps the most significant parliamentary role in monitoring proposed legislation for conformity with the Convention comes in when litigation in the sphere of the Bill's subject matter is pending before the European Commission or the Court. Thus even when litigation against the United Kingdom at Strasbourg has not reached its culmination, any findings up to that date by the Commission(48) provide an obvious objective yardstick for parliamentary criticism of such legislation. For example, in the recent controversial 'closed shop' legislation - the Employment Bill, 1980 - there was much reference by MPs to the Three Railwaymen case(50) which had been referred at that time (1980) by the Commission to the Court.

It is arguable that even the finding of admissibility against the United Kingdom by the Commission in an area which forms the subject matter of concurrent legislation may be influential in Parliament (if not in government) in inspiring amendments to such legislation, even if that legislation was originally in no way initiated as a means of aligning United Kingdom law with the Conventions' obligations. The problem here, of course, is that a finding of admissibility is not necessarily indicative of the ultimate conclusion of the Commission on the merits. This aspect is to be seen recently in the House of Lords' debate on the Mental Health Act (Amendment) Bill, 1982, where it was proposed(51) that s.141 of the 1959 Mental Health Act (which limits the rights of mental patients to sue staff(52)) should be amended to lighten the burden of proof on the patient. At the Report stage, the Government spokesman, Lord Elton, referred to a case then pending against the United Kingdom on this matter which less than three weeks beforehand had been declared admissible.(53) In rejecting the proposed amendment he criticised the premature nature of such parliamentary concern by stating:

"I would not invite noble Lords to anticipate the judgment which they [ie the Commission] will now consider on the merits. I do not consider it sensible to amend our law at the very moment when the Commission... has the opportunity to consider it in relation to an individual's application to them".(54)

In other recent instances it has been evident that the mere lodging of an application to Strasbourg on a currently controversial issue - or even a statement of intent to do so by the aggrieved party - has been enough to instigate pressure in Parliament for a statutory change in the existing law, particularly if the issue has also been subjected to judicial criticism in the domestic forum for alleged infringement of the Convention.

A recent example of the former - the 'trigger' effect of the mere lodging of an application - can be seen in the controversial area of telephone tapping where Art.8 (right to privacy) has been used as a weapon(56) in challenging the Telecommunications Bill over its omission to contain a clause imposing statutory control on such activities. Here the Government has decided against legislation on the issue, largely influenced, it appears, by the Diplock Report(57) (which makes only laconic reference to the Convention).(58) This was despite the fact that in the 1979 Malone case,(59) where the Metropolitan Police had been unsuccessfully sued for telephone tapping, Sir Robert Megarry had stated that such control (in the light of the Convention) cried out for legislation.(60)

In 1979, before the Bill was debated in Parliament, Mr Malone had lodged his application (under Art.8) with the Commission.(61) And, at least one MP made reference to this fact in respect of obligations under the Convention.(62)

A recent example of the latter factor - the mere threat to lodge a complaint with Strasbourg - to activate parliamentary interest can be seen to have arisen out of the Harman case, (63) 1982, where Lord Scarman in his dissenting judgment in the House of Lords had opined that to make a solicitor guilty of contempt of court in supplying to a journalist copies of documents (obtained by an order for discovery), could be inconsistent with the United Kingdom's obligations under the Convention. As a backdrop to parliamentary pressure to amend the 1981 Contempt of Court Act or provide for this situation in the new Administration of Justice Bill, 1982,(64) has been the well-publicised announcement of intent by Miss Harman to lodge a complaint in Strasbourg over the issue.(65)

4. What Use has been made of the Convention by Small 'Interest Groups' in Campaigning for Statutory Change in the United Kingdom?

It is not difficult to observe that sponsorship from several small extra-parliamentary 'ginger groups' in the United Kingdom concerned with civil liberties has lain behind some of the more significant individual applications from the United Kingdom to Strasbourg. Prominent amongst these has been the NCCL,(66) MIND,(67) the Howard League for Penal Reform,(68) and STOPP,(69). All such organisations have also made liberal use of the European Convention in advocating changes of the law through reports and discussion documents. Indeed in one very recent instance, a group calling itself the 'Childrens' Legal Centre' appears to have been influential(70) in the last-minute Government decision to introduce an amendment to the Criminal Justice Bill, 1982, over the practice of 'locking up' children in care without access to the courts.(71) In effect, therefore, the European Convention has given such groups a potent additional weapon in their national campaigns in the United Kingdom to amend the law.(72)

5. The Impact of the Convention in the United Kingdom in the Absence of Relevant Litigation:

It is particularly difficult to gauge what persuasive influence the European Convention may have had in the case of legislative change in areas of human rights which have not been tested out in specific litigation at Strasbourg; for it has not been United Kingdom practice to refer openly to the impact of the Convention in framing new legislation and rules(73) apart from exceptional circumstances. Thus all that can be said here is that in a general way it can be assumed that all Government departments in the United Kingdom would have regard to such an international treaty obligation when framing new laws where the Convention might impinge.(74)

In consequence, usually the only explicit acknowledgment of the influence of the text of the Convention is to be found, if at all, in the travaux preparatoires which led up to the legislative or other legal change in question.

A good example of this can be seen in the 1972 Diplock Report on legal procedures to deal with terrorist activities in

Northern Ireland.(75) This Report makes frequent reference to the Convention, and cites Art.6 thereof as laying down "certain minimum requirements for a criminal trial in normal times".(76) Thus, on the vexed question of the admissibility of confessions based on subjection of the accused to "torture or to inhuman or degrading treatment", the Report clearly acknowledges that the wording of its recommendation has been adopted from Art.3.(77) The impact of the Convention of this recommendation adopted in s.8 of the Northern Ireland (Emergency Provisions) Act has received subsequent judicial affirmation in R v McCormick.(78)

Apart from references to the European Convention by the occasional ad hoc body considering legislative change,(79) there appears to be a growing tendency for the Law Commission, which is a standing body concerned with law reform in the United Kingdom, to refer to the Convention in some specific instances. But it should be noted that in every instance the Law Commission's attention to the relevant articles of the Convention appears to have been sparked off by either litigation at Strasbourg or domestic judicial reference in the particular sphere.

For example, in its Working Paper No.72,(80) the Law Commission refers to the question of whether the Incitement to Disaffection Act 1934 complies with Art.10(1) of the Convention - a matter given publicity in Arrowsmith case(81) at Strasbourg.(82) More recently, in its Working Paper No.19(1981),(83) the Law Commission in considering the existing offence of blasphemy as interpreted in Whitehouse v Lemon, 1979,(84) noted that the defendant in that case had appealed to the European Commission alleging inter alia, that his conviction contravened Arts.9 and 10 of the Convention and referred to the interpretation by Lord Scarman in the case concerning these articles.(85)

The only other aspect of the travaux preparatoires to legislation which may usually reveal what attention the Government has paid to the Convention's text is where a parliamentary question forces an answer on the issue. But as already seen,(86) such parliamentary probing is very occasional, and particularly so where there has been no litigation against the United Kingdom at Strasbourg on the issue. None the less, isolated instances are to be found in Hansard.(87)

6. The Impact of Litigation against Other Parties to the Convention:

The most obvious way in which United Kingdom legislation may be influenced in this instance is where successful cases brought against other parties contain issues which are similar or identical to those in cases pending against the United Kingdom at Strasbourg.(88)

Mental health law is an area where existing United Kingdom legislation has been shown to be deficient in such a way. For in 1972, in the Winterwerp case(89) against the Netherlands the applicant inter alia alleged that his detention as a mental patient was in breach of Art.5(4) inasmuch as he was not heard by the judge who had authorised the continuation of his detention. Very shortly afterwards the Commission was seized of four applications against the United Kingdom(90) involving similar issues to those in Winterwerp. Because of the similarity, the United Kingdom attempted to intervene when Winterwerp reached the European Court in 1979 and to persuade the Court to hear argument from the United Kingdom on the interpretation of Art. 5(4).(91) For the Netherlands had conceded an interpretation of Art.5(4) which was of great concern to the United Kingdom in the light of its own mental health legislation.(92)

In the event, the Court did allow the United Kingdom to put in a written statement of its views(93) - a seemingly unprecedented concession.(94) But it well illustrates the interest which the United Kingdom may have in the scrutiny at Strasbourg vis a vis other parties to the Convention with similar legislative provisions to those in the United Kingdom. For here an adverse finding has an obvious 'knock-on' effect for United Kingdom legislation, quite apart from the litigation in the same aspect against itself. It may thus be speculated that even in the absence of the present spate of litigation against the United Kingdom at Strasbourg in the mental health area,(95) existing United Kingdom legislation on this matter would have been amended. Indeed, the Winterwerp case was cited in parliamentary debate on the recent Mental Health Act (Amendment) Bill as an authoritative interpretation of the United Kingdom's obligations to provide legal aid for mental patients appearing before mental health review tribunals.(96)

An example of litigation against other parties where no proceedings are pending against the United Kingdom in the particular subject area and which appears(97) to have influenced recent legislative changes in the United Kingdom concerns military discipline. Here in the aftermath of the Engels case(98) (against the Netherlands) before the Court, and the Eggs case (against Switzerland) before the Commission, important changes in the United Kingdom statutes seem to have been prompted in an area which was formerly considered to be outside the ambit of the Convention.

Of the two cases, Engels would be the more influential on United Kingdom practice as it proceeded to the European Court.(99) It concerned conscripts in the Netherlands' armed forces who were punished for breaches of the rules of military discipline, and the complaints to the Commission were essentially based on Arts.5 and 6.(100) In 1976 the Court made the important finding that the European Convention did apply to members of the armed forces; that a penalty or measure does not escape the terms of Art 5 when it takes a form such as strict arrest; that what belonged to the 'criminal' sphere for the purposes of Art.6 included deprivation of liberty liable to be imposed as a punishment in appropriate circumstances; and that hearings before the Supreme Military Court in camera were a violation of Art.6(1).

In the Eggs case, in a similar instance, there had been no referral to a court at any stage in the disciplinary proceedings; and after an examination on the merits in 1977, the

Commission found, not surprisingly (in the light of Engels), that Switzerland was in breach of Art.5(1), and implicitly also in breach of Art.5(4).(101)

Both Dutch and Swiss military law was changed as a result of these cases.(102) And amendments to analogous provisions in sections 78(5) and 79(6) of the Army and Airforce Act, 1955 in the United Kingdom have now been effected in the 1981 quinquennial Armed Forces Act. The gist of the United Kingdom changes is summed up in the 'Explanatory Memorandum' to the Bill, which explains that the change of wording in the relevant sections was to make it clear that "when a comanding officer in accordance with s.78 ... or an appropriate superior officer, in accordance with s.79, comes to the view that an accused is guilty of an offence and that a punishment other than one of the most minor kind is appropriate (in which circumstances he is required to offer the accused the opportunity of a court-martial) he has not made a formal determination of guilt."(103) As is so typical of United Kingdom practice, there is no reference to European Convention's influence in bringing about these statutory changes either in the Bill's 'Explanatory Memorandum' or in the parliamentary debates on the Bill.(104)

7. The Impact of Litigation against the United Kingdom:

(a) Before the European Commission:
The Commission, unlike the Court or Committee of Ministers, has no mandatory powers at all,(105) its primary function being to try to effect a friendly settlement under Art.28. So, strictly speaking, a finding in the Commission's Report under Art.31 as to a breach of the Convention has only morally persuasive value for the State concerned. But despite the Court of Appeal's recent decision in Guilfoyle v The Home Office(106) which has branded the Commission as a purely investigative body not exercising any judicial functions,(107) it does undoubtedly exercise quasi-judicial functions.(108) As one witness(109) put the matter before the Home Affairs Sub-Committee on Race Relations.(110)

"The Commission is not bound by its earlier opinions under any Convention rule. However, like any body that has to make a series of decisions, it must have regard to the common elements in the various situations brought before it and so form and express reasonably consistent opinions..."(111)

Despite this, the past official United Kingdom attitude towards the findings of the Commission seems to have been one of blissful disregard. This, for example, comes out clearly from the evidence given by Home Office officials to the above-mentioned Home Affairs Sub-Committee that only an affirmative decision by the Committee of Ministers(112) or the Court(113) would be considered sufficient to force a change in United Kingdom law.(114)

This strict view of the Commission's competence(115) hides the realities of power which the Commission has in applying moral pressure on a State party to amend its laws. This pressure has been highlighted in one way by the tendency of the Commission to refuse to endorse a friendly settlement (under Art.28) in cases where a 'public interest' dimension is seen to be involved, unless there is evidence that the State has agreed as part of the 'package' to amend the non-conforming aspect of its domestic law.

An early instance of this can be seen in the Alam case(116) concerning alleged breaches of Arts.6 and 8 in respect of United Kingdom immigration practice. Here, as part of the friendly settlement, the Government informed the Sub-Commission that an Immigration Appeals Bill(117) and a draft Aliens (Appeal) Order had been introduced into Parliament in November 1968.(118) Although, as seen,(119), this legislative activity was ostensibly the result of a domestic recommendation - the Wilson Report, 1967 - it seems clear that without such a speedy change in the United Kingdom's immigration appeals legislation, a settlement acceptable to the Commission might not have been achieved.

Another example can be seen in the Knechtl(120) case concerning a prisoner's right to correspond with his solicitor with a view to bringing civil proceedings against a prison doctor (Art.6(1). In the Commission's report of 1972 it noted "in particular" that under the terms of the friendly settlement between the applicant and the United Kingdom, the Government had laid a White Paper (concerning the right to consult a solicitor in such a case) before Parliament on December 10, 1971.(121)

More recently, it may be noted in X v UK(122) concerning corporal punishment in an English school, that the follow-up to the friendly settlement has been an official circular to all education authorities in England and Wales informing them of the implications of the European Convention on such a form of punishment.(123)

Where no friendly settlement has been achieved,(124) the mere process of the Commission drawing up a Report (under Art.31) stating that in its opinion there has been a breach, is another means by which the Commission may apply some pressure on the Government to make legislative changes. For the recipient of the report is the Committee of Ministers which has the power to make the final decision (unless the case is referred to the Court).

The importance of this procedure is two-fold. First, it is at this stage that the content of the Commission's Report may be made public under Art.32(3); and even publicity in itself may be a "powerful sanction"(125). Second, the practice of the Committee of Ministers has been to endorse the opinions of the Commission,(126) so that in effect any adverse finding by the Commission against the United Kingdom constitutes a 'writing on the wall' for the prospective Committee of Ministers' stage. The result of this has been that parties to the Convention have tended, in some cases at least, to take remedial domestic measures before the Committee of Ministers becomes seized of the matter.(127)

A good recent illustration of this situation can be seen in Hamer v UK(128) and X v UK(129) concerning the right of prisoners to marry, where the United Kingdom accepted at an early stage the unanimous finding by the Commission (in reports of 1979(130) and 1980(131) respectively) that the applicants' ability to exercise their right to marry had been substantially delayed by the combined effect of United Kingdom national law and administrative action (Art.12). Thus despite the absence of a friendly settlement, the Prison Department was reported to have relaxed its policy on this matter in guidelines issued in October 1980,(132) and on April 2, 1981, shortly before the Committee of Ministers was due to consider the two cases, it was announced in Parliament that the Government had decided to amend the marriage laws so as, inter alia, to allow prisoners to be married in prison "having regard to the recent deliberations of the European Commission of Human Rights".(133)

In consequence, the United Kingdom was able to inform the Committee of Ministers that it "accepted the Commission's Report"(134), that it had "changed its practice" with regard to the marriage of prisoners, like Mr Hamer, serving a determinate custodial sentence;(135) and that it hoped that there would be an early opportunity to amend United Kingdom marriage laws.

(b) Before the Committee of Ministers or the Court:
Under Arts.32 and 53 respectively of the European Convention, the decisions of the Comittee of Ministers (where an affirmative vote has been attained) and of the Court are binding on the parties to the treaty concerned.(136) So that any decision of either body (unlike the Commission(137)) may have direct implications for legislative change in United Kingdom domestic law, even if there are adademic doubts about how far, if at all, the Court itself may decree any such remedial change.(138)

Of course, not all cases which have gone against the United Kingdom in either body have involved the necessity for any change in United Kingdom law;(139) but most have, and some specific examples will be examined in the next section.

An interesting point arises in connection with the Committee of Ministers' supervisory powers over execution of

a Court's decision where a State party has purported to amend
its domestic law by legislation to comply with the Court's
decree in a 'general interest' situation. For there may be some
doubt as to whether the legislative change does in fact ensure
conformity with the Convention, and the Committee of
Ministers, as a non-legal body, may have difficulty in deciding
whether a violation has been remedied.(140)

A similar problem for the Committee of Ministers can
arise under Art. 32 following an adverse report from the
Commission where it has to decide without reference to the
Court whether there has been a violation (under Art. 32 (1));
and if there is, whether the State in question has taken
"satisfactory measures" (which may again include legislative
change) within the prescribed period.(141)

As will be seen, (142) there is as yet no provision in the
Convention enabling a State to submit its draft legislation to
the Commission or the Court to obtain advance clearance on
conformity. Without such assistance, what the Committee of
Ministers has tended to do in respect of its supervisory powers
over the Court's judgment under Art. 54 is simply to "take
note of"(143) or express "satisfaction"(144) at the legislative
action taken by the party in question. It has thus avoided
expressing an opinion on the substance of the matter, i.e.
whether the legislation has effectively remedied the
breach.(145)

The Sunday Times case(146) illustrates this problem in
respect of the United Kingdom. For here, almost two years
after the Court's judgment, the Committee of Ministers felt
able to dispose of the case (under Art. 54) by simply "taking
note" of the summarised statement from the Government that
the Contempt of Court Bill then proceeding through
Parliament was "designed, inter alia, to prevent futher
conflict... with the provisions of the ...Convention as
interpreted by the Court in this case".(147) It is not clear
from the appendix to this resolution whether the United
Kingdom actually submitted the Bill's relevant clauses. Even
if it did, this would have been somewhat premature in the light

of possible amendments to the Bill during the legislative process (as indeed happened)(148) or failure of the whole Bill to achieve enactment.(149) It can be argued from this that the Committee of Ministers should delay finalising its supervisory functions until the requisite harmonising legislation is actually on the statute book.

The above considerations apply a fortiori where the United Kingdom Government merely informs the Committee that it intends to bring in amending legislation in the future and therefore cannot even produce a draft bill for this body to scrutinise, as recently happened (albeit under the Art.32 procedure) in the prisoners' marriage rights cases.(150) For here the Committee accepted the United Kingdom's statement of intent to amend the marriage law at an early opportunity. As a result there can be no guarantee that even if such legislation is introduced its contents will be of a sufficiently remedial nature to satisfy the Convention. Rather than prematurely washing its hands of the issue, it may be suggested that the Committee should have used its "prescribed period" powers under Art. 32(2) so as to pressurise the Government into early action which could be adequately monitored.

8. Recent Important Areas of Human Rights' Litigation(151) against the United Kingdom at Strasbourg with an Impact on Domestic Law:

(a) Mental health:
In this area there has been a concerted multi-pronged attack in Strasbourg on existing United Kingdom practice, particularly under the 1959 Mental Health Act. In consequence, several amendments have had to be made in the Mental Health Act (Amendment) Bill, 1982;(152) and yet further amending legislation may be necessary if further adverse decisions result from the Committee of Ministers or the Court as a result of other pending applications.(153)

It has been Art. 5(4) which has made the greatest impact on the 1959 Act as a result of applications to date.(154) Here, the United Kingdom's attitude was made evident in its intervention in the <u>Winterwerp</u> case(155) - that only the formal lawfulness of a detention order need be judicially reviewed.(156)

In the most important of these applications, <u>X</u> v <u>UK</u>,(157) the legality of existing United Kingdom procedures under the 1959 regime has been tested by the European Court in the context of Arts 5(1)(e), 5(2) and 5(4).(158) In its 1981 decision, the Court, although finding no breach of Art. 5(1) (unjustifiable deprivation of liberty), determined unanimously that the United Kingdom had breached Art. 5(4) and that its habeas corpus procedure did not provide a sufficient remedy in the circumstances.(159)

Coincidentally,(160) new legislation on a broad area of mental health law in the United Kingdom was introduced into Parliament shortly after the publication of the'<u>X</u>'case on November 10, 1981. Typically, there was no reference to the European Convention's requirements in the explanatory memorandum to the Bill - the Mental Health Act (Amendment) Bill - and at the Bill's second reading in the House of Lords the Government's spokesman(161) stressed the domestic influences behind the Bill,(162) particularly the Butler Report.(163) Even the White Paper accompanying the Bill made only brief reference to the '<u>X</u>' case.(164)

The most notable omission in the Bill's central aims of increasing the powers of mental health review tribunals and the possibilities of review of detention was quickly pointed out by MIND(165) and in Parliament, namely that the Bill failed to accommodate the situation in '<u>X</u>' concerning a <u>restricted mental patient</u>. Some official admission by the Government that the rights of such patients might have to be yet further improved in the light of the recently decided '<u>X</u>'case was not surprisingly made in para. 52 of the above-mentioned White Paper. This pointed out:

> Under the present law, the Home Secretary must refer the cases of restricted patients to a Tribunal periodically if they ask him to do so, but the Tribunal

can then only advise the Home Secretary whether to discharge the patient. It cannot itself order discharge. The Government has decided not to include any amendments to the 1959 Act which relate to the issue in [the 'X'case] until the judgment of the Court has been studied.

At the Bill's second reading in the House of Lords, the Government promised to bring in amendments at the Committee stage to remedy the defects shown up in 'X', and indicated that the broad drift of such amendments might be to "seek to give to the mental health review tribunals a power to discharge in the case of restricted patients as well as others"; and that it intended to ensure that each tribunal panel would include an experienced lawyer.(167)

Accordingly, important amendments to the Bill were announced at the Second Reading stage in the Commons.(168) These were stated to be necessary to enable "[United Kingdom] law to take account of the recent judgment of the European Court" and were to enable restricted patients to apply direct to a tribunal for a review where the power to discharge would be independent of the Home Secretary.(169)

A further important point arising out of the 'X' case concerns the applicant's complaint that he was not informed promptly of the reasons for his arrest when he was recalled to a mental hospital in 1974, in alleged breach of Art. 5(2). The Commission, in its report, found there had been a violation of this Article:(170) and seemingly to meet this deficiency, at the end of 1980 ministerial circulars were issued to relevant authorities in the United Kingdom announcing a new two-stage information procedure for the recall of patients "in order to meet the criticisms made by the European Commission".(171) When this matter was again taken up before the Court, the Court took note of these new procedures. In the circumstances the Court found it not necessary to examine the case under Art. 5(2) as it considered this amounted to no more than one aspect of the complaint which it had already examined under Art. 5(4).(172)

Apart from the issues in the 'X'case, several other aspects of United Kingdom mental health law have also been recently questioned on their conformity with the European Convention's obligations. These are:

(1) Legal representation:

In the Winterwerp case(173) the applicant had contended that in view of the special situation of persons of unsound mind, there was a right for them to be legally assisted to be read into Art. 5(4), but the Court in its 1979 judgment appears not to have made any express ruling in this regard. None the less, it has been recently suggested in the United Kingdom that the effectiveness of the new legislative review procedures will not be assured unless patients are legally represented at the hearing; and that as legal aid was under existing law not available in such circumstances, the new amending mental health legislation would be open to challenge at Strasbourg.(174)

Thus during debate on the Mental Health Act (Amendment) Bill there was strong parliamentary pressure for the addition of a clause guaranteeing legal aid and representation before review tribunals. Not only were references made to decisions of the European Court on this issue - in particular Winterwerp and more generally, Airey (against Ireland)(175) - but also to the pending application against the United Kingdom in Collins(176) on this very matter before the Commission. This plea soon found some favour with the Government. In the House of Lords it was stated to be under "urgent consideration",(177) and a subsequent concession by the Government - implemented at the Standing Committee stage of the Commons - will extend legal aid, advice and assistance to patients appealing to review tribunals.(178)

(ii) Treatment at United Kingdom mental institutions:
There has been a batch of cases alleging before the Commission that the applicants have suffered inhuman and degrading treatment in United Kingdom mental hospitals in breach of Art. 3.(179) In one of these, A v UK(180), a patient

in Broadmoor hospital who had undergone solitary confinement received in 1980 an ex gratia payment of £500 as a result of the friendly settlement. An important aspect to the settlement was the issue of guidelines to govern the use of seclusion at Broadmoor.(181) In a further letter of April 29, 1980, the Government had indicated generally that guidelines on this matter would be kept under review and that further improvements which might appear possible in the light of experience would receive "proper consideration".(182) But the official view of these guidelines is that they clarify previously unwritten practices rather than introduce changes.(183)

(iii) The right to sue: s.141 of the Mental Health Act:

An important set of applications(184) involve s.141 of the 1959 Act which, inter alia, limits the right of mental patients to sue (for unlawful detention or alleged wrongs done to them during detention) to circumstances where there is a "substantial ground" for the contention that the defendant acted in "bad faith or without reasonable care".(185) And a High Court judge's permission for institution of proceedings on this basis must be obtained.

Surprisingly, the Mental Health Act (Amendment) Bill, as published, contained no proposed amendments to s.141, though the 1978 White Paper did advocate modest reform to the extent that the section should be changed to require only "reasonable" rather than "substantial" grounds for permission to sue.(186) In effect, the present rule may require a patient to prove his case in advance of trial, and, as such, this may conflict with the 'fair trial' provisions of Art. 6 of the Convention. The deficiencies of United Kingdom law in this regard have been highlighted in Kynaston v Secretary of State for Home Affairs(178) in 1981.

Predictably, at both the Report stage and the Third Reading in the House of Lords of the Bill, determined efforts were made to amend the existing law, spurred on by the fact that during the currency of parliamentary debate on the new Bill one of the 's. 141' applications was found to be admissible at Strasbourg (on the basis of Arts. 5 and 6) in the Ashingdane case.(188) The basic aim of these proposed amendments was to make "much less severe" the burden of proof on a patient contemplating legal proceedings.(189) However these efforts proved unsuccessful, and the Government made it clear that it was not prepared at that stage of the Strasbourg proceedings(190) to change the law. If, therefore, the Ashingdane case proceeds in due course to an adverse conclusion for the United Kingdom at Strasbourg, a separate piece of legislation will be needed to harmonise United Kingdom law with its international obligations.

(iv) Undue length of review proceedings:

The existing mental health legislation is also alleged to violate Art. 5(4) (apart from the alleged deficiencies mentioned above) because of the length of the proceedings for discharge from a United Kingdom mental hospital. On this question the application in Barlay-Maguire v UK(191) has recently been declared admissible by the Commission.(192)

(b) Homosexuality:

Of the applications to date(193) alleging that United Kingdom sexual offences legislation is not in conformity with the European Convention, the most important has been Dudgeon v UK.(194) Here the applicant complained that the laws in force in Northern Ireland prohibiting male homosexual activity constituted an interference with his private life under Art. 8 and discrimination under Art. 14 both in respect of his private sexual life being subject to greater restrictions than female homosexuals and heterosexuals and because male homosexuals elsewhere in the United Kingdom are not subject to such restrictions.

In October 1981, the European Court found, as had the Commission,(195) that the Northern Irish laws contravened Art. 8. The finding of the Commission alone, however, was enough to prompt the Government to go through the unusual procedure of issuing a draft statutory instrument on this matter in 1979 as a form of 'working paper' to elicit comments on possible legal changes. This, no doubt, was because of the strong political pressure which exists in Northern Ireland against amending the law on homosexuality in any way. When in 1979 the Secretary of State was questioned in Parliament as to when this draft order - the Homosexual Offences (Northern Ireland) Order(196) - was to be laid before Parliament, he replied that such legislation was traditionally left to the initiative of private members' bills and that he would reconsider the law "if there were any developments in the law which were relevant".(197)

Thereafter, in its Report of March 5, 1981,(198) the Northern Ireland Standing Advisory Commission on Human Rights recommended that the Government should reconsider its stance on the issue. Referring to Dudgeon, where the Commission had decided "substantially in favour of the applicant", the Report said:

"[R]ather than pursue the case to the European Court, the Government [should] act upon the decision of the European Commission and announce its intention to lay a draft....Order before Parliament".(199)

After the Court's judgment of October 1981 on the basis of Art. 8,(200) the Government came under renewed pressure to change Northern Ireland's homosexuality laws (where the 1967 Sexual Offences Act never applied)(201). The Northern Ireland Office studied the judgment, and it was announced in Parliament on February 24, 1982, that the Government had "noted" the decision, and would be taking steps to bring the law in Northern Ireland "into line with that of the rest of the United Kingdom."(202) In April, 1982, a draft Order - The Homosexual Offences (Northern Ireland) Order was duly laid before both Houses, and on October 25, 1982 it was approved by the House of Commons.

A further potential problem for the Government arises in the case of the law relating to homosexuality among the armed forces. For by s. 1(5) of the 1967 Sexual Offences Act the armed services and the merchant navy are expressly excluded from that Act's amending provisions. In the recent

Armed Forces Bill(203) a move to liberalise the relevant legislation was rejected by a Commons Standing Committee.(204) However, the legal issues here are similar to those in Dudgeon, and at least one application has now been lodged in Strasbourg by a former serviceman (dismissed from the forces for homosexual behaviour while on leave).(205) Significantly, it was reported in December 1981(206) that a soldier convicted by court-martial of a homosexual offence had both his conviction and sentence quashed by an Army Board. Although no reasons were given for this unusual move, it may be speculated that the Strasbourg proceedings in Dudgeon may have been influential, especially as it has also been reported that new instructions on homosexuality have been issued to commanding officers of all three armed services so as to bring their procedures in this area more into line with the civilian viewpoint.(207)

(c) Corporal punishment in schools:

Two sets of applications - from Scotland and England -have so far effectively reached culmination in Strasbourg. These are Campbell & Cosans v UK(208) and X v UK.(209)

(i) Campbell & Cosans:

These two applications were from parents concerning corporal punishment in Scottish schools attended by their children. They complained that the use or threatened use of corporal punishment infringed both Art. 3 of the Convention and Art. 2 of Protocol No. 1 because it was not in conformity with their philosophical convictions. Although neither the Commission (in its Report of May 16, 1980)(210) nor the Court (in its judgment of February 25, 1982)(211) found the threatened use of corporal punishment to be a breach of Art. 3, both found that the education authorities' refusal to guarantee the non-use of such punishment on the applicants' children violated Protocol No 1. Thus the Court found there to be a breach of the second sentence of Art. 2 of the Protocol in the case of Campbell, and an additional breach of the first sentence of the same article in the case of Cosans.(212)

(ii) X v UK

This application concerned corporal punishment of a girl pupil in an English school. It was declared admissible by the Commission on July 12, 1978, and thereafter the Government sought a friendly settlement of the issue. On February 27, 1982, the terms of a friendly settlement were announced which involved payment to the applicant of £1,200 as compensation.(213)

(iii) The impact of these two cases on United Kingdom law:

As a result of the Court's decision in Campbell & Cosans, the Government is, at the time of writing, considering the implications of the judgment.(214) As far as Scotland is concerned (whence this set of cases came), it appears that the Scottish educational authorities were advised to abolish (by July 1984) the use of the 'tawse' (the implement of punishment) even before the Court had given judgment.(215) But obviously this litigation has implications for all United Kingdom schools where corporal punishment is currently practised - not only in the public sector but also possibly in the private sector as well.

New legislation may, therefore, be necessary to amend the existing 1944 Education Act as it is clear that the Department of Education itself has no power to dictate schools' disciplinary policy even in the state system (where such matters are determined by the local education authority, the managers or governors of the school and the head teacher.)(216)

The result of any such amending legislation may be to abolish corporal punishment throughout the public sector as it may be administratively inconvenient, if not impossible, to devise a system involving both corporal and non-corporal systems of discipline within one school, or to hive off certain schools as strictly 'non-corporal punishment' institutions in an attempt to respect the philosophical convictions of parents. In point of fact, the use of corporal punishment in schools is already on the wane, as at the present time about one third of the local education authorities in England and Wales have

abolished   (or   are   committed   to   abolishing)   such
punishment.(217)

In addition, the result of the friendly settlement in the
'X'case has been the official circularisation of all English
education authorities with a warning that the use of corporal
punishment in schools in certain circumstances amounts to
inhuman or degrading punishment under Art. 3.(218) A copy of
the Commission's Report in the case was enclosed.

The combined effect, therefore, of Campbell & Cosans and
'X' is likely to be to force a legislative change in this area of
educational   practice,   particularly   now   that   further
applications on this matter are pending at Strasbourg.(219) An
important side effect of these cases may also be to strengthen
the impact of the Tyrer case(220) (the Manx birching case) on
the broader question of judicial corporal punishment in the
United Kingdom.   Thus in the instance of the recently-
attempted amendments to the Criminal Justice Bill to re-
introduce corporal punishment for perpetrators of crimes of
violence(221) it is significant that the educationally-oriented
body called 'STOPP' urged MPs on the Commons Committee
concerned to oppose these moves on the ground that this would
be a breach of the United Kingdom's obligations under the
Convention.(222)

(d) Immigration:
The earliest important Strasbourg proceedings over United
Kingdom immigration legislation arose in the East African
Asians cases.(223) These concerned applications from persons
of Asian origin from East Africa who were, as United Kingdom
passport holders, denied entry into the United Kingdom.

Here the Committee of Ministers failed to get the
necessary two-thirds majority to uphold the Commission's
findings (in their Report of 1973) that the United Kingdom had
breached Art. 3 in the case of 25 applications (by citizens of
the United Kingdom and Colonies) and of three applications
under Arts. 8 and 14 taken together. For this technical reason
the Committee decided that no further action was called for

in these cases.(224) None the less, it may be speculated that had the necessary two-thirds vote been obtained, the Committee would have endorsed the Commission's findings in toto.(225)

The official United Kingdom attitude, however, has been to treat the case as one from which it is impossible to glean any legal principle. Strangely, for example, the memorandum by the Home Office to the Sub-Committee on Race Relations and Immigration, makes only laconic reference to the case.(226) Indeed, the tendency of Home Office evidence to the Sub-Committee was towards treating these important cases as ones that turned on their own particular facts.(227)

The above-mentioned Sub-Committee had been set up after anxiety had been expressed in Parliament concerning the conformity of the proposed new immigration rules (in the 1979 White Paper)(228) with the European Convention. The evidence submitted to it was centred on Rule 50 (entry of husbands), Rule 52 (entry of fiances) and Rule 48 (entry of parents and grandparents).(229) One of the most prestigious legal witnesses, Lord Scarman, stated bluntly that he could see "no difference in legal principle" between the East African Asians cases and the proposed rules which would refuse entry to husbands.(230)

In their First Report, the Sub-Committee merely attempted to set out the principal arguments adduced in evidence before them without forming any judgment.(231) But the Report did strongly stress the suggestion of witnesses that the immigration proposals were most vulnerable in relation to Art. 8 coupled with Art. 14 on the grounds of sexual and/or racial discrimination:(232) also that if the Commission were of the opinion that the new rules were racially discriminatory, this might lead to a breach under Art. 3 (degrading treatment) on the basis of the East African Asians' case.(233) There were, therefore, strong hints in the Report that the new rules would infringe the Convention (as was also suggested in the later parliamentary debate on December 4, 1979).(234) Despite this, the finalised new immigration rules remained virtually intact.(235)

It is not, therefore, surprising that several applications are now pending before the Commission arising from the new rules;(236) and that in 1982 some have been found to be admissible.(237) As a result, the rules have currently undergone further review by the Home Office,(238) and it seems likely that at least one of the controversial rules will be changed when the new Nationality Act becomes law at the beginning of 1983,(239) despite strong political 'back-bench' pressure against this. The main impetus for the change seems undoubtedly to have been the recent findings of admissibility in three of the Strasbourg 'test cases'.

9. Conclusions:

It seems clear from the above survey that the past practice of official reticence in acknowledging the impact of the European Convention in forcing or influencing changes in United Kingdom law is beginning to subside under the unprecedented welter of cases which have now gone against the United Kingdom at Strasbourg. Indeed, as seen, several pieces of pre-emptive legislation have occurred seemingly to avoid any ultimate public condemnation at Strasbourg; so that even the (non-mandatory) findings of the Commission are now being treated with greater apparent sensitivity than before.(240)

Because of increasing official and public awareness of the Convention's impact, any new legislation touching a human rights' field, even as yet unlitigated against the United Kingdom, will be subject to increasing scrutiny for possible non-compliance so as to ensure that it is "Strasbourg-proof".(241) Furthermore, it is perhaps an irony that in certain areas where the United Kingdom Government has feared to tread in reforming existing law for fear of public protest - as in the case of the Northern Irish homosexuality laws - the interposition of an adverse finding at Strasbourg can actually facilitate the passage of domestic legislation. For here the impetus for change has come from an external source, and the resulting reform can thus be blamed on "a collection of foreign jurists".(242)

There remains the problem, however, of whether there is adequate monitoring by the supervisory body - the Committee of Ministers - of such remedial legislation in the aftermath of litigation at Strasbourg. The present weaknesses in the system, as discussed earlier, can mean that the 'rubber stamp' of approval given to remedial legislation on a particular issue in one case by the Committee may with hindsight prove to be over-generous when the same issue is successfully litigated again, despite the intervening amendment of United Kingdom law.

This situation could, for example, arise over the new contempt of court legislation in the United Kingdom;(243) and it does actually seem to have occurred in the controversial sphere of prison correspondence following the Golder case.(244) For here the consequential amendment to the Prison Rules - Rule 37A - despite getting approval from the Committee of Ministers - arguably did little to remove the objectionable features of Rule 34(8) (whereby communications from prisoners required leave of the Secretary of State in connection with any legal business). Thus with the advent of the Silver case,(245) the amended rules have now been re-amended on the question of the right of prisoners' correspondence.(246)

The United Kingdom, of course, does not as yet possess any domestic standing body (as do other parties to the Convention)(247) to scrutinise any draft legislation or rules for conformity with the Convention, and the one example of pre-legislative scrutiny to date - on the revised immigration rules - was done purely on an ad hoc basis.(248) The possibility of a standing body of this sort being set up in the United Kingdom has been considered briefly in the 1977 Report of the Standing Advisory Commission on Human Rights in Northern Ireland (albeit in the context of incorporation of the Convention into United Kingdom law). As they stated:

"In principle we would welcome the introduction of some suitable mechanism for scrutinising the potential effect of pending legislation ...[W]e do not think that there is any practical scope for introducing a new scrutiny stage as part of the Parliamentary process itself because of the undue strain which it would impose on the Parliamentary machine...We doubt whether the introduction of such a mechanism would be feasible unless there were radical changes in the machinery of Parliament...What would, in our view, be feasible...would be to authorise the proposed Commission for Human Rights [recommended to be set up under the Report] to make recommendations about the compatibility of existing and proposed legislation with the protection of human rights".(249)

As the United Kingdom courts themselves have, as seen, no power to assess legislation subsequent to enactment for conformity with the European Convention, at present only Parliament can perform a public watchdog service in a pre-legislative way to "protect the national interests of the British people by witholding approval of a measure which would result in violations of the Convention by the United Kingdom...".(250) But, as seen, such a domestic monitoring device is at present very haphazard.(251)

Thus the setting up of a new standing body - as suggested by the Standing Advisory Commission supra - to scrutinise draft United Kingdom legislation for conformity with the Convention, and indeed, the United Kingdom's broader human rights obligations (such as under the 1966 UN Covenants) would seem to be a desirable reform, albeit one with important constitutional implications.

Another possibility might be reform of the Strasbourg machinery so that either the Commission(252) or the Court could be empowered to give its opinion on any party's draft legislation or decree as regards conformity with the Convention. Unfortunately, such a reform would be hedged by practical difficulties, as has recently been convincingly stated by a Steering Committee for Human Rights considering revision of Protocol No. 2 in respect of conferring competence on the Court to give advisory opinions.

As the 1980 Report noted:

The proposed procedure would require the Court to give
an abstract and general assessment of the compatibility
of the draft law with the Convention and not in a
concrete case. However, in many cases it is the way in
which the law is applied in practice which is important
and not the way in which it has been drafted. If the
Court had given a favourable opinion on a draft law,
this could prejudice the position of the Commission and
the Court and prove very embarrassing in the event
that a subsequent complaint came before them of an
alleged violation of the Convention arising from the law
which had been interpreted and applied after it had
entered into force".(253)

FOOTNOTES

(1) See on this Nedjati, <u>Human Rights under the European Convention</u>, 1978, p.4.

(2) See <u>Malone v Commissioner of Police of the Metropolis (No.2)</u> [1979] 2 All ER 620, 647.

(3) See Robertson, <u>Human Rights in Europe</u>, 2nd ed 1977, p27; and the dictum in the <u>De Becker</u> case (Yearbook 2,234) cited by Jacobs in <u>The European Convention on Human Rights</u>, 1975, p10.

(4) Robertson, op cit at p27.

(5) See infra fn 136.

(6) See, eg Art. 13 ("effective remedy") and Art. 57 (furnishing explanation of how internal laws ensure effective implementation) discussed by Robertson, op cit at pp30, 77, 105 and 269.

(7) Though UK courts do increasingly refer to the Convention as an aid to interpreting ambiguous domestic statutes. See, eg Duffy, "English Law and the European Convention on Human Rights" (1980) 29 ICLQ 585. More circuitously, by dint of the European Court of Justice taking account of human rights contained in the European Convention in interpreting <u>EEC</u> law, such principles may become <u>directly applicable</u> EEC law.

(8) See, eg the recent complaint by Lord Wade during parliamentary debate on the 1982 Mental Health Act (Amendment) Bill: <u>Hansard</u> (HL) vol 427, col 876.

(9) <u>The Times</u>, July 13, 1982.

(10) According to <u>The Times</u>, July 9, 1982.

(11) See supra, essay at p 283.

(12) See more particularly infra s 8.

(13) By Lord Kilmarnock : <u>Hansard</u> (HL), vol 427, col 875. For others, see infra s 8(a).

(14) Ibid, col 878. See also the comment of Lord Wade, ibid, col 876 ("... we have to rely on issues relating to the convention <u>point by point</u> as they arise") (emphasis added).

(15) See <u>The Times</u>, June 7, 1982 and infra fn 71.

(16) At the Third Reading of the Bill in the Lords on October 12, 1982: see <u>The Times</u>, October 11, 1982.

(17) See infra fn 251 and accompanying text.

(18) But note that not all UK government departments have their own 'legal section'. Thus, eg in the case of human rights issues arising from the armed services (see infra s 6), it has been the Treasury Solicitor's department which has seemingly given the legal advice (the Ministry of Defence having no legal department of its own). The handling of issues under the European Convention in so many different government departments seems unsatisfactory, and may in some cases lead to an inter-departmental difference of view - for example with the Foreign Office.

(19) See, eg Mann, "Britain's Bill of Rights", (1978) 94 LQR 512, 521.

(20) HC 1979-80, 394 (February 20, 1980).

(21) <u>Proposals for Revision of the Immigration Rules</u>, HMSO Cmnd 7750 (1979).

(22) On December 4, 1979: see Hansard, (HC) vol 974, cols 256, 428. See also the repetition in the First Report of the Home Affairs Committee 1979-80 - Proposed New Immigration Rules and the European Convention on Human Rights : HC 434 (February 11, 1980).

(23) See infra fn 236 and accompanying text.

(24) See Hansard (HL) vol 415, col 665.

(25) See, eg, the express reference to the Convention in the explanatory memorandum to the legislation amending the Austrian penal code on August 3, 1971: Stocktaking, 1977 (DH(77)3), p40. See also the attitude of Norway, discussed in Morrisson, The Developing European Law of Human Rights, 188, 189.

(26) No 2991/66: 10 Yearbook, 478.

(27) The Immigration Appeals Act, and the Aliens (Appeal) Order, 1969.

(28) Mr Callaghan: Hansard (HC), vol 776, col 469 (January 22, 1969).

(29) Report of the Committee on Immigration Appeals, Cmnd 3387, 1967.

(30) Reference is mostly to potential EEC obligations arising from the policy of freedom of movement (para 141), though there is also vague reference to the idea of 'due process' embodied in "certain international conventions" (ibid). The relevant conventions cited in the Appendix (No IV, p84) do not include the European Convention. None the less it was affirmed in Parliament that the new legislation fulfilled the international obligations referred to in the Report: Hansard, (HC) vol 776, col 528.

(31) See supra essay at p 318.

(32) (1979) 2 EHRR 245.

(33) Cf the 'domestic' background to the new Mental Health Act (Amendment) Bill, 1982 infra fn 163.

(34) Hansard (HL), vol 415, col 659.

(35) See eg, Hansard (HC) vol 1000, col 43; Hansard (HL) vol 415, col 660. This aim of the Bill was made clear both in the preamble and the explanatory memorandum.

(36) Hence Parliament cannot be relied upon to act as a watchdog of the public interest in this respect.

(37) Also MPs tend not to be conversant with the technicalities of the Convention, and thus, eg, easily confuse the Commission with the Court: see the example in Hansard (HC), vol 2, col 326.

(38) For a plea to ignore such international obligations, see the incredible statement of one MP (Mr Stanbrook) during debate on the new immigration rules: Hansard (HC), vol 974, col 349 ("We may forget about any breach of the convention. The overriding law is what we take to be in the national interest of the British people").

(39) ECHR Series B, 24.

(40) See infra fn 208.

(41) At the Committee Stage of the Criminal Justice Bill 1982: see The Daily Telegraph, February 4, 1982. The proposed amendment was duly rejected: see The Daily Telegraph, March 24, 1982.

(42) See The Daily Telegraph, March 24, 1982.

(43) See, eg, the statement of Mr Whitelaw in the Commons on February 18, 1982 that it would be "completely contrary" to the UK's international

obligations: Hansard (HC) vol 18, col 397.
(44) See, eg, the statement of STOPP (infra fn. 222): The Guardian, March 23, 1982.
(45) See The Times, August 31, 1982.
(46) See infra fn 210 and accompanying text.
(47) Cf the legal opinion of September, 1982, prepared by the Association of Governing Bodies of Public Schools: The Times, August 31, 1982.
(48) See further infra fn 115 and accompanying text.
(49) See, eg, Hansard (HL) vol 411, col 912. At the Second Reading in the Lords, the Lord Chancellor affirmed that the wording of the Bill was intended to conform with the provisions of the European Convention: see ibid, at col. 931 (July 7, 1980).
(50) See supra essay at p 283 and Hansard (HC) vol 974, cols 219, 220.
(51) By Lord Wallace of Coslany. See the Third Reading in Hansard, vol 427, 1418 and the Report Stage, ibid, col 917 (February 23, 1982). See also the proposed amendment of Lord Winstanley (ibid, at col 1421) who stated that the House should "not allow the Government merely to sit back passively awaiting condemnation from the European Court".
(52) For fuller discussion, see infra fn 186 and accompanying text.
(53) Ashingdane v UK: see infra fn 188.
(54) Hansard (HL), vol 427, col 919.
(55) Cf the influence of Strasbourg litigation on the deliberations of the Law Commission - for example, the Arrowsmith case, infra fn 81.
(56) See The Times, April 3, 1982.
(57) Report on the Interception of Communications in Great Britain, Cmnd 8191, March 1981. For official statements on this decision, see The Times April 1 & 2, 1981.
(58) At p3.
(59) Malone v Commissioners of Police of the Metropolis (No 2) [1979] 2 All ER 620.
(60) Ibid at p 649.
(61) No 8691/79. See (1982) 4 EHRR 293.
(62) Mr Mikardo. See Hansard (HC) vol 2, col 326. For the proposed amendment (Clause 47 of Pt 1) see Hansard (HC) vol 2, cols 292, 331, 332 & 333.
(63) Home Office v Harman [1982] 1 All ER 532, 547.
(64) See respectively Hansard (HC) vol 18, col 589 and The Times, April 8, 1982.
(65) See The Daily Telegraph, February 11, 1982.
(66) The National Council for Civil Liberties which, eg, has helped sponsor the recent immigration cases (infra fn 236): see The Times March 1, 1982. See also their recent statements on telephone tapping (The Times, March 4, 1981); the 'sus' law (s.4 of the 1824 Vagrancy Act) (The Times, December 9, 1980); and homosexuality (The Times, October 23, 1981).
(67) Concerned with the important mental health applications: see infra fn 157 et seq.
(68) Concerned with the prisoners' rights applications. See supra, essay at p 352.

(69) The 'Society of Teachers Opposed to Physical Punishment' who have backed the recent 'corporal punishment' applications: see infra fn. 210 et seq.
(70) See The Times, July 21, 1982.
(71) This course has been preferred to introduction of a separate Bill. Under the amendment, local authorities are to be required to get authorisation from a magistrate for locking up children in their care after 7 days' detention.
(72) See Thorold, "Britain Facing another Caning from Europe", The Times, March 2, 1982.
(73) Supra fn 25 and accompanying text.
(74) See supra fn 18 and accompanying text.
(75) Report of the Commission to Consider Legal Procedures to Deal with Terrorist Activities in Northern Ireland, Cmnd 5185, 1972. This makes early general reference to the European Convention at p5.
(76) Ibid, at para 12, p8.
(77) Ibid, at para 90, p 32. See also the references to Art 6 of the Convention in paras 22 & 61.
(78) [1977] NILR 105. For comment, see Boyle, Hadden & Hillyard, Ten Years on in Northern Ireland, 1980, at p47; and Greer, "The Admissibility of Confessions under the Northern Ireland (Emergency Provisions) Act, (1980) NILQ 205, 212.
(79) See also recently the 1979 Report of the Committee of Enquiry into the UK Prison Services, Cmnd 7673 which at para 1.15, p 5, states that the Committee had before them the "main international instruments", including the European Convention, and the 5th Report of the Home Affairs Committee on the Law Relating to the Public Order Act, vol II (HC 756 - i (1979-80), pp.xiv, (para 36) and xlviii (para 37) (reference to Art 11 on the right to peaceful assembly).
(80) Codification of the Criminal Law: Treason, Sedition and Allied Offences, para 93.
(81) No 7050/75.
(82) The European Commission's Report found no violations of Arts 5, 9, 10 or 14 (October 12, 1978). The Committee of Ministers endorsed this in Res DH(79) on June 12, 1979: see (1981) 3 EHRR 218.
(83) Offences against Religion and Public Worship.
(84) [1979] AC 617, 664.
(85) See para 6.6, p 80. The Strasbourg application (No 8110/79) arising from this 'Gay News' case was declared inadmissible by the Commission in 1982: see Communique B(82) 21, p 2. In appropriate circumstances, the UK Government seems content to rely on the Law Commission to consider any 'European Convention' perspectives thrown up by domestic courts. See eg, the query by Lord Wade in the Lords as to whether the Government intended, in the light of dicta in Gleaves v Deakin [1979] [1980] AC 477 2 All ER 497, 498, to amend the law of criminal libel so as to "bring it into line with the European Convention"; Hansard (HL) vol 401, col 1625. The Government spokesman replied (ibid, at col 1626) that the law here was currently under review by the Law Commission. But note that where litigation is pending at Strasbourg on the area of investigation (as in the 'Gay News' application,

supra) the natural tendency of the Law Commission has been to put the topic into 'cold storage' until the European Commission has finally determined the issue.

(86) Fn 37 and accompanying text.

(87) See, eg, Lord Wade's query re prospective legislation supra fn 85. An example on pending legislation can be found during debate on the 1976 Education Bill with reference to Art 2 of the First Protocol, where the laconic ministerial reply was that the article had been considered and that the Bill was "not inconsistent" with this international obligation: Hansard (HC) vol 915, col 189 (July 14, 1976).

(88) See, eg, the query by the Home Affairs Sub-Committee on Race Relations and Immigration at p.20 of their Report (supra fn 22) as to whether complaints involving immigration had been brought before the Commission involving other European States. A similar influence can be seen in the situation where successful litigation against the UK in one sphere focuses attention of the possible impact of the Convention on other analogous spheres (where no actual litigation against the UK (or any other party) has yet transpired). See, eg, the impact of the 'X' case (concerning mental health detention infra fn 157) on the law relating to detention of children (supra fn 16) and its potential impact in other areas, such as immigration and parole: see comment in (1982) 45 MLR 459, 464, and the reaction of MIND: The Times, November 6, 1981.

(89) Series A, No 33.

(90) Nos 6850/74, 6871/75, and 7099/75. See Stocktaking, 1979, at pp 108, 109.

(91) In November 1978 there had been an exchange of letters between the UK and the Court's Registrar on the matter.

(92) See infra fn 155.

(93) See Series A, No 33, p 6.

(94) There is some provision for a State not party to proceedings before the Commission to intervene before the Committee of Ministers: see Robertson, op cit supra fn 3 at p 250.

(95) See infra s.8(a).

(96) Hansard (HL) vol 427, col 889. Cf the parliamentary reference to the West German Klass case (No 5029/71) in an attempt to amend the Telecommunications Bill to cover phone tapping: Hansard (HC), vol 2, col 326.

(97) See the comment supra in the text accompanying fn 25.

(98) No 5100/71: Series B, No 20, 15.

(99) See infra fn 136 and accompanying text.

(100) Series B, No 20, at p 133.

(101) No 7341/76: See paras 72, 75 and 76 of the Commission's Report, 1979.

(102) See Stocktaking, 1977, at p 23 (Netherlands); Res DH(79) 7, Yearbook (1979), 467, 468 (Switzerland).

(103) See also the Bill's Second Reading: Hansard (HC), vol 998, col 791 (February 10, 1981). The Act came into force on July 28, 1981 (Chap.55).

(104) Nor, it seems, in the Select Committees: see (1981) 44 MLR 693, 700, 701.

(105) See Robertson, op cit supra fn 3 at p 184.

(106) [1981] 1 All ER 943.

(107) Ibid at p 946.

(108) See supra the essay at p 247.

(109) Professor Fawcett.

(110) See infra fn 228 and accompanying text.

(111) In response to the question as to what extent the Commission was bound by the precedents of its previous decisions: supra fn 22, p 62; see also ibid, at p 13, para 48 ("not bound by their own decisions").

(112) See the Report of the Sub-Committee supra fn 22 at p 12, para 52.

(113) See, eg, ibid at p 12, and parliamentary official statements, eg, Hansard (HL) vol col 931.

(114) See further fn 138 infra.

(115) A fortiori in the case of a mere finding of admissibility. See supra fn 54 and accompanying text.

(116) No 2991/66: 10 Yearbook 478.

(117) See the Immigration Appeal Act, 1969, Ch 21.

(118) See Stocktaking, 1979, pp 35, 36.

(119) Supra fn 27 and accompanying text.

(120) No 4115/69.

(121) 13 Yearbook, 738 (1970). See Harris, Cases & Materials on International Law, 2nd ed, 1979 who comments (at p 554) that the Strasbourg application was seemingly "not totally irrelevant" to the change. For the subsequent Strasbourg saga on prisoners' correspondence rights, see supra essay at p 352. and infra fn 244 et seq.

(122) See infra fn 209.

(123) See The Times, March 6 1982. See also infra fn 181 for another example.

(124) Under Art 28.

(125) Robertson, op cit supra fn 3 at p 243.

(126) See ibid at pp 184, 185, 249.

(127) Ibid at pp 254, 258.

(128) No 7114/75.

(129) No 8186/78.

(130) Res DH(81) 5 (April 2, 1981).

(131) DH(81) 4. See [1981] Public Law, 149.

(132) See The Times, March 9, 1981.

(133) Hansard (HC) vol 1, col 283.

(134) See supra fns 130 and 131.

(135) Supra, fn 130.

(136) See respectively Arts 32(4) and 53.

(137) See supra fn 105.

(138) See Robertson, op cit supra fn 3 at pp 208, 209. But note that the Court's power to make some scrutiny of remedial domestic legislation under the "just satisfaction" procedure of Art 50. Thus in the recent X v UK case (infra fn 157), the Court in its second judgment of October 18, 1982 said it was "taking note" of the draft legislation - the Mental Health Act (Amendment) Bill 1982: see The Times, October 19, 1982.

(139) See eg, the Tyrer case and Res DH (78) 6 (April 25, 1968), Appendix VIII, p 22; Ireland v UK, Res 78(35) (June 22, 1978).

(140) See Robertson, op cit supra fn 3 at p 263.

(141) As Robertson, op cit, points out (at p 248), para 2 of Art 32 does not "authorise the Committee... to prescribe what measures must be taken; it is rather left to the Government concerned to draw its own conclusions". But see Rule 5 of the Rules on Art 32 adopted in 1969.

(142) Infra, s.9.

(143) See, eg, the Sunday Times case: Res DH(81) 2, (April 2, 1981).

(144) See, eg, the Second Vagrancy case (v Belgium): Res DH(72) 1.

(145) See Robertson, op cit, at pp 260, 263.

(146) No 6538/74.

(147) Supra fn 143 (Appendix): (1981) 3 EHRR, 615.

(148) See supra, the essay at p 318.

(149) See comment in [1981] Public Law, 145, 146.

(150) See supra fns 128 & 129.

(151) Apart from those contained in specific essays in this book.

(152) No 151.

(153) See particularly fns 176 & 188 infra.

(154) See, eg, B v UK (No 6870): Communique B(81)50, p5.

(155) See supra fn 89.

(156) For which purpose habeas corpus was alleged to be sufficient.

(157) No 6998/75.

(158) See The Times, November 6, 1981.

(159) Paras 47 & 62.

(160) There is no indication in the legislative history to indicate that the Strasbourg proceedings in any way instigated or even expedited the legal changes (cf supra fn 35 and the Contempt of Court Bill).

(161) Lord Elton.

(162) Hansard (HL) vol 425, col 934. See also ibid, col 941.

(163) Report on Mentally Abnormal Offenders, 1975, Cmnd 5244. It is also based on the DHSS consultation document on review of the Mental Health Act of 1976.

(164) "Reform of the Mental Health Legislation", Cmnd 8405, para 52.

(165) See The Times, November 12, 1981; also Muchlinski, "Mental Health Patients' Rights and the European Human Rights Convention", (1980) 5 Human Rights Review, 90, 107.

(166) Hansard (HL) vol 425 col 970.

(167) See Hansard (HL) vol 425 cols 934 & 940. On December 9, 1981, the Under-Secretary of State for Scotland affirmed that the 'X' case also necessitated an amendment to **Scottish** legislation on the same matter: The Times, December 10, 1981.

(168) On March 22, 1982: Hansard (HC) vol 20, col 692.

(169) Ibid. But ironically the rights of unrestricted patients were to be correspondingly reduced for fear of falling foul of Art 14: see Hansard (HL) vol 427, col 1397. For criticism of this, see Mr Gostin's letter to The Times, January 28, 1982 and Hansard (HL) vol 427, cols 863 & 1394; (HC) vol 20, col 717.

(170) See Communique B(80)36, p5; and The Times, September 12, 1980.
(171) See para 16 of the Court's judgment on November 5, 1981. And see also the parliamentary statement in Hansard (HL) cols 934, 935 & 941.
(172) Ibid, para 66.
(173) See supra fn 96.
(174) See The Times, November 14, 1981, and Hansard (HL) vol 425, cols 958 & 970.
(175) Cited by Lord Hooson: Hansard (HL) vol 427, col 892. See also the second reading in the Commons: Hansard (HC) vol 20 cols 709 & 715.
(176) See The Times, February 23, 1982.
(177) Hansard (HL) vol 427, col 894; see also ibid col 1433.
(178) See The Times, April 24, 1982.
(179) Eg, Nos 6840/74, and 6870/75. See The Times, November 13, 1981.
(180) No 6840/74.
(181) See (1981) 3 EHRR 131.
(182) Ibid at p 134.
(183) Ibid.
(184) See The Times, December 23, 1980 and November 13, 1981; also Muchlinski, supra fn 165 at pp 110, 111.
(185) See Ch 7 of the 1978 White Paper supra fn 164.
(186) Para 7.6, p 83.
(187) The Times, February 19, 1981.
(188) No 8225/78 (see Communique C(82) 5, and The Times, February 16, 1982).
(189) See Hansard (HL) vol 427, cols 1418 & 1421; also (HC) vol 20, col 709.
(190) See supra fn 54. There has been strong opposition from the health union, COHSE, and members of the medical profession to any change: see The Times, February 5 and April 24, 1982.
(191) No 9117/80.
(192) See Communique B(82)2 (January 26, 1982).
(193) The first important application - No 7215/75 - failed: see Stocktaking, 1979, p122. But in its evidence to the Commission in this case, the Government indicated that the law on homosexuality was currently under review by two official bodies in the UK: see 'Case of X', p 4.
(194) No 7525/76.
(195) See Annual Review, p15 (1980); The Times, October 23, 1981.
(196) This was made public at the beginning of the consultation period (three months).
(197) Hansard (HC), vol 969, col 466 (Written Answers).
(198) Sixth Report: 1979-80:HC 143 (1980-81).
(199) Paras 26 & 27.
(200) See para 63 of the judgment: (1982) 4 EHRR 149.
(201) See, eg, the NCCL statement: The Times, October 23, 1981. For a comparison of the respective English and Northern Irish laws, see paras 14 - 17 of the judgment.
(202) See Hansard (HC) vol 18, col 387 (Written Answers).
(203) See supra fn 103.

justice have not been observed, and anyway that two of the judges, Megaw and Waller LJJ, thought that certiorari would not lie against a disciplinary decision of a prison governor.

The final area where Art 6 has been relied upon, though without success, has been in relation to security and release on parole licence. In Brady the applicant argued that the fact that Category A status is decided by a Committee, whose membership is secret and before whom there is no right to make representations, meant that the procedure is unfair and in breach of Art 6. However, the decision regarding the security classification was characterised by the Commission as administrative, and so within Art 6.

Just as loss of remission does not count as a deprivation of liberty according to the Commission, it seems from Brady and X v UK(68) that granting parole would not amount to more than an administrative discretion. The Commission in these cases seems to have adopted the more rigid judicial/administrative distinction such as existed in this country before Ridge v Baldwin,(69) while the English courts now seem to be saying that there is a general duty on administrative bodies to act fairly, but that the content of that duty will vary according to the function to be carried out.(70) In fact, there is probably little difference in outcome between the Commission's approach and that of the English courts. In Payne v Lord Harris,(71) the Court of Appeal refused to grant a declaration that a prisoner was entitled to know the reasons for being refused parole by the Parole Board, in order to be in a position to make representations for his release; and that it was contrary to natural justice for him not to be informed of the reasons. While the Parole Board are under a duty to act fairly, there is no duty imposed on them to disclose their reasons for refusing to recommend parole. Indeed, Brightman LJ stressed that the function of the Board is merely to recommend, it is the Secretary of State who makes the actual decision. The broad principle followed by the English courts therefore seems wider than that of the Commission, but in practice, the same results are reached.

Article 8: Freedom of correspondence etc.

The very nature of imprisonment means that some aspects of a person's private and family life will be adversely affected, but the question is one of degree. The Commission has received numerous complaints from prisoners who argue that the prison authorities have acted in breach of Art 8, particularly in relation to respect for correspondence. The proviso to Art 8, enables public authorities to interfere with the exercise of the right to correspondence if in accordance with law, and if necessary in a democratic society. The cases have considered whether certain restrictions imposed by imprisonment are in fact necessary. According to Beaven,(72) there has been a shift in the approach of the organs of the Convention, away from reliance upon a doctrine of inherent limitations of prisoners towards examining the "margin of appreciation" left to States by the proviso clauses. It is now up to the State to show why it thinks a restriction is necessary within the proviso, and no longer enough to argue that the fact of imprisonment itself means the authorities need not even rely upon the proviso.(73) The Court then retains for itself the final decision on whether the restriction is reconcilable with the right guaranteed by the relevant Article.

A prisoner is entitled to write and receive one letter per week, but more are allowed at the discretion of the governor or Secretary of State (r 34(3),(7)). Unconvicted prisoners may have unlimited correspondence (r 34(1)). By r 33(3), every letter or communication to or from a prisoner may be read or examined by the governor or prison officer deputed by him, and the governor may, at his discretion, stop any letter or communication on the ground that its contents are "objectionable" or of "inordinate length". The rationale for censorship of letters has been suggested by Cohen and Taylor to be to forestall "escape plots, plans for new criminal enterprises, arrangements to smuggle in illicit goods".(74) It seems reasonable to assume that knowledge that a letter may be censored does have a deterrent effect in so far as details about escapes, for example, would be unlikely to be spelled out in a letter. Hitherto, however, complaints about the prison system were also regarded as objectionable and censored, and the rationale for such censorship has little to do with prison security and much more to do with the fear of criticism reaching the outside world. This is borne out by the fact that, until recent changes in standing orders, letters containing complaints or requests concerning prison treatment could only be sent once the issue had been aired internally.

Prisoners have found little help forthcoming from the English courts on the issue of censorship. In Guilfoyle v Home Office,(75) the plaintiff wished to correspond with his solicitor in respect of alleged assaults suffered while in custody after the Birmingham pub bombings. The governor stopped a letter containing a green form from the solicitor, who thereupon lodged an application with the European Commission alleging breaches of Art 6 and 8. Guilfoyle sought a declaration that he was henceforward a party to legal proceedings and that his correspondence could not be either read or stopped, by virtue of r 37A(1). The Court of Appeal unanimously refused, being of the opinion that proceedings before the Commission are not legal proceedings. The Court said that the Commission's task is to investigate the facts of the application and report to the Committee of Ministers. Since these proceedings are not judicial, then they are not legal proceedings, following Lord Scarman in A G v BBC.(76) The Court of Appeal noted that there is a European Agreement(77) relating to persons participating in proceedings under the Convention, which recognises that the authorities may examine prisoners' correspondence, but provides that there is to be no delay in its despatch nor alteration of its contents. Clearly then, the Convention envisages that letters will be read. It may be noted that there is nothing in the Prison Rules which specifically governs correspondence with the Commission, and the prisoner is at the mercy of the goodwill and efficiency of the Prison Department in pursuing his application. This is even plainer after Guilfoyle, since if proceedings under the Convention are not legal proceedings, then r 37A does not apply at all.

At Strasbourg, in the earlier cases, e.g. X v UK,(78) the Commission upheld the authorities' right to censor letters on the ground that limitation on correspondence "is a necessary part of a person's deprivation of liberty which is inherent in the punishment of imprisonment". Since the Golder case, however, the Commission has been much more prepared to investigate complaints about censorship. A number of applications concerning censorship were dealt with together, and are awaiting determination by the Court of Human Rights under the name of Silver.(79) The report of the Commission on these cases was notable for its publication of the relevant standing orders and circular instructions used by the Prison Department and also of the censored letters, enabling the reader to make his own judgement on whether they contained objectionable material. The Commission considered that the right under Art 8 to respect for correspondence "envisages the free flow of such communications, subject only to the limitations prescribed by Art 8(2)". It followed the Court in Golder in rejecting the contention that a prisoner's right to correspondence is subject to implied limitations by virtue of his situation. It also rejected the Government's argument that letters intended for publication are not "correspondence".

There was dispute as to the meaning in Art 8(2) of "in accordance with the law". The Commission rejected the Government's argument that this phrase means "in accordance with the domestic law", and preferred to interpret it as not merely a reference to domestic law but also "to the rule of law, or the principle of legality" common to democratic societies. In the Sunday Times case,(80) the Court held that the law must be adequately accessible, and sufficiently precise to enable a citizen to foresee the consequences which a given action may entail, if necessary with legal advice. While r 33 and r 34(8) are public and known to prisoners, and therefore accessible, the restrictions contained in the secret standing orders and circular instructions were neither accessible nor foreseeable, and the issue was therefore whether their effects could be reasonably deduced from the Prison Rules.

The second matter in dispute was the meaning of "necessary in a democratic society". The Commission followed the Court in the Handyside Case(81) which noted that

(232) Ibid, at paras 14-16, p vii.

(233) Ibid, at para 18.

(234) Hansard (HC) vol 974, cols 312, 329.

(235) See the Statement of Change in Immigration Rules, Cmnd 394, February 20, 1980 and the consequential amendments to Rules 50 & 52.

(236) See The Times, March 24, 1981 and May 10, 1982.

(237) Nos 9274/80 ('X'), 9473/81 (Cabales), & 9474/81 (Balkandali): see Communique C(82) 25 (May 14, 1982).

(238) See The Times, May 10, 1982. Earlier, in March 1982, six Tory MPs had tabled an 'early day' motion stating that they believed the new rules breached the Convention: see The Times, March 26, 1982.

(239) See The Times, July 12, 1982. It seems that the proposed amendment (published in a White Paper of October 25 1982) will allow all British citizens - but not mere residents in the UK - to bring in foreign spouses: see The Times, October 19, 1982. It is significant that this proposed change will only affect one of the three cases found admissible at Strasbourg (where the applicant has British citizenship): The Times, October 26, 1982. On the conformity of the Nationality Act itself with the Convention, see comment in (1981) 30 ICLQ 247, 255.

(240) See eg, supra fns 125, 53 et seq and s.7(a). The gibe of Viscount De L'Isle on government insensivity to the Commission's findings (during debate on the Employment Bill) now seems less apposite: see Hansard (HL) vol 411, col 912.

(241) Lord Belstead: Hansard (HL) vol 427, col 1397.

(242) The Times, March 2, 1982.

(243) Supra fn 31 et seq. It appears that the Sunday Times now wishes to complain again to the Committee of Ministers over the governmental policy of "minimum compliance": Sunday Times October 3, 1982.

(244) Series A, No 18.

(245) See Communique C(81) 21. It is now pending before the Court.

(246) Standing Order No 5: see Hansard (HC) vol 14, col 100 (December 1, 1981).

(247) See the memorandum of Mr Lester to the Home Affairs Sub-Committee, supra fn 22, pp 34, 35.

(248) See supra fn 226 et seq and accompanying text; and the comment by Warbrick in (1980) 130 NLJ 852 on such "institutional possibilities".

(249) Emphasis added: Cmnd 7009, para 7.17. Cf the suggestion of Duffy in "English Law and the European Convention on Human Rights", (1980) 29 ICLQ 585, 618.

(250) Mr Lester, supra fn 22, at p 41.

(251) Section 3.

(252) See the question put by the Home Affairs Sub-Committee; supra fn 22, pp 11 & 62.

(253) H (80) 1, January 15, 1980, at p 5.

(204) On May 10, 1981: see The Times, May 11th, 1981.
(205) See The Times, May 8, 1981.
(206) See The Times, December 18, 1981.
(207) See The Daily Telegraph, February 5, 1982.
(208) Nos 7511/76 and 7743/76.
(209) No 7907/77.
(210) See Communique C(80) 43.
(211) See The Times, February 26, 1982; (1982) 4 EHRR 293.
(212) See Communique C(82)7, p 1.
(213) See The Times, February 28, 1982.
(214) See Hansard (HC) vol 19, col 227 (Written Answers) and col 482 (March 4 & 11, 1982 respectively); also ibid, vol 20, col 41 (Written Answers), March 15, 1982 (corporal punishment in schools for mentally handicapped children to be banned?); and the letter from the PM's office to STOPP (The Times, August 27, 1982).
(215) See The Times, February 25, 1982.
(216) See the UK admission in the 'X' case supra (Doc 27.07 - 06.2). Note that the new Eduction (School Information) Regulations, 1981, (SI No 630) in force in May, 1981, which require local authorities to provide information to parents on, inter alia, disciplinary policy, in each school, do not appear to have any connection with the Strasbourg proceedings.
(217) A recent circular to Church of England voluntary aided schools has also advised phasing out corporal punishment there: see The Times, July 23, 1982.
(218) See supra fn 123.
(219) See The Times, September 1, 1982, where a 16-year old schoolgirl has alleged in her complaint that corporal punishment in UK schools constitutes an administrative practice.
(220) See Res 78(35) of the Committee of Ministers (June 22, 1978). The ineffectiveness of the UK Government's communication to the Manx authorities that judicial corporal punishment would be in breach of the Convention was highlighted on July 20, 1981, when a 16-year old youth was sentenced to a birching (though this was quashed on appeal: see The Times, October 7, 1981). No steps to change the Manx legislation on this matter seem to be contemplated at present.
(221) See supra fn 41.
(222) See supra fn 44.
(223) 13 Yearbook 928, (1970). But see also the Alam case supra fn 26.
(224) See Res DH(77) 2.
(225) See the memorandum of Mr Lester to the Home Affairs Sub-Committee supra fn 22, p 38 ("The Committee of Ministers cannot be regarded as having over-ruled the Commission's findings of violation").
(226) See supra fn 22 and the comment of Professor Jacobs at para 95.
(227) See ibid, pp 10-12, & 43.
(228) See supra fn 21.
(229) Supra fn 22, para 9, p vi.
(230) Ibid, at para 17.
(231) Ibid, at para 20, p viii.